THE BIRTH OF THE *Beat* GENERATION

VISIONARIES, REBELS, AND HIPSTERS, 1944–1960

CIRCLES OF THE TWENTIETH CENTURY

Also by Steven Watson

The Harlem Renaissance: Hub of African-American Culture, 1920–1930

Strange Bedfellows: The First American Avant-Garde

THE BIRTH OF THE *B*EAT GENERATION

VISIONARIES, REBELS, AND HIPSTERS, 1944–1960

Steven Watson

PANTHEON BOOKS NEW YORK

All rights reserved under International and Pan-American
Copyright Conventions. Published in the United States
by Pantheon Books, a division of Random House, Inc.,
New York, and simultaneously in Canada by Random
House of Canada Limited, Toronto.

Permissions acknowledgments are on pages 383–85.
Illustration credits are on pages 385–87

Book design by Jo Metsch & Cheryl Cipriani

Endpaper illustration by James Steinberg

Interior map designed by Eric Hanson

Manufactured in the United States of America

Library of Congress Cataloging-in-Publication Data

Watson, Steven.
  The birth of the beat generation: visionaries, rebels, and
hipsters, 1944–1960 / Steven Watson.
      p.   cm.   (Circles of the twentieth century)
  Includes bibliographical references and index.
  ISBN 0-679-42371-0
  1. American literature—20th century—History and
criticism.   2. Beat generation.   3. United States—
Civilization—20th century.
I. Title.   II. Series: Watson, Steven. Circles of the
twentieth century.
PS228.B6W38   1995
810.9'0054—dc20   95–13259

First Edition
9 8 7 6 5 4 3 2 1

To William S. Burroughs, Allen Ginsberg, and
Herbert Huncke:
present at the birth of the Beat Generation,
and surviving still

CONTENTS

FOREWORD "The history of the world is the history not of individuals, but of groups," wrote the eminent African-American polemicist W. E. B. Du Bois.[1] Henry James echoed this sentiment when he wrote, "The best things come, as a general thing, from the talents that are members of a group; every man works better when he has companions working in the same line, and yielding the stimulus of suggestion, comparison, emulation."[2]

As these very different figures suggest, key moments of cultural transition are driven not only by the individual artists and writers who give birth to new ideas but also by a complex nexus of editors, patrons, critics, and hostesses who introduce these ideas to the world. Before modernism had its own institutions, social constellations played the most instrumental role in its growth. Group affiliations were sometimes concretized in manifestos of revolutionary aesthetics, or inclusion in little magazines, or sometimes in less formal connections founded on personal relationships and

Complex works of art speak not through individuals but ensembles.
—Paul Rosenfeld

*Artists to my mind are the real architects
of change, and not political legislators
who implement change after the fact.*
                                    —William Burroughs

common enterprises. Whatever form they took, cultural "circles" were essential midwives of modernist culture, providing sources of psychological and financial support, organs for disseminating aesthetic formulations, and the group identity necessary for fomenting revolutionary cultural change.

The convention of parsing history in biographies of single figures, or dispensing theory in the gnomic vocabulary of academe, springs from the conception of the history of art and literature as a tale of individual genius, independent of social context. *Circles of the Twentieth Century* embarks on a task that complements the work of biographers, presenting history-in-the-round and offering individual lives within the complex social constellations that shaped them. These books are directed at both the general reader and the scholar. General readers will find a condensed and readable narrative that depends on neither extensive prior knowledge of the subject nor the stamina required to navigate a voluminous tome devoted to a single life. Scholars will find not only the useful academic apparatus (footnotes, chronologies) to which they are accustomed but also less conventional materials, such as diagrams of circles, maps, and glossaries of the period slang that freshly illuminate their periods. The scholar will probably discover little new about his subject of expertise, but he might discover something new about the milieu in which that subject thrived.

These books are, of course, indebted to the research of well-known scholars, whose work is credited in the notes and bibliography. Without such pioneering researchers on the Beat Generation—Ann Charters, Barry Miles, Ted Morgan, Gerald Nicosia, Michael Schumacher, Tom Clark, and John Tytell, for example—this volume would have been impossible. *Circles of the Twentieth Century* offers vivid and synthetic overviews intended to introduce fascinating subjects that have been the province of scholars to broader audiences.

BEATS ALL

Overleaf:
Hal Chase, Jack Kerouac, Allen
Ginsberg, and William Burroughs
enacting a Dashiell Hammett fantasy on
the Upper West Side, ca. 1946

*B*EAT" TO "BEATNIK": THE EVOLUTION OF A WORD   The word "beat" originally derived from circus and carnival argot, reflecting the straitened circumstances of nomadic carnies. In the drug world, "beat" meant "robbed" or "cheated" (as in "a beat deal"). Herbert Huncke picked up the word from his show business friends on the Near North Side of Chicago, and in the fall of 1945 he introduced the word to William Burroughs, Allen Ginsberg, and Jack Kerouac. He never intended it to be elevating, but the opposite: "I meant beaten. The world against me."[1]

The word acquired historical resonance when Jack Kerouac, in a November 1948 conversation with fellow writer John Clellon Holmes, remarked, "So I guess you might say we're a *beat* generation." Appropriating this conversation, Holmes introduced the word to the mainstream public four years later, in a November 1952 article for the *New York Times Magazine*, entitled "This Is the Beat Generation." "It involves a sort of nakedness of mind, and, ultimately, of soul," Holmes wrote, "a feeling of being reduced to the bedrock of consciousness."

Humility is indeed beatness, a compulsory virtue that no one exhibits unless he has to.
—William Burroughs

By the early 1950s, Kerouac and Ginsberg had begun to emphasize the "beatific" quality of "beat," investing the viewpoint of the defeated with mystical perspective. "The point of Beat is that you get beat down to a certain nakedness where you actually are able to see the world in a visionary way," wrote Ginsberg, "which is the old classical understanding of what happens in the dark night of the soul."[2]

"Beat" became widely disseminated after the publication of Kerouac's *On the Road* in 1957, when the media promoted the Beat Generation as a cultural phenomenon. *San Francisco Chronicle* columnist Herb Caen coined the term "beatnik" after the October 1957 launching of the Russian "sputnik," asserting that the satellite and the new bohemian type were "equally far out."[3] This deprecating incarnation of "beat" stood for a species of avant-garde camp follower who invariably wore a black beret, goatee, and black jeans (if male) or black tights (if female), played bongo drums, drank cheap Chianti, and smoked marijuana. Beatniks liked Charlie Parker, Lord Buckley, and Lenny Bruce, hung out in coffee houses, and said "Dig," "Cool," and "Crazy!"

The faddish commercialization of the Beat Generation began in the fall of 1957 and reached full force in *Life* and *Time* two years later. In 1959, the Beat Generation became a B movie by that name, and the beatnik was epitomized by the goateed Maynard G. Krebs, a character on the popular television series *The Many Loves of Dobie Gillis*. The fad had already begun to wane by the early 1960s, and a few years later beatniks were considered quaintly nostalgic artifacts; their moment had peaked quickly. Most strikingly, the Beat phenomenon infiltrated American popular culture more widely and effectively than any avant-garde phenomenon prior to Andy Warhol's Factory. But while Warhol intended such a foray into commercial culture, the Beats did not. At the time of this writing, images of Beat Generation figures still appear in advertisements for jeans and sneakers.

For an entry in the *Random House Dictionary*, Jack Kerouac provided an apt historical definition: "Members of the generation that came of age after World War II, who, supposedly as a result of disillusionment stemming from the Cold War, espouse mystical detachment and relaxation of social and sexual tensions."[4] As the twentieth century draws to a close, the Beat Generation has outlived that historical moment, surviving notoriety and media blitz to become classic literature for succeeding generations.

By avoiding society you become separate from society and being separate from society is being BEAT.
—Gregory Corso

BEAT LIVES, BEAT LITERATURE By the strictest definition, the Beat Generation consists of only William Burroughs, Allen Ginsberg, Jack Kerouac, Neal Cassady, and Herbert Huncke, with the slightly later addition of Gregory Corso and Peter Orlovsky. By the most sweeping usage, the term includes most of the innovative poets associated with San Francisco, Black Mountain College, and New York's Downtown scene. Using the broad definition, the Beat Generation is marked by a shared interest in spiritual liberation, manifesting itself in candid personal content and open forms, in verse and prose, thus leading to admiration for Walt Whitman, William Carlos Williams, and other avant-garde writers.

The Beats' identity has as much to do with literary aesthetics as with their collective biography. Their intertwining lives provided a basis for Beat literature, and this can be seen in the work of William Burroughs, Allen Ginsberg, and Jack Kerouac. They transformed the details of everyday life, snatches of remembered conversations, and personal friends into highly idiosyncratic narratives that sometimes seemed to have been dictated from an uncensored consciousness. Burroughs narrated his first years of heroin addiction using a dry, spare "Factualist" voice in *Junky* and a nightmarish black comic voice in *Naked Lunch*. In a series of sometimes Benzedrine-driven or marijuana-inspired writing bouts, Kerouac set down

Neal: His names were long and will never be forgotten.
Lucien: All our intelligence was in him.
Allen: All his sorrows were more than ours.
Bill: All our courtesy was most in him.
Joan: Her madness was all our own.
—Allen Ginsberg, on his friends

in "spontaneous bop prosody" the picaresque narrative of his life. His writing marathons resulted not only in his most famous novel, *On the Road*, but in the continuing epic of his life that he called "the Legend of Duluoz." In his notable and notorious poem "Howl," Ginsberg created the epic apologia of his generation. The lives, the legend, and the literature begin to fuse.

The Beat fraternity, forged a decade before the world began to glamourize it, provided their entry into the world of writing. The intimate circle was both subject matter and audience—and, because autobiography was transformed into art, the fictional characters have lived on long after their prototypes died. This collective of characters, both fictional and real, exemplifies a pivotal paradigm in twentieth-century American literature: finding the highest spirituality among the marginal and the dispossessed, establishing the links between art and pathology, and seeking truth in visions, dreams, and other nonrational states.

The Beats were not the first Americans to revolt against literary tradition, nor were they the first to entwine their lives and their art. Like their avant-garde forebears, who experimented in every arena from dress to drugs to politics and sex, the Beats conducted their lives in a state of countercultural experiment.

At the time of their original notoriety, during the Eisenhower era, the Beat Generation touched a raw nerve. Succeeding generations—the hippies of the 1960s, the punks of the 1970s—regarded them as cultural antecedents, and their work continues to be discovered anew. In 1951 Allen Ginsberg wrote Jack Kerouac. "I can't believe that between us three already we have the nucleus of a totally new historically important American creation."[5] At the time, Ginsberg's pronouncement sounded like the arrogance of youth; a half-century later it sounds like bemused prophecy.

Allen Ginsberg divides the history of the Beat Generation into four phases: 1) The key writers meet and are spiritually liberated. 2) The liter-

In the U.S. you have to be a deviant or die of boredom.
—William Burroughs

We are now contending technicians in what may well be a little American Renaissance of our own and perhaps a pioneer beginning for the Golden Age of American Writings.
—Jack Kerouac

But listen . . . do you realize (this is apropos) that a new literary age is beginning in America?
—Jack Kerouac

ary artifacts are written. 3) The battle against censorship is waged. 4) Publication is followed by notoriety and renown.[6] The history recounted here follows that rough outline.

YOUNG WILLIAM BURROUGHS One of the earliest vignettes about William Burroughs—"Billy" at the age of eight—comes from a childhood playmate. He recalled Billy's hideaway beneath the back steps of the family house, equipped with a box, a candle, spoons, and instruments for investigating the forging of hard metals for weapons. The atmosphere in that nether hideaway was both captivating and conspiratorial, and Billy, although a year and a half younger than his playmate, dominated their activities through his dark, purposeful curiosity.[7]

During this same year, Burroughs had his first experience with shooting guns and writing fiction—activities that would dominate his life. He called his first work "Autobiography of a Wolf," and the ten-page story described an animal who lost his mate and was killed by a grizzly. When adults tried to correct him—surely the youngster meant "Biography of a Wolf"?—he was coolly adamant. As he recalled seventy years later. "No, I meant the autobiography of a wolf and I still do."[8]

How had young Billy developed an intense identity with this feral creature that lives outside society? The seeds of alienation are not readily apparent in his surroundings. The Burroughs family lived in a well-kept three-story, red brick house at 4664 Pershing Avenue in St. Louis, Missouri, surrounded by large trees whose dappled light was cast on freshly mowed lawns with beds of carefully tended peonies, irises, and roses and a small fishpond. Given the choice of playing in these elegant surroundings or in the dark below the stairs, Billy chose the latter.

When William Seward Burroughs II was born on February 5, 1914, Mortimer and Laura Burroughs had the means to provide their sec-

William Burroughs as a child on Pershing Avenue, St. Louis, Missouri

Here once the kindly dope fiend lived.
—Jack Kerouac, on William Burroughs

ond son with a privileged life. The family fortune came from William Seward Burroughs I, and they named Billy after his grandfather, who had invented and, in 1888, patented the first key-operated recording and adding machine, the Arithmometer, which became the basis for the highly profitable Burroughs Adding Machine Company. Burroughs company investors reaped millions, but the inventor had sold most of the company's stock. Mortimer retained some and presciently sold it for $276,000 three months before the Crash in 1929. But the fortune had largely dwindled by the time it accrued to the inventor's grandson.

Mortimer and Laura Burroughs' financial position did offer the comfort of *haut bourgeois* existence—a family staff that included a maid, nanny, cook, and gardener, a summer house in a beach town on Lake Huron—but their social position remained equivocal, good enough for the St. Louis Social Register but not sufficiently elevated for the St. Louis Country Club. "Of course we were invited to the *larger* parties," Burroughs recalled. "But when the WASP elite got together for dinners and lunches and drinks nobody wanted those ratty Burroughses around."[9]

Billy's parents seemed to be a complementary and faithful couple. Laura was a willowy, refined-looking beauty whose manner was both brutally forthright and ineffably sad. She was funny, smart, psychic, and vain. She was not only the architect of the Burroughs gardens but an accomplished flower arranger, commissioned by Coca-Cola to write three books on the subject. She was devoted to Billy, her favorite, and cherished his odd jokes. After repeatedly bailing her son out of legal problems she could still chuckle, "He's just the funniest person I know," and admit to him, "I worship the ground you walk on."[10]

Mortimer was the eldest and stablest member of a family that included an alcoholic sister and a morphine-addicted brother. After graduating from MIT, he founded a plate glass company. His mild façade was impenetrable and his manner often taciturn, but Mortimer consistently

A Note on Beat Slang

The slang of the Beat Generation combined and transformed the vocabulary of many worlds. Incorporated into their conversation and writing are expressions from the argots of jazz musicians, drug users, carnival and circus workers, homosexuals, hipsters, and African Americans. The language became a cliché of the late 1950s and 1960s, but in its earlier years it was a means to express an underground world. It gave voice to the marginal, the hip, the dispossessed urban dweller. A 1948 article on hipster language described its functions: "to re-edit the world with new definitions . . . jive definitions." In the bottom corners of the pages that follow are examples of Beat and hipster talk, gleaned from conversations, letters, and literature.

committed small acts of kindness and displayed genuine interest in his sons. He excluded Billy from his basement toolshop but introduced him, early on, to guns and hunting, and he actively encouraged his son's verbal skills by reading to him and asking him to use five new words each day. The Burroughses jointly supported their son's intellectual development and enrolled him in the progressive Community School.

A Welsh nanny interrupted Billy's sunny childhood. Like a witch in a dark fairy tale, she taught the four-year-old occult curses, nasty rhymes, hoots that brought toads from beneath their rocks, incantations that could send a blinding worm into the eye of an enemy. The dark intimacy of Billy's relationship with the nanny was so compelling that he could not abide being separated from her on her days off. On one such day, she took Billy along with her veterinarian boyfriend on an outdoor expedition. Throughout his life, Burroughs would recall the foreboding of that afternoon: "I hear the dark mutterings of a servant underworld."[11] Something happened in those woods that, years later, he vainly tried to recall in psychoanalysis and hypnosis. He could only summon up disjointed bits of the boyfriend's smiling face, his pants pulled down, the coaxing voice of the nanny, the feeling of being pushed, the boyfriend screaming in pain. He didn't tell his parents, but the sense that something awful had happened would linger in his mind. At the age of forty-four, undergoing psychoanalysis, he had formulated a version of the childhood trauma: "I witnessed a miscarriage, by Mary the evil governess, and the results were burned in the furnace in my presence. That is the 'murder.'"[12]

Neighbors and schoolchildren regarded Billy Burroughs as an odd child and an unhealthy influence. His sallow complexion, withdrawn manner, unathletic frame, and sinus problems all set him apart. "That boy looks like a sheep-killing dog," observed a schoolmate's father, and another altered it to, "That boy looks like a walking corpse." Burroughs' identity was stamped early: sepulchral, dark, and very smart. Even children

Hip: originally an adjective describing a drug user: "When we get where the Yage is, we'll dig a hip cat and ask him, 'Where can we score for Yage?'" [Burroughs] But it also meant knowing, possessing knowledge of particular information: "Hip is the affirmation of the barbarian." One can become **hip to** a particular experience: "In the 1940s pre-med students and nurses were getting hip to amphetamine to help them through their long days." [Huncke] It is also used as a verb, meaning to introduce: "Keep diggin' the all-night, all-frantic one over WMCA—570 first on the dial—and I'll hip you to all the things that are jumpin' off. Your boy, Symphony Sid."

shunned him. "You're a character," said a schoolmate, "but you're the wrong kind."[13] Billy lived up to his reputation, aiming his Eversharp pencil at classmates as if it were a gun, creating homemade bombs. One blew up in his hands when he was fourteen (sending him to the hospital for six months), and another was thrown through his school principal's window (it failed to explode).

Burroughs was certain that he had been born with sexual feelings for men, but as he reached adolescence he gave his desires a name, and his attractions emphasized his sense of dark isolation. It came as a wondrous relief when, at the age of thirteen, he happened upon the memoirs of a thief–hobo–drug addict who called himself Jack Black. Between the red cardboard covers he discovered a world of con men and safecrackers, morphine and opium, and the title seemed to embody the youngster's nihilist sentiments: *You Can't Win*. Billy called it "the Good Red Book"[14] and found in it a pantheon of heroes and anti-heroes, an underworld argot far more colorful than Missourian plain speaking, and a set of outsider values that seemed more authentic than the hypocrisy of St. Louis's country club set.

The adolescent Burroughs playacted expertly. He imaginatively thrust himself into the personae of fictional characters—invariably thieves, pirates, low-lifes, decadent writers in pongee suits, drug addicts, and scroungers. Just as books had provided the source for his imaginative identification, his newly found "family," his stories offered an outlet for his dark imagination. Even his high school juvenilia reveal the themes and sardonic humor of his later work. Aspiring to write pulp crime fiction, he turned out sagas of severed hands, mandatory marijuana injections, ominous fortunetellers, blood-spattered bodies, and lynched figures twisting slowly against red sunsets. Writing for *True Confessions* was his aspiration. Burroughs fantasized writers as figures who lounged around in opium stupors and sampled the bizarre fruits of exotic locales. His first published

"If God made anything better, he kept it for Himself," I said . . .
—William Burroughs

Just when you think the earth is exclusively populated by Shits, you meet a Johnson.
—William Burroughs

Cop: *to pass a capsule of heroin to someone, hand to hand. "'Get ready to cop,' I said, and dropped the caps into his hands." [Burroughs]*

work, appearing when Billy was fifteen, was called "Personal Magnetism," and in the brief essay he noted, "I would like to know how to control others at a glance."[15]

Burroughs spent his high school years at Los Alamos Ranch School, where he learned to shoot rifles and throw knives, and where several events foreshadowed his later life. At sixteen, Burroughs bought a bottle of chloral hydrate at the local drugstore, ingested it, nearly died, and later claimed he "just wanted to see how it worked." Although the schoolmaster assured his parents, "I doubt if he will try anything like it again,"[16] it was precisely this investigative act of self-medication that the psychic explorer would repeat, in many variations, throughout his life.

As Burroughs' hormonal drives accelerated in his last years of high school, strong and ritualized associations developed between his homosexual desires and the act of writing. Following obsessive sexual fantasies and masturbation, writing became a fetishized vehicle for personal expiation. Homosexual desires were purged on the page just as his semen was spilt in masturbation, and his diary became a confessional. His infatuation with a fellow student—Burroughs could not hide his own slavelike and unreciprocated devotion—aroused jeers, taunts, and whispers. Although he had learned to survive without peer approval, Burroughs couldn't abide the unremitting teenage flak. Two months short of graduation, he demanded his parents remove him; and, as always, they came to his rescue.

Burroughs was concerned that his diary not fall into the hands of classmates, who could torture him everlastingly with this black-and-white evidence of his sexual deviance. He read the tortured words he had confided to its pages, and the emotions seemed so melodramatic that they aroused in him a rush of humiliation and nausea. He burned each page. "The act of writing had become embarrassing, disgusting, and above all, *false*," Burroughs recalled. "The sight of my words written on a page hit me like the sharp smell of carrion when you turn over a dead dog with

At age fifteen, William Burroughs, an unhappy student at Los Alamos Ranch School, New Mexico

Capable boy—needs to develop more group spirit—good student and will become better when he has made a place for himself in groups of boys.
—Teacher, on William Burroughs' report card

a stick, and this continued until 1938. I had written myself an eight-year sentence."[17]

Los Alamos provided its final evaluation of Burroughs: "His interest is in things morbid and abnormal, affects his sense of proportion in his work, making spotty and uneven results. His brain power, if rightly used, seems sufficient to get him to college, but there is doubt about his ability to direct himself."[18]

After a stint in a St. Louis school designed to get its students into good colleges, Burroughs enrolled at Harvard in September 1932, and quickly learned to hate the exclusive club atmosphere of the WASP upper class. Sexually, he remained frustrated and astoundingly naive—he was a virgin until his senior year and lacked the most rudimentary knowledge of sex. (Babies, he thought, entered the world through a woman's navel, and when he learned about sexual intercourse, he quoted Chesterton, "The pleasure is momentary, the pains are infinite and the posture is ridiculous."[19])

Instead of participating in campus life, he holed up in his room with his favorite possessions, a .32 revolver and a pet ferret named Sredni Vashtar (after a ferret in a Saki story that had been trained to kill a domineering nanny). Charwomen were afraid to clean his Claverly Hall room, but a circle of fellow outsiders gathered in his chamber for Burroughs' Sunday afternoon open houses. But even friends entered his domain warily. Once, when fooling around with his revolver, Burroughs nearly blew away a classmate's stomach; the gun barrel, diverted at the last moment, produced a gaping hole in the wall.

Burroughs' chief pleasure during his undergraduate years came from a handful of English classes. He discovered the notebooks of Samuel Taylor Coleridge and Thomas De Quincey detailing opium's phantasmagoric effect on their writing. Without access to such mind-altering drugs, and still fearful of reawakening the shame he'd long associated with

If Harvard doesn't bother me, I won't bother Harvard.
—William Burroughs

William Burroughs , Harvard yearbook, 1935

writing, Burroughs simply stored his memories. At the end of his under-graduate years, he skipped graduation ("It didn't mean a fuckin' thing"[20]), and the yearbook listed only his name and address. In a later one-paragraph biography, he described the period: "Harvard 1936 A. B. No-body ever saw him there but he had the papers on them."[21] For graduation, Mortimer and Laura gave their son a trip to Europe that lasted a year, and a $200 monthly stipend that provided a financial safety net for the next twenty-five years.

Thus began the period that the historian of psychoanalysis Peter Swales calls "Burroughs in the Bewilderness."[22] Burroughs had graduated from America's most prestigious university, but he wasn't educationally prepared to support himself with a profession. He had studied English and loved literature, inhabiting its characters and exotic locales, but he was paralyzed in the act of writing. Nor could he pursue a medical degree, for he lacked the undergraduate requirements of mathematics and physics. He thought that perhaps his niche in life was to become a psycho-analyst. He had seen, and would continue to see, the profession from the perspective of the couch; before he came into the company of Ginsberg and Kerouac, he had had six psychoanalysts, and as an analysand he re-peatedly found that he was better read in psychoanalytic theory than most of his therapists.

Burroughs' Grand Tour of Europe that summer was dark—he saw Nazis everywhere, the beautiful boy-ridden Romanische Baden in Vienna, a homosexual hotel in Budapest, gypsy cafés in Yugoslavia. By the fall he had decided to stay in Vienna and study medicine as a preliminary step to becoming a psychoanalyst. Burroughs lived in a combination hotel and Turkish bath, studied, and underwent a treatment for syphilis. As Vienna became increasingly saturated with Nazis, Burroughs realized he could not remain there and dropped his courses in medicine. He did an unex-pected thing: in July 1937 he married a thirty-five-year-old Jewish woman

The only possible ethic is to do what one wants to do.
—William Burroughs

I could have been a successful bank robber, gangster, business executive, psychoanalyst, drug trafficker, explorer, bullfighter, but the conjuncture of circumstances was never there.
—William Burroughs

John: *one who buys a prostitute, treated with the respect appropriate to the situation: "A sucker is just to be taken. But a John is different. You give him what he pays for." [Burroughs]*

who had befriended him. Her name was Ilse Klapper, and their union was strictly a marriage of convenience, to allow Klapper to escape persecution as a Jew by emigrating to the United States. Burroughs' act was without apparent selfish intent or ulterior motive, for it did not endear him to his parents and he gained nothing from the deed but the doing itself. Despite the fears of Laura and Mortimer Burroughs, Ilse Klapper moved to New York and never asked for any money. Burroughs would later divorce her in Mexico, but by that time there was a second Mrs. Burroughs.

Burroughs returned to America and pursued psychoanalysis through another route. During the next four years both at Harvard University and Columbia University he registered in courses in psychology and anthropology—both as backdoor means to eventually study psychoanalysis—but in each case he dropped out before completing his courses. At Harvard he rented a white frame house with his old friend Kells Elvins, and the two began acting out skits on their screened porch, trading dialogue, and getting into laughing jags. "I hadn't laughed like that since my first tea-high at eighteen," Burroughs recalled, "when I rolled around the floor and pissed all over myself."[23] Their sketch was inspired by the sinking of the *Titanic* and the *Morro Castle,* and they called it "Twilight's Last Gleaming." From the skitlike method of its creation and its mosaic of grotesques to the first appearance of the scabrous Dr. Benway, "Twilight's Last Gleaming" represents Burroughs' first literary step beyond juvenilia. Looking back years later, Allen Ginsberg called it "the whole key of all his work, like the sinking of America."[24] The piece begins in true Burroughs fashion: "A paretic named Perkins sat askew on his broken wheelchair. He arranged his lips. 'You pithyathed thon of a bidth!'"[25] Burroughs and Elvins submitted the piece to *Esquire,* which rejected it as "too screwy." Burroughs again stopped writing, this time for seven years.

For his first regular boyfriend, he chose, in late 1939 at the age of twenty-five, a shallow blond office boy named Jack Anderson who, on the

The most dangerous thing to do is stand still.

—William Burroughs
to Allen Ginsberg

My affections, being concentrated on a few people, are not spread all over Hell in a vile attempt to placate sulky, worthless shits.

—William Burroughs

side, hustled both men and women. Burroughs' homosexual attraction triggered old feelings of subservient humiliation, and the boyfriend both willingly and inadvertently tortured him. With only the thinnest of apartment walls separating them, Burroughs heard the grating and orgasmic sounds of the boyfriend's affairs. Burroughs couldn't abide his feelings of vulnerability and anger, but rather than expressing them, he went on "a Van Gogh kick."[26] For $2.71 he bought a pair of stainless steel poultry shears that reminded him of his grandmother's Thanksgiving dinners. He looked in his dresser mirror, "composing his face into the supercilious mask of an eighteenth-century dandy," and severed the tip from the little finger on his left hand. He briefly watched the blood spurt, bandaged the finger, and put the joint in his vest pocket. "I've done it," he said to himself, and noticed that "a lifetime of defensive hostility had fallen from him."[27] The euphoria continued until his psychiatrist convinced him to go to Bellevue and he was then transferred to Payne-Whitney. This incident marked the end of his student career to become a psychoanalyst.

Burroughs found his niche in Chicago's disreputable North Side, where he moved in September 1942. Herbert Huncke, whom Burroughs would meet three years hence, described the area this way: "I tell you what made up the near North Side: dikes, faggots, a certain so-called hip element, the swish places and the she-she places."[28] It resembled life in the pages of Jack Black's memoirs. Burroughs joined Sunday crap games, he heard prison tales, and he felt like he was one of the crowd. He polished his own imagined identity as a criminal with his revolver in a sock and his dreams of swindling the commercial world of its money. Obsessive make-believe dominated his plans—to locate the manholes in Chicago and install bombs that would detonate as Brinks trucks passed over them, for instance. None of his schemes came to fruition.

In rapid succession, Burroughs landed a repetitive factory job and boring work apprehending store employees who stole merchandise. But it

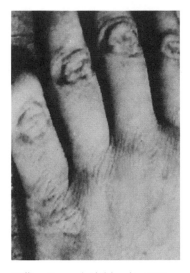

William Burroughs' left hand in 1963, showing the digit he severed with stainless steel shears in 1940

Daddy, Daddy-O, Daddy O: African-American slang of the 1920s—a woman called her lover **Daddy**; a man called someone he liked and respected **Daddy-O**—was transformed in the bebop period of the 1940s to indicate a hip male: "Get with those technicolor peyote kicks Daddy O. . . ." [Burroughs]

Safety lies in exterminating the type that produces the environment in which you cannot live.
                                    —William Burroughs

was at A. J. Cohen, Exterminators, that he found the job that would hold him for eight months—longer than any other in his life. Tooling through Chicago's streets in his black Ford V-8, he could gain entrance to apartments by ringing the bell and popping the always pertinent question: "You got any bugs, lady?"[29] He was a walking toxic pharmacy, carrying kerosene, pyrethrum powder, fluoride, phosphorus paste, and arsenic. He earned $50 a week plus knockdown jobs, set his own hours, and took sufficient pride in his work that he became an expert on the nefarious habits of bedbugs.

In the fall of 1942, Burroughs' old St. Louis friend, thirty-one-year-old David Kammerer, and the object of his obsession, eighteen-year-old Lucien Carr, arrived in Chicago. In St. Louis, Burroughs had witnessed the relationship between the two men grow into a version of *The Blue Angel*. Tall, red-headed, with a prominent nose and weak chin, the black sheep son of a respectable St. Louis family, Kammerer displayed charming manners and cultured speech punctuated by notes of superiority, wit, and mockery. Kammerer had taught English at Washington University and run a play group for grade school boys, and it was here that he had met young Lucien Carr. He subsequently became Lucien's Boy Scout master, following him through adolescence, from St. Louis to Phillips Andover to Bowdoin College to the University of Chicago.

Lucien had a slender five-foot-nine frame, a hairless chest, and muscled thighs, slanted catlike green eyes, modeled cheekbones, and a thatch of yellow hair. Though not homosexual, he possessed enough charisma to enthrall Kammerer and later Allen Ginsberg and Jack Kerouac.

Burroughs saw plenty of the pair, although their volatility sometimes caused him trouble—when they urinated from Burroughs' window and ripped the room's Gideon Bible, for example, Burroughs' landlady expelled him. In the spring of 1943, Lucien Carr put his head in an oven. Whether it was a suicide attempt, a means to avoid military service, or a

Solid: a popular word from the 1940s on, often emphasized with a hand gesture. It can be a simple affirmative: "The waiter nodded. 'That's two dry martinis and two orders of shish kebab. Right, gentlemen?' 'Solid, Pops.'" [Burroughs] Or it can be an adjective for a well-ordered but not boring existence: "Everything was solid that year. I had a pad on tenth street living with a gone little chick from Newark." [Kerouac, imitating hipster, 1950]

work of art (as he later asserted) remained unclear, but he ended up in Cook County Hospital. After leaving the hospital, Lucien Carr and David Kammerer separately decided to move to New York. The rootless William Burroughs followed them.

Burroughs arrived in New York in the spring of 1943. At the age of twenty-nine his physical presence had evolved into the singular identity that would remain unchanged for many years:

> Lee's [Burroughs's frequent pseudonym] face, his whole person, seemed at first glance completely anonymous. He looked like an FBI man, like anybody. But the absence of trappings, of anything remotely picturesque or baroque, distinguished and delineated Lee, so that seen twice you would not forget him. . . . His face had the look of a superimposed photo, reflecting a fractured spirit that could never love man or woman with complete wholeness.[30]

JACK KEROUAC: THE BEGINNINGS Gabrielle Kerouac gave birth to Jean-Louis Lebris de Kerouac on a large brass bed in the second-story bedroom of a rented frame cottage in the French-Canadian section of Lowell, Massachusetts. The baby was strong and chubby, prompting the family to call him Little Thumb. Years later Jack Kerouac claimed to remember that late afternoon of March 12, 1922, right down to the beads and lace curtains, and the "red light and the sadness."[31] Above him hung a black lacquered crucifix.

"Memory Babe" was a nickname Kerouac acquired during his childhood and cherished throughout his life. Despite Kerouac's prodigious recall, such memories are unlikely. They do, however, embody essential elements of his legend—the aura of Catholicism, predetermined loss, and damnation. Jack—or "Ti-Jean" (Little Jean), as the family called

I was born, my damned sin began. I wonder when it began.

—Jack Kerouac

Jack Kerouac at ca. eleven, Lowell, Massachusetts

him—was the last of three children born to his working-class parents, Leo and Gabrielle. The motto emblazoning the family's blue and gold ancestral shield read: *Aimer, Travailler, et Souffrir* (Love, Work, and Suffer). Until he was five years old, the baby of the family spoke only a Franco-American tongue known as *joual*, a patois spoken because Gabrielle knew so little English. The Kerouacs passed through a succession of rented whitewashed houses and upstairs apartments with shaky porches in Lowell or Pawtucketville, its French-Canadian ghetto. During the first years of his life, he was restricted to the house, often with his mother. In the morning he smelled oatmeal cooking on the coal stove, and in the evening he smelled hamburger, boiled potatoes, and smoke from his father's Cuban cigar. The points of his compass were the linoleum-floored parlor, the crib upstairs, the porch, and the second-story windows poking through the short slope roof. The cloistered house became the private screen on which he projected his hopes and fantasies, and many of them revolved around his older brother, Gerard. As Jack put it years later: "For the first four years of my life, while he lived, I was not Ti Jean Duluoz, I was Gerard, the world was his face, the flower of his face, the pale stooped disposition, the heartbreakingness and the holiness and his teachings of tenderness to me."[32]

"Ti-Jean" Kerouac at three

Gerard was five years older than Jack and physically his opposite; the family called the fraternal pair "bread and butter." Gerard was tall and thin, his feet turned inward, and his blue eyes looked out from hollows in his wan face. Gerard was born with a rheumatic heart, and Leo often patted him on the head and sighed, "Me poor lil Wolf, you were born to suffer."[33] After Gerard was stricken ill with rheumatic fever at the age of seven, Gabrielle channeled her grief into ministering to him. Each day before Leo returned from work, she lit a devotional candle in her kitchen, prayed to Saint Martha, and filled the home with prayer cards and images of Saint Thérèse. Leo regarded Gerard's impending death as bitter con-

Sound: *to voice an opinion, inquire: "I sounded the cat was he holding" (I asked him if he had any drugs).*

firmation of his tragic sense of existence. He took no solace in religion and publicly greeted a priest at his door with the brusque command: "Get lost."[34]

Gerard faced impending death with the equanimity of those sustained by the belief that real life begins after death; his want of physical vitality seemed to nourish a disembodied spirituality. One day at school he had a vision, which he reported to the presiding nun: the Virgin Mary had come to transport him to Heaven in a little white wagon pulled by lambs. Thereafter, Gerard was invested with magical powers by his family and neighbors, by the St. Louis de France nuns, and most of all by his younger brother. Jack revered him as a saint who communicated with birds, with God, and with angels. According to the Kerouac mythology, Gerard was the first victim of the travails that doomed the family. Gerard died one July day when Jack was four years old. Despite his vivid memory, Jack could barely summon up the event. The last thing he could remember about Gerard was being slapped by him. He did recall running down the sidewalk along Beaulieu Street and yelling "'Gerard est mort!' as tho it was some great event that would make a change that would make everything better."[35] The funeral was held in a church basement, and beneath a large concrete cross, colored light streamed through the stained glass onto the open casket where Gerard lay, grasping a solid silver crucifix. Jack later recalled the funeral as a vast movie starring Gerard and directed by God.

Gerard's presence continued to hover over his younger brother, not only in the portrait that hung on the mantelpiece but in the idealized role of martyred saint. Jack began to hallucinate white dots swarming before his eyes, mimicking Gerard's hallucinations during the last months of his life. Jack retreated to his mother's bed, and during his childhood years an emotionally over-close relationship developed between Gabrielle and her remaining son. The vision of his mother enfolding him in her worn brown bathrobe, offering him a butter-and-sugar sandwich, would remain

I believe my brother was a saint, and that explains all.

—Jack Kerouac

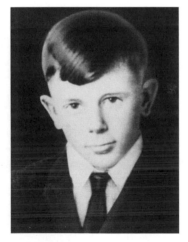

"Saintly Gerard" in a hand-tinted family portrait

throughout his life—as would the bitter sound of his mother's chilling words, "You should have died, not Gerard."[36]

Years later, describing a recurrent dream of Gerard in his coffin, Kerouac wrote: *"Write in honor of his death."*

Jack soon developed a solitary life that worried his parents. His imaginative explorations began with enacting wordless "silent movies"— pantomimes—in the darkened family parlor, playing all the characters against the backdrop of mambos and Sousa marches on the wooden crank Victrola, with the glowing Jesus looking down from the wall. The plays became long-running serials, like the Saturday movies that would soon become a staple of Jack's childhood. By the age of eight, his serial pantomimes had been transferred to paper. (The first of these roughly drawn comic strips that developed into complex sagas was called "Kuku and Koko at the Earth's Core.")

Only after Gerard's death did Jack venture beyond the house, into a world where English was spoken and severe discipline was exacted by Catholic nuns. Although he was an ardent student and earned good grades, he was extremely shy in the classroom and cut off by the barrier of language. As a classmate recalled, "He was like a tomb—all closed in."[37] Inspired by an English teacher, he became devoted to writing words. His literary awakening came at the age of twelve, when he began recounting his personal history. These writings were long, secret, semiecstatic outpourings that often culminated in masturbation—a habit that would continue through his life. From the beginning, writing was not only aimed at an end product but was also a self-stimulating process.

At school, he recalled a film the nuns showed; the fabricated magic of the cinema caused a stone statue of Saint Thérèse to move her head. A few years later, he saw his mother's statue of Saint Thérèse turn her head, this time without the magic of film. Shortly thereafter he experienced a ghostly vision of a dead playmate shuttling among other shrouds. The line

Judas is me, Jesus is Gerard.
—Jack Kerouac

How I loved my mother! How the baby loves his mother! How good it is to be a good mammal.
—Jack Kerouac

He was an angel, I was a mortal; what he could have brought to the world, I destroyed by my mere presence; because if I had not lived, Gerard would have lived.
—Jack Kerouac

You are destined to be a man of big sadness and talent, it'll never help to live or die, you'll suffer like the others, more.
—Joe Kerouac to his nephew Jack

I believe that memories are inseparable from dreams.

—Jack Kerouac

Jack Kerouac, as a track star at Lowell High School, 1939

between the emblematic and the actual, he believed, was permeable. He kept his flickering experiences of the netherworld to himself.

Gradually, Jack began to enter the universe of his father. Leo was swarthy and feisty, frustrated and alcoholic, his world dominated by print shops and rough sports. The public domain of Lowell began to replace Jack's darkened rooms and religious shrines, and he heard the polyglot languages whose sounds fascinated him. The Merrimac River, which ran through the city, provided Kerouac with a metaphor for freedom through escape.

Leo Kerouac suffered a sharp business downturn during the Depression, and Jack was struck ever more clearly by the disparity between classes. Gabrielle worked all day at a skiving machine in the local shoe factory and returned each evening to quietly and stolidly rule the home. Leo encouraged his son to typeset his one-page racing form sheet and introduced him to race tracks outside Lowell. There he first witnessed the "exciting cities of great neon, Providence, the mist at the dim walls of great hotels."[38]

It was Kerouac's physical prowess that eventually provided him a ticket out of Lowell. At the age of sixteen he developed a stocky frame, muscular arms, and thick legs. To his father's pleasure, he made the varsity football team, and even substituted for a halfback in the season's first game. In his first season, Kerouac eluded pursuers to score several touchdowns, and he quickly became a local hero. The football coach played Jack infrequently, however; he was sometimes described as "the twelfth man on the Lowell High School Eleven." But the crowds chanted "We want Kerouac!" and football scouts grew keenly interested in his athletic future. Kerouac was also the fastest dash man on the school track team, and he helped Lowell High School to become the state champions in the 300-yard relay. The adolescent began to feel the disparity between his private thoughts, directed to writing and memory, and his high school persona as a gridiron star. Football scouts from Boston College and Columbia made offers of athletic scholarships; since the former hired Leo Kerouac for printing jobs, Jack felt some pressure to go to Boston. "Never mind us," counseled his mother. "Go to Columbia."[39]

Forget this writing stuff, Jean, it'll never pay. You're such a good student—sure you'll go to college, get a job. Stop dreaming!
—Leo Kerouac to his son Jack

YOUNG ALLEN GINSBERG At thirteen, Allen Ginsberg was the smallest boy in his class, and his heavy glasses, braces, and highly developed intellect inspired his classmates to dub him "The Professor." Tests revealed a vocabulary that exceeded the verbal repertoire of most high school graduates, and his motto—"Do what you want to when you want to"[40]—foreshadowed his liberationist philosophy. Ginsberg characterized himself as "an atheist and a combination of Jeffersonian Democrat–Socialist Communist."[41] He later described his youthful self as "a kind of mental ghoul, totally disconnected from any reality, existing in a world of newspapers and aesthetics: Beethoven, Leadbelly, Ma Rainey and Bessie Smith."[42] When Nathan the local tailor saw Ginsberg many years later, he recalled the child: "You had the brain of an 80 year old man and so much alive, so full of joy, your eyes shined as if they had stars in them."[43] Allen's prematurely adult taste, political iconoclasm, and literary ambition came naturally to a child born of the poignant union of Louis and Naomi Ginsberg. "Is he a poet by nature or nurture?" Louis rhetorically asked years later. "I think both."[44]

When they married in 1919, Louis and Naomi shared bohemian interests and leftist beliefs. He was a Socialist, she was a Communist, so they named their firstborn after Eugene Debs. Active in Greenwich Village poetry circles that revolved around Alfred Kreymborg's little magazines, they knew such archetypal bohemians as Joe Gould and Maxwell Bodenheim. (Naomi, in fact, later tortured her husband with claims that she had slept with Bodenheim.) They made an attractive and earnest

Either I'm a genius, I'm egocentric, or I'm slightly schitsophrenic [sic] probably the first two.
—Allen Ginsberg, at age fourteen

Crazy: *either great or unusual: "Crazy, man!"*

Naomi Ginsberg's oil-on-paper portrait of Allen recalled as a child, painted in the hospital

couple—dapper, tall Louis with a toothy smile, wavy hair, and a Rutgers diploma, paired with energetic, svelte Naomi, always ready with a rousing song or a paean to the working classes. The mysterious symptoms of Naomi's schizophrenia (then known as dementia praecox), which would eventually sever their twenty-nine-year marriage, first appeared in 1919. Naomi's family could not understand her new hypersensitivity to light and sound, symptoms that lasted only a few months. Seven years later, Irwin Allen Ginsberg, their second child, was born on June 3, 1926.

Naomi's next schizophrenic episode came after years of fully functioning as an activist and a mother, a wife and a teacher of disadvantaged children. Naomi signed herself into a sanatorium, leaving behind three-year-old Allen and eight-year-old Eugene. Thereafter she revolved in and out of psychiatric institutions. During her periods of schizophrenic decompensation, Naomi grew more vocal about her Communist beliefs and more insistent about practicing nudism at home. She transformed family conflicts into grand plots, with wires planted in the ceiling of their rented home and sticks inserted in her back; eventually Hitler, Mussolini, and Roosevelt became part of her paranoid design. The professionals of the day diagnosed a "nervous breakdown," but they offered no cure. Naomi underwent a traumatizing barrage of shock therapies: more than forty treatments of insulin shock, electroshock, and Metrazol. Private sanatoriums were costly and ineffectual, and her stays at the state hospital at Greystone induced Louis's guilt. Little Allen couldn't understand why his mother abandoned the family for those strange places where vacant-looking people in institutional smocks played croquet on expanses of green lawn. When Naomi returned home, the medications had altered her metabolism, and the figure Ginsberg would recall as the "beautiful Garbo of my Karma"[45] was bloated and fleshy. Fourteen-year-old Allen wrote in his journal that she had "lost her girlish laughter and figure. I don't blame her for her condition."[46]

Naomi and Louis Ginsberg at Coney Island, ca. 1919

Groove: *on the beat, swinging, from jazz slang; Glenn Miller's "In the Groove." Used as a verb, it means to be fascinated by: "Groove on that hip chick!"*

Four-year-old Allen Ginsberg in New Jersey

As Naomi experienced longer and more intense periods of schizophrenic decompensation, Allen became increasingly torn between his parents. As he later described his confusion: "I *received* & *submitted*, with *awareness* of a true nature, to my mother's paranoid emotions. . . . *Then,* listening to my father's complaints, I identified myself with his emotions: the result was that in *one* hour, I was on her 'side' and 'his' & continually felt called to make a decision."[47] Allen sometimes stayed home from school, acting as his mother's caretaker and confidant. He listened to her paranoid fantasies—Louis was poisoning the soup, pots must cover her ears to shield her from evil, invisible bugs and assassins from Newark threatened. At times Allen unconsciously colluded—for how could an adolescent sort out his mother's irrational ideas from her deeply felt emotions?

Allen and his older brother Eugene were shuttled between run-down apartments in noisy Paterson neighborhoods, never certain how their mother would behave. Allen recalled a childhood sustained by generosity and love, though his repertoire of family memories bore little resemblance to the customary nuclear family of the interwar period: his mother taking her sons to Communist meetings, where he learned his first songs ("The Red Flag" and the union rouser "On the Line"); Naomi playing the mandolin, singing "Last Night the Nightingale Woke Me," and spinning leftist fairy tales about princes helping the working classes; visits to a Communist-run summer camp called Camp Nicht-Gedeiget (Yiddish for "no worry"); and Sunday mornings with the *New York Times* spread on the floor as Louis marched through the room reciting Milton and Keats while finishing household chores. When, at the age of eleven, he staged a puppet show called "A Quiet Evening with the Jones Family," it was a fantasy stab at normalcy. Amid all the uncertainty, Louis strove to maintain a stable home for his two sons; after days teaching English at Paterson's Central High School, he bought take-out borscht and kasha at the S & Z

Lay on: *coined in the 1940s, a verb meaning to tell, inform: "I laid on him my understanding of Genesis." It also means to give, especially money: "He laid a C-note on me." [Huncke]*

restaurant, and on weekends he shuttled his sons to family get-togethers. Allen lacked any semblance of conventional family life, but he experienced the generosity of spirit and the ad hoc community that he would later foster in his own life.

In spare moments, Louis sat at his corner desk, beneath a gooseneck lamp, writing lyric, rhyming poems that abstracted and idealized his Job-like existence. He called himself "Paterson's Principal Poet" and not only published in little magazines such as *The New Masses* and the local newspapers but was anthologized in Louis Untermeyer's *Modern American Poetry* (which Allen regarded as "my schoolboy poetry bible when I was twelve years old").[48] Despite the straitened finances—during the Depression his salary was cut by one-third—Louis went into debt to subsidize Horace Liveright's publication of his collection of poems, *The Everlasting Minute.*

Allen was frequently frightened by fearsome shadows and dark hedges, by ghosts in the alleys and the "shrouded stranger" that would later appear in his poems. He escaped into the imagination world of movies, music, radio plays, and books. Louis recalled his son confronting an anti-Semitic bully on the playground and rendering him powerless through his pointed language: "I believe that my son then felt the power of words."[49] At age eleven Allen first set his thoughts down in a leather-covered diary that he locked with a key.[50] Allen recorded dreams, favorite movies, fights with his brother, and his mother's hospitalizations, all recounted in the same tone. Words became one of the few things he could control, and their artful deployment echoed the poetry written by both his father and his older brother. At fourteen, he prophesied in his journal: "I am writing to satisfy my egotism. If some future historian or biographer wants to know what the genius thought and did in his tender years, here it is. I will be a genius of some kind or other, probably in literature. I really believe it. (Not naively, as whoever reads this is thinking.)"[51] Allen's journal writing became one of

If at first you don't succeed, try a little ardor.
Is life worth living? It depends on the liver.

—Louis Ginsberg, from "Keep an O'Pun Mind"

Allen Ginsberg visiting his mother, at Greystone, ca. 1937

ALLEN GINSBERG

"Professor" is the philosopher
and genius of the class . . .
hopes to study law . . . Talent
Club President, Criterion, Big
Brother, Senior Mirror . . .
fiend for Beethoven and Charlie
Chaplin . . . indulges in music,
politics, history, literature . . .
Gold "P" . . . hates dull
teachers and Republicans.

Allen Ginsberg.
June 24, 1943

Allen Ginsberg's yearbook photograph, annotated by Ginsberg and a classmate, Eastside High School, Paterson, New Jersey, 1943

the most consistent features of his life and continues to the present day. "Now, from the cracked and bleeding heart,/Triumphantly, I fashion—Art!"[52] opened one of his early journals.

Allen also sought consolation and assurance in the most tangible expressions of love. Physical contact became such a strong need that Louis dubbed Allen a "little kissing bug."[53] By the age of seven he was conscious of sexual feelings, which he called his "baser emotions,"[54] and through his childhood and adolescence they grew prodigiously. He shared a bed with his older brother, who pushed Allen away as he tried to burrow against Eugene's flesh, and he sometimes climbed into bed with Louis, aroused as he rubbed against his father's leg. "I must have been a sexpest to the whole family," he later observed.[55] Sometimes his inchoate hunger for flesh focused on boyhood friends, and the usual preadolescent crushes took the form of infatuations with muscular boys and neighborhood gang leaders. Fantasizing about one of these crushes—"dreamy Earl/you Prince of Pa-

High: *in a euphoric state (from drugs, alcohol, aesthetic ecstasy, or sex); used by African Americans in the 1930s, subsequently by hipsters: "Sure, man, that cat's real high on tea! Look at those big, staring eyes." [Holmes]*

terson"—Allen stood behind his porch rail and exposed himself to the passing traffic on Haledon Avenue. (No one noticed.) "Perhaps my whole character is exhibitionistic," Ginsberg observed as he looked back on that incident.[56] He daydreamed about boys and, at the age of sixteen, sought an explanation for his desires at the Paterson Public Library. He furtively opened the volume of Kraft-Ebbing's *Psychopathia Sexualis*, read case studies of homosexuals, and asked, "Am I a homosexual?"[57] Looking back thirty years later, Ginsberg observed that his desires set him apart and served as "a catalyst for self-examination."[58]

The masturbatory images he carried in his mind were transformed into hero worship: "My high school mind hero, jewish boy who became a doctor later—then silent neat kid"[59] was a boy named Paul Roth, a half year ahead of Ginsberg. "I spent all the time I could with him," Ginsberg recalled, "but in a very shy way."[60] Ginsberg dreamed of following his hero to Columbia, which Roth attended on scholarship. As he ferried across the Hudson in 1943 to take the university's entrance examination, Allen stood at the prow of the Hoboken ferry and vowed to devote his life to the working classes.

COLUMBIA UNIVERSITY To the west of Columbia University stretched Riverside Drive, the home of the Jewish/academic aristocracy, and to the east, separated by Morningside Park, lay Harlem. Chartered in 1754, Columbia had grown into a large Ivy League school, presided over since 1902 by Nicholas Murray Butler. Of particular interest to its new undergraduate students, Jack Kerouac and Allen Ginsberg, it boasted one of the nation's finest English departments.

Jack Kerouac arrived at Columbia in September 1940, a year older than most of his 500 classmates. After graduating from Lowell High School, he had spent a year at Horace Mann Preparatory School building

Brains and brawn found a happy combination in Jack.
—Horace Mann yearbook entry for Jack Kerouac

up his weight for football and raising his scholarship to Columbia standards. Wearing his blue and white beanie, Kerouac listened to President Butler's welcoming speech about "The Joy of Work," and thereafter he embarked on the split-identity, zigzag course that would characterize the rest of his life.

Every afternoon Kerouac practiced football at Baker Field as a running back. Acquitting himself honorably in the season's first two games, he even returned one kickoff for ninety yards. But a few days later he cracked his right tibia, and Kerouac's gridiron career was henceforth enacted off the field. Hobbling around campus on crutches, the dark jock with soulful good looks presented such an appealing image to the Columbia undergraduate imagination that he was voted class vice president and tapped for Phi Gamma Delta, one of Columbia's prestigious fraternities. (Refusing to wear the pledge beanie, however, he didn't last.) At least superficially, Kerouac could successfully impersonate an Ivy League collegian.

To balance this outgoing persona, Kerouac expressed his solitary nature inside his dormitory room in Livingston Hall, smoking a pipe, listening to classical music on WQXR, and gazing out his window at Butler Library's stone frieze of great writers. But the writer who most thoroughly captured his imagination had nothing to do with class assignments. After reading *Look Homeward, Angel*, Kerouac systematically devoured the rest of Thomas Wolfe's novels. He discovered a kindred spirit in these massive autobiographical fictions by a fellow outsider who cherished the gargantuan promise of the raw young nation and expressed himself in unabashedly poetic language.

Kerouac's relationship to Columbia was as erratic as his football career and classwork, which ranged from A's in literature to an F in chemistry. When he returned a day late for football practice at the outset of his sophomore year, the coach greeted him coolly. Before the season's first game, Kerouac simply left practice and hopped a southbound bus, his suit-

Go into the American night, the Thomas Wolfe darkness, the hell with these bigshot gangster football coaches, go after being an American writer, tell the truth, don't be pushed around.
—Jack Kerouac

case full, only to return briefly to Columbia and the football team a year later. Deprived of players during wartime, the coach telegraphed Kerouac and offered him one last chance to play, but Kerouac didn't last the week. He was too light, and he couldn't successfully execute Coach Furey's signature play. While listening to Beethoven's Fifth Symphony, Kerouac vowed that he would be an artist, skipped practice, and never returned. He thereby walked away from his football career, from his scholarship to Columbia, and from the ladder of conventional achievement, and he never returned.

Jack Kerouac, "Weird Self-Portrait at Sea," ca. 1941

Before re-entering the orbit of Columbia, as a nonstudent, he plied many trades—grease monkey, merchant seaman, and short-order cook. He signed up to join both the Marines and the Coast Guard, panicked, drank, vomited, passed out in a public men's room in downtown Boston, woke up afraid to face his parents, and shipped out as a scullion en route to Greenland.

Kerouac joined the Navy in February 1943, but he could tolerate the boot camp routine—uncomfortable hammocks, prohibitions against smoking, and compulsive inspections—for only a few months. One afternoon at drill he simply laid his gun on the ground and quietly walked away to the library, where he was apprehended in the act of reading. At the hospital the psychiatrist asked his identity, and Kerouac replied, "I'm only old Samuel Johnson."[61] He meant that he was a man of letters and therefore cherished his independence, but the reference was lost on the Navy psychiatrist, as was Kerouac's assertion that he was "dedicating my actions to experience in order to write about them, sacrificing myself on the altar of Art."[62] Finally he was honorably discharged from the Navy with the "diagnosis" of "indifferent character."

A letter Kerouac wrote from the Navy hospital reflected his own version of his divided psyche, which he hoped to mend through writing:

> My schizoid side is the Raskolnikov–Dedalus–George Webber–Duluoz side, the bent and brooding figure sneering at a world of mediocrities, complacent ignorance, and bigotry exercised by ersatz Ben Franklins; the introverted, scholarly side; the alien side.
>
> My normal counterpart, the one you're familiar with, is the halfback-whoremaster-alemate-scullion-jitterbug-jazz critic side, the side in me which recommends a broad, rugged America; which requires the nourishment of gutsy, redblooded associates; and which lofts whatever guileless laughter I've left in me rather than that schizoid's cackle I have of late.[63]

My life is like a sea, my memory the boat.

—Jack Kerouac

Throughout his peripatetic chaos, Kerouac was able to maintain a ritualized writing discipline. He kept journals in small notebooks, he read incessantly, carefully annotated H. G. Wells's *Outline of History*, and worked on a neatly handprinted novel, *The Sea Is My Brother* (whose title echoed his quest to replace the lost Gerard). Kerouac returned to the Columbia milieu in September 1943, and he entered the orbit of apartment 15 at 421 West 118th Street. The two women who lived here—Edie Parker and Joan Vollmer—and their friends would alter his life. As Kerouac put it, "In start coming the characters of my future life."[64]

A man of letters is a man of independence.

—Jack Kerouac to a Navy psychiatrist

ENTER ALLEN GINSBERG That same fall of 1943, Allen Ginsberg arrived at Columbia University. The seventeen-year-old freshman was supported by a CIO (Congress of Industrial Organizations) scholarship and a $100 stipend from the university. His already vast reading helped equip him to consort with fellow undergraduates who were older, WASP-ier, and more experienced in the ways of the world. Eager to fit in, he immediately found a niche in the English Department, where he studied with Raymond Weaver, Pulitzer Prize–winning poet Mark Van Doren, and Lionel Trilling. His plans to become a labor lawyer were quickly forgotten as he absorbed the Western literary canon delineated by Lionel Trilling. As Ginsberg put it, Trilling "tried to revive the humanistic solidarity and good manners of mid-nineteenth-century England. Mahogany Matthew Arnold."[65] Ginsberg felt close to his new mentor "because we were both Jewish and he sort of empathized with me."[66] Allen became a model student who studied diligently at Butler Library, wrote rhymed lyrics that appeared in the *Columbia Jester Review*, and participated in the Philolexian debating club. In contrast to the cadets who sat in the back rows and yawned, the zealous student with the horn-rimmed glasses and nasal voice was a pleasure to teach; both Trilling and Van Doren became Ginsberg's

*Fruit: homosexual, from the 1930s, usually used by heterosexuals pejoratively: "All girls go fruit, black girls go fruit for mexican girls." [Kerouac] Homosexuals used the word in a camp context: **fruit salad**, meaning a homosexual gathering; **fruit-bowl queen**, meaning a homosexual athlete.*

supporters. They even encouraged his poetry, although for them poetry did not include Walt Whitman, William Carlos Williams, or Ezra Pound. Since they claimed no place in his father's universe of poetry, Ginsberg initially did not even notice the omissions.

Lucien Carr on the Columbia University campus, facing Butler Library, 1944

Know these words and you speak the Carr language: fruit, phallus, clitoris, cacoethes, feces, foetus, womb, Rimbaud.

—Allen Ginsberg, on Lucien Carr

ENTER LUCIEN CARR Shortly before Christmas 1943, Allen was wandering down the seventh-floor hall of his deserted dormitory. From behind a wooden door at the end of the long corridor came the sounds of Brahms Trio No. 1. When Ginsberg knocked to ask the name of the composer, he recognized the face of a classmate from Lionel Trilling's class. "Well, well! A little oasis in this wasteland," said Lucien Carr.[67] Ginsberg stepped into a small room that was self-consciously stamped with the freshman's personality. Posters of paintings by Rousseau and Cézanne covered one wall, and a bookcase was crowded with titles that attracted Ginsberg: Flaubert, Rimbaud's *Une Saison en enfer*, Spinoza's *Ethics*. Sensing Carr's worldliness and cynicism, Allen felt "jejune" by comparison. Recalling Ginsberg, Carr exclaimed, "Naive, he was incredibly naive! He was just an eager young Jewish kid from Paterson who wanted to know everything about books and writers and art and painting, who knew nothing about the serious things in life such as wenching and drinking!"[68] Ginsberg invoked Yeats when he recalled their first meeting: "the most angelic-looking kid I ever saw, with blond hair, pale and 'hollow of cheek as though he drank the wind and took a mess of shadows for his meat.'"[69] Carr and Ginsberg celebrated their mutual sense of discovery by pouring two glasses of burgundy.

They adopted personas—Lucien dubbed himself Claude de Maubris and Allen became Gillette—and they waged endless undergraduate conversations about the meaning of art, the necessity of political action, and the emptiness of bourgeois life. Lucien was the first of Allen's college infatuations, although he would not reveal his homosexuality to

Carr for three years. It was not only Carr's spoiled dandy good looks that attracted Ginsberg but also his bold personal style (red bandanas and red shirts), his library, and his iconoclasm. As Ginsberg wrote in his journal, "He is in youth a 'genius of life.'"[70] Lucien's effect on Ginsberg was vitally important, as he noted, five years later in his journal: "As long as I have thought of us as artists, it has been Claude [Lucien] who I thought of as central to any active inter-inspiring school or community of creation."[71]

Among Lucien Carr's "fetishes" that Ginsberg noted in his journal was "William Burroughs at 48 Morton."[72]

GINSBERG MEETS BURROUGHS Shortly after Christmas 1943, Lucien Carr and Allen Ginsberg hopped a subway to Greenwich Village, carrying on a discussion about what they called the "New Vision." The two found David Kammerer conversing with William Burroughs, his old friend and current neighbor, and the first words Ginsberg heard Burroughs utter were in praise of a lesbian who was "straightforward, manly, and reliable." Burroughs was twenty-nine at the time; to the seventeen-year-old Ginsberg he seemed impossibly old and wise. His watery blue eyes behind glasses, his seersucker suit on a spindly frame, his sinus-driven snuffling, his sallow skin and thin sandy hair all added up to an impression of a man preternaturally mature. "I wondered who this intelligent aristocrat was," Ginsberg recalled.[73] Seated on an upturned log, he listened to Lucien recount a recent fight between Kammerer and a painter that had climaxed in Carr's biting the painter's earlobe. Burroughs responded to this lurid tale by quoting an obscure and apposite passage from the first act of *Troilus and Cressida*: "In the words of the immortal Bard, 'tis too starved a subject for my sword.'"[74] At this moment, impressed by the older man's effortless verbal grace, he put to Burroughs the question he and Lucien had been debating on the IRT: What is art? Burroughs drily replied, "Art is a three letter word."[75]

Lucien Carr's Fetishes, Noted in Allen Ginsberg's Journal
The West End
Pernod
People
The Rack
Clothes (sweater, shirt)
Shaving
Music (Brahms, Mahler)
The Face-Mask
Knives
Greenwich Village
Burroughs at 48 Morton
Streets
Stores
Alleys

Hipster: In the late 1930s, this word meant one who used drugs, and that meaning persisted, but it also implied one who possessed underground wisdom: "Huge apocalyptic novels by homosexual hipster." [Ginsberg, on discovering Genet, 1949]

Do you realize Hubbard [Burroughs] is somewhat like Sherlock Holmes's older brother?

—Irwin Garden (Ginsberg-based character), on William Burroughs

KEROUAC MEETS CARR When Jack Kerouac first saw Lucien Carr across the smoky West End bar at Broadway and West 113th Street, he remarked to Edie Parker, "Looks like a mischievous prick."[76] His initial hostility was doubtless colored by jealousy (Edie and many other women were fascinated by Carr) and by Carr's blond aristocratic grace, so different from his own working-class style. Drinking together helped erode the barriers between the two men, and after they ended a drinking bout at the West End by Carr rolling his new friend in a barrel along the sidewalks of upper Broadway, the relationship was cemented. Kerouac idealized Carr's impetuous acts—tossing a plate of veal parmesan over his shoulder, singing bawdy songs and chewing on shards of a cocktail glass, ripping up Burroughs' seersucker suit. "Never before had I felt that way about life and the times as I did that summer," Kerouac recalled. "It was because Claude's [Carr's] sensibilities were affixed to his charm, and vice versa, and both had captivated me. He was unlike most people in that he never concealed the nature of his sensibilities—he wore them on his sleeve in place of a heart."[77] Carr's discussions about the vision unique to the writer encouraged Jack's literary vocation. Kerouac in turn represented to Carr a writer-in-the-flesh, both a lure and a threat; although Carr wrote little, Kerouac had already written half a million words. Theirs was a charged brotherhood of opposites—light and dark, aristocrat and working-class. As Carr recalled, "Each person who came along was someone for Kerouac to love."[78]

Ignu: Coined in the late 1940s by Allen Ginsberg and Jack Kerouac after Dostoyevsky's The Idiot, *this word meant a holy idiot, an angel in comical form.*

GINSBERG MEETS KEROUAC The "romantic seaman who writes poem books"[79] became a frequent subject in Carr's daily conversations with Ginsberg. That idealized figure, Ginsberg found, was less romantic in person. He met Kerouac in the spring of 1944, while Kerouac was in the middle of a late breakfast of eggs and bacon. Kerouac offered his guest a beer. When Ginsberg replied, "No, no. Discretion is the better part of valor," Kerouac looked at the freshman four years his junior and barked, "Aw where's my food!" Kerouac later described that moment in a novel: "Turns out it took years for Irwin [Ginsberg] to get over a certain fear of the 'brooding football artist yelling for his supper in big daddy chair' or some such."[80] That morning's conflict played off their contrasting styles—Jew–Canuck, macho–intellectual, man of the world–nerd—but it did not last too long. When the two next met, walking through the Columbia campus, Ginsberg began a conversation that quickly became more nakedly revelatory than his talks with Lucien—he recounted his childhood fears that ghosts populated the hedges and the alleys. Kerouac responded, "Gee, I have thoughts like that all the time."[81] Ginsberg suddenly felt a link to Kerouac based on vulnerability—"that if I actually confessed the secret tenderness of my soul he would understand nakedly who I was."[82]

Ginsberg quickly fell in love with his new friend, although several months passed before he bluntly confided in Kerouac. "Jack, you know, I love you, and I want to sleep with you, and I really like men."[83] Kerouac let out an uncomfortable groan, but he didn't reject Ginsberg, and the revelation subsequently opened the way to intimate discussion of their mutual nightmares. Ginsberg recalled Kerouac as "a slightly older person and someone who I felt had more authority, his tolerance gave me *permission* to open up and talk."[84]

KEROUAC MEETS BURROUGHS In February 1944, David Kammerer brought William Burroughs to Jack Kerouac's apartment, ostensibly to gather information about the merchant marines. In Burroughs' eyes, Kerouac—damp from a shower, wearing only dirty chinos—looked the part of the seaman, and he launched into a series of queries. Kerouac was baffled,

Nobody can actually like Burroughs.
—Jack Kerouac

It's a finkish world.
—William Burroughs to Jack Kerouac

not by the questions, but by the mere presence of this inscrutable, intellectual man in his apartment. He detected in Burroughs "a little of the wistful German Nazi youth as his soft hair fluffles in the breeze,"[85] and he surmised that Kammerer and Burroughs were "the most evil and intelligent buncha bastards and shits" he had ever encountered.[86]

When Ginsberg and Kerouac later visited Burroughs, Ginsberg recalled, "We were like ambassadors to the Chinese emperor, making a delegation of ourselves to inquire into the nature of his soul. Quite literally and directly. Who is Burroughs? Why is he so intelligent? Will he be friendly or unfriendly?"[87] Burroughs treated his new acolytes (his first) with unusual interest. They were intrigued by his personal knowledge of Budapest and Vienna, his patrician style, and his catholic literary appetite. And, as Kerouac observed, "He has *finish*."[88] Burroughs' taste contrasted with both Lionel Trilling's and Mortimer Adler's canon; prominent on Burroughs' bookshelves were Jean Cocteau's *Opium*, Hart Crane's *Collected Works*, the histories of Vico and Pareto, and Oswald Spengler's *The Decline of the West*. Before they departed, Burroughs gave each a gift: Yeats's *A Vision* to Allen, Spengler's *Decline of the West* to Jack. The two concluded that what they had taken for aloofness was actually shyness and wondered whether Burroughs would become a mentor. Ginsberg compared him to a bust of Dante and wrote in his journal: "Bill has always been the wise, warm, friendly old father confessor."[89] Jack Kerouac called Burroughs "the grandest mirror in which I can stare at myself."[90] Burroughs seemed to be the most intelligent man alive.

Eddify yer mind, me boy.
—William Burroughs to Jack Kerouac, on giving him Spengler's *Decline of the West*

Head, pot head, tea head: *a marijuana user, term used from 1940s to the present: "Like Proust be an old tea head of time." [Kerouac]*

THE NEW VISION Beginning in 1944 Ginsberg, Kerouac, and Carr talked about "the New Vision" and "the New Consciousness." The terms carried overtones of youth (with its untried faith in vision and consciousness) and of the avant-garde (which used "new" to evoke modernity). Ginsberg recently described the literary underpinnings of the New Vision in "works of late civilization" which had been suggested by Burroughs. Among the primary texts were Yeats's *A Vision*, Auden's *The Age of Anxiety*, Kafka's *The Trial*, André Gide's *Lafcadio's Adventures*, and Camus's *The Stranger*. Kerouac, Ginsberg, and Carr also read Giovanni Vico and Vilfredo Pareto on the cycles of history, Joyce's *Finnegans Wake*, and, most important, Oswald Spengler's *Decline of the West*. Ginsberg recently described the genesis of the New Vision:

> It was a very rich reading list, which we were not getting in college, just the opposite of college, because college was the American Empire, and this was the decline of Empire. . . . To put it right down very much on the ground, it [the New Vision] comes out of Spengler's *Decline of the West*, which speaks of the end of the culture and the beginning of the high civilization, which is a degenerate sophistication and exfoliation of the primary culture, simultaneous with the rise of a second religiousness. . . . The new vision assumed the death of square morality and replaced that meaning with belief in creativity. I think we were quite moralistic in a way.[91]

The New Vision reflected a dark historical moment in which civilization was in decline, the West was at war, and the atomic bomb had been dropped. They all could quote the closing lines of Yeats's "The Second Coming": "And what rough beast, its hour come round at last,/Slouches towards Bethlehem to be born?" The New Vision also provided an arena in which Ginsberg and Carr could examine questions of morality and aesthetics, as suggested by a parody dialogue in Ginsberg's journal:

> Carr: I tell you that I repudiate your little loves, your little derivative morality, your hypocritical altruism, your foolish humanity

When will we go, beyond the beaches and the mountains, to greet the birth of the new task, the new wisdom, the flight of tyrants and demons, the end of superstitions; to adore—the first ones! Christmas on Earth?

—Arthur Rimbaud

List of "News"
("New," along with "little," "free," "revolution," and "renaissance," is a buzzword used, beginning in the 1910s, as a declaration of modernity.)
The new woman
The new paganism
The New Republic
The new verse
The New Freewoman
The new art
The New Negro

obsessions, all the cares and tenets of your expedient little modern
bourgeois culture.

Ginsberg: And I reply that I repudiate your priggish cynicism, your
own equally coerced amorality, your escapist egotism, your foolish
obsession with your narrow personal devices, all the petty appurte-
nances of your neurotic escapist mechanism.[92]

Ginsberg attempted to synthesize their conversations into a philosophy that granted art a powerful political role: "political in the highest
sense—humanitarian."[93] He valued most highly those figures who saw life
from multiple perspectives. "Art for art's sake is a delusion. The satanist,
the moralist, the poet, the politician are all poor fools. Only the dilettante
is the exemplar of realism."[94]

The New Vision not only offered an alternative to the well-culti-
vated terrain presented by Lionel Trilling and Mark Van Doren, it also introduced concepts that would later prove central to the Beat Generation:
1) Uncensored self-expression is the seed of creativity. 2) The artist's consciousness is expanded through nonrational means: derangement of the
senses, via drugs, dreams, hallucinatory states, and visions. 3) Art super-
sedes the dictates of conventional morality. "The highest and most creative
world is a world of artists," Ginsberg wrote in his journal in 1944, and
when he read the sentence a half-century later he said, "I still believe
that."[95]

Derangers of the Senses in the Service of Art
Antonin Artaud
Hector Berlioz
Jean Cocteau
Samuel Taylor Coleridge
Thomas De Quincey
The Hashish Eaters Club
Aldous Huxley

AUGUST 13, 1944 The events that began on Sunday morning, August 13, 1944, and continued into the next morning reverberated for years
among the new circle of friends. By the end of this twenty-four-hour period, there was a corpse, a killer, and two accomplices, inextricably bound
in a weird covenant exacted by manslaughter.

The oldest of the five participants, thirty-three-year-old David Kammerer, rolled out of his bed in his tiny Greenwich Village apartment at 48 Morton Street and put on his habitual combination of cheap Sixth Avenue shirt, frayed Sulka tie, and rumpled tweed suit. As he lit his first Lucky Strike of the day and put on his steel-rimmed glasses, Kammerer conjured up the tantalizing image of his beloved, Lucien Carr.

Since following Carr to New York, he had scaled the walls of Columbia's Warren Hall to spy on the sleeping Lucien and crashed Village parties to be near him. "This is silly, Dave, what you're doing is selfish," warned William Burroughs. "You're not really interested in him, you're interested in yourself, and what you're trying to accomplish is not at all to his advantage."[96]

Lucien Carr sometimes desperately wanted Kammerer to give up his pursuit, but few suspected it from seeing the two together. Carr appeared to welcome Kammerer's adoration—especially at moments when the older man could ghost a term paper, for example—and Carr's girlfriend, Celine Young, believed that he considered it a point of pride that Kammerer dogged his footsteps. In August 1944, however, Carr observed, "I feel like I'm in a pond that's drying up and I'm about to suffocate."[97] The atmosphere of crisis heightened as Lucien made plans to ship out to sea with Kerouac.

Earlier that week, inspired by watching Jean Renoir's *La Grande Illusion*, Lucien Carr and Jack Kerouac had envisioned an escape from their respective romantic pursuers. Although Kerouac's pursuer, Edie Parker, displayed none of Kammerer's mania, her hints about marriage nevertheless alarmed Jack. In order to put an ocean between them and their pursuers, Carr and Kerouac planned to ship out as normal workers. The plan was kept secret from David Kammerer. for they imagined him pursuing Carr to foreign shores. En route to the ship they signed a petition

Gone: *According to Herbert Huncke, this positive adjective originated in Midtown New York among zoot-suiters and jazz musicians in the late 1930s: "Let's buy some tubes and go over to Ronnie's. They have some gone numbers on the box." [Burroughs]*

with pseudonyms, Arthur Rimbaud (Carr) and Paul Verlaine (Kerouac), that reflected their literary and bohemian frame of mind. (Carr had recently developed a habit of chanting Rimbaud's line "Plonger au fond du gouffre . . . ciel ou enfer qu'importe?") The chief mate of the *Robert Hayes*, however, sized up the pair as uncooperative adolescents and threw them off the ship (Kerouac seeming to prove the mate's perspicacity by yelling "Fuck you all!" as he made his way to the gangplank).

That Sunday morning of August 13, Lucien Carr felt desperate and disconsolate in the wake of the *Robert Hayes* fiasco. He wandered down the hall to Allen Ginsberg's dorm room, found him gone, and opened his journal. There, in Ginsberg's barely decipherable handwriting, was an entry entitled "Essay in Character Analysis: Lucien Carr."

> He would hate to be known as a mere boor, an eccentric, crankish fool, or a worthless bull-like, stupid, oafish exhibitionist. His ego demands intellectual recognition. Thus he adopts the postures and attitudes of the intellectual with which he is familiar—the Bohemian. All the appurtenances of the Bohemian become his and this pathogenic dread of non-self recognition and non-social recognition drives him to red shirts, wild songs, drink, women, queer shoes, loud talk, arrogance, infantilism on a high intellectual level. It is thus vicarious intellectual recognition. It is a palliative to his scarred ego. Either he is a genius or he . . . but he can recognize no other alternative. He must prove that he is a genius.[98]

Bebop: Beginning in the 1940s, this style of jazz was described as "the third stage in jive music." Mating the intricate African rhythm to European harmony, bebop was applied to Charlie Parker, Dizzy Gillespie, and Thelonius Monk.

In the margin, Lucien wrote: "Notice the tears in your most definitive work." (He later told Ginsberg that it wasn't tears: "I was sweating like a bitch." Ginsberg replied, "The truth hurts, eh?"[99])

*Jack Kerouac and Lucien Carr,
Columbia University, August 1944, a
few days before they were scheduled to
ship out to sea*

A few hours later, crossing upper Broadway, Ginsberg encountered David Kammerer. In the middle of the traffic island Kammerer unburdened himself about his fear that Carr would ship out and declared that he would follow Lucien. He urged Ginsberg to join them. The following exchange took place:

> Kammerer: Oh Ginsberg, heed the call of the artist. Reverend sybarite, forsake thy calling.
> Ginsberg: Art waits on humanity at the moment.
> Kammerer: That's right. Burroughs called you the bourgeois Rimbaud last night.[100]

Early in the evening, Lucien Carr dined with his mother in the Victorian living room of her East Fifty-Seventh Street apartment. Frail and bright-eyed, she railed against David Kammerer as a diabolic Iago figure who tracked her son "purely for love of evil." She then produced an artifact from the spring of 1943—the certificate of Lucien's stay on Cook County Hospital's psychiatric wing. When Marion Carr instructed her son to burn the certificate, he bargained with her: if she would put a $20 bill inside as it burned; if he could burn it on the carpet. Carr lost both his demands and finally agreed to burn the certificate in a large ashtray. Mother and son turned out the lights, struck a match, and giggled as the paper went up in flame.

Later that evening, Jack Kerouac and Allen Ginsberg went to their favorite haunt, the West End. Kerouac and Ginsberg were sitting in one of the dark oak booths when Lucien reeled in through the revolving door, past the jukebox and cigarette machine, and announced he was ready for more Canadian Club whiskey. As he described burning his hospital certificate, Ginsberg offered his condolences: "You've lost the only family heir-

Kick, kicks: *immediate gratification of desires: the Sunday* New York Times' *review of* On the Road *was called "In Pursuit of 'Kicks.'" Sometimes refers to a state related to getting high on drugs or drunk or any such derangment of the senses. "'See? See?' cackled Dean, poking my ribs, 'I told you it was kicks. Everybody's kicks, man.'" [Kerouac] Also means a particular driving interest: "1955 Chevrolets, that's his kick."*

loom that you had."[101] Kerouac retired at midnight, believing—yet again—that he could sign up to ship out the first thing Monday morning. Cutting across Columbia's campus en route to Edie Parker's apartment at 421 West 118th Street, Kerouac ran into David Kammerer and told him that he'd find Lucien Carr at the West End.

Kammerer stuck his head into the bar and engaged Lucien in conversation. Long after Ginsberg went home to read Karl Marx, Kammerer's pleas to Lucien continued. The jukebox played the summer's hit song, "You Always Hurt the One You Love," as the two talked until Johnny, the big bartender, announced the last call for drinks. Kammerer and Carr staggered out and headed west toward Riverside Park.

The volatile combination of whiskey, the day's unhinging events, and Kammerer's desperate fear of separation proved fatal. The two men argued on the dark grassy banks of the Hudson. After Kammerer reportedly made a sexual advance and threatened to hurt Lucien's girlfriend, Carr pulled his white-handled Boy Scout knife from his pocket and stabbed Kammerer twice in the heart. Fearing that the blood-spattered corpse would rise and walk, Carr pushed the 185 pounds of dead weight to the river's edge, removed the laces from Kammerer's shoes, pulled off his belt, and tore Kammerer's bloodied white shirt, and loaded the corpse down with rocks. Carr stripped completely and entered the river up to his chin, pushing the corpse before him. David Kammerer would not sink. He floated slowly downstream.

Columbia Student Kills Friend and Sinks Body in Hudson River.
—*New York Times,* August 17, 1944

Lucien's first thought was to seek the counsel of the wisest man he knew: William Burroughs. Carr hailed a taxi on Riverside Drive and instructed the cabbie to go to Greenwich Village. When Burroughs answered the door in a bathrobe, Carr blurted out, "I just killed the old man." He flashed a bloody pack of cigarettes and offered Kammerer's last Lucky Strike. Burroughs' flat voice and gray, deadpan face betrayed nei-

The Man: *A flexible drug-world term from the 1940s on, it can mean the chief drug pusher or, on the other hand, the police or a narcotics agent.*

ther outrage nor fear as he mused to himself, "So this is how Dave Kammerer ends."[102] Carr was sure he would get "the hot seat," but Burroughs cannily appraised the situation and offered his advice. "Don't be absurd," he drawled. "Get a good lawyer and do what he tells you to do. Say what he tells you to say. Make a case for self-defense. It's pretty preposterous, but juries have swallowed bigger ones than that."[103] He gave Carr a $5 bill and sent him on his way.

Alone with the memories of his dead friend, Burroughs tore up the cigarette pack and flushed the shreds of bloodied tobacco and paper down the toilet but gave little thought to informing the authorities. He was no stool pigeon. He silently mourned Kammerer and fondly recalled Toots Shor's comment on seeing Mayor James J. Walker in a casket: "Jimmy, Jimmy, when you walked in, you brightened up the joint."[104]

Cool: *a multipurpose word from the 1940s, used by hipsters to mean someone who was not judgmental and not affiliated with the law: "Don't worry, he's cool." It later became a staple word of the caricatured beatnik (Mademoiselle story: "Flaming Cool Youth of San Francisco Poetry"); a positive exclamation ("Cool!" "Cool shit!"); also a general positive adjective ("a cool time," "a cool sweatshirt"). Cool also describes an attitude of "second-removism" sometimes adopted by hipsters: "A raw mind and a cool mind are two different minds. The raw mind is usually associated with the physical life, whether athletic, work, or just beat (like Huncke); the cool mind is the intellectual emphasis and the physical counterpart of it is a kind of gracefulness . . . a gracefulness that is almost effeminate." [Kerouac]*

Lucien Carr taxied to 421 West 118th Street and walked up six flights to apartment 62, where Jack Kerouac was sleeping in the living room with Edie Parker. Lying on his stomach with one arm raised over his head, Kerouac rolled over, blinked his blue eyes, and ran his hand through his dark brown hair as Carr tossed the dead man's steel-rimmed glasses on the table and blurted out his story. Kerouac quickly dispatched Edie to get breakfast and threw on his chinos and white tee-shirt. He and Carr headed off to nearby Morningside Park, where Kerouac drew attention away from Carr by urinating on a bush, while Carr buried the glasses in a shallow hole. Walking up 125th Street, Carr knelt over a subway grate and theatrically dropped the murder weapon, the white-handled Boy Scout knife.

Two days later, accompanied by a lawyer, Lucien Carr turned himself in. Both the police and the district attorney's office were taken aback by Carr's intellectual presentation. "At first he was nervous," reported the

New York Times, "but as he completed his amazing recital he became astonishingly calm and self-possessed."[105] Carr remained in the district attorney's office all night, although he was not formally charged, reading Yeats's *A Vision*. When the Coast Guard's initial report failed to find the body, they thought Carr was a lunatic, but David Kammerer's body was sighted that afternoon, floating off West 108th Street. The manslaughter story was soon played out in the tabloids as "an honor slaying." Indicted for second-degree manslaughter, Lucien entered the "Tombs" in lower Manhattan carrying two books under his arm: Yeats's *A Vision*, and Gerald Heard's *The Third Morality*.

Both Kerouac and Burroughs were booked as material witnesses. Mortimer and Laura Burroughs promptly put up $2,500 bail for their son, but Leo Kerouac was less sanguine about his son's plight. He declared Jack a disgrace to the family and refused to rescue him from the Bronx City Jail. While the tabloid pages treated Carr as an intellectual prince of darkness, Kerouac was portrayed as merely a minor hoodlum. Lying on a board-and-mattress bed, he read Aldous Huxley's *Brave New World*, felt the wound of his father's rejection, and was shocked when he was taken to the morgue and drawer 169 was pulled out to reveal the naked, bloated, blue corpse of David Kammerer.

Kerouac struck a deal—not with the DA but with his girlfriend: if Edie Parker would put up bail money, he would marry her. She did, and he did, on August 22, in a City Hall ceremony with a prison plainclothesman as best man and Carr's girlfriend, Celine Young, as maid of honor. "The tragic events of the past few weeks, I believe, catapulted us into a badly timed union," Kerouac wrote Edie's mother, "but a bad beginning might augur a successful ending."[106] Shortly thereafter, Jack and Edie took the train to Grosse Pointe, Michigan, where they were met by a chauffered Packard limousine and driven to the Parker family's home at 1407 Somerset. Amid chandeliers, lace, china, and a butler, Kerouac feared that he

"Student Accused as 'Honor' Slayer," Daily News, *August 17, 1944*

Uncool: *adjective describing one who doesn't take appropriate precautions, leaves himself open to the attention of the law: "It is uncool to give your home as a forwarding address for packages from Mexico."*

had traded the Bronx City Jail for a more elegantly upholstered prison. Wearing a leather jacket and heavy boots, he informed Edie's family friends that his profession was "artist," and when he wasn't working in a ball-bearing factory, he holed up for hours in the bathroom, handprinting on a yellow tablet a novel about his childhood. But he feared that he would find no raw material for fiction: "There's no tragedy in Grosse Pointe."[107]

Lucien appeared in homicide court neatly dressed in a pressed cocoa-brown suit, his hair plastered to his skull. In his right hand he carried Yeats's *A Vision*, and for most of the hearing he stared at the book, apparently oblivious to the courtroom proceedings. He pleaded guilty to second-degree manslaughter and received an indeterminate sentence in the Elmira Reformatory, which he entered on October 9, 1944. From behind bars he reviewed his actions and reported to Ginsberg that he still maintained that morality was an internal matter, that intellect was powerful but now seemed slightly less important, and that he was pondering the meaning of the spirit.

And now, this curtain has been rung down! Everything I have loved of the past year has fled into the past. My world is no longer the same.
—Allen Ginsberg, after David Kammerer's death

Only Allen Ginsberg escaped the legal net, but he was emotionally shaken. An unrelenting headache developed as he pondered the events in his journal. "Kammerer Dead! Another lover hits the universe! Life—it moves!—? Like all sad people, I am a poet."[108] His first year at Columbia, his polemical discussions with Lucien Carr, his new friendships, now took on a darker cast: "But the acceleration of life was the passing climax of a longer pleasure: it was the prelude to the decay of this life. Now the omened deed is done. The shadow has closed down on us and engulfed us all. . . . The libertine circle is destroyed with the death of Kammerer. If Carr is released, it can never be the same. Only I will remain faithful to the past."[109]

419 WEST 115TH STREET: JOAN VOLLMER'S APARTMENT Although the circle of friends disbanded in the wake of David Kammerer's death, the horrific event irrevocably branded them as members of the same unsavory tribe. Columbia University thereafter designated Kerouac "an unwholesome influence on the students" and more informally as "a lout," while Ginsberg was regarded with suspicion.[110] Within the next year, Burroughs, Kerouac, and Ginsberg would each try to portray the murder in fictional form. Ginsberg's version, composed for a creative writing class, was halted by Columbia's associate dean, who deemed it "smutty." At Kerouac's urging, he and Burroughs began writing alternating chapters of a Dashiell Hammett–like novel entitled "And the Hippos Were Boiled in Their Tanks." Kerouac described it at the time as "a portrait of the 'lost' segment of our generation."[111] Their joint effort was never published, although Kerouac made attempts to sell it up to 1952. More important, the collaboration stimulated Burroughs to attempt his first writing in nearly a decade, and it offered Kerouac the opportunity to work with the wisest man he knew. "We make a good team," he wrote.[112]

Surrounded by a number of friends, Ginsberg, Kerouac, and Burroughs were drawn back to the Columbia milieu in 1945: Burroughs returned from St. Louis, and Kerouac separated from Edie Parker after a few months. For the year following the summer of 1945, the trio experienced their most concentrated period of communal living: As Ginsberg recalled, "It was very warm, very friendly, very family."[113] They pooled their money for home-cooked communal meals; they slept together, both chastely and not; they conducted "Dostoyevskian confrontations" and enacted vaudeville routines; and they engaged in psychoanalysis. The center of the activity—and the crucible for their coming of age—was a rambling, high-ceilinged, five-bedroom apartment at 419 West 115th Street rented by Joan Vollmer for $115 a month.

Joan's old-fashioned flat became the unofficial hangout for the

We are all sealed in our own little melancholy atmospheres, like planets, and revolving around the sun, our common but distant desire.
—Jack Kerouac to Allen Ginsberg

Joan is the nicest woman I know; "the greatest" as they say in hip-talk.
—Allen Ginsberg, on Joan Vollmer

group that had previously clustered around Lucien Carr at the West End. Celine Young, Carr's girlfriend at the time of his arrest, observed that they would find other people "to fill in the place he created for himself." They were complemented by a shifting constellation of a half-dozen people, only one of them, a clean-cut anthropology student named Hal Chase, a matriculated student at Columbia.

Kerouac came to the apartment late in 1945, lured once again by the presence of Edie, whom he treated more as his girlfriend than his wife. Edie supported them by working as a cigarette girl in such nightclubs as the Zanzibar and 21, but she soon fled to a more stable life with her grandmother. But Kerouac remained a fixture in Joan's apartment.

When Allen Ginsberg moved into Joan Vollmer's apartment in March 1945, he was a sexually inexperienced eighteen-year-old who had just been suspended from Columbia. Like many of the pivotal episodes in his life, his suspension was linked to Kerouac. Late one night in early 1945, Kerouac arrived at Ginsberg's dorm room following an encounter with Burroughs. In objective tones that could inspire anxiety, Burroughs had declared that Kerouac was fixated on his mother. Kerouac needed to discuss this all too apt observation with Ginsberg. After talking until 2 AM, Jack climbed into Allen's bed, each stripped to his underwear. They remained chaste through the night but awakened to the self-righteous knock of a Columbia dean, whereupon Kerouac buried himself under the bedcovers of Ginsberg's absent roommate. The infraction that prompted the unexpected visit was two short statements Allen had etched into the grimy dust on his dorm room window: [Columbia President] BUTLER HAS NO BALLS and FUCK THE JEWS—accompanied by a cock and balls beside a skull and crossbones. The delinquent and perhaps anti-Semitic cleaning lady for whom the message was intended reported it to the university. The administration took such umbrage that they billed

Nowhere: the opposite of hip; unenlightened, out of it, lacking special knowledge: "I never seen such nowhereness, no s-h-i-t, why don't he just go somewhere and fade, um." [Kerouac] It can also be used to describe a place or event: "Every time I hit Panama, the place is exactly one month, two months, six months more nowhere, like the course of a degenerative illness." [Burroughs]

Ginsberg $2.63 for an overnight guest, suspended him from all Columbia classes and activities, and wrote Allen's father that the infraction was so grave that it "cannot be repeated in a letter."[114] Allen showed up at the dean's office prepared to deny homosexual activity with Kerouac, but the idea proved so unspeakable that it was not mentioned.

At this remarkable juncture, Ginsberg was struck not only by the level of institutional denial of homosexuality but also by the hysterical reaction to an undergraduate's words. Despite the support of his professors, Lionel Trilling and Mark Van Doren, Associate Dean Nicholas McKnight suspended the undergraduate for a year and remanded him to psychiatric counseling. Ginsberg concluded that it was the Columbia administration whose sanity should be questioned, and he soon chose as his analyst William Burroughs. Moving the half-block from Columbia to Joan Vollmer's apartment, Allen embarked upon a remarkably different sort of education, based on reading lists from William Burroughs. "So it was kind of funny," he recalled, "because the conversation in the house was a lot more elegant than the classroom conversation, a lot more curious and investigative and psychically moving."[115]

One bedroom remained free in Joan Vollmer's apartment, and Ginsberg and Kerouac urged William Burroughs to rent it, since he wanted something better than the furnished room over a Columbus Circle bar that he occupied in 1945. They also thought Burroughs and Joan might make ideal friends and possibly mates. "They were both older than us, slightly, and we thought they were kind of intellectual, sardonic equals," Allen recalled, "because they both had a laconic sense of humor and both were completely untyrannized by normative American stereotypes."[116] Soon after Burroughs moved into the apartment in early 1946, he became Joan's lover, as well as the apartment's resident teacher and analyst. In this unlikely way, Burroughs' desire to be a psychoanalyst was finally enacted.

He tried unsuccessfully to psychoanalyze me. It was mistaken psychoanalysis but it was an interesting experience.

—Allen Ginsberg, on William Burroughs

Flip: *verb from 1940s and 1950s, meaning any extreme mood from a fit of intense enthusiasm to a psychotic break, as in "flip your wig," "flip your lid": "She's a whole lot and not a little crazy—she's having therapy, has apparently very seriously flipped only very recently. . . ." [Kerouac]*

Kerouac joined Ginsberg as Burroughs' analysand. For several months, it became a daily practice to lie on the couch, free-associate, and consider Burroughs' periodic interpretations. His observation of Jack at the age of twenty-three, for example, foretold the emotional dependency that would dominate Kerouac for the rest of his life: "Trouble with you Jack is you're too hung up on your mother's apron strings. You're going around in circles. Are you man enough to break away?"[117] What most struck Kerouac at the time was Burroughs' observation that Kerouac would abort success, needing to punish himself for his childhood wish that Gerard would die, as he then did. "Now all I can remember about Gerard, for instance, is his slapping me on the face," he wrote his sister, "despite all the stories Mom and Pop tell me of his kindness to me."[118] But formal psychological self-exploration was not a process that Kerouac could long endure, and he offered this description to Ginsberg: "There we are, with our unvarying pistols, firing the same shots at each other, wearing the same facial expressions, a puppet show run by a mad bore, and it's never going to end."[119]

In contrast, Ginsberg was primed to ventilate his pent-up feelings, and he emoted with such intensity that Burroughs grew uncomfortable. "Nobody loves me, nobody loves me, nobody loves me," Ginsberg wailed. Burroughs thought to himself, "Why should anyone love you?"[120] Although he lacked formal credentials, Burroughs had honed his human remove to the fine point of objectivity that befitted an analyst. Since the age of twenty-six he had been under the care of psychiatrists, one of them, Dr. Louis Federn, an intimate colleague of Freud. Most recently, hypno- and narcoanalysis under the guidance of Dr. Louis Wolberg had exhumed several distinct personalities. Just below the surface lurked a simpering lesbian English governess who commandeered her charges. On the next layer was a sharecropper tobacco farmer named Luke who cherished his shotgun and possessed the charm and menace of a psychotic redneck sheriff. Burroughs' bottom nature revealed a Chinese man sitting and starving

Whom I love most in the world, in this order:
Neal
Eugene
Jack
Bill—I should die for these—
Lucien
Joan
Huncke
Neal

—Allen Ginsberg

on the banks of the Yangtze, revealing neither ideas nor feelings, a chilling and utter blank. Although it is not clear whether Burroughs considered these personalities split-offs of a clinical multiple personality disorder, he has never repudiated their ontological authenticity.

The afternoon free associations evolved into evening skits that mixed vaudeville routine and psychodrama. The three played out their own submerged personalities and interacted with one another in Mitteleuropeische dialect and cracker twang. Ginsberg played an oily Hungarian preying on Kerouac, who wore his father's straw hat to enact an American innocent in Paris—or, in a variation on this theme, the absent Lucien Carr meeting the well-oiled Hungarian. Wearing Joan's dress, Burroughs became an imperious countess. "I was playing an Edith Sitwell part," he said. "I got in drag and looked like a sinister old lesbian."[121] Burroughs laughed so hard he fell on the floor, and Ginsberg was so impressed that he planned to write a novel-length rendition of their Walpurgisnacht theatrics, in which "the three of us, Jack, Bill and myself would charade spontaneously and be transformed into our alternate personalities."[122] Placed before a camera forty years later, he and Burroughs launched into those routines as if they had been rehearsed the night before.

One evening in the fall of 1945, Ginsberg and Hal Chase lay on one bed, while Burroughs and Kerouac lay on another. Their wide-ranging talk led to a group epiphany: Kerouac and Chase were dubbed the "Wolfeans," while Burroughs and Ginsberg were the "non-Wolfeans" (also known as the "Baudelairians" or the "Black Priests"). The former identified with the epic sweep of Thomas Wolfe, and the macho pioneers who believed in the promise of a new frontier; they were at home in America. The "non-Wolfeans" represented the cosmopolitan, sacerdotal Old World, associated with homosexuality, Jewishness, socialism, and intellectualism. The four were struck by the insight, but after they came down from the benzedrine, Ginsberg was troubled by the anti-Semitism and rejection of

Mud: *a pre-1930s term for opium: "I take a bang or some mud in coffee now and then, and I pick up on gage right smart" (I take a shot of heroin and some opium in coffee, and I smoke marijuana frequently). [Burroughs] Opium is also called* **Cocteau's kick:** *"At present I have a quantity of Cocteau's kick. . . ." [Burroughs]*

We long ago realized our flesh happily, while you and Bill used to sit under white lamps talking and leering at each other.
    —Jack Kerouac to Allen Ginsberg

You could dip into the set at any point and stay with it for days on end.
    —Hal Chase, on Joan Vollmer's apartment

They didn't want to learn, they wanted to emote.
    —Hal Chase, on the residents of Joan Vollmer's apartment

Dollies: Dolophine (brand name for methadone), used as a substitute in kicking heroin: "Both chippying with dollies. . . ." [Burroughs]

homosexuality implied by the distinction. "That was painful, like putting a transparent sheet or wall between us, the Wolfeans and the non-Wolfeans."[123]

The "Night of the Wolfeans" became a common reference point, not just for the season at Joan Vollmer's apartment, but for years afterward. It crystallized the duality within the group that Ginsberg had described as early as the summer of 1945. "We are of different kinds," he wrote Kerouac. "Jean, you are an American more completely than I, more fully a child of Nature and all that is of the grace of the earth." Ginsberg considered himself "alien to your natural grace, to the spirit which you would know as a participater [*sic*] in America. . . . I am not a cosmic exile such as Wolfe (or yourself), for I am in exile from myself. . . . I wish to escape from myself, I wish to obliterate my consciousness and my knowledge of independent existence, my guilts, my secretiveness."[124]

When Kerouac looked back on that dark season two decades later, he declared it "a year of evil decadence."[125] But Hal Chase observed, "Jack spent the rest of his life trying to duplicate that kind of discussion."[126] The transcendent moments and the episodes of Benzedrine psychosis on West 115th Street were driven by drugs, and the urge to distinguish the two is probably misguided. The epiphanies, the baring of souls, and the stand-up psychodrama routines would eventually find their ways into the writing of Kerouac, Burroughs, and Ginsberg.

BURROUGHS MEETS JUNK Shortly before moving to West 115th Street, Burroughs was introduced to morphine. He was working as a bartender and a small-time fence, a line of work that offered entrée to the criminal world that excited him. Among the hot goods from the Brooklyn Navy Yard were sixteen yellow boxes of morphine tartrate syrettes. Burroughs accompanied a friend to the Lower East Side apartment of Phil

White and Herbert Huncke and stepped into a black and yellow room with a Chinese red ceiling. Burroughs seemed "like a fish out of water"[127] in this tawdry environment, Huncke observed. He was dressed in his customary uniform of Chesterfield overcoat over a conservative gray suit, snap-brim fedora, gray gloves. Huncke thought of exclaiming, "Jesus Christ, get him out of here, man! This guy is heat!"[128] The atmosphere became easier after assurances were made and his coat was removed, and when Burroughs pulled several morphine syrettes from his pocket, Phil

Herbert Huncke in his room, New York, ca. 1953

White inquired whether Burroughs would mind if they shot up. Burroughs replied, "You know, I'd like to try that myself. I've always sort of had an interest in that kind of thing."[129] Huncke and White shot up in the bedroom, and when Burroughs' turn came, he rolled his shirtsleeve up as far as possible, dabbed alcohol on his vein with a cotton swab, and inspected the needle to make sure it was sharp. Huncke and White regarded his hygienic deportment with amusement. Burroughs averted his head as the morphine was injected. Pins and needles pulsed through his system in waves, from the back of his legs to the back of his neck; his face flushed, and he seemed to float, without discernible corporeal outline. Burroughs looked around and coolly observed, "Well, that's quite a sensation."[130]

Burroughs sold Huncke and White four boxes of the seventy-five half-grain syrettes (for $1.50 a grain) and took twelve boxes back to his $15-a-week apartment. A few nights later he injected himself. He awoke the next morning filled with fear and vomited until noon. That evening, when Phil White arrived at Burroughs' apartment to buy his full supply of morphine, Burroughs retained eight syrettes for his own use. White looked into Burroughs' gray face, shook his head sadly, and said, "It's bad stuff. The worst that can happen to a man. We all think we can control it at first. Sometimes we don't want to control it."[131]

Burroughs initially shot up out of curiosity, then he shot up whenever he could score. "I felt his approach came from a purely scientific standpoint," Huncke recalled. "He became a drug addict principally as a result of research."[132] Burroughs described his progress from intellectual interest to addiction in this way: "You become a narcotics addict because you do not have strong motivation in any other direction. Junk wins by default."[133]

By the time Burroughs moved into Joan Vollmer's apartment, he knew some heroin dealers, and one of the city's junky hangouts was convenient—just twelve blocks downtown, on the traffic island at Broadway and

A junky spends half his life waiting.
—William Burroughs

I think it no exaggeration to say it takes about a year and several hundred injections to make an addiction.
—William Burroughs

103rd Street. Despite their varied age and race, the habitués were brothers in junk: sallow faces topped by the inevitable snap-brim hats, thin bodies animated by stiff-fingered gestures. Their favorite prescriber, a senile doctor whose last vestige of pride derived from his always full waiting room, practiced a block away. When he became so senile that pharmacies no longer honored his prescriptions, the addicts trekked out to another doctor in Brooklyn. In addition to learning the ropes of scoring heroin, Burroughs sharpened his paranoid sensitivity to the enemy (stool pigeons, junkies about to crack, cops, and pushers who cut their drugs or gave short counts). "Junk is not a kick," Burroughs concluded. "It is a way of life."[134]

JOAN VOLLMER At the pivotal moment when Burroughs became addicted, he also met the woman who would become his common-law wife. The women who popped in and out of the Beat saga played supporting roles as sexual partners, mother figures, and saviors. As Ginsberg recorded in his journals: "The social organization which is most true of itself to the artist is the boy gang."[135] The chief exception was Joan Vollmer (Adams), the sole female equal in an otherwise all-male cast. Both men and women looked up to Vollmer, and as Huncke recalled, "Her remarks never failed to start action of some kind."[136] Edie Parker considered Joan the most intelligent woman she knew and admired her Garboesque aura. Herbert Huncke counted her "one of the most charming and intelligent women I've ever met."[137] And Burroughs recalled four decades later, "Her intuition was absolutely amazing."[138] In a journal entry from the 1940s, Ginsberg wrote that Joan "has high consciousness—she chooses to live forsaking ambition & pride."[139] One of the apartment residents, Hal Chase, observed that she had more style than any of them, and her verbal command intimidated Kerouac.

A former Barnard journalism student, Joan Vollmer had a high

Chick: the female counterpart of **cat** (a **chick** can be of any age). Developed in the late 1940s as an attempt to include both sexes in the hip world ("a hot chick and a cool cat"), the word acquired sexist implications. It is sometimes said with implications of ownership: "Only my mother is still great but whether she likes it or not Edie and I are re-uniting again, my own mad chick." [Kerouac, on Edie Parker]

Joan Vollmer, New York, ca. 1946

brow and tipped nose, a delicately cream-colored complexion and ma-
hogany bangs. By her early twenties, her taste and sardonic style were already formed. She wore silky garments casually draped, peasant blouses
worn off the shoulder, and tightly bound bandanas; she read Proust, Joyce,
and Kant; she listened to classical music, indulged in morning-long bub-
ble baths, and read every edition of every New York newspaper. Her favorite cartoon, drawn by William Steig, depicted a downcast character
who said, "My mother loved me, but she died."[140] She questioned both traditional and progressive orthodoxies. "And," Herbert Huncke observed,
"she took to the underworld types like a natural, too."[141]

    Joan revolted against the boredom of her upper-class bourgeois up-
bringing, escaping into marriage to a law student named Paul Adams, who
was drafted at the outset of World War II. Not the sort to remain celibate in
his absence, Joan got pregnant by a Columbia student and wanted to carry
the baby to term. She hatched a plan to be admitted into Bellevue, in
order to lure her husband home, have sex with him, and convince him
that the baby was his. She aimlessly walked around Times Square in the
rain, one foot in the gutter, muttering to herself in front of the Horn and
Hardart. Her plot worked, and Julie was born early in 1943. After that incident, Joan bought a diaphragm, which she put on in the bathtub, but
sometimes she'd "forget" to insert it, and over the course of the academic
year she had two abortions. She keenly appreciated what she called "cocks-
manship"; Edie Parker observed that Joan was not wild but she was promis-
cuous. She offered advice to her friends about abortions and sex.

    William Burroughs' brilliance attracted Joan, and she wanted to se-
duce the resident genius-as-sex-object. When Burroughs moved into her
rambling apartment, Joan gave him the prize room, where he set up a bed,
desk, and bookshelves. Burroughs sized up Joan as the smartest member
of the group and the only one capable of inspiring him to take up new
pursuits. (Her observation that Mayan priests possessed telepathic powers

**Allen Ginsberg's List of Bars,
1946**
Queer bars:
    Main Street Bar
    McDouglas
    Astor Men's Bar
    Cerudi's
    Ralph's
    Beggar's
    Jimmy's at 43rd
    Tony Pastor's

Intellectual bars:
    West End
    Minetta's
    George's
    Beggar's

Jazz bars:
    White Rose
    Vanguard
    George's
    Downbeat

particularly piqued his interest.) He liked her dry humor and her psychological clarity, and they discovered that they shared the same favorite short story, Conrad Aiken's "Silent Snow, Secret Snow." Most of all,
he was drawn to the resolute iconoclasm described by Ginsberg: "almost
self-annihilating in her refusal to partake of any sacrament, literary or
political."[142]

Burroughs took Joan, Kerouac, and Ginsberg on group "dates," as
Joan wrote, to "fruity men's bars in the Village."[143] She gave him high
marks for his sexual prowess: "You're supposed to be a faggot, you're as
good as a pimp in bed."[144] Above all, she adored his intelligence. After he
uttered one of his dryly lascivious remarks, stretched out on a long couch,
Joan would encircle his gaunt figure in her arms and exclaim, "Oh,
Bill!"[145] For long hours, they would lie on her huge bed and talk. "We had
these, in retrospect, very deep conversations about very fundamental
things," Burroughs recalled.[146] But Joan also realized that sex made Burroughs feel uneasy. "Of course there are certain things he can't do,"
she observed to Ginsberg about psychoanalysis with Burroughs. "I don't
suppose he could really analyze anyone's sex problems. He'd be too
discomfited."[147]

THE CREW Joan Vollmer's commune was poised midway between
the Ivory Tower and the Lower Depths. One pole of orientation was the
Columbia campus a half-block away; the other was seventy-three blocks
south, in Times Square hangouts like the Angle Bar and the Bucket of
Blood. The apartment became an Uptown outpost for an elite group of
prostitutes, addicts, and thieves. Most of them had grown up in upper-
middle- to upper-class environments—the overcoat thief who was a scion
of a prominent Philadelphia banking family, for example, and the red-
headed gun moll–cum–prostitute whose father was a judge. Some were

Charge: marijuana, word used in the
1940s and 1950s. "Then we picked up
on charge. . . . Then we got more charge
out & blasted." [Ginsberg]

crashers; some were paying roomers in the apartment atmosphere that mixed scholarship, patrician manners, and street smarts. The Times Square contingent—Herbert Huncke, Phil White, Bill Garver, and Vicki Russell—entered the scene in the spring of 1946.

Bill Garver lived a few blocks away on West 109th Street and entered the fold through Herbert Huncke, with whom he had shared a cell on Riker's Island. A middle-aged, skeletal figure with dangling arms and soft-spoken formal manners, William Maynard Garver was the son of a prominent Philadelphia banker who paid him a monthly remittance to stay away. He had been expelled from Annapolis for drunkenness and throwing a bag of water out the window. He attended Harvard and then devoted the rest of his adult life to morphine addiction. Garver devised a novel means of financing his habit. He would arrive in a restaurant, dressed in suit and tie, and order a cup of coffee. After surveying the overcoats on the rack, he'd walk out wearing one and quickly pawn it for $10 or $12. He called his modus operandi "boosting bennies."[148] Although he had been arrested ten times for petty larceny, this method served him well for many years.

Priscilla Arminger renamed herself Vicki Russell because it sounded like an appropriate moniker for a classy, six-foot, red-headed, $100-a-trick prostitute, as well as distancing her from her father, a Detroit judge. She was funny and demonically energetic and, in Ginsberg's opinion, "as attractive as any woman I know."[149] She engaged in both Reichian therapy and drug addiction. She kept her johns in line: "If he has any sort of body at all, say, 'Oh don't ever hurt me,'" and "If you really want to bring a man down, light a cigarette in the middle of intercourse."[150] It was Vicki Russell who introduced to Joan Vollmer's apartment the cheapest way of getting a Benzedrine high: buy over-the-counter Smith, Kline, and French inhalers—meant to last six months—crack the inhaler, remove the three-quarter-inch Benzedrine-soaked accordion strip of paper, and drop it

Miss Green: code term for marijuana: "I am of course indulging in a perfect orgy of Miss Green & can hardly see straight right at this minute, whoo! 3 bombs a day." [Kerouac] "A curious illusion I get lately when I am a little lushed and swing on Miss Green's unnatural tit, I feel that there is another person present." [Burroughs]

in a cup of coffee or simply swallow it whole. Vicki was ingesting two strips a day when she taught her method to Jack Kerouac.

Benzedrine became Kerouac's drug of choice. Wrapped in chewing gum, the induced euphoria and energy buoyed his Wolfean jaunts through New York's boroughs, culminating in jazz joints, where he heard Charlie Parker and Thelonius Monk play the bop jazz that was just becoming popular. At the time, Kerouac was obsessed with finding a "method" for writing. He first set up scenes in his mind, allowed them to gestate while listening to the radio, then, from his self-absorbed trance, dashed to his typewriter to type out 100 words a minute. He tried to viscerally imprint his mind on paper before its contents evaporated. If he felt that he had missed a word, he crumpled the paper and started all over; he regarded revision as a form of censorship. His frenzied method, apotheosizing spontaneity, assumed a religious quality. Prior to moving to the 115th Street apartment, he had engaged in a nightly ritual of expression and purgation.

He would write by candlelight and finish each page by feeding it to the flames. He characterized the process, which he called Self-Ultimacy, as a means of creating a new "artistic morality."[151] In the month Lucien Carr went to prison, Kerouac remained absorbed with the New Vision, writing Ginsberg, "Out of the humankind materials of art, I tell myself, the new vision springs."[152] The following month he cut himself, using a piece of string as a tourniquet, and wrote in his own blood: "The Blood of the Poet."[153] Kerouac calculated that he had already written nearly half a million words. When Burroughs came upon Kerouac in his lair, he glanced at the candles and paraphernalia and snorted, "My God, Jack, stop this nonsense and let's go out and have a drink."[154] Although Burroughs encouraged his younger acolyte, he privately thought that if Kerouac could write a publishable novel, anyone could. "He liked to think of me as a teacher,"

Speedball: *cocaine mixed with morphine or heroin: "But I was off the junk now. Still a shot of morphine would be nice later when I was ready to sleep, or, better, a speedball, half cocaine, half morphine." [Burroughs]*

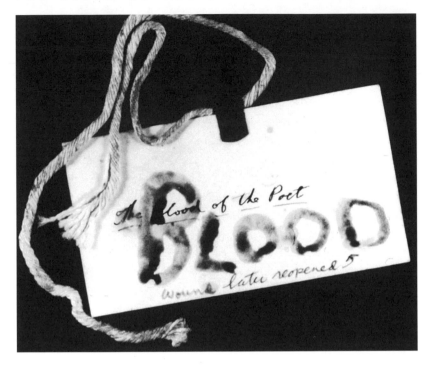

The apex of Self-Ultimacy: Kerouac writes in his own blood, November 1944

Burroughs said. "He pushed these categories onto people—you're going to be my teacher."[155]

Benzedrine physically transformed Kerouac—his muscles turned to flab, his hairline receded, his swarthy skin grew deathly pale. (His pallor was sometimes so striking that Vicki Russell applied pancake makeup to his face before he was exposed to the harsh fluorescent light of the IRT.) His early Benzedrine experience climaxed in December 1945, with a five-day-and-night jaunt through the city accompanied by Allen and Hal Chase. At the trip's end, Kerouac insisted that his exhausted companions hike to the Brooklyn Bridge. Kerouac hoisted Ginsberg on his back and carried him a mile to the Seventh Avenue subway, while Ginsberg

Croaker: a doctor: "I wouldn't let them croakers up there treat my corn let alone my psyche." [Burroughs, on psychiatrists, 1949]

*I wish you, Jack, not well, because there always is
A wound; and the most deeply cut of such
Is this futility of consciousness
That hoping for your joy is vanity—
I wish you nothing but necessity.*
            —Allen Ginsberg, "To Kerouac
                in the Hospital"

sang Bach's Toccata and Fugue in D minor. Shortly thereafter, Kerouac collapsed.

He was admitted to Queens VA Hospital, where thrombophlebitis was diagnosed. On his release he moved to his parents' apartment in Ozone Park, Queens—they had recently moved from Lowell—ending his stay at Joan Vollmer's commune. The pull of family was always strong, and Jack now shared with his father the experience of bed-ridden illness: Leo Kerouac was dying of stomach cancer. Jack tended him while Gabrielle supported the family by working in a shoe factory. Jack stayed up after his parents retired and ingested Benzedrine to inspire his writing. As Leo's death neared, Jack felt closer to him and more vulnerable to his prejudice and advice. "Beware of the niggers and the Jews," he warned his son, and he extracted the promise that would guide Kerouac the rest of his life: "Take care of your mother whatever you do."[156]

In Leo's eyes, Jack was a failure—a son who couldn't support himself, whose friends were decadent, whose literary vocation seemed ridiculous. After burying his father in Lowell, Massachusetts, next to Gerard, Jack put another sheet of paper in the typewriter and summoned up the past in order to redeem it. He began to write the family saga that, four years later, would become his first published novel: *The Town and the City*.

Artist shmartist, ya can't be supported all ya life.
            —Leo Kerouac to his son Jack

During his year in Joan Vollmer's apartment, Allen Ginsberg held a variety of jobs—washing dishes at Bickford's cafeteria, clerking at Frances Steloff's Gotham Book Mart, shipping out with the U.S. Maritime Service. He also read voraciously and wrote one of his first long poems, "The Last Voyage." His journal entries from this period were filled with character sketches and dream reports, snatches of overheard conversations and ruminations about the intense desires of a homosexual virgin. "I spend my lifetime rushing out meeting people," he wrote, "connecting

Working the hole: *robbing drunks on the subway: "Now he peddled from time to time and 'worked the hole' (rolling drunks on subways and in cars) when he couldn't make connections to peddle." [Burroughs]*

with facts & dramas; I do not need to know the facts and I am not a good actor."[157] Others recalled Ginsberg at this time as a highly charged, intellectual kid brother. As he wrote in his journal, his manner of presentation altered with each of his friends: "I will be sweet to Trilling; sharp & unfathomable to Bill, cute & annoyingly & superficial & profound & overrational to Joan; insignificant to Jack. . . . But I am frenzied really."[158]

Kerouac became the chief object of Ginsberg's yearning for love and tenderness. After one of their long evening walks, the two ended up near the waterfront, and there, shielded between two parked trucks, they masturbated one another. But Kerouac remained uncomfortable with homosexuality, and Ginsberg became one of the targets for his ambivalence. Kerouac's attacks mirrored the prevailing social condemnation of homosexuality, which encompassed Louis Ginsberg's view of homosexuality as "a menace to society."[159] Even Burroughs, an avowed homosexual, had formed a heterosexual domestic partnership. Ginsberg felt alienated from the "high teacup" style of the homosexuals who met at the Astor bar and listened to Edith Piaf records. (Calling someone "Astorish" meant the person was ostentatiously homosexual.) Ginsberg later described it as "a manneristic fairydom that depends on money, chic, privilege and exclusive, monopolistic high style."[160] Distanced from both the straight world and the fashionable homosexual milieu, Ginsberg's struggle to embrace his sexual identity was played out in the 115th Street commune. Allen's sexual fantasies involved his roommates, Kerouac and Hal Chase. Chase called him "a sociological homosexual"[161] who subscribed to the belief that the only way to succeed in the arts was to be homosexual, and he heard in Ginsberg's intellectual discussions attempts to ferret out the "hidden homosexual" in his roommates. Lacking a model of positive homosexual expression, Allen's self-esteem sometimes hit bottom. He wrote in his journal: "I am really the lowest of the low, *really*, no one is useless & unlovable as myself; really can't escape that."[162]

The cow ate the cabbage: faux-folksy term for having oral sex: "Well, about five nights ago he caught me when I was drunk and horny, and one thing led to another and I ended up showing him how the cow ate the cabbage. . . ." [Burroughs]

Like when I was the cheapest thief in New York and Phil [White] and I made a teenage sailor for his locker key and came home with a bag of dirty laundry, and I smelled the handkerchiefs to see if the kid had jacked off in them, lust flickering like heat lightning through junk haze. Ah ma folle jeunesse!
—William Burroughs

THE DISPERSAL By the summer of 1946, the apartment residents had begun to disband, and life went haywire for those who remained. Drug paraphernalia–used No. 26 half-inch hypodermic needles, eyedroppers, teaspoons—littered the kitchen and the bathroom, and a hodgepodge of hot goods (dresses, guns, luggage lifted by Herbert Huncke and his friends) was stashed throughout the apartment. After a stool pigeon informed on Huncke, he began another three-month stint at Riker's Island, and the presence of the law hovered ominously over the apartment.

In pursuit of morphine prescriptions, Burroughs began to forge a signature on prescription blanks stolen from Dr. Greco. His careless misspelling of "Dilaudid" aroused the suspicion of the prescribing pharmacy, and in April 1946 Burroughs was arrested. Fingerprinted and mugshot, Burroughs began a painful withdrawal in the Tombs, crying to himself, "Forty years! Man, I can't do no forty years!"[163] Joan Vollmer bailed him out and eased his junk sickness with Nembutal. Burroughs uneasily awaited his trial, working more and more desperately to sell enough dope to support his daily three caps at $3 each. For a nerve-wracked week he worked with Phil White as a shill while his partner rolled drunks on the IRT subway, and he peddled the purest caps of morphine available (16 percent pure). "What a crowd," he later wrote. "Mooches, fags, four-flushers, stool pigeons, bums—unwilling to work, unable to steal, always short of money, always whining for credit."[164] When the judge confronted the well-spoken addict two months later, he benevolently remanded Burroughs to his parents' care in St. Louis as part of a four-month suspended sentence.

Joan Vollmer, meanwhile, ingested more Benzedrine inhalers than any of her roommates. She developed sores all over her body, and her Botticellian complexion turned startlingly pale. With a whisk broom she compulsively swept the apartment for hours at a time. She heard the voices of an elderly couple downstairs, and she entertained her housemates by re-

Chippy: *to use heroin occasionally, but not frequently enough to become addicted: "I have a little chippy habit."* [Huncke]

counting their conversations with such apparent accuracy that she was entirely believable. The frenzied but benign hilarity of the couple's battles sometimes turned dark—the couple called Joan a whore, for instance, and her roommates dope fiends—and Joan panicked when she heard the husband chasing his wife around the room with a knife. Ginsberg and Kerouac rushed downstairs, only to find the apartment empty. "She was nonplussed," Ginsberg recalled. "She said, 'Well, then I must be hearing voices.'"[165]

Things grew worse as spring turned to summer, as Joan's roommates departed and back rent piled up. Hal Chase was the first to leave, overwhelmed by the stolen goods and the drug taking. Huncke went to jail, Burroughs to St. Louis, Kerouac to Ozone Park to tend his dying father, Ginsberg to his father's home back in Paterson. Once again "the libertine circle" was broken.

The only ones left were a car thief from Pittsburgh, a handsome but stupid blond safecracker named Whitey, Joan, her three-year-old daughter Julie, and a succession of desperate characters who boarded there. Missing Burroughs, Joan began "a flash affair" with Whitey. When Huncke was released from jail, he tried to protect her, offering to raise the rent money by stealing luggage. But by fall she had been evicted from the apartment and Whitey had landed in jail. Joan's body grew thin, her laughter became more bitter, and she spent her days knitting on the bed. Kerouac visited her one day and found her "out of her fuckin' mind on Benzedrine." She stripped and asked, "Who are you, strange man?"[166] Not long thereafter, in November, she was picked up in Times Square and taken to Bellevue. Her first Bellevue stay four years earlier had been a ruse, but this episode was for real. It may also have been an attempt to lure Burroughs back into her life.[167]

Burroughs loyally drove East in early December in his station wagon to spring Joan from her ten-day stay in Bellevue. They took a room

I saw Joan last week-end. She seems to be losing her mind. It's a shame don't you think?
—John Kingsland to Allen Ginsberg

Lush: *any liquor: "Despite the temptations of Mexico I am still on the lush wagon." [Burroughs] Other terms for liquor include* **juice, white lightnin'** *(corn whiskey),* **Regal** *(a New Orleans beer): "I Regal up every chance I get." [Burroughs]*

in a Times Square hotel room, where they conceived a child (William Burroughs III would be born July 21, 1947). Burroughs proposed a plan for the family. They would buy a ninety-nine-acre ranch forty miles north of Houston and raise the perfect cash crop: marijuana.

As 1947 began, Joan Vollmer wrote her old roommmate, Edie Parker Kerouac: "Let me have your news. Make it Mrs. W. S. Burroughs, New Waverly, Texas."[168]

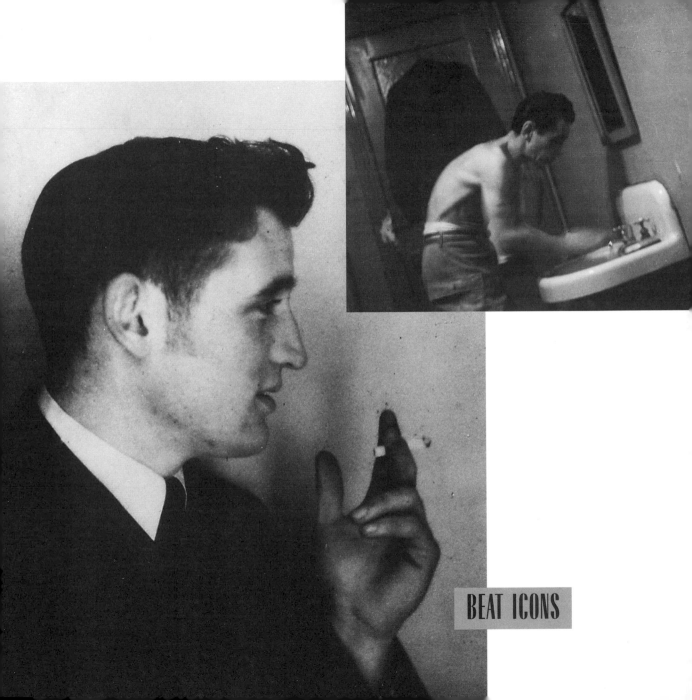

BEAT ICONS

$\mathcal{B}$EAT ICONS Paired with William Burroughs, Allen Ginsberg, and Jack Kerouac—the chief writers of the Beat Generation—were three men who produced only scraps of published writing. As muses and Virgilian guides, however, Herbert Huncke, Carl Solomon, and Neal Cassady played vital roles in the Beat saga. By all conventional standards, each embodied a facet of the dark underbelly of American life: the first could be described as a heroin-addicted thief, the second as a schizophrenic genius, and the last as a rapaciously sexual car thief. But Ginsberg, Burroughs, and Kerouac discerned in these figures qualities that were bracingly authentic, humane, commonsensical, and even seraphic. In one of his poems, for example, Ginsberg wrote of his circle of friends: "Holy Peter holy Allen holy Solomon holy Lucien holy Kerouac holy Huncke holy Burroughs holy Cassady."[1]

The Beats did not invent the tradition of turning the lowest into the highest—they had models in such pioneering modern writers as Baude-

"He's mad," I said, "and yes, he's my brother."

—Jack Kerouac, On the Road

*The hip-bohemian criminal-poetic
conformism is a brotherhood of useless
agony.*
　　　—Carl Solomon to Jack Kerouac

laire, Dostoyevsky, Céline, and Genet. The notion of the anti-hero as icon—the underworld beatifed—had already been partly codified. Kerouac, for example, thought the great American of the future would be "the hitchhiking Negro saint."[2] By the late 1940s the three had even spawned a vocabulary. For example, Kerouac and Ginsberg coined a word, "ignu" (splicing together "ignoramus" and "gnosis"), that meant a holy figure out of the Dostoyevsky novel *The Idiot*. For William Burroughs, the term of highest praise was a "Johnson," a word derived from a family of thieves that Burroughs knew from Jack Black's memoir, *You Can't Win*. Jack Kerouac idealized the disenfranchised and wrote, "the only people for me are the mad ones, the ones who are mad to live, mad to talk, mad to be saved."[3]

Through Beat literature, Huncke, Solomon, and Cassady were transformed into literary icons—Ginsberg once pleaded guilty to thinking of them as metaphors, and Kerouac would call Cassady "the archetypal American Man."[4] But long before literature and history transformed them into cultural icons, these three men led real "beat" lives.

*Tell me of Huncke. Man of enigma-
knowledge and despair of aggression.*
　　　—Jack Kerouac, on Herbert Huncke

HERBERT HUNCKE In 1946, when Herbert Huncke introduced the word "beat" to his friends, he couldn't have imagined that it would become a portentous, historical term. It was simply one of the words he had picked up on his picaresque travels. "Talking is my stock in trade," he recalled a half-century later. "I think that led me to the road."[5]

Huncke was physically unprepossessing—a birdlike frame and a puppyish manner, an oversized head dominated by sympathetic, liquid hazel eyes, sallow skin that appeared to be permanently ingrained with soot. Huncke found his niche in a world ruled by pimps, prostitutes, thieves, drunk rollers, and dealers. The cops knew him as "the creep," and his fellow hustlers and addicts referred to him as "the Mayor."

Born of hard-working, middle-class parents, he recalled his never-satisfied father as "a miserable bastard"[6] and his mother as beautiful, hysterical, and resentful of the adolescent joys that she had missed. Neither could offer the emotional nurturing their only son needed. Many years later, introducing Huncke's autobiography Burroughs wrote: "The protagonist is thrown into the water to sink or swim. So he learns something about the water."[7]

"I actually ran away from home at twelve," Huncke said. "I used the whole terminology and everything."[8] He rode Chicago's trolleys and streetcars to the southern end of the line and started hitchhiking with a dime in his pocket and a map in hand. A hundred miles out of Chicago, he was introduced to oral sex by a stranger who thrust a $10 bill into his hand and sped off. Huncke fell into hustling without even knowing what it was. His sole outfit grew rumpled and his hair oily, so the twelve-year-old presented a more suspicious figure by the side of the road. On a warm summer afternoon he was standing by an onion field near Geneva, New York, and the sense memory of the onions' smell was so pungent that it remained with him the rest of his life. "I thought this is the smell of real freedom," Huncke said. "I never dreamed it could smell so penetrating, so physical." At that moment a policeman picked him up, installed him in a local jail cell, offered two cigarettes, and called his father in Chicago. "There was nothing to be scared of there, it was a nice cell all painted white," said Huncke. "I started to cry I was so mad. That was my first time behind bars."[9]

It would not be the last. Huncke would spend many months of his life in jail, and at first he thought he would prefer it to home, where his father judged him "always the weak sister."[10] Huncke recalled entering jail in his young adulthood: "I thought at least there I wouldn't be self-conscious, I'd have all these guys all under the same pressure. At least we'll all be friends. My God! How wrong can you be! Jesus! Come through the door!"[11]

Alas—such is the luck of a Huncke.
—Herbert Huncke

At age sixteen, Huncke met a freak show "hermaphrodite" named Elsie John. He worked as her shill for her midway act, and he also delivered pot for her (seven high-quality joints for a quarter). A massive creature, Elsie shaved, powdered, and creamed half of her body, applied mascara and green eye shadow, and wore her hennaed hair in a Veronica Lake bang; on the other heavily muscled side, Elsie brushed her hair back, exposing a prominent sideburn. Whether performing in a sideshow arcade or lounging in her cheap theatrical hotel, Elsie John wore a leopard skin, a spangled skirt, and one high-heeled shoe, and three toy Pekinese dogs attended her. She was also a heroin addict, and Huncke was fascinated by her glistening eyes after she shot up. She wouldn't allow Huncke to become involved in dealing heroin ($28 an ounce), but she did offer him the small quantities of heroin that would lead to his first habit. Huncke last saw Elsie John in the South State Street Jail, surrounded by hoods who were exposing themselves, while Elsie screamed, "I'm a hermaphrodite and I have papers to prove it." (Years later, Elsie John became the subject of Huncke's first accomplished story.)

For the next six years (1934–1940), Huncke drifted around the country. He ran errands, hustled, bellhopped, broke into cars, befriended the marginal figures who supplied him with small jobs and drugs. Hitchhiking and riding the tops of freight cars, he neatly stored his worldly goods—a pair of socks, handkerchief, toothbrush, and razor—in a small cigar box. He used amphetamines and heroin and marijuana when he could afford it, but he avoided addiction because his drug use was sufficiently irregular and varied. Times Square became his headquarters in 1940. "I was always quick in picking up on the scenes, and I took to 42nd Street," he recalled. "I was a natural for it."[12]

Times Square held a special place in America's psyche, seminal not only to Huncke but to his new friends, Burroughs, Kerouac, Ginsberg. "The new social center had been established on Times Square—a huge

room lit in brilliant fashion by neon glare and filled with slot machines, open day and night," wrote Ginsberg. "There all the apocalyptic hipsters in New York eventually stopped, fascinated by the timeless room."[13] A few bastions of propriety—like the *New York Times* and the McGraw-Hill building—looked onto the street life, but more typical were the single-room-occupancy hotels, the Laff Movie, the Horn and Hardart, and the Pokerino palaces. The floating all-night all-day population of prostitutes, sailors, dealers of drugs and hot goods, and newspaper hawkers made its headquarters at Bickford's cafeteria. This crossroads came to symbolize the decline of American empire to Kerouac and Ginsberg. "It was a hyperbolic spookiness all taking place in an undersea light of Pokerino freak shows of Times Square," Ginsberg recalled. "At the center of empire, the very square of time."[14] Against this backdrop, Kerouac pictured Huncke in an oversize black raincoat, smoking through a cigarette holder, and Ginsberg recalled neon-lit "all-night vigils"[15] over coffee at Bickford's talking with Times Square's "intelligent Melvillean street wanderers of the night."[16]

A tougher Times Square hangout was the Angle Bar, where Huncke began, in early 1946, to meet William Burroughs. Huncke and his friend, Phil White, soon became Burroughs' guides to the drug world. He accompanied Huncke and White to the Angle Bar and the Bucket of Blood, learned the symptoms needed to elicit morphine prescriptions, to pick the pockets of drunks, and to steal prescription blanks. Throughout this tutelage, though, Huncke held private reservations about Burroughs: "I had him pinned for a mark."[17]

CARL SOLOMON Carl Solomon nostalgically recalled his years growing up in a red house in the Bronx, where the extended family read Marx and Freud, cheered the Yankees, and played pinochle. Carl's closest playmate was his father. They fished and fought duels with wooden

Blow: *originally a jazz term, a verb meaning spontaneous expression in music: "Dig, now, out of the corner of your eye and as we listen to Wyonie [Blues Harris] blow about his baby's pudding." [Cassady] Used by Jack Kerouac and subsequently Allen Ginsberg to describe writing spontaneous prose: "how right you are, that was the first time I sat down to blow it came out in your method, sounding like you, an imitation practically." [Ginsberg to Kerouac, on writing "Howl"]*

swords. Moe wanted his son to be "an officer and a gentleman," so he taught Carl to prize medieval romance, to practice chivalry, to hum patriotic airs, to brush his teeth, and to salute every American flag he passed. When Carl was eleven, Moe died, leaving his son bereft. Decades later he observed, "If I appeared Beat, this [death] and not gratuitous despair was the reason for my 'Beatness.'"[18]

Solomon took refuge in books and his prodigious intellect. The press cited him as a seven-year-old prodigy who had memorized the batting averages of all the players in the National and American leagues, and he leapfrogged through public school for the academically gifted, skipping four grades in the process. At the age of fifteen, facial hairs just beginning to sprout, he enrolled at City College of New York. He learned to fire an M-1 rifle and drilled in his ROTC khakis, and simultaneously he became membership secretary for a Communist front organization called American Youth for Democracy. He lunched with the World Federalists and guitar-playing Socialists, and he lost interest in earning good grades. At the age of seventeen, before most people have even begun college, Solomon rejected it: he shipped out with the U.S. Maritime Service and saw many ports in Europe and Africa. He began reading existentialim, Rimbaud, symbolism, surrealism, *Partisan Review*, Gide, *Horizon*, while listening to jazz.

One hot July evening in 1947, wandering along Paris's rue Jacob looking for existentialists, Solomon came upon a crowd gathered outside a gallery. A black-haired turbaned figure began screaming, and Carl saw a finger directly pointing at him. The scabrous words were written by Antonin Artaud, who would soon become Solomon's literary model. Artaud declared psychiatry a means of social control that branded lunatics because their minds were superior, lucid, and disturbing. Solomon later recalled, "Artaud said: 'If I am told one more time that I'm crazy, I'm going to commit a crime.' That sentence knocked me out when I was twenty. Everything else just followed naturally."[19]

To act out deviant behavior, Solomon began committing Dadaist

Carl Solomon's Bookshelf
Antonin Artaud (especially *The Man Suicided by Society*)
Jean Genet
Louis-Ferdinand Céline
André Gide's *Lafcadio's Adventures*
Partisan Review
Horizon
Le Dictature Lettrice

Bum kick: *the opposite of gratified desires: "For a real bum kick you should hear a decaying, corseted tenor singing 'The Hanging of Danny Deever,' followed by 'Trees' as an unsolicited encore." [Burroughs]*

"crimes," what he later described as "a most inflexible scheme of opera-
tions derived on my part from the last stages of surrealism."[20] For example,
he attended a lecture on Stéphane Mallarmé and threw potato salad at the
lecturer. "Very, very often I seemed on the brink of losing my reason,"[21]
Solomon recalled. He repeatedly considered suicide as a valid existential
act. "THE THING THAT I HAVE UNDERSTOOD IS THAT MAD-
NESS ENTAILS NO OBLIGATIONS," he later wrote Ginsberg.
"THERE'S NO NEED TO KILL PEOPLE IN ORDER TO PROVE TO
THEM THAT YOU ARE INSANE. THEY KNOW IT ALREADY."[22]

His most significant "crime" was enacted in the Brooklyn College
cafeteria: he stole a peanut butter sandwich and then surrendered himself
to a policeman. The officer turned him over to a psychiatrist. In March
1949, on his twenty-first birthday, Solomon appeared on the granite steps
of Columbia Psychiatric Institute, his head shaved. He demanded a lobotomy. This symbolic suicide of the mind was Solomon's homage to Artaud,
but the psychiatrists refused to play their part in Solomon's drama. Instead
they diagnosed him as clinically depressed and admitted him to the hospital. He resided on the sixth floor, and before long he began a regimen of
insulin shock treatments.

We are all guttersnipes. Gratuitousness is the spirit of the age. Gide and Cocteau have made us what we are.
—Carl Solomon

A western kinsman of the sun, Dean [Moriarty].
—Jack Kerouac, on Neal Cassady

NEAL CASSADY   Neal Cassady was born on the road on February 18,
1926. En route from Des Moines, Iowa, to California, his recently married
parents pulled their top-heavy Ford house-truck into Salt Lake City, where
Maude Cassady gave birth to her ninth child in a charity hospital. After
the Cassadys arrived in Hollywood, Neal Cassady, Sr., opened a barbershop on the corner of Hollywood and Vine, and the future looked promising. But the Cassadys' prosperity quickly gave way to alcoholism, and the
marriage soon followed suit. When Neal Jr. was six, he and his father
moved to Denver and began living in a $1-a-week cubicle—shared with a

double amputee named Shorty—in a condemned, five-story flophouse called the Metropolitan. Most of the 100 residents were derelict winos who begged on the streets for money to keep them in rotgut liquor ("canned heat") to supplement their meals at the Citizens' Mission. Each morning, young Neal awoke on a sheetless mattress, went to the communal bathroom, encountered men with the D.T.'s along the way. He dressed himself and made his way to the Mission, sat on stainless steel benches, and consumed a breakfast of oatmeal, bread, and coffee. He watched the poker and pinochle games in the Metropolitan's lobby, and each Saturday he went to the Zaza barbershop, where his father, smelling of pomade and talcum, worked the third chair.

Neal thrived in the flophouse atmosphere. "For a time I held a unique position: among the hundreds of isolated creatures who haunted the streets of lower downtown Denver there was not one so young as myself. . . . I alone, as the sharer of their way of life, presented a replica of childhood."[23]

I became the unnatural son of a few score of beaten men.
—Neal Cassady

Neal recalled this as the idyllic period of his youth. It ended when he moved into the Snowden Apartments with his mother, his baby sister, and his twelve-year-old half-brother, Jimmy. Although "the castle of my childhood"[24] ostensibly offered a more nurturant setting for a child, Jimmy was a sadist. He had previously drowned cats in toilets, and he now incarcerated Neal in the family's Murphy bed. Trapped in the dark and narrow cavity between the bed and the wall, Neal was afraid to yell out because his brother might torture him more aggressively, and screaming could cause suffocation. His mother offered no protection. Neal adapted, transforming his terror into a visionary experience. Locked up in the bed, he felt time was moving triple its normal speed, "a loose fan-like vibration as it rotated into ever-tightening flutter."[25] The deranged sensation resembled the experience that he would later summon up with marijuana and LSD.

Cassady was sexually initiated at the age of nine. He accompanied

Nannybeater: *a gay basher, used without regret: "I was a nannybeater and fresh as a daisy too. . . ." [Kerouac]*

his father to the home of a drinking buddy, whose oldest son led his brothers—and Neal—in sexual intercourse with as many sisters as they could hold down. All boundaries of sexual decorum evaporated. Neal "sneak shared" women with his father, he slept with grandmothers and prepubescent girls in abandoned buildings, barns, and public toilets.

Cars, theft, and sex dominated Cassady's adolescence, all linked in what he called "Adventures in Auto-Eroticism."[26] Between the ages of fourteen and twenty-one, he stole some 500 cars. Arrested ten times and convicted six, Neal spent fifteen months in reform schools. Eternally unrepentant, he would be released, glimpse a flashy Mercury or Oldsmobile sedan, and resume the "soul-thrilling pleasures"[27] of joyriding through the streets of Denver in a hot car.

Kerouac would later observe that for Neal "sex was the one and only holy and important thing in life."[28] He masturbated six times a day and also had sexual intercourse. Cassady was physically desirable and athletically able: thin-hipped and hard-bellied, he did fifty chin-ups at a clip and could throw a football seventy yards. Kerouac compared Neal's face to a young Gene Autry's, with green eyes, a firm jawline, and jutting chin beneath an all-enveloping smile. He couldn't afford good clothes, but, as Kerouac recalled, "his dirty workclothes clung to him so gracefully, as though you couldn't buy a better fit from a custom tailor but only earn it from the Natural Tailor of Natural Joy."[29]

Neal's seductions, directed at both men and women, followed naturally from his finely honed con man skills. His flattering, manic patter was inflected with a mild western accent and sounded like a 33⅓ rpm record played at 45 rpm. A friend recalled that part of his modus operandi was an "insinuating grin involving his jaw and nose (the architecture of his face once seen, never forgotten)."[30] Other witnesses remarked on the size of his penis, reported to be eight inches long, and thick. Every woman was his darling, about whom he could always find something to sincerely

I see no greatness in my self. . . . I'm a simple-minded, child-like, insipid sort of moronic and kind of awkward feeling adolescent.
—Neal Cassady

I have thought of Neal as being a psychopath for quite some time. To me he is nothing more than a series of incidents.
—John Clellon Holmes to Allen Ginsberg

adore, if only for the moment. And every man had the potential to teach him something.

In short, Cassady was a perfect natural sociopath: unrestrained by guilt and fueled by hedonism. If he had been only a sociopath, however,

Neal Cassady, Denver
"I'm a big show-off, but it's a good view of the lot and the cars in the background look good."

But you must also stop feeling like the student, the novice—he who is taught by the Justins & Allens. This is your own form of Oedipus complex, to take on the role of he who's being helped, to "flirt."

—Jack Kerouac to Neal Cassady

LuAnne Henderson, the fifteen-year-old bride of Neal Cassady (photograph reconstructed from torn scraps)

He came to the door stark naked and it might have been the President knocking for all he cared. He received the world in the raw.

—Jack Kerouac, on Neal Cassady

he might have ended up like the residents of the Metropolitan. During one of his reform school stints, in the fall of 1942, he dreamed of himself as a middle-aged loser with thinning hair and a bloated face, trying to sell a mattress to buy rotgut liquor. Upon awakening the next morning, he began a course of compulsive self-improvement. He used his solitary hours in reform school to absorb the Great Books, and between his day jobs he read Schopenhauer and Proust at the Denver Public Library. Knowledge became a higher form of seduction. He talked about philosophy and literature with the same speedball riff that characterized all his conversation.

One day in a Walgreen's drugstore booth he spotted a fifteen-year-old ringleted blonde and declared, "That's the girl I'm going to marry."[31] A few weeks later he did marry LuAnne Henderson. In December 1946, in a blinding blizzard, the newlyweds impulsively set out for New York with a stolen $300 and a stolen car. They arrived in Times Square with only $35, a satchel of clothes, and a collection of Shakespeare and Proust.

CASSADY AND KEROUAC MEET By the time Neal Cassady hit New York, a few months after Joan Vollmer's apartment commune had broken up, Ginsberg and Kerouac were primed for new excitement. They had heard tales from their friend Hal Chase of an "unbelievable crazy quixotic man,"[32] and, as Kerouac recalled, "my life hanging around the campus had reached the completion of its cycle and was stultified."[33]

On first meeting Cassady, Kerouac was disappointed. Neal's revved-up jive and intellectual name-dropping sounded especially caricatured in an Upper West Side apartment filled with former Columbia students. But Kerouac's second meeting with Cassady proved electric. When he knocked on the door of a cold-water flat in Spanish Harlem, Neal answered in the nude, fresh from having sex with LuAnne. Kerouac and Cassady began talking and didn't stop until dawn.

To Cassady, Kerouac represented the great writer he aspired to become. He implored Kerouac to teach him to write. Kerouac quickly understood the request as a con, but he was nonetheless seduced by Cassady's desperate drive to learn. Kerouac, too, had done his time in solitary with the Great Books, and both men were athletes—fast runners and football players. But the link forged that night transcended the autodidactic and athletic interests they held in common. Cassady became "a new kind of American saint,"[34] in Kerouac's view. "He reminded me of some long-lost brother; the sight of his suffering bony face with the long sideburns and his straining muscular sweating neck made me remember my boyhood."[35]

What is all the holy feeling I have for holy Neal, maybe he's my brother at that; it was you first said we were Blood brothers, remember?
—Jack Kerouac to Neal Cassady

CASSADY AND GINSBERG MEET On January 10, 1947, while Allen Ginsberg was visiting Vicki Russell, Kerouac and Cassady dropped by to score some marijuana. (Cassady had never smoked it.) Already high, Ginsberg looked at Cassady and was enthralled. Evoking their encounter that night, Kerouac wrote, "Two piercing eyes glancing into two piercing eyes—the holy con-man with the shining mind, and the sorrowful poetic con-man with the dark mind."[36] For the next few weeks, Kerouac scarcely saw either of them.

During this time, Cassady and Ginsberg talked endlessly. Cassady's rapid patter, jumping manically and modifying endlessly, fascinated Ginsberg. Cassady called his style "sixteen thoughts down," meaning that sixteen associations were operating simultaneously. Ginsberg figured his own rational train of thinking only went "4 thoughts down," and he apotheosized Cassady's panoramic perception: "Neal's is awareness, mine is consciousness. The consciousness is shallow; awareness is all embracing."[37]

In mid-January, Ginsberg and Cassady decided to sleep overnight following a late party on West 104th Street. Feeling vulnerable and excited, Ginsberg turned his back to Cassady and huddled on the edge of the

Perhaps you are a temptation rather than an angel. Yet you have a star in your forehead. . . .
—Allen Ginsberg to Neal Cassady

Don't you remember how you made me
stop trembling in shame and drew me to
you? Don't you know what I felt then, as
if you were a saint . . . ?
—Allen Ginsberg to Neal Cassady

Neal is his God-Bone.
—Jack Kerouac, on Allen Ginsberg

cot. Cassady curled his arm around his friend and tenderly pulled him near. That Whitmanesque, brotherly gesture in the middle of the night marked the beginning of Ginsberg's sexual education.

Ginsberg's previous homosexual experiences had been either uncomfortable (with Kerouac) or emotionally empty. In contrast, his first experiences with Cassady were passionate, operatic, and tender. Cassady regarded sex, Ginsberg recalled, as "a sort of joyful yoga . . . an ultimate exchange of soul."[38] (Ginsberg either romanticized his new lover, or Cassady's sex with Ginsberg was less sadistic than his relations with women—or both.) Within a few short weeks, Allen began to embrace his desires, and thus began the sexual turnaround that would lead Ginsberg to become one of poetry's frankest celebrators of homosexuality. Cassady was the ideally experienced and comfortable teacher, and Ginsberg learned quickly. In his journal, he left an explicit recording of his sexual education: "I will try to think on those sexual positions with Cassady which would please me. Try his laying me again. Try breast to breast position. Try 69 again, coming both at once. Try sitting on his chest and making him blow me. Try laying his mouth, French kissing, etc. Make him give me a trip around the world. . . . I want some real hip sex. What is it?"[39]

Ginsberg and Cassady's honeymoon did not last long. Although each offered qualities that seemed to complete the other, their extraordinary differences—in status and desire—soon dominated the relationship.

Ginsberg also recorded in his journals the doubts that followed their physical operatics. "I have had an increased feeling that the nearer we come to understand each other, the less he is attracted sexually, whatever the fluctuations of brotherliness."[40] By the time Cassady returned to Denver on March 4, Ginsberg had concluded, "Neal & I are not evenly mated."[41]

Both Kerouac and Ginsberg accompanied Cassady to the Greyhound bus station for the 6:30 PM departure. With an air of rueful affection, the three stepped into a photo booth and snapped a picture, and Neal cut the strip into pictures for each of them. Cassady stepped onto the bus that would take him out West to Colorado wearing a secondhand charcoal pin-stripe three-piece suit, the first he had ever owned. On returning to his room, Ginsberg wrote, "No tears, some melancholy, but mostly a peace & Grace."[42] Two long-running romances—one sexual, one literary—had been set in motion. Both would propel Beat history.

DENVER INTERLUDE: NEAL AND CAROLYN AND ALLEN AND JACK

Feeling abandoned after Cassady's departure, Ginsberg relentlessly examined their relationship in letters and made plans to travel to Denver. But the recipient, frightened by Ginsberg's ardor, responded with a brutal frankness: "I *really don't* know how much I can be satisfied to love you, I mean bodily, you know, I somehow disliked pricks & men & before you, had consciously forced myself to be homosexual. . . . I don't want to be unconsciously insincere by passing over my non-queerness to please you."[43]

The apparent candor of Cassady's letters did not extend to mentioning his new girlfriend, Carolyn Robinson, whom he had met a few weeks after returning to Denver. Dressed in his pin-stripe suit and a white tee-shirt, Neal had raked her over appraisingly, instantly impressed by the qualities she possessed that LuAnne had lacked. Three years older than Neal, Carolyn had grown up in Nashville, graduated from Bennington, and was now pursuing an MFA in Theater Arts at the University of Denver. Her blond hair wound in braids and her good looks and subdued clothes reflected taste and breeding. Neal wooed her with ardent politeness and discreet hand holding, suggesting that he had studied at Columbia with two college buddies, Allen and Jack. Emblematic of the Beats' propensity for love triangles, Cassady courted her by copying in ballpoint pen some of Allen's love poems to him. Only a few days before Allen ar-

Pick up: to drink alcohol, to use marijuana, opium, nembutal, or other drugs: "He laid claims to apocalyptic visions and heuristic discoveries when he picked up. . . ." [Anatole Broyard]. It applies not only to drug or alcohol use, but to mental pick-up: "To pick up means to get a lift out of things right now." [Huncke] It can also mean to score drugs: "If you asked me to cop grass I could pick up for you." [Huncke]

rived, Cassady finally acknowledged her existence: "She is just a bit too straight for my temperment [sic]; however, that is the challenge."[44]

Carolyn would become the only enduring female figure in the Beat saga. From the outset, her perspective on her romance with Neal was severely, sometimes even comically, limited. She worried that Neal lacked physical passion, for example, and she had no idea that during his courtship Neal was also sleeping with LuAnne and conducting an epistolary romance with Allen.

When Ginsberg arrived in Denver in July 1947, Neal introduced him to Carolyn as an old friend. Since Allen had no money, he moved into the Colburn Hotel room Carolyn shared with Neal. She felt embarrassed to sleep with Neal in a double bed two feet away from Allen's couch, but—always a good sport—she tolerated the cramped quarters for the sake of Neal's "college buddy." Neal first had sex with her only after Ginsberg's arrival. She submitted to his insistent thrusts but wondered, "Who was this animal raging in lust?"[45] She wanted to scream or cry but didn't want to wake Allen. He, meanwhile, heard each kiss and sigh from the couch "as I lay there jealous heart sick & crying trembling alone listening to love's noises."[46]

Carolyn couldn't understand the tension she felt within the threesome or the odd intensity that filled the room one afternoon while Allen read his poetry as she sketched Neal in the nude. And why—each night—was Neal rushing around? To satisfy his three lovers, Cassady maintained a grueling schedule. After finishing his day job transporting shoppers in a jitney, he spent the early evening with Carolyn and then surreptitiously crept out to see LuAnne. She agreed they should divorce, but in the meantime she wanted sex. He dashed back to the Colburn Hotel to sleep with Carolyn until 6 AM. At this point he went to see Allen, who had taken a graveyard-shift job vacuuming the third floor of the May Company and lived in a dank basement flat on Grant Street. "Remind Neal to ditch a few women," Ginsberg wrote in his journal.[47]

Boogie: to dance, to live hedonistically: *"If you can't boogie, I know I'll show you how."* [Kerouac] Derived from African-American slang, it also meant second-stage syphilis or musical harmony.

Traveling to Denver at the urging of letters that Neal signed "Your brother," Jack Kerouac arrived on the scene of this manic roundelay. He had ample time to explore the habitat of his new hero/comrade, but he saw little of Neal and felt shut out by the private language and intensity of the relationship between Ginsberg and Cassady. One evening Jack and Neal escorted Carolyn, whom Neal proudly introduced as the woman he would marry, to a downtown tavern. Neal kept the jukebox supplied with coins as Jack danced with the bride-to-be. In Jack's arms, Carolyn experienced the shy, brooding romanticism that she longed for, and she felt both disturbed and warmed by his whispered regret: "It's too bad, but that's how it is—Neal saw you first."[48] As the jukebox played "Too Close for Comfort," Carolyn had no idea that Jack fell in love with his buddies' girlfriends, or that, as he wrote Neal, he considered her "hardly your type—she's too pale and furtive."[49]

Devastated by Neal's mania and the closed-off route to his "secret heart," Allen experienced waves of rage and spontaneous weeping. He began to hallucinate telephone calls from Cassady. He wrote a long letter to Neal that was by turns angry and pitying. "I am the only one capable of mastering you right now and moving you by will and intelligence and insight and presumption out of the sterile round of self-destructive love and work and activities and emotions, the whole impasse of your existence."[50] In his journal, he wrote, "My *fault*, my *failure*, is not in the passions I have, but in my lack of control of them."[51]

Ginsberg's suite of poems from that summer, "Denver Doldrums," reflected his abject depression. On one of his last days in the city, looking out Carolyn's hotel window, he "word-sketched" the view, dominated by a bare-chested bricklayer with yellow hair and a smudged red hat eating a brown-bag lunch. Four years later, rearranged under the influence of William Carlos Williams, these lines would become his first poem in the natural, objective style that led to his mature poems.

One morning in mid-August, the balls Neal juggled came crashing

Cottons: the cotton used to absorb heroin prior to shooting. Containing some residue, it is often saved by addicts in cases of emergency: "I was out all out of junk at this point and had double-boiled my last cottons." [Burroughs]

down as Carolyn walked into her hotel room to find on her bed Neal bracketed by LuAnne and Allen. She could barely comprehend what she was seeing—she especially couldn't fathom the sight of two nude men together—and vowed never to see Neal again. At the same time, she later wrote, "Somehow I knew positively that our relationship *was* predestined."[52]

Soon after this farcical scene *en flagrante delicto*, Ginsberg and Cassady began hitchhiking to New Waverly, Texas, the new home of William and Joan Burroughs (although there was never an official ceremony, Joan considered herself a common-law wife and called herself Joan Burroughs). When they reached the hot, dusty plains of Oklahoma, traffic grew sparse. Alone with Neal, Allen compulsively analyzed their relationship, demanding that they unite, and the discussion culminated in an ersatz ceremony. Ginsberg later described that moment:

> We kneeled together on the road in Oklahoma, in the middle of a four way cross of dirt roads, on an endless plain at night fall. I hadn't imagined such a place or such an eternal vow: fidelity, union, seraphic insight, sights of America, everything I could imagine. He accepted it all, just a poor lost soul, an orphan in fact, looking for a father seraph and I was looking for a seraphic boy.[53]

I thought it was a little paradise. So fucking bucolic.
             —Herbert Huncke

TEXAS INTERLUDE To get to William and Joan Burroughs' farm, the visitor left the highway at the five-block-long town of New Waverly, Texas, and headed twelve miles through bayou country, up a pitted macadam road, past armadillos, persimmon trees, and elderly Negroes sitting on weathered porches. At the end of a dirt logging road stood the Burroughses' house. One first saw the dilapidated barn, much bigger than the house, and then the corrugated roof that overhung the one-story cabin. It was small, but provided a room each for William, Joan, four-year-old Julie, and Herbert Huncke. Along the front ran a swaying wooden porch set with kerosene lamps, ending at a large blackberry bush and a wild-rose bush. Pine and moss-covered oak surrounded them, and two hundred yards down a twisty path was a bayou used for bathing. There was no plumbing, electricity, or heat. On this spread of ninety-seven acres, Burroughs hoped to make his fortune. He originally planned to set up a mail-order citrus business. "Money to be made here like picking fruit off the trees," Burroughs wrote Ginsberg. "Grapefruit that is."[54] But soon after the Burroughses moved in during January 1947, he decided that marijuana would be the perfect cash crop, one that was always in demand.

Life on the Burroughs farm was relaxed and rudimentary. William would rise and read in his separate room and emerge about 10:30 to look at the mail and the papers. He occasionally glanced over his glasses and announced to Joan, "Well I see Peaches Browning got another divorce here."[55] His outfit rarely varied: he wore khaki pants and shirts, a felt hat with a sweatband pushed back on his head, a black vest with a key chain, and work boots. Aside from newspapers and conversation and domestic chores, the chief business of the day was killing scorpions and shooting. Burroughs fired his .22 target pistol at bottles, possums, and dead tree trunks, and he occasionally shouted, "Hey, the redcoats are comin'!" into the deserted landscape. At five began the cocktail hour followed by barbecued steaks. After dinner, Burroughs would shoot and then the group would listen to music on the tinny wind-up Victrola. The selection was impressive—from Prokofiev's *Alexander Nevsky* Suite, to Billie Holiday's blues, from Viennese waltzes to a favorite album called *52nd Street Jazz*, featuring Charlie Parker, Coleman Hawkins, and Lester Young. Neighbors beyond the pine forest speculated on the identity of this crew of Easterners who played music and shot guns, and one day a local druggist told Burroughs and Huncke that locals imagined them to be gangsters shooting off

Shooting is my principal pastime.
—William Burroughs

*Cranked: high, excited. According to Herbert Huncke, **crank** was an early version of **crack**.*

machine guns. ("That just tickled the shit out of Burroughs," Huncke recalled. "Such strutting was never known."[56])

As summer came to the farm, Joan's pregnant figure grew fuller with the child she and Burroughs had conceived in the Times Square hotel room. In the heat of the day she reclined in the water in a nearby pond. "She was so beautiful there," Huncke recalled, "the water lapping on her belly, Joan playing Earth Mother."[57] After using amphetamine inhalers, she would clean the little house, care for Julie, prepare meals, and polish the kerosene lanterns.

Bill and Joan slept in separate rooms and had little physical contact. (She knocked at his door one night and said, "All I want is to lie in your arms a little while."[58]) William Burroughs III was born on July 21, 1947, in characteristically unplanned fashion. "I think it's time," Joan said, and she and Bill set off in their Jeep for the nearest hospital, twenty-seven miles away. Joan did not breast-feed her child, knowing that her milk would be laced with amphetamines, from the two inhalers a day she had used throughout the pregnancy. Billy was born addicted and spent his first days on earth in withdrawal. (Meanwhile, Allen Ginsberg celebrated the event by composing an extended "Birthday Ode" to Billy and writing to Lionel Trilling that he "will be almost another brother to me."[59]) Joan's paranoia grew. At night, by the light of a kerosene lamp, she would inspect her skin with a hand mirror, looking for white wormlike filaments that she regarded as symptoms of postnuclear contamination.

The last member of this ersatz family was Herbert Huncke, recently released from the Bronx jail. Burroughs had asked Huncke to bring a Mason jar of marijuana seeds, from which he hoped the Burroughs dope dynasty would flower. The plan didn't work. Huncke had been so drugged up when he boarded the bus to Texas that he forgot the jar. He spent the trip kicking heroin, and Burroughs kindly met him at the Houston bus station with a shot of an opium derivative called Pantopon.

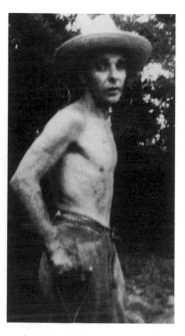

Herbert Huncke at work, New Waverly, Texas, summer 1948

Huncke became the farm's chief factotum because, he recalled, "Burroughs was busy in his usual fashion shuffling around and playing landed gentry."[60] Huncke hauled firewood and water each day, invariably muttering to himself about the heat, the chiggers, and the goddamned Viennese waltzes. He became the link between the farm and Houston's drug world. He scored Benzedrine inhalers by the gross for Joan, paregoric for Bill, Nembutals for himself, and marijuana seeds for the farm's chief crop. He enclosed the porch with screen so he could doze off to sleep watching the moon and listening to armadillos.

The marijuana crop required little labor; it was one of the only things that would grow in the dry soil. When locals admired the unfamiliar-looking crop, Joan explained that it was "some new kind of animal feed."[61] As a moneymaking cover for their illicit herb, they also grew tomatoes, peas, and cotton. Burroughs conducted scientific experiments for weed concentrates.

Two visits punctuated the Burroughses' pastoral routine. Shortly after William III was born his grandparents arrived, under the impression that their son had kicked both drugs and the influence of figures like Herbert Huncke. About twenty minutes after their morning fix, Huncke and Burroughs encountered Mortimer and Laura, stranded in their station wagon that was too big to make it down the dirt road. The senior Burroughses were dressed as if they were arriving at a country club, while Huncke wore denims and tee-shirt; Burroughs introduced him as a neighbor, Huncke said "How do you do?" in his best neighborly manner and promptly disappeared. The parental visit was short and genial, and when the senior Burroughses left a few days later, they maintained their convictions that their son was on the right track. For the cabin Laura sent yards of patterned cretonne that eventually hung in swags at the windows, and two large cupboards that dwarfed the rooms.

Neal Cassady and Allen Ginsberg arrived in New Waverly on

Naturally, I thought the guy was just kiddin.
—Herbert Huncke, on Burroughs' request for a Viennese waltz

It was a house full of pretty frantic people.
—Herbert Huncke

Henry and Charly: Charly is cocaine, and **Henry** is heroin: "When you shoot Henry and Charly you can smell it going in." [Burroughs]

August 29. The sexually frustrated Ginsberg hoped for miracles from their idyll in Texas: "When we got here, I expected this happy holiday of God given sexuality," Ginsberg wrote the day after arriving, "but where was the royal couch?"[62] Huncke worked with Ginsberg to create one by joining two cots. Cassady looked on at what he called "the symbolic bed" and periodically observed, "I don't care, brrp, brrp."[63] As soon as he and Ginsberg lay down, the bed collapsed. It seemed to be an omen for their relationship as well. Ginsberg's "petitionary masochistic lust"[64] so threatened Cassady that he rejected even Ginsberg's touch. "And man," he told Kerouac, "I'd never been that way, you know, but, man, he was all opening up and I was all . . ."[65]

The last day of their roller-coaster romance was spent in Houston. Ginsberg planned to sign on as a messman bound for Dakar. He was broke, so Burroughs lent him money, and Huncke had maneuvered a full suite at the Brazos Hotel for the single-room rate. After going to black jazz clubs, high on marijuana, Cassady dropped Huncke on the street and Ginsberg at the hotel. Neal sped off in the Jeep, swallowing Nembutals. He picked up a teenage girl just released from a mental hospital and took her to the hotel. She waited while he angrily tried to satisfy Ginsberg's sexual needs. Huncke witnessed Cassady's thrusts and concluded they were aimed to humiliate rather than satisfy lust. Soon Cassady passed out. No one was satisfied.

Shipping out September 7, on the S.S. *John Blais*, Ginsberg observed, "The sacramental honeymoon is over."[66]

Back on the farm, Burroughs put Cassady to work, but socially he was barely tolerated. Huncke was offended by his parasitical behavior and Joan deflected his flirtatious attentions with "blasé brittleness" and "sharpened laughs."[67] (As Neal later described it to Kerouac: "Man, relationship completely a stone wall between me and June [Joan], as far as that goes, see, although I don't want to be that way, naturally, but I mean I'm not

But no such happy forest of Arden seems to be in sight in Texas . . .
—Allen Ginsberg

Rap: *a primarily one-way communication; coined in the 1930s, widely used in the 1960s: "It may be kind of an idea, you have a little conversation piece that goes with it, and that's your rap." [Huncke]*

ah—. . . ."[68]) But Burroughs needed Cassady to transport the nearly mature marijuana crop to New York because he feared night driving and didn't trust Huncke at the wheel. On September 30, with Cassady at the wheel, Burroughs in the front passenger seat, and Huncke squeezed between duffel bags of freshly harvested marijuana, they set out. Three nonstop days later, they arrived in New York. Neal hung around a few days for a planned rendezvous with Kerouac, but they just missed one another. Joan, Julie, and little Billy were supposed to meet them at Grand Central Station, but Joan appeared so odd to the police—who thought she was about to abandon her children—that they sent her to Bellevue for her third stay. When Burroughs informed hospital officials that he was the husband and father and a member of the Harvard Club, Joan was released.

Peddling the marijuana crop proved more difficult. A bellboy toked a sample and yelped, "Hey, man, that's awful, that's green tea. Jesus, it's terrible shit, it's not even cured."[69] The scientific Burroughs had failed to take this crucial step, and he quickly set about baking batches of marijuana until his product reached a greenish-brown color. Huncke and Burroughs reconnected with Vicki Russell, recently returned from working with a Philadelphia–based madam, and Bill Garver, still stealing overcoats. But neither offered much help, and Garver supplied Burroughs with enough heroin to get rehooked. The sheer bulk of the marijuana posed yet another problem—Burroughs likened it to hauling around a bale of alfalfa. They finally wholesaled most of the crop for $100, left a suitcase full in a Grand Central locker, ate a slice of pizza, and headed back to New Waverly. The gentleman farmer's marijuana scheme had proved to be a comic fiasco.

Throughout his adult years, Burroughs was forced to move on, periodically, after running afoul of the law. In Texas, his infraction was making love to Joan by the side of the road in their Jeep. The local Beeville sheriff, Vail Eenis—a character right out of Burroughs' imagination—

Elitch: code word for smoking pot, used as verb or noun, coined by Jack Kerouac and Neal Cassady in summer 1950: "Elitch is bad for muscles unless you keep going like you do all day." [Kerouac] Also, **Elitch's Gardens**, meaning a field of marijuana.

quipped to the local judge. "This here feller was disturbin' the peace while tryin' to get a piece."[70] Burroughs lost his driver's license for six months and stayed in the Beeville jail until his parents wired $173 to pay his fine. It was time, Burroughs concluded, to move on. "I detest limitations of any kind," he later wrote Ginsberg, "and intend to establish my ass some place where I am virgin on the police blotter."[71] Burroughs' principle would dictate his subsequent moves from Texas to New Orleans to Mexico City to Colombia to Tangiers. His biographer, Ted Morgan, aptly dubbed him "the Wandering Wasp."[72]

BEAT LIVES, BEAT LITERATURE

*F*INDING A VOICE: JACK KEROUAC WRITES *THE TOWN AND THE CITY*
"Until I find a way to unleash the inner life in an art-method, nothing about me will be clear," Jack Kerouac wrote Allen Ginsberg in
the fall of 1945. About the New Vision, he observed, "The fact was I had
the vision . . . I think everyone has . . . what we lack is the method."[1] He
spent the next six years seeking that method. During this time Ginsberg
and Burroughs also developed their writing voice, but neither pursued it
with the self-consciously agonized drive of Kerouac.

Jack Kerouac looked on all his novels as a single autobiographical
epic—"running Proust"—called "the Legend of Duluoz." The seeds of his
epic chronicle could be seen in Kerouac's May 1, 1945, notes for a novel
evoking his move from Lowell to the dissolute big city of New York. But
the first words weren't typed for nearly a year, while Leo Kerouac was
dying of stomach cancer. The novel's panoramic scope and its title, *The
Town and the City*, suggested Jack's hero, Thomas Wolfe. Kerouac's ambitions were impossibly large: to prove that he was not the failure that his fa-

*I am going to marry my novels and have
little short stories for children.*
—Jack Kerouac

Death hovers over my pencil . . .
—Jack Kerouac

*My subject as a writer is of course
America, and simply, I must know
everything about it.*
—Jack Kerouac

**Pinned to Jack Kerouac's Wall to
Inspire His Writing**
*Art is the highest task and the proper
metaphysical activity of this life.*
—Nietzsche

*Read Jack's Novel last week, and think it
is very very great, Alas! that we should
have been so true.*
—Allen Ginsberg

ther considered him; to capture all of America; to express the New Vision in an autobiographical narrative; to throw out "all this overlaid mental garbage of 'existentialism' and 'hipsterism' and bourgeois decadence"[2] and replace it with directly observed experience. He wanted to write the Great American Novel his first time out.

Returning from his father's funeral to Gabrielle's apartment in Ozone Park, Kerouac set his typewriter on the kitchen table and buried himself in writing. "I associate home and mother and farms and the *Town and City* etc. with a kind of childish immortality (the 'genius' etc. who will be redeemed)."[3] Returning to the religiosity of his "Self-Ultimacy" period, he wrote hymns in his journal and said a prayer before penitentially beginning to write. "When this book is finished, which is going to be the sum and substance and crap of everything I've been thru throughout this whole goddam life," he wrote, "I shall be redeemed."[4]

Writing *The Town and the City* proved to be the most sustained act of Kerouac's life. He drew upon concrete memories of his Lowell childhood and conflated them with the stories of his childhood friends (especially Alex Sampas, whose sister he would marry near the end of his life). In September 1948, he finished a first draft of 380,000 words. Carrying his 1,183 pages of typed manuscript in a battered doctor's bag, Kerouac made the rounds of his friends.

He divided the sprawling narrative of the Martin family into five books and the mind of Jack Kerouac between the five Martin brothers. The Kerouac family was seen through a veil of nostalgia, and some of the most virtuosic writing portrayed Jack's football stardom. The long *bildungsroman* picked up considerably when the protagonist moved from the town to the city and the darker narrative of friendship began to unfold. Lucien Carr, Allen Ginsberg, William Burroughs, and Herbert Huncke appeared as central figures, and David Kammerer's death was portrayed as a suicide.

At this stage of his writing, Kerouac felt no responsibility to record events exactly, and his later dictum—"first thought, best thought"—held no sway; the novel underwent several drafts. After later disenchantment with his first published work, Kerouac stated that it had been dictated by Columbia's literary strictures. The novel read like the work of a writer trying both to create something new and simultaneously to impress his teachers and evoke his literary models. His intricate interweaving of motifs, his repetition of key symbolic words, and his adjective-ridden prose earnestly strained for lyricism. Many of the problems critics ascribed to this first novel were apt: it is adolescent, sprawling, and diffuse. Kerouac's biographer Gerald Nicosia described *The Town and the City* as an apprentice work, but already Kerouac's characteristic vocabulary—"glee," "lost," "rain," "dream," "vision," "sad"—appeared. Amid the lushness of overwritten sentences was Kerouac's extraordinary ear for sound and rhythm.

I feel like writing a huge novel about all of it. Just think—these people I mentioned, and us, and Bill, Joan, Huncke, Allen and Lucien & Celine, and Vicki and Normie, and all the places & things of New York. Where could I begin?

—Jack Kerouac

Just a little boy who wants to be a novelist.

—Alan Ansen's chiding description of Jack Kerouac

ALLEN GINSBERG'S VISION In the summer of 1948, Allen Ginsberg sublet an apartment at 321 East 121st Street. He worked two hours a day as a file clerk and idled about the rest of the day. Without telephone or friends, surrounded only by egg-crate bookshelves and the view over East Harlem, Allen felt his isolation.

Jack Kerouac rarely visited; he was holed up in Ozone Park completing *The Town and the City*. But he did share sections of his manuscript with Ginsberg, who felt that the tumult of the last four years was justified because it had been given permanent literary form. "I also felt my own failure as an artist to conclude a large and, if not mature, at least complete and internally perfect work."[5]

On April 1, Neal Cassady had married Carolyn Robinson, then four months pregnant. "So O.K. Pops, everything you do is great," Ginsberg angrily responded. "The idea of you with a child and a settled center

I was so sick that I found myself worrying about the future of man's soul, my own in particular.

—Allen Ginsberg

of affection—shit."[6] Cassady suggested cutting off all correspondence: "You and I are now farther apart than ever. Only with effort can I recall you."[7] Allen's hopes of being loved were dashed: "I figured I'd never find any sort of psychospiritual sexo-cock jewel fulfillment in my existence!"[8]

Ginsberg took long self-questioning strolls in the baked-in summer heat of Harlem, his thoughts turning to his ill-defined future and his utter aloneness; as he later put it, "I gave up, I shut down the machinery, I stopped thinking, I stopped living."[9] For the first time, he had no circle of friends, no confidant, "no New Vision and no Supreme Reality and nothing but the world in front of me, and of not knowing what to do with *that*."[10]

Profoundly unmoored, he buried himself in books. Many of them—by Saint Teresa of Avila, Saint John of the Cross, and William Blake—propounded mystical visions. One July day, while reading Blake's "Ah Sunflower," Ginsberg's eyes wandered to the cityscape at dusk. He had just finished masturbating when he experienced a series of visions so overwhelmingly vivid that they dominated the next fifteen years of his life.

He heard from within his solitary flat "a voice of rock . . . like the voice of the Ancient of Days"[11] intoning the poem. Ginsberg immediately knew that Blake was speaking, looked down at the poem, and felt he had become one with the sunflower. At the same moment the view from his window appeared transformed: his eyes traveled from the nineteenth-century gargoyles and cornices that crowned the Harlem apartment buildings to the sky at dusk. In its blue infinity, Ginsberg saw God. "I suddenly realized that *this* was *it*! . . . This was the moment that I was born for."[12]

Bop prosody: *a term coined by Jack Kerouac in 1951 to describe a process of writing spontaneously, improvising in a manner akin to jazz-playing: "the use of mixtures containing spontaneity, 'bop prosody,' surreal-real images, jumps, beats, cool measures, long rapid vowels, long long lines, and the main content, soul." [Corso, on the Beat literary aesthetic]*

Blake's voice returned several minutes later, intoning "The Sick Rose." This time Ginsberg's vision was slightly different. He became the sick rose, the worm of death housed within himself. He felt the inevitable doom of the universe and an edge of fear, but the vision remained awesomely beautiful.

He heard Blake's voice a final time that day reciting "The Little Girl Lost." Ginsberg hypnotically focused on a repeating refrain:

> Do father, mother, weep?
> Where can Lyca sleep?
>
> How can Lyca sleep
> If her mother weep?
>
> If her heart does ache
> Then let Lyca wake;
> If my mother sleep,
> Lyca shall not weep.

Ginsberg realized that he was Lyca; by awakening, the veil clouding eternity could be lifted to reveal heaven.

    Blake's visitations did not end that day. Later that week, Ginsberg experienced flashes of euphoria, and he tried several times to conjure up the vision. One day in his old-fashioned kitchen, next to the bathtub-sink, he began shaking his body, whirling, and moving up and down. "Dance! dance! dance! dance! spirit! spirit! spirit! dance!" Ginsberg chanted. A creepy, paranoid fear suffused him, and "suddenly I felt like Faust, calling up the devil."[13] He abruptly ended his dance, and never repeated it.

    The dark side of the vision returned a few days later, in the Columbia bookstore, while Ginsberg was reading Blake. "The apparition of an evil, sick unconscious wild city rose before me in visible semblance, and about the dead buildings in the barren air, the bodies of the soul that built the wonderland shuffled and stalked and stalked and lurched in attitudes of immemorial nightmare all around."[14] The customers in the bookstore turned into a common army of tormented souls, hiding their pain and their consciousness behind twisted, grotesque masks of rejection and self-

I want to be a saint, a real saint while I am young, for there is so much work to do.
—Allen Ginsberg to Mark Van Doren

Sticks, steeazicks: *marijuana cigarettes, derived from African-American slang of the 1930s and 1940s.* **Steeazicks** *is* **sticks** *transformed by carny pig Latin: "a couple of steeazicks from Panama as big as your thumb" [Kerouac].*

deception. "The main insight I had at that time was that everybody knew. Everybody knew completely everything."[15]

Coming on the heels of crisis and rejection, lacking a vessel for psychological ventilation, Ginsberg's ego disintegrated in successive waves of euphoria and paranoia. His vision bore all the classical marks of a psychotic break. He vowed to himself: "Never deny the voice—no, never *forget* it, don't get lost mentally wandering in other spirit worlds or American or job worlds or advertising worlds or earth worlds."[16]

Wherever I go I see myself in a mirror— it used to be my own selfblood, now it is god's.

—Allen Ginsberg

When Allen recounted his vision to friends, they responded with skepticism and fear. Louis Ginsberg interpreted it as a sign that his son had inherited Naomi Ginsberg's schizophrenia and blamed the break on Cassady. In a two-word letter Louis counseled his son: "Exorcise Neal."[17] Burroughs was skeptical, Kerouac tried to be understanding, but Joan Burroughs was the only one who intuitively understood. "I've been claiming for three years that anyone who doesn't blow his top once is no damn good," she later wrote him. "When I refer to it as top-blowing, I'm sure you know what I mean. No percentage in talking about visions or super-reality or any such lay terms. Either you know now what I know (and don't ask me just what that is), or else I'm mistaken about you and off the beam somewhere—in which case you're just a dime-a-dollar neurotic and I'm nuts."[18]

Ginsberg took as his mission breaking down the masks that set tormented souls apart from one another; he must avert "the possibility of the sick rose coming true and the atom bomb."[19]

Script: a doctor's prescription for drugs: "As a habit takes hold, other interests lose importance to the user. Life telescopes down to junk, one fix and looking forward to the next, 'stashes' and 'scripts,' 'spikes' and 'droppers.'" *[Burroughs]*

While carrying on with his daily life—attending classes, wearing a black tie, and maintaining an A average—Ginsberg tried to recapture his experience in poetry. After months of writing, he knew that he had failed. His poetic repertoire relied on private symbols, archaic attitudes, and decorative flourishes, "overwritten coy stanzas, a little after Marvell, a little after Wyatt."[20] Ginsberg had discovered the pathway to expanded consciousness through deranged senses, but he lacked the voice to describe it.

THE CASSADYS' MARRIAGE Carolyn Robinson and Neal Cassady were married on April Fool's Day 1948. The bride wore a light green woolen dress under her loose navy blue jacket to conceal her four-month pregnancy. Her ring, plate silver set with rhinestones, came from Woolworth's.[21] Judge Clayton Golden performed the $10 ceremony, and the newlyweds toasted with two beers in a grimy diner, where the bride picked up the tab. Over the next few years Carolyn ruefully looked back on that afternoon, "as my 'wedding day' became more and more a grotesque parody of my youthful dreams."[22]

Despite the inauspicious beginning, the Cassadys' became the only long-running marriage among the Beats. They remained married for the next fourteen years, raised three children, and bought a suburban home with its own swimming pool and patio. Of all the people associated with the Beats, Neal and Carolyn Cassady struggled hardest to meet the demands of the "real" workaday world. But such evidence of marital continuity and bourgeois trappings doesn't reflect Neal's desertions and desperation over the years. His impersonation of a suburban homeowner was overshadowed by his sexual mania, depression, and addictions, shifting from drugs to religion.

The Cassadys' marriage offers a narrative in which the tabloid plot is always the same. Neal would work and remain home for a while and then either go off with a girl in a hotel room or go off with boys in a car. The woman might be LuAnne or a stranger, and the car might be a Ford or a Hudson. Each time Carolyn would be surprised and would always take him back with one of her timeworn rationalizations.

That initial difference between the two of you must undoubtedly be ironed out, that is, her kind of serenity, and your restlessness and blood-brother craziness.
—Jack Kerouac to Neal Cassady, on the Cassadys' marriage

Don't worry about your boy Neal, he's found what he wants and in her is attaining greater satisfaction than he's ever known.
—Neal Cassady, on Carolyn Cassady

Suffice to say I just eat every 12 hours, sleep every 20 hours, masturbate every 8 hours and otherwise just sit on the train and stare ahead without a thought. . . .
—Neal Cassady

Neal and Carolyn Cassady shortly after being married, San Francisco, April 1, 1948

Neal described marriage as "a combination of willful blindness, a perverted sense of wanting to help the girl, and just plain what-the-hell."[23] His gaudy adventures provided the marriage's frenzied plot, but it was Carolyn who ruled the marriage—by simple determination. And she was very determined. Beneath her blond maternal façade, she pushed ahead with steely, masochistic, controlling nerve. She felt she had to, for her children depended on her.

In addition to his first wife, LuAnne, who periodically returned, Neal had a third wife, Diana Hansen, whom he bigamously married. Hansen was a well-born model, infatuated with Cassady and pregnant with his child. Two hours after she married him, on July 10, 1950, he used his brakeman's pass to catch a train back to Carolyn. Neal had countless transitory sexual encounters and intense affairs. Every time Neal deserted her, Carolyn picked up the cards, wherever they lay. But as Kerouac observed, "He went back to the woman that wanted him the most."[24]

KEROUAC GOES ON THE ROAD In the fall of 1948, after completing *The Town and the City*, Jack Kerouac was depressed, angry, and isolated. "I am lost," he wrote Ginsberg. "The only thing to do is to give up—I am giving up."[25] Instead, he began a new book. He described it as "an American-scene picaresque, 'On the Road,' dealing simply with hitch-hiking and the sorrows, hardships, adventures, sweats and labours [*sic*] of that."[26] At the center would be two boys headed West.

Neal Cassady's letters, passionately affirming that the pair were "blood brothers," inspired him.[27] The two men fantasized about buying a ranch where they would live together with their respective women ("Your mother [Bless her] & Carolyn [Bless her] are exactly alike," Neal observed.[28]) They even envisioned a communal home that would house William Burroughs and Herbert Huncke. Kerouac found in Neal a model for the energy and ambition that he often lacked, and Neal suggested that the two should go "into action as one."[29] It didn't matter that Neal already had a wife and two children; male bonding superseded all.

On December 15, 1948, Jack picked up the telephone and heard, long distance, a "mad Western excited voice over the phone, 'Yes, yes, it's Neal, you see . . . I've got a '49 Hudson.'"[30] Cassady planned to head East to pick up his buddy and drive him West. The spontaneous gesture swept away, for the moment, Jack's fears about his future; now he was in Neal's impulsive hands.

Cassady arrived at the home of Kerouac's sister, in Rocky Mount, North Carolina, driving a brand-new mud-spattered maroon Hudson. He was unshaven and wore a pair of stained white gas-station coveralls. His motley cohorts included his ex-wife LuAnne (sporting waist-length dirty blond hair) and a friend named Al Hinkle, who had started the trip as a honeymoon with his new wife, Helen. (She had been summarily dumped in Arizona. "She had started wanting to stay at motels at night and stopping for food and such nonsensical things as that,"[31] LuAnne recalled.) The cross-country trip in an unheated car depended on breakneck speeds, sponging money, stealing gas, cadging food from hitchhikers, as LuAnne put it, "hocking all the way across" America.[32] (The newlywed Helen Hinkle meanwhile made her way to the Burroughses' home in Algiers, Louisiana, where she waited for her husband to pick her up on the return swing.) The travelers celebrated Christmas with the Kerouacs, but Cassady wanted to keep moving. He transported Gabrielle's furniture from Ozone Park to North Carolina, traveling another 2,000 miles in three days.

The crew spent New Year's Eve in New York, partying with the old crew, crowding into Allen Ginsberg's apartment. The newly rehabilitated Lucien Carr had been sprung from the Elmira Reformatory, and Jack presented Neal to him as the mythic figure Carr had been a few years earlier. Looking at Kerouac and Cassady, LuAnne was reminded of eleven-year-

What's your road, man?—holyboy road, madman road, rainbow road, guppy road, any road. It's an anywhere road for anybody anyhow.
        —Neal Cassady, as Dean Moriarty
        in *On the Road*

I have almost real reason to perhaps almost believe that he stole the car, but I don't know.
        —Jack Kerouac, on Neal Cassady

I went with him for no reason.
        —Jack Kerouac, on Neal Cassady

Lucien in New York amazingly bright, like future glory when he reborn—a Super Liberace Billy Graham Nature Boy Prophet of Gold.
        —Jack Kerouac, after Lucien Carr's
        return from prison

Neal Cassady at the wheel

old kids "getting their first buddy, their arms around each other over the shoulder type of thing."[33] In the drunken, Dionysian, marijuana-stoned romantic roundelay of the opening days of 1949, life became a nonstop party, whose participants included LuAnne, Neal, Allen Ginsberg, a friend named Alan Ansen, Kerouac and his new girlfriend, Pauline. It seemed like a brief return to former high times, and during one of those parties Kerouac expanded on his notion of "beat": if the present generation was beat, it would soon become beatific. This was Kerouac at his most optimistic.

Plans changed frequently during the first weeks of January—the tight band of Jack, Hinkle, LuAnne, and Neal would go to New Orleans; they would stay in New York with Allen; they would ship out to sea. The chaos—and the adrenaline of uncertainty—aptly reflected Kerouac's mind at this pivotal point in his life.

The next move was determined by a call from William Burroughs. The forgotten Helen Hinkle had been stranded in the very strange Burroughs household since January 3, and Burroughs looked forward to the time when Hinkle "gets tired of fiddle fucking around N.Y."[34] so that he could pick up his wife.

The only thing to do was go.
—Jack Kerouac, On the Road

The foursome—Neal, LuAnne, Jack, Al—left New York on January 19, 1949, inspired by Neal's dictum: "We should realize what it would mean to us to UNDERSTAND that we're not REALLY worrying about ANYTHING."[35] This trip to San Francisco would become the centerpiece of *On the Road*. Neal silently coasted into gas stations in the middle of the night, filled the tank, and turned the meter back; they washed dishes in exchange for food; they stole gas, cigarettes, and food; they sold the spare tire for gas money. Gunning the car to eighty, turning up the radio to full volume, banging on the dashboard until it was dented, they tooled through the South. Along the way they told each other their intimate life stories. As they neared New Orleans, they picked up the Chicken Jazz 'n Gumbo disk jockey show. "Don't worry 'bout *nothing!*"[36] the deejay instructed.

We were all delighted, we all realized we were leaving confusion and nonsense behind and performing our one and noble function of the time, move.
—Jack Kerouac, On the Road

LOUISIANA INTERLUDE: THE BURROUGHSES Before arriving at the Burroughses' house in Algiers, Louisiana, Jack dressed up in black cotton pants and a white shirt. He was trepidacious about seeing William Burroughs. Helen Hinkle recalled the thick atmosphere as the foursome walked in and Jack's anxious response: he began making crêpes suzette. The Hinkles repaired to another room to argue (Burroughs invoked Robert Burns to capture her mood: "Gathering her brows like the gathering Storm,/Nursing her wrath to keep it warm"[37]). LuAnne drifted in and asked if they were going to screw. She liked to watch, she said.

The crew stayed a week, long enough to get a sense of life around the Burroughses' household. Burroughs spent most of his time sitting in a rocking chair, playing with his seven cats, and shooting Joan's empty Benzedrine inhalers with his air gun. He would periodically repair to the bathroom with a black necktie and works to shoot up. Burroughs showed them the arsenal of guns he kept in his drawer and demonstrated knife throwing while Joan puttered around the dilapidated house, raked lizards from the single dead tree in the yard, and tried to mother the two children she loved but couldn't manage (Julie bit herself, Billy a.k.a. "the Little Beast"[38] ran naked through the barren yard). The Burroughses' marital relationship appeared to Kerouac both unfathomable and profoundly close. They talked long into the night, communicating "their own set of subtle vibrations."[39] Jack concluded simply, "Love is all."[40]

Confronted by his two gurus, Cassady and Burroughs, Jack felt torn. With his "Whoo!" and his "Yes, yes, yes!" Neal's trip across the continent had the aura of a religious pilgrimage—the drive through the American landscape became a magic dream. Burroughs regarded both the trip and Cassady skeptically. Why was Jack following these grifters on such a meaningless trip? "Obviously the 'purpose' of the trip is carefully selected to symbolize the basic fact of purposelessness," Burroughs wrote Ginsberg. "Neal is, of course, the very soul of this voyage into pure, abstract meaningless motion. He is The Mover, compulsive, dedicated, ready to sacrifice family, friends, even his very car itself to the necessity of moving from one place to another."[41]

Jack could offer no rational response to Burroughs—reason had

She loved that man madly, but in a delirious way of some kind.
—Jack Kerouac, on Joan Vollmer and William Burroughs

[Bull] seems to me to be headed for his ideal fate, which is compulsive psychosis dashed with a jigger of psychopathic irresponsibility and violence.
—Dean Moriarty (Neal Cassady) on Bull Lee (William Burroughs)

nothing to do with it—and he resumed the trip with Neal and LuAnne. The Hinkles stayed on in New Orleans. Watching as the figures of the Burroughses receded into the distance, Jack observed, "But we lean forward to the next crazy venture beneath the skies."[42]

ONWARD The Hudson's ball bearings were broken, the dashboard was dented from Cassady's manic drumming, and half a continent stretched ahead as the threesome drove through the day and through the night. They imagined meeting blues-moaning Negroes in bayou jazz joints, they saw actual fires. As they traversed the endless plains of West Texas at a steady seventy miles an hour, they took off their clothes and headed into the dusk with LuAnne sandwiched in the front seat between her two beaus. (Truck drivers looked down from their high cabs and briefly swerved.) The white blacktop divider whizzed by as they drove through the desert of the Southwest and then swung north toward San Francisco, Neal at the wheel, Jack observing the swiftly passing landscape through the window, LuAnne loving both men. The specifics of the voyage—the cowtowns, drawling cops and shopkeepers, Okie accents, diners and railroad hotels, mountains, potato patches, and the blue Pacific—merged into a kaleidoscopic metaphor, a Wolfean riff on the American panorama, at once literary and entirely real.

Finally, the amorous trio reached San Francisco, penniless and exhausted. "No more land!" Neal yelled. "We can't go any further 'cause there ain't no more land!"[43] At the corner of O'Farrell and Grant, where Neal deposited Jack and LuAnne, the pilgrimage ended as suddenly as it had begun. Neal returned to his domestic life with Carolyn, and Jack and LuAnne were adrift and penniless. "Neal will leave you in the cold any time it's in his interest," said LuAnne.[44]

"Oh, smell the people!" yelled Dean with his face out the window, sniffing. "Ah! God! Life!"
—Jack Kerouac, *On the Road*

I mean, man, whither goest thou? Whither goest thou, America, in thy shiny car in the night?
—Jack Kerouac, *On the Road*

Drive your Chevrolet, through the USA, America's the greatest land of all!
—Dinah Shore, Chevrolet advertisement

GINSBERG: TO THE MADHOUSE When Neal Cassady, Jack Kerouac, and LuAnne Henderson drove off in the maroon Hudson in January 1949, Allen Ginsberg felt stranded in the straight, workaday world. He earned $30 a week as an Associated Press copy boy, and he missed his friends.

Less than a month later, a link to his lost circle reappeared in the person of Herbert Huncke. Ten days out of Riker's Island, where he had served time for marijuana possession, Huncke appeared at Allen's door at 8 AM on a snowy morning. Surviving on a diet of coffee, doughnuts, and Benzedrine, he was delirious and suicidal, his soaked, cracked shoes housing bloody, blistered feet. Huncke was most worried about his psychological health: "Sure, I'm old, and I'm evil, and I'm ugly, and I'm tired," he told Ginsberg. "But that isn't it. I've been this way for ten years, and I'm all down the main line now."[45]

At first, Ginsberg turned him away—his last contact with Huncke a year before had resulted in the robbery of $200 worth of a friend's books, silverware, and records—but he soon relented. Averting his eyes, Ginsberg bathed Huncke's feet. He housed and fed him and tried to fan the merest spark of life. For two weeks Huncke lay on Ginsberg's couch, the shades drawn as he slept, awoke, blinked, and bit his lips for minutes on end. He had developed a rash below his mouth. "It appeared to do no harm," Ginsberg wrote, "other than to complete the destruction of the dark beauty of his face."[46]

From a distance, Allen had once regarded Huncke as a glamorous petty criminal; up close, Ginsberg wrote, "I see that he suffers, more than myself, more than anyone I know of perhaps, suffers like a saint of old in the making; and also has a 'cosmic' or suprasensory perception of an extraordinary depth and openness."[47] Kerouac, Burroughs, and Carr all warned against Huncke's parasitism, but Ginsberg had worked himself into a psychological impasse. He viewed his boarder in the same guilt-ridden light as Naomi—a victim/saint. "He was my experiment, my love, my teacher, my dog," wrote Ginsberg, "and if I renounced him I renounced at the

In all probability committing suicide would be the proper course yet I find myself reluctant to take the final step.
—Herbert Huncke

Wig: *the mind (as in "flip your wig"), or an eccentric figure: "I also look forward to usual Frisco wigs like seeing Leonard Hall the Buddhist and Cris McLaine and the crazy twisted poets. . . ." [Kerouac] Used as a verb, it means to go crazy: "What's with you? You wig already and remove our dry goods inna public hall?" [Burroughs, on Ginsberg's stripping at a poetry reading]*

same time my own dignity and ineffable senses of taste and justice."[48] He assumed responsibility to revive Huncke, and, once revived, Huncke took great interest in the apartment. He rearranged Allen's furniture, dusted, burned sticks of incense, and left notes to "watch your ashes."[49] He began wearing Ginsberg's clothes, sleeping in his bed, filling Ginsberg's drawers with his own trinkets, and confining Allen's goods to a bureau drawer in the living room.

Within a month of his arrival, Huncke had also insinuated his Times Square cronies into the apartment. Vicki Russell, the tall redhead Allen had known from Joan Vollmer's apartment, had recently been nursed through heroin withdrawal by her boyfriend, Little Jack Melody, an elfin, twenty-six-year-old Sicilian-American safe robber with, as Ginsberg put it, "a doe-like gentility."[50] The apartment filled up with stolen objects —a carved foyer cabinet, two dark wooden chairs, tarnished silverware, Vicki's perfume bottles, clothes of all sizes, and many small radios. Little Jack Melody's portrait of Vicki hung in the living room, on the mantel sat two opium pipes from Chinatown, and in the middle of the kitchen stood a massive cigarette machine. Ginsberg didn't halt the transformation of his apartment into a warehouse of hot goods, but he harbored feelings of dread.

Anticipating a police raid, Ginsberg wanted all incriminating diaries and letters moved to his brother's apartment. On April 22, 1949, he accepted Little Jack Melody and Vicki Russell's offer of a ride in a stolen car filled with hot goods. Around 4 PM, Little Jack was flagged down for turning the wrong way on a one-way street in Bayside, Queens. He swerved around the squad car and began a sixty-mile-an-hour chase that ended six blocks later when the car jumped a curb, caromed off a telephone pole, and rolled over twice. Ginsberg recalled singing, "'Lord God of Israel, Isaac, and Abraham,' from the *Messiah*, like invoking the Hebraic father-figure authority divinity to come and get me."[51] When the car came to rest upside down, Ginsberg found his glasses broken, his papers

The more obligation Huncke is under to anyone, the more anyone has done to help him, the more certain he is to steal from or otherwise take advantage of his benefactor.

—William Burroughs,
on Herbert Huncke

Copper jitters: *exaggerated paranoia about the police: "Sooner or later you get the 'copper jitters,' and everybody looks like a cop." [Burroughs]*

*All my geniuses are in jail, Alan—
Burroughs, Huncke, Allen (innocent
Ginsberg), the big redneck Vicki, maybe
Neal & LuAnne, for all I know.*
　　　　　　　—Jack Kerouac, April 1949

strewn about among stolen furs and overcoats. The siren's din in his ear, seven cents in his pocket, clutching his 1943–1945 journal, Ginsberg myopically fled. "I had a complete, final, and awful sense of what I might call Divine Wrath. It seemed clear, as things flashed through my mind that I was now in a position that I had fantasized and dreamed about and dreamed myself into."[52] He bummed money for a subway token and a phone call and warned Huncke to clean up the apartment. When Ginsberg arrived home, he found Huncke in the kitchen sweeping up cigarette butts and bottle caps, with opium pipes still on the mantel. Looking into Ginsberg's terrified face, Huncke stoically continued his sweeping and said, "Why get hung up? It's hopeless now. I've been through this so many times."[53]

The newspaper coverage of the arrest described Ginsberg as a writer doing criminal research to capture "realism" for a story. To avoid prison, his Columbia mentors, Lionel Trilling and Mark Van Doren, advised him to plead insanity. He pleaded psychological disability and was required to enter psychoanalytic therapy (without charge) at Columbia Presbyterian Psychiatric Institute.

*I admire you for delivering yourself to
an actual bughouse. It shows your
interest in things and people.*
　　　　—Jack Kerouac to Allen Ginsberg

"THIS IS A REAL MADHOUSE" The day before Allen Ginsberg was scheduled to enter the Psychiatric Institute, he celebrated his twenty-third birthday in Paterson and surveyed his life in his journal. "I am 23, the year of the iron birthday, the gate of darkness," he wrote. "I suddenly realized that my head is severed from my body, I realized it a few nights ago." The same journal entry contained elements of desperate hope: "My wrath must end. All my images now are of heaven. I dream of incomprehensible love and belief."[54]

A few weeks later, following a bureaucratic delay, Ginsberg sat in the hallway of the Psychiatric Institute's sixth-floor north ward, awaiting assignment to a bunk bed, third tier up.[55] Cradling the Bhagavad-Gita in his arms, he believed that he, like Oedipus, had brought this tragedy on himself.

Tall, newly obese, twenty-one-year-old Carl Solomon peered at Ginsberg through thick glasses, his head wrapped in a towel from the insulin shock treatment he had just undergone. He had gained sixty pounds since entering the hospital in March, demanding a lobotomy. Just unstrapped from an insulin bed, unmoored by hypoglycemic coma, his body and mind ached as he asked the new patient's identity. "I'm Myshkin," Ginsberg mumbled, invoking the saintly, disturbed figure of *The Idiot*. "I'm Kirilov," countered the young man, invoking the cynical nihilist of *The Possessed*. As Solomon recalled that moment, "the cadence of the superreal was never challenged. . . . Not one of us would dare assume responsibility for a breach of the unity which each hallucination required."[56]

Ginsberg recognized the instantaneous connection he had felt on meeting the seminal figures in his life—Cassady, Carr, Burroughs, Kerouac. In a gesture of identification, Ginsberg recounted his vision of Blake. "He accepted me as if I were another nutty ignu," Ginsberg reported to Kerouac, "saying at the same time, with a tone of conspiratorial glee, 'O well, you're new here. Just wait awhile and you'll meet some of the other (repentant) mystics.'"[57]

Allen began an eight-month period of self-inquiry: What would he do with his life? Was he a poet? Was he homosexual? He couldn't decide whether he was facing a difficult life transition, or—like his mother—was insane. "I have manoeuvered myself to a position I have always fancied the most proper and true for me," he wrote Kerouac. "I really believe, or want to believe, really I am nuts, otherwise I'll never be sane."[58] Kerouac responded, "I'd say you were always trying to justify your ma's madness as against the logical, sober but hateful sanity."[59]

Ginsberg's days passed in utterly routine fashion, marked by a time

*When I came out of Electric Shock
All I could see was the end
Of my nose.*
—Carl Solomon, "Electric Shock"

*I am now become a BLEAK PROPHET—
bleak thoughts, bleak eyes, bleak smile.*
—Allen Ginsberg, from Columbia
Psychiatric Institute

to shave, to eat, to sunbathe, a time for occupational therapy. During the afternoons he watched ships float lazily beneath the George Washington Bridge, which became "a symbol of all that is permanent and real."[60] He wrote poems, some of which would be published years later in *The Gates of Wrath* and *Empty Mirror*.

The psychiatrists diagnosed Ginsberg as bright and extremely neurotic; he engaged in psychotherapy two to three times a week. His therapists encouraged Ginsberg to conform to America's legal and sexual rules. Carl Solomon observed that the doctors cared nothing about a patient's madness so long as it remained socially acceptable; they objected only when the insanity assumed concrete form (when Solomon offered his doctor a handful of marbles, for example, so that he would swallow them and die). The therapists refused to discuss Ginsberg's visions, discouraged all homosexual expression, and labeled his acts of individuality as eccentric. "I was trying to explain to him where I was at," Ginsberg recalled, "and I said, 'It's like the telephone is alive.' Now, had he been a doctor of any kind of wit, like they had in the old days, he would have said, 'And what does the telephone say, Allen?' But instead he got annoyed and stamped his foot and said, 'The telephone is not alive.' So he didn't know where I was at all."[61] The therapists' vision of sanity sharply differed from that of his previous analyst, William Burroughs, and Ginsberg began to think of Burroughs as a deranged Faustian master. "O Bleak Bill," Ginsberg wrote Kerouac. "He is afraid that I will find out that he is crazy, that his analysis of me was a tragic farce—not an absurd farce, but a tragic real one—that he has led me astray."[62]

Ginsberg's new therapists' proffered alternatives were no more satisfactory. They insisted on Ginsberg's ordinariness, denied his gift as a poet, and prescribed conventional behavior. "I am torn between putting aside my loyalty & love directed to the past (the under-world, the mythical symbols of tragedy, suffering and solitary grandeur) and the prosaic com-

Carl Solomon in Allen Ginsberg's apartment, ca. 1953

munity of feeling which I might enter by affirming my own allegiance to those bourgeois standards which I had rejected," Ginsberg confided to his journal. "How easy it is to reverse these values entirely and consider myself the patient and forbearing wiseman in a nation of madhouses."[63]

Carl Solomon provided an in-the-flesh antidote to the psychiatrists' prescriptions for sanity. He frequently cited Antonin Artaud's dictum that a lunatic "is a man who has preferred to become what is socially understood as mad rather than forfeit a certain superior idea of human honor."[64]

Solomon peppered his speech with oblique references that sounded like surrealistic aphorisms: "Every man lives by a set of rules to which he is the only exception. And this he understands."[65] (When Ginsberg transcribed such pronouncements in his small notebook, Solomon regarded this activity as a symptom of "the writer's disease.") Solomon smuggled in magazines and books from the outside (convincing the staff that the Harvard literary journal, *Hound and Horn*, was a field and stream magazine) and concealed Trotsky's *Permanent Revolution* and Ann Balakian's *Literary Origins of Surrealism* in fake dust jackets. He introduced Ginsberg to Jean Genet and Louis-Ferdinand Céline. The two hatched schemes that were put down to "ward nuttiness." They wrote an unmailed letter to T. S. Eliot that closed: "Before saying farewell, we want to assure you that we know a good literary dictator when we see one: A smart young fellow like you, a real hustler."[66]

Their dayroom discussions often led to verbal sparring, for the two played with diametrical positions, and Solomon thrived on polemic. Upholding Artaud's image of the poet as brute, Solomon derided Ginsberg's Wordsworthian sensitivity as the ravings of a "dopey daffodil."[67] Solomon called Walt Whitman a political revolutionary and Ginsberg called him a sexual revolutionary. Solomon described their bracing relationship: "Myshkin is a talent but so is Kirilov, and Kirilov will always heckle Myshkin, and we will always have a well-rounded earth."[68]

When Ginsberg walked out of the Psychiatric Institute on February 27, 1950, two months after Solomon's discharge, he vowed to begin a new season in the real world. He would get a job, become a labor journalist, value the quotidian over the visionary, and form sexual relationships with women. On the day of his discharge he wrote Kerouac a note that revealed his stern resolve: "A turning point has been reached in that I am no longer going to have homosexual affairs: my will is free enough now to put this in writing in a final statement."[69]

Blasting: *smoking marijuana; also* **bliazasting***, its carny pig Latin transformation: "Bliazasted a moment ago" [Kerouac].*

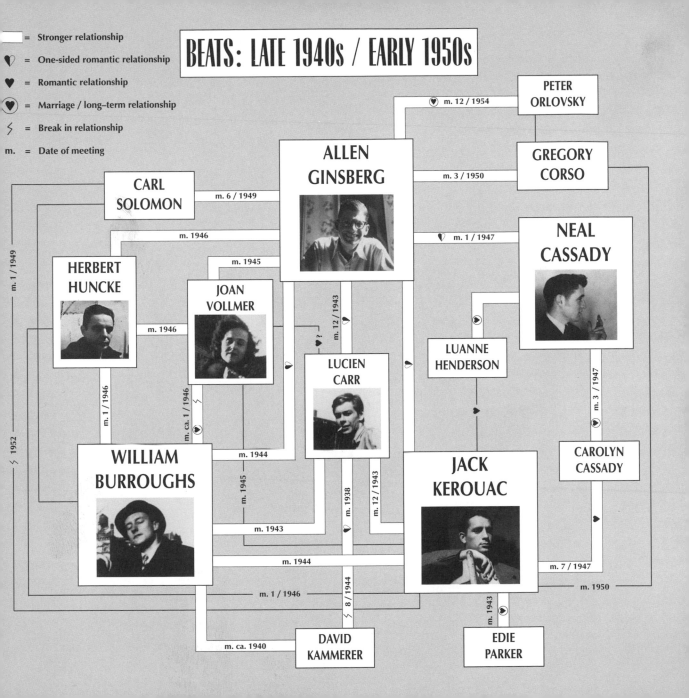

Ginsberg also planned to write poetry that presented a more ordered vision of the real world—"with sentence structure & thought determining stanza, each stanza a statement, each line in place in reference to the others."[70] But one of his first journal entries after leaving the hospital reflects the underbelly of his new resolve: "Write a long poem about a man whose pride is swallowed by oblivion. Impulses reverse of normalcy —mine the dregs. Write secret fantasy."[71]

You say you have found out you are just a human like other humans. Human, Allen, is an adjective, and its use as a noun is in itself regrettable.
— William Burroughs to
Allen Ginsberg

AFTER THE HOSPITAL: THE NORMALCY PROGRAM AND THE SAN REMO

After leaving the hospital, Allen Ginsberg returned to his father's home and pursued normalcy: he found jobs, he avoided thinking about the metaphysical, he slept with women. Ginsberg's earnest reconciliation with the quotidian world was—in part—successful.

The event that went most smoothly was, surprisingly enough, Allen's loss of heterosexual virginity. Three months after his release, he met Helen Parker, a woman in her mid-thirties with two children, who impressed Ginsberg with her appreciation of William Carlos Williams' poetry. At first Ginsberg self-consciously re-enacted his well-groomed Hungarian character from the charades in Joan Vollmer's apartment, but he gradually felt more comfortable playing himself. When he first slept with Helen Parker, the experience felt both natural and tonic. "The first days after I lost my cherry—does everybody feel like that?" he asked Kerouac. He denounced his homosexuality as "camp, unnecessary, morbid, so lacking in completion and sharing of love as to be almost as bad as impotence and celibacy, which it practically was anyway."[72]

Square: conformist, Organization Man, a solid citizen, from the 1940s on: "A square is some guy who forces himself arbitrarily into a square auto-life mold."
[Corso]

Despite his denunciation, Ginsberg continued to enjoy homosexual fantasies. But his sexual relationships for the next five years were primarily heterosexual; initially driven by rationalized control, they continued by desire. The most stable of his heterosexual relationships, with a "really gone sweet girl"[73] named Dusty Moreland, even led to a marriage

proposal. But he described the relationship in nonerotic terms: "We talk a
lot, sleep once in a while, but never screw."[74] Hoping to reconcile his homosexual desires and his plan to share his life with a woman, he came
upon a novel solution in a dream: "Two cocks will solve the problem."[75]

Ginsberg encountered more trouble with employment. "Existing
and plucking fruits from trees is work enough for me," he wrote Lionel
Trilling in the prehospital days. "Too bad they tore down all the trees."[76]
Allen was fired from the *Labor Herald*, an American Federation of Labor
newspaper, a ribbon factory, and a literary agency. On the ribbon assembly
line he became transfixed in thought, at the agency he typed sloppily, he
was inattentive and diffident—he concluded that he would always end up
messing up a job. "Truly the real world is my downfall," he wrote Cassady.[77] He was more successful as a market researcher for an advertising
firm, where he pondered the question: What sells Ipana toothpaste?

Ginsberg balanced the demands of the real world with the warmth
of his friends. His tight circle included some old Columbia friends (Lucien Carr, Kerouac), some new poet friends (Philip Lamantia, Richard
Howard, John Hollander and his prospective wife, Ann Loeser), a Harvard
Law School graduate named Bill Cannastra, and Carl Solomon. Allen
also circulated among a larger network of acquaintances represented by
the habitués of the San Remo bar. This now legendary Greenwich Village
hangout became a point of social reference altogether different from his
therapists' aspirations or his employers' demands. Just as Joan Vollmer's
apartment had once provided Ginsberg's intimate society, the San Remo
provided a broader coterie society in which bohemians, artists, homosexuals, writers, and hipsters came together.

By the way what ever became of Al's normality program? . . . I certainly was glad to see him pull out of that let's-take-our-place-in-a-normal-society dive.
—William Burroughs, on Allen Ginsberg

In such places as Greenwich Village, a ménage-à-trois was completed—the bohemian and the juvenile delinquent came face-to-face with the Negro, and the hipster was a fact in American life.
—Norman Mailer

THE SAN REMO Founded in 1925 as a working-class bar, the San
Remo, with its scarred wooden booths, black and white tile floor, and-
pressed-tin ceiling intact, became a hipster hangout after World War II.

*Do the sad souls of the Remo wittingly
defy a fiendish system, and when they
love each other, do they overcome it
triumphantly?*
            —Judith Malina, on the San Remo

**SAN REMO REGULARS
(early 1950s)**
James Agee
Julian Beck
Maxwell Bodenheim
Chandler Brossard
Anatole Broyard
John Cage
Gregory Corso
Merce Cunningham
Miles Davis
Dorothy Day
Paul Goodman
Joe Gould
John Clellon Holmes
Chester Kallman
Jack Kerouac
Judith Malina
Harold Norse
Frank O'Hara
Jackson Pollock
Larry Rivers
Gore Vidal

The bar sat at the northwest corner of Bleecker and MacDougal, just south of Washington Square. Since the 1910s, Washington Square had been the center of American bohemia, offering affordable rents, a tolerant Italian community, cheap food, and former stables that provided ideal studios. Bohemian styles changed with the decades, as did their emblematic hangouts. In the 1930s they were cafeterias like Stewart's and the Life Cafeteria, in the 1940s it was George's Bar, and, from World War II to the mid-1950s, the San Remo. Chandler Brossard, a regular there, described its significance to bohemians and hipsters this way: "The San Remo bar on MacDougal Street is a divine and exclusive retreat. It is Gargantua's mother's bra. It is the rowboat that George Washington successfully fled the country in. It is our Great Wall of China."[78]

For many Villagers, the San Remo offered an extension to their tiny cold-water flats. One could sit in isolation among a crowd sipping what was called "the strongest espresso this side of Sicily,"[79] nurse fifteen-cent beers, or drink hard liquor. Martinis, dispensed by members of what was called "the Minor Mafia," were the most popular drink because they delivered the most alcohol for a buck. Over the bar hung a photograph of Maxwell Bodenheim, the poet-bohemian-bum par excellence.

The younger generation of bohemians regarded the San Remo as the closest thing in New York to a Paris bar, an addiction and a nightly hangout that continued into the early hours of the morning. The members of Judith Malina and Julian Beck's Living Theater went there after rehearsals, Paul Goodman's therapy group continued talking there after their sessions, and homosexuals used it as a pickup joint, especially on Thursday nights. (One noted distinct antipathy between "the dope fiends and the queers."[80]) Visitors encountered painters (Jackson Pollock, Larry Rivers), poets (Frank O'Hara, John Ashbery) and novelists (James Agee), sailors and grifters. Amid the discussion of Reich and existentialism, jazz and marijuana, a comfortable *maudit* atmosphere reigned, causing some

to refer to the bar as the San Remorse. "The center of my universe?" Judith
Malina asked herself.[81]

Allen Ginsberg called the bar habitués "subterraneans" (Kerouac
appropriated the term as the title of his novel about the San Remo crowd),
but the more widely used term was "hipster." This social type, first defined
in print after World War II, embraced a compendium of existentialism,
drugs, and jazz. It offered the Beat Generation America's most trenchant
model for bohemian nonconformity. Anatole Broyard described the hipster as "the illegitimate son of the Lost Generation,"[82] and Norman Mailer
called him "the White Negro." He (and the species was typically male) rejected middle-class life, favoring personal id over societal superego. He
had little of the innocence and idealism of the romantic bohemian rebels
of the 1910s; he was, in Norman Mailer's words, "a psychic outlaw" rather
than a countercultural utopian. He looked to Harlem for inspiration.

Hipsterism had little to do with Marxism but propounded a revolution of life style. Mailer observed, "The hipster represents the first wind of
a second revolution in this century."[83] He spent his adolescence in World
War II and entered adulthood in the wake of the Holocaust and the first
atomic bomb. Instead of the literary canon he read a combination of texts
that one observer listed as: "Rexroth and Rimbaud, Henry Miller and *Mad
Comics*, Sartre and science fiction, jazz magazines and jerkoff magazines."[84] He affected a "cool" attitude of existential neutrality; one writer
described the hipsters as "the draft-dodgers of commercial civilization."[85]
Marijuana was sought after, jazz was ubiquitous, and affect was cool. A
raised finger stood for a wave, brushed palms for a handshake. The hipster's movements were slow and catlike. His favored color was black
(sweaters, turtlenecks, leotards), dark glasses covered his eyes, and he
danced strictly to the off-beat. The hipster was America's version of the
underground man, or, as Norman Mailer put it, "the rebel cell in our
social body."[86]

Symptoms of the Hipster
Likes jazz, specifically bebop, especially
    Charlie Parker
Beret
Goatee
Formal wear: "padded shoulders, thirty-
    one inch pegs, two and seven-eighths
    inch brim on the hat, roll collar, dark
    glasses"
Smokes marijuana
Drinks strong espresso coffee
Does nothing
Hangs out at the San Remo
Knows existentialism
Drinks heavily
Jeans
Black turtleneck
Black sweater
Likes Lord Buckley

Wild mad eastside funny Gregory.
   —Jack Kerouac, on Gregory Corso

ENTER GREGORY CORSO Across the street from the San Remo, Gregory Corso was born in 1930. His eighteen-year-old mother, Michelina, sailed back to Italy six months after his birth and his father, Fortunato, placed him in foster care. The agency that arranged for foster parents believed it was unhealthy for a child to develop filial attachments. When Gregory returned to his father at the age of ten, he had lived with three sets of parents. His two-year stint with his father and stepmother proved to be painful, because both loudly ridiculed Gregory's frequent bed-wetting. At twelve, charged with stealing a neighbor's radio, he was sentenced by juvenile court to four months in the Youth House. Here he was beaten up so often that he despairingly thrust his hands through a window and was sent to the Bellevue Hospital children's observation unit. From there he went to a Christian Brothers home, and finally, a few months later, he began living on the street. He slept in subways and on rooftops, snatched lunches from schoolgirls, and stole small articles to survive. His formal education stopped at the sixth grade.

At sixteen, Corso and two cohorts organized a robbery that was more sophisticated and profitable than his earlier petty thefts, coordinating the use of walkie-talkies to rob the Household Finance office. With his share of $7,000, Corso went to Florida. His partners went on a spree, were caught, and informed on Corso. The police independently detected something odd about a homeless adolescent vacationing in Florida in a zoot suit, and Corso was apprehended. He was sent upstate to Dannemora, home of Clinton State Prison. He was one of the youngest inmates in an environment more threatening than any he'd been in before, but Mafia inmates advised him and he used clowning to make his way.

Like Neal Cassady, Corso educated himself during his three years in prison. He began by studying a 1905 dictionary, and then, guided by an older inmate, he read *The Brothers Karamazov*, *Les Misérables*, and books of classical Greek history. His favorite was Shelley, who described poetry as

Blow your top: to go insane, either from a psychotic break or from excessive use of marijuana: "The weed available in the U.S. is evidently not strong enough to blow your top on and weed psychosis is rare in the States." [Burroughs]

the stimulation of "unapprehended combinations of thought" to improve the moral faculty of mankind.[87] Corso began to write poems as an ethical act to redirect the downward course of society, creating "a state in which he can find no wrong, and so hold love and sympathy for all things."[88]

When he was released from prison in 1950, Corso moved to New York and took a furnished attic room on West Twelfth Street. In a nearby Greenwich Village lesbian bar called the Pony Stable, Allen Ginsberg first saw Corso seated at a table accompanied by a stack of his typed poems. Pleased to encounter a fellow poet in such an unlikely setting, and admir-

If you believe you're a poet, then you're saved.

—Gregory Corso

Poet Gregory Corso, Paris

ing the twenty-year-old's edgy, dark looks, Ginsberg struck up a conversation. He began reading Corso's poems and found much to like. He was particularly struck by a line: "The stone world came to me, and said Flesh gives you an hour's life."[89]

This meeting through poetry offered the key to opening intimacies between the two men. Ginsberg, in Beat confessional tradition, related his life story and Corso responded in kind. Finally Corso described his nightly ritual: from his darkened room he looked across West Twelfth street into the fourth-floor apartment of a young woman, and while she took her bath and then made love to her boyfriend, Corso masturbated. He fantasized someday introducing himself to her. As Corso told the story, it dawned on Ginsberg that Corso lived directly across from his girlfriend, Dusty Moreland, and the unlikely fact that Corso had witnessed Ginsberg's heterosexual lovemaking with her added to the relationship a further erotic *frisson*. The next day, Ginsberg fulfilled Corso's fantasy by introducing him to the woman of his voyeuristic pleasure.

Ginsberg soon introduced Corso to Kerouac, John Clellon Holmes, and other writers, and he was quickly accepted as part of the writers' community. "To me, friends were very hard to make, especially in prison," Corso said. "But coming out of prison, you're a poet and the other guy's a poet, automatically you were friends, you see. I didn't see it that way. It took a little while before I became friends with these guys."[90] Corso was most strongly affected by Ginsberg, who provided encouragement and occasional lodging, and Kerouac, whose spontaneous prose he emulated. Corso later described Kerouac as "a Beat Christ-boy" and, following Kerouac's death, wrote a moving elegy for his friend: "How inseparable you and the America you saw yet was never to see."[91]

Corso's poetry combined an obsession with destructive forces and his romantic belief in poetry's redemptive power. He mixed seemingly disparate and random images to evoke beauty and alter consciousness. Dur-

Because Jack, like me, we speak the unspeakable. And we feel free. We're Americans, why not?

—Gregory Corso

Viper, dope fiend: *terms from the 1920s that preceded* **junky** *to describe a drug user*

ing his wanderings of the 1950s, he was often separated from his fellow Beats. In the mid-1950s, for example, poet Bunny Lang brought him to Cambridge, where he moved in Frank O'Hara's orbit. When City Lights published his collection *Gasoline* in 1958 Corso was recognized, and he did several readings with Ginsberg and Peter Orlovsky. His poems reflected his role as "an independent trickster hero who provides a lot of common sense."[92] In Ginsberg's words, "One reason I dig Gregory—he'll write about anything, socks, army, food, Arnold, Looney—so he also now writes the ONE GREAT POEM about the Bomb. He's extended the area of poetic experience further out than anyone I know."[93]

If you have a choice of two things and can't decide, take both.
—Gregory Corso

FINDING A VOICE: GINSBERG MEETS WILLIAM CARLOS WILLIAMS A month after Allen Ginsberg's discharge from the Psychiatric Institute, he heard William Carlos Williams read at the Guggenheim Museum. Four years earlier, he had reviewed Williams' *Paterson (1)* for the *Passaic Valley Examiner* and primarily concluded that "the book and I have little in common."[94] Hearing Williams in person at the Guggenheim excited him, although Williams felt resistance in the crowd and not long after wrote about his thwarted desire to *move* the audience. "But they don't move," he wrote. "It's like moving anything, you've got to get it rocking first, then lift it onto your knees, then heave it. But the only thing they'll rock to is the old religious swing. And that they can have."[95] Ginsberg, however, was impressed: he hoped to meet the poet that night but ended up just waving. Two days later he sent the sixty-six-year-old poet a long letter. "I would like to make my presence in Paterson known to you," he wrote Williams, "and I hope you will welcome this from me, an unknown young poet, to you, an unknown old poet, who live in the same rusty county of the world."[96] He enclosed a sheaf of poems he had written during his hospital stay, some rhyming lyrics, and a mad song "to be sung by Groucho Marx to a Bop

Beat mentor William Carlos Williams in his office in Paterson, New Jersey, by Eve Arnold

background."[97] Ginsberg announced portentously, "I envision for myself some kind of new speech."[98]

In his search for new speech, Ginsberg could not have found a more appropriate poet in all of America, and their geographical proximity was felicitous. More industriously than the other members of his generation, Williams promoted the continuing American poetry avant-garde, and his history stretched back to the epochal Armory Show in 1913. Perhaps inspired by seeing the modern art exhibition, Williams wrote *Poetry* magazine about its fellow art form, modern poetry: "It's the new seed, the one little new seed that counts in the end: that will ultimately cover fields with vigorous growth."[99]

The generation of American poets who launched the revolution of the word in the 1910s included such pivotal members of the twentieth-century modernist canon as Ezra Pound, T. S. Eliot, Wallace Stevens, and Marianne Moore. But it was William Carlos Williams who worked most actively to carry on the tradition of modern American poetry. In the 1910s and 1920s, Ezra Pound and Amy Lowell had acted as poetry's impresarios, while T. S. Eliot reigned as a tastemaking editor of *The Criterion* and Faber publishers. But Lowell died, Eliot converted to Catholicism and became known as "the Pope of Russell Square," and Pound aptly declared that "after the age of fifty, one cannot be a telephone directory of younger writers."[100] Williams, however, continued to support younger poets. He read and reviewed their work, wrote reviews and introductions to their collections of poetry, and corresponded with succeeding generations. Within two months of Ginsberg's letter, for example, William had received his first correspondence from two key members of the youngest generation: Charles Olson and Robert Creeley. From the 1910s to the 1950s, Williams acted as an instrumental intergenerational networker, and he would pass the mantle on to Allen Ginsberg.

Williams so enjoyed Ginsberg's letter that he printed it in Book Four of his epic, *Paterson*, and signed the letter "A. P." (Did that signify "Allen Paterson"? Ginsberg asked, and Williams responded, no, it meant "A Poet.") Ginsberg became a source of new vitality for Williams, who, at sixty-seven, felt his creative life was coming to an end. As he wrote Robert Lowell, "I've become interested in a young poet, Allen Ginsberg, of Paterson—who is coming to personify the place for me."[101] In Ginsberg's poems, however, Williams found little that sounded new. Although the young poet displayed an above-average grasp of rhymed verse, Williams gently and pointedly counseled, "In this mode, perfection is basic."[102] Until Ginsberg could write idiomatically and root his work in objects and details of quotidian life, Williams could not encourage the direction of Ginsberg's poetry.

Kerouac also encouraged Ginsberg to create a mosaic of details,

Younger Poets Admired by William Carlos Williams
Robert Creeley
Charles Henri Ford
Allen Ginsberg
David Ignatow
H. H. Lewis
Charles Olson
George Oppen
Kenneth Patchen
Kenneth Rexroth
Muriel Rukeyser
Charles Tomlinson
Parker Tyler
Louis Zukofsky

Deep form: *Jack Kerouac's term for a writing process that resolved both metaphysical vertical depth and horizontal narrative movement*

using the "sketching" method that he began in 1951, recording straightforwardly what the eye sees and not attempting to forge something poetic. Ginsberg had made precisely such detailed observations in his journals, interspersed with diaristic confessions, dream records, self-analysis, and preliminary drafts of poems.

Attuned to the counsel of Kerouac and Williams, Ginsberg selected descriptive passages from his journals, isolated the most intense fragments, and arranged them like one of Williams' poems. Framed by the page, with the lines broken by breath length or syllable, the isolated fragments took on a new power. Many years later, looking at his 1947 Denver journal description of dungareed bricklayers at lunch, now reconfigured as a poem, Ginsberg declared that he had unintentionally created "a little shiver of eternal space."[103] In the closing three lines—"it is darkening as if to rain/and the wind on top of the trees in the/street comes through almost harshly."[104]—Ginsberg felt he had finally evoked the transcendental moment he had unsuccessfully tried to express in his sonnets about his Blakean vision. But he didn't recognize his achievement until he'd sent off his newly configured journal entries to William Carlos Williams in January 1952. At that moment, Ginsberg feared that he had reached a dead end as a writer.

Williams responded with extraordinary enthusiasm: "You *must* have a book, I shall see that you get it. Don't throw anything away. These are *it*."[105] Ginsberg exulted to Cassady and Kerouac that not only would his poems be published (by New Directions, he thought, with a dedication to Herbert Huncke) but they *all* could now get books published: "We'll have a huge collected anthology of American Kicks and Mental Museeries. The American Spiritual Museum, a gorgeous gallery of Hip American Devices."[106] The poems Williams promoted wouldn't be published for nearly a decade, under the title *Empty Mirror*, and by that time Ginsberg was an international celebrity. But in 1952, at a moment Ginsberg was

Paste this in yr. hat, Ginsberg is the great poet of the Jews of the 20th Century in America.
—Jack Kerouac, on Allen Ginsberg

Tea, T: *marijuana, word used from the 1920s onward: "Let's sip some tea."* [Huncke] *Code variations include* **Orange Pekoe**.

ready to stop writing, Williams' enthusiastic response opened a new door to writing naturalistically.

Ginsberg's new style shared some of the characteristics of Imagism, the movement that had initiated the modern poetry revolution in America. Ginsberg wrote Cassady that his new verse "strips yakking down to modern bones."[107] As the 1910s poets had used the Imagist mode to rid themselves of the formal intricacies and rhetorical excesses of Romanticism, Ginsberg's journal style helped him shed the archaic forms he had inherited from his father and from Lionel Trilling. Although the new work cleansed his rhetorical palette, it couldn't accommodate the expansiveness of Ginsberg's imagination and desire. Allen first consummated this marriage over a year later: "First time I let my imagination and desire dominate over what, in the mental hospital, I had been taught to accept as an adjustment to reality."[108] The poem that Ginsberg called a "first breakthrough"[109] was a heroic attempt to reconcile his conflicted romance with Neal Cassady. Ever since their parting in Houston six years before, Ginsberg and Cassady had corresponded—in love, hate, sadness, and remorse. Now, in thirty-four stanzas, he proceeded to incorporate his feelings into a newly imagined history of the relationship, to "make up a legend of my poor sad summer with you, and try to create some recognizable human-angelic ideals story, too."[110] He called it "The Green Automobile," a reference to Oscar Wilde's wearing of the green carnation: "Neal, we'll be real heroes now/in a war between our cocks and time:/let's be the angels of the world's desire/and take the world to bed with us before we die."[111]

ON THE ROAD I: THE ROMANCE OF THE ROAD After his cross-country trip with Neal Cassady, Jack Kerouac returned to his mother's house in the spring of 1949 and plunged into writing *On the Road*. At first he couldn't settle on the story's hero. He vacillated between Ray Smith,

The Three Imagist Rules, Set Down by Ezra Pound
1. Direct treatment of the "thing," whether subjective or objective.
2. To use absolutely no word that did not contribute to the presentation.
3. As regarding rhythm: to compose in sequence of the musical phrase, not sequence of a metronome.

I'll have seen 41 states in all. Is that enough for an American novelist?
—Jack Kerouac

based on Kerouac, and "Red" Moultrie, the former athlete–prison inmate turned footloose truck driver and seaman, based on Neal Cassady. "Red" Moultrie grew more dominant, and *On the Road* became a religious allegory about Moultrie's search for self in the vast landscape of America. Ray Smith was transformed into an idealistic follower and observer of the wandering hero.

Kerouac wrote some 5,000 words a day, and the narrative became increasingly intricate. But his attempt to create a piece of American realism grew overburdened with writerly devices and spiritual metaphors. He built narrative bridges to *The Town and the Country*, developed intricate color and season symbolism, and linked Neal's quest to American history. In his attempts to capture "panoramic consciousness," the narrative took on so much freight that it sank.

Before he set the novel aside, Kerouac struggled to transcend adolescent realism, conventional narrative, self-consciousness. In a letter of May 1949, he proclaimed his first important literary theory: truth couldn't be described as universal but only "from moment to moment incomprehensible, ungraspable, but terribly clear."[112] Over the next few years, working on the novel in spurts, he tried to find a voice that expressed his ontological vision.

Kerouac was periodically revived by direct and indirect contact with Neal Cassady. When he took his mother to Denver in 1949, for example, he hitchhiked to Larimer Street to hang out in the same pool hall where Neal had played, and he listened to the cowboy sound of Denver speech. In July, Neal sent Kerouac a long letter, noting that a rift had developed between them. Whereas Cassady identified himself with Huncke as a destined loser, he thought Kerouac had been saved. Throughout Kerouac's struggles, Cassady observed, "Your deep anchor has been this involvement with writing, which unerringly threw you into the other camp."[113] In the next letter, Cassady begged him to visit and promised him

Proposed Titles for *On the Road*
Down the Road Night
American Road Night
Look Out for Your Boy
Boy on the Road
Hit the Road
Lost on the Road
Souls on the Road
Love on the Road
In the Night on the Road
Home and the Road
Along the Wild Road

Americans should know the universe itself as a road, as many roads, as roads for traveling souls.
                    —Walt Whitman

bop, crazy happenings, and smutty jokes. Kerouac found a driveaway car and set out to see Neal and Carolyn Cassady in San Francisco. As he crossed the border from Colorado into Utah, he discerned in a formation of cumulus clouds the finger of God pointing west toward California.

GETTING PUBLISHED I: *THE TOWN AND THE CITY* Kerouac and Ginsberg and Burroughs believed in the revolution of the word, a tradition that had begun in America in the 1910s and had altered twentieth-century literature. But literary revolutionaries were never easily published, and depended on little magazines. They thrived during the 1910s and 1920s, but the little magazines were fewer in number when the Beats began writing. They looked to mainstream publishers, high and low. The utterly respectable Harcourt, Brace published Kerouac's first novel, and the utterly mass-market paperback Ace Books published Burroughs' first novel. Only Ginsberg relied on alternative publishers, first appearing in the little magazine *Neurotica* (edited by Jay Landesman, 1948–1952) and later with the small press City Lights.

Jack Kerouac was the first to run the gauntlet of publication. After reading the manuscript of *The Town and the City*, his friends had been very encouraging; Ginsberg, for example, called it "a major literary event."[114] Publishers showed less enthusiasm. Scribners quickly rejected it, and Little, Brown considered it too long. Acting as Kerouac's voluble unpaid publicist, Allen Ginsberg touted the novel to everyone he knew as a masterpiece. Brom Weber, Kerouac's writing teacher at the New School, asked his colleague Alfred Kazin to promote the novel to Harcourt, Brace. On March 29, 1949, they agreed to publish the novel and paid Kerouac a $1,000 advance on royalties.

Kerouac naively regarded the advance from a mainstream publisher as a promise of fame, fortune, and comfortable living on his royal-

Little Magazines of the American Avant-Garde
Poetry (Harriet Monroe) (1912–present)
The Little Review (Margaret Anderson, Jane Heap) (1914–1929)
Others (Alfred Kreymborg) (1915–1919)
The Dial (Scofield Thayer and Marianne Moore) (1920–1929)
Hound and Horn (Lincoln Kirstein) (1927–1934)
Blues (Charles Henri Ford) (1929–1932)
View (Charles Henri Ford, Parker Tyler) (1940–1947)
Neurotica (Jay Landesman) (1948–1952)
Origin (Cid Corman) (1951–1982)
Black Mountain Review (Robert Creeley) (1954–1957)

Let's you and I revolutionize American letters and drink champagne with the Hollywood starlets.
—Jack Kerouac to Neal Cassady

Jack Kerouac's Bookshelf
Thomas Wolfe
Fyodor Dostoyevsky
Herman Melville
Marcel Proust
James Joyce

*I want us all together before it is too
late, before the Season dies from neglect
(as they always do in time).*
—Jack Kerouac to Allen Ginsberg

Opposite page:
Jack Kerouac, by Elliott Erwitt, ca. 1950

ties. In one of his fantasies about normal life, he imagined buying a ranch
in Colorado, where he would live with his mother, wife, and children.
Such idyllic domestic plans, periodically batted about, were usually harm-
less, but with money in his pocket they turned dangerous. In late May
1949, he moved to Denver and rented a $75-a-month prefab home in sub-
urban Westwood. He moved his mother and his sister and brother-in-law
into the small home, pleased finally to act the role of family provider. Not
surprisingly, the plan for the family domicile was a disaster. Gabrielle felt
stranded without friends and her work in the shoe factory, and she feared
mud sliding down from the mountain.

Jack stayed on in Denver after his mother returned East in June,
and his editor, Robert Giroux, came out to help revise the manuscript.
Kerouac dreaded the prospect of impersonating the public role of author,
which he imagined as a serious, well-mannered figure utterly unlike himself. Swinging between grandiosity and anxiety, Kerouac worried that his
dust-jacket photo—with suit and tie, neck button fastened, slicked-down
hair—made the author look like a "faggot." He also dreamed that the
book's movie rights would be sold to David O. Selznick. (In his journal,
Kerouac even imagined the classic novels he would adapt for film, including *Huckleberry Finn, Look Homeward, Angel,* and *The Brothers Karamazov.*) In order to appear as an "author," he purchased three new outfits,
ranging from a pearl gray suit to a jaunty wine-colored sport jacket. He was
now ready for the imagined rounds of cocktail parties and book signings.

The Town and the City was published on March 2, 1950, to re-
spectfully mixed reviews. (In his hometown, however, the *Lowell Sun* objected to the portrayal of the town and the author's "cheap style."[115])
Within a month of publication, the book's sales had virtually dried up, and
Harcourt, Brace stopped advertising. After counting on regular royalties to
sustain him, Kerouac confronted the grim fact that he wouldn't recoup his
advance. He projected his disappointment and anger onto his publisher

My book has not sold at all. It is not even discovered. What can I say, except that the world is no good anyway and we all know it.

—Jack Kerouac, 1950

I know literature and I would bet all on you instead of Harrington, Holmes, Allen & even Bill & Lucien, for all their finesse. Yours is the gaunt soul of a Dosty. Believe me.

—Jack Kerouac to Neal Cassady

and editor, claiming that the guts of the manuscript had been excised. Never again, he declared, would he compromise his writing. It would be seven years before Kerouac saw his next book published.

WRITING *ON THE ROAD* II: THE SCROLL   On December 27, 1950, Jack opened a thick, typed envelope from Neal. "To have seen a specter isn't everything," it began, "and there are death-masks piled, one atop the other, clear to heaven. Commoner still are the wan visages of those returning from the shadow of the valley. This means little to those who have not lifted the veil."[116] Neal's letter continued for 23,000 words, mixing stories of lost loves, miscarriages, dwarfs, mentally unstable women, and homosexual exploits. For three afternoons and evenings, high on Benzedrine, he had set down line after line and he had not altered a word. One story inspired another, as Cassady digressed and returned to the main narrative—the Pilgrim's Progress of Cassady's "soul."

Kerouac declared the letter "the greatest story" ever written by an American, superior to Wolfe and Céline, equal to Joyce and Dostoyevsky at their best. He declared that Cassady would inspire a new American Renaissance. American outcasts now had "a vision all their own, eloquent, confessional, sublime, and pure,"[117] and Neal became "a colossus risen to Destroy Denver!"[118] Ginsberg concurred that the letter was "almost pure masterpiece,"[119] but Cassady didn't take their encomiums too seriously: "All the crazy falldarall you two boys make over my Big Letter just thrills the gurgles out of me, but we still know I'm a whiff and a dream."[120]

The evidence that remains of the legendary "Joan letter" (as it is known in Beat hagiography) is only partial; many parts of it were lost. The extant narrative pulses with speed-driven randomness, assuming complete responsibility for reporting his actions and none for the psychology behind them. Neal's letter became Kerouac's fetish-text, providing him with permission to follow his own riff-driven narrative images, to further pursue a full-confessional style, grounded in unblinking accounts of lived events. Over the two weeks after receiving the "Joan letter," Kerouac wrote Neal long, confessional letters about his early years and his guilt over the death of Gerard; nothing in Kerouac's long correspondence with Cassady compares with this sustained outpouring. "You and I will be the two most important writers in America in 20 years," wrote Kerouac. "That's why I see no harm in addressing my next ten novels & possible lifework to you and you alone."[121]

Neal's letter also aroused fraternal jealousy in Kerouac, exacerbated by Cassady's failure to comment on *The Town and the City*. When Neal finally told him, "You're the kind of writer who'll go on forever!"[122] Jack interpreted it as an insult. At this moment, when Cassady would have his greatest effect on Kerouac's writing, the relationship was poised in a state of dynamic tension between jealousy and identification, admiration and hurt.

Shortly before Kerouac received the "Joan letter," he married Joan Haverty, a twenty-year-old woman he had known for a few weeks, and the circumstances leading up to the marriage were gruesome. Joan had been Bill Cannastra's girlfriend. A Harvard graduate, a habitué of the San Remo, and a friend of both Ginsberg and Kerouac, Cannastra was a bright, destructive, handsome, alcoholic homosexual trying to go straight. Nothing in his life was as vivid as his death. On October 12, 1950, as the No. 6 subway train was pulling out of the Bleecker Street station, he drunkenly began to climb out the window and, as friends tried to pull him in, his head struck an iron pillar. At the time of Cannastra's death, Kerouac had never met Cannastra's girlfriend, Joan Haverty. A month later they were married, and on February 16, 1952, a baby named Janet Michelle was born. Kerouac's husbandhood lasted only months, but his fatherhood was longer-lived and more difficult. Kerouac dodged child sup-

Rather, I think one should write, as nearly as possible, as if he were the first person on earth and was humbly and sincerely putting on paper that which he saw and experienced and loved and lost; what his passing thoughts were and his sorrows and desires.
—Neal Cassady to Jack Kerouac

Make: *to act: "make the scene"; also means to have sexual intercourse: "I made a hot chick last night."*

port payments, saw his daughter twice (at ages nine and fifteen), and denied paternity (despite the unmistakable physical resemblance).

In early 1951, John Clellon Holmes brought Jack Kerouac the manuscript of his just completed novel, *The Beat Generation* (published in 1952 as *Go*). Holmes had borrowed the term from Kerouac and lifted much of his novel's narrative directly from the lives of Ginsberg, Kerouac, Cassady, and Huncke. Holmes wasn't exactly an interloper—he had been a friend of Kerouac and Ginsberg since the summer of 1948—but Holmes observed from the sidelines. Disconcerted to find the lives of his friends so directly portrayed, Kerouac thought about *On the Road*. "You know what I'm going to do?" Kerouac said to Holmes. "Just write it down as fast as I can, exactly like it happened, all in a rush, the hell with these phony architectures."[123]

In early April 1951, Kerouac sat at his rolltop desk at 454 West Twentieth Street, stocked up with Benzedrine inhalers. He had recently read sections of Burroughs' in-process manuscript, "Junk" (later published as both *Junkie* and *Junky*; hereafter *Junky*), and recalled that initially he "was imitating a kind of anxious Dashiell Hammett of Wm. Lee."[124] Then he invented a way to write nonstop. He taped together rolls of tracing paper, so that his writing trance would not be interrupted by inserting new pages in the typewriter. He began a now legendary bout of continuous writing that lasted three weeks. His wife, Joan, waitressed each day and returned home to fuel him with coffee, pea soup, and cigarettes, and she slept behind a screen that was erected to shield her from the harsh light at the desk. Kerouac sweated profusely and went through a dozen tee-shirts a day, which were washed and hung to dry throughout the little apartment. Nothing stopped his typing—not paragraphs, not periods—and he roared on as if the 120-yard-long scroll of paper was an endless highway. By April 20, he had written 186,000 words—the novel that had tested him so sorely for the last two years was virtually complete. "Rolled it out on floor," he wrote Cassady, "and it looks like a road."[125] A few days later, he immodestly remarked to John Clellon Holmes that he was thrilled to help introduce "a new trend in American literature."[126]

I've telled all the road now. Went fast because road is fast . . .
—Jack Kerouac, on writing
On the Road

Jack Kerouac's letter to publisher A. A. Wyn: "I submit this as my idea of an appealing commercial cover expressive of the book."

I'm the bop writer.
                        —Jack Kerouac

It's the only way to write.
    —Jack Kerouac, on verbal sketching

WRITING *ON THE ROAD* III: THE DISCOVERY OF SPONTANEOUS PROSE Six months after completing the "scroll" version of *On the Road,* Jack Kerouac experienced the breakthrough he later called "the great moment of discovering my soul."[127] In early October 1951 he had just heard bop alto player Lee Konitz at Birdland, when his Columbia friend Ed White, over dinner in a Chinese restaurant, had advised him to begin "sketching" in words. Dressed in a red shirt, carrying *Remembrance of Things Past* as his talisman, Kerouac worked *in situ,* jotting fifteen-minute bursts of notation in his "scribbled secret notebooks."[128] He tried to convey, uncensored, his field of perception at the moment of composition, eradicating the gap between experience and its written evocation. He described the process as an "undisturbed flow from the mind of personal secret idea-words, *blowing* (as per jazz musician) on subject of image."[129] Sketching proved exhilarating, and soon Kerouac no longer required external stimuli; as he later put it, "The object is set before the mind."[130] He had discovered another means of deranging the senses—a central element in the New Vision—by descending into the maelstrom of his sensorium. "Sometimes I got so inspired I lost consciousness I was writing." Kerouac wrote in the spring of 1952.[131]

He soon called the exercise "wild form" and codified it in 1957 as "Essentials of Spontaneous Prose." He believed "wild form" transcended the restricted form of the traditional novel. He described the new method as standing—egoless and unjudging—inside the world of sensation and memory, refracting sequential experience through a train of associations. Kerouac's drive to capture the immediate present by recording his process of discovery had forebears in the automatic writing of William James and Gertrude Stein, the trance writing of William Butler Yeats, and the Surrealists' automatic writing, and there were contemporary counterparts in Action Painting (Abstract Expressionism), and Method Acting. But most important was jazz.

Strip your psyche to the bare bones of spontaneous process, and you give yourself one chance in a thousand to make the Pass.
                    —William Burroughs

Kerouac had frequented Harlem music joints since his undergraduate days, and in 1951 they inspired "bop prosody." Kerouac's model was a "tenor man drawing a breath and blowing a phrase on his saxophone, till he runs out of breath, and when he does, his sentence, his statement's been made . . . that's how I therefore separate my sentences, as breath separations of the mind."[132] Jazz's improvisatory method reflected his belief in "moment to moment" truth, and its riffs provided a loose structure for his novel's dialogue ("18 bars, bridge, and take-out 8 bars"). If a character seemed inspired, Kerouac allowed him to continue, to "blow" freely for a few extra choruses.

"Wild form," "bop prosody," and "spontaneous prose" offered not simply technique but Kerouac's version of a writer's religion. Surveying America's pop culture and its down-at-the-heels theater marquees, jalopies, and diners, Kerouac transformed these physical stimuli through the act of spontaneous writing, pushing the limits of expressiveness to reach ecstasy and redemption.

Carolyn Cassady's ink drawing of Neal at the typewriter, trying to write his memoirs, San Francisco, late 1951

With his newfound literary credo, Kerouac's twenty-day version of *On the Road* now seemed overly dependent on linear time, geography, and surface; it was too "horizontal"; he described it as "those transcontinental wildtrips written in simple old prose."[133] To round out the iconic figure of Neal Cassady as "an archetypal American Man,"[134] Kerouac began writing inserts that provided "vertical" shafts of memory and metaphysics. Before long, the inserts took over; they became a final version of *On the Road*, eventually published in 1972 as *Visions of Cody*. In the process of writing, Kerouac felt so close to Cassady that he longed to be in his physical presence. Cassady urged him to visit their home in San Francisco, "'cause life so simple, good and easy here, that it's actually unreal seeming, like a joke or dream."[135]

Arriving two days after Christmas 1951, armed with a tape recorder, Jack was greeted at the door by Neal in the nude. Jack took up

Blow as deep as you want to blow.
                          —Jack Kerouac, on sketching

The Fifties' Enshrinement of Spontaneous Process
Jackson Pollock's all-over drip painting
The rise of Method Acting at the Actors' Studio
Charles Olson's projective verse
Helen Frankenthaler's poured paintings
The first "happening" at Black Mountain College
Cinéma vérité

residence in the Cassadys' large, unfinished attic, sparsely furnished with a bed, an ersatz desk constructed from orange crates, and the eleventh edition of the *Encyclopaedia Britannica*. He neatly organized his notebooks and buried himself for a final time in the life of Neal Cassady.

In the flesh, Cassady presented the antithesis of Kerouac's iconic free spirit: he was unemployed, depressed, and carless, caring for his daughters while Carolyn supported the family. Kerouac tape-recorded long drunken and stoned conversations with Neal and transcribed them. They not only became an inspiration for Kerouac's writing but also formed the central section of the book. At the same time, encouraged by Allen and Jack, Neal managed to write segments of an autobiography, but the more he thought of himself as a writer, the more blocked he became. The utter lack of self-consciousness that fueled his breakneck panoramic style was now hampered by being A Writer.

By May 1952, when Kerouac left to see Burroughs in Mexico City, he was satisfied that he had finally captured Cassady—even though his iconic fiction bore little resemblance to the current reality. The final lines of the novel provided Kerouac's elegiac farewell to Cassady: "Adios, you who watched the sun go down, at the rail, by my side, smiling—Adios, King."[136]

KEROUAC AND WOMEN During Kerouac's 1952 visit to the Cassadys, Jack began a romantic relationship with Carolyn Cassady that can be described as representative of his serial relationships with women. They invariably followed a pattern: he became infatuated with a woman associated with a male buddy; he fantasized domesticity; he drove away in a car; he proposed marriage; he returned to his mother. The pattern began during his Columbia days, when he dated Lucien Carr's girlfriend, Celine Young, and it continued to the end of his life, when he married the sister of a close childhood friend, Sammy Sampas.

Ball: *to go all the way, with sex or with speed*

When Kerouac visited the Cassadys at the end of 1951, Carolyn resented her exclusion from the intimate fraternity—but she also felt attracted to Jack. To enter his attic room, Kerouac passed through Neal and Carolyn's bedroom, and the sexual atmosphere sometimes became heated. About to leave on a two-week-long railroad stint, Neal grinned at his wife and Jack and said, "You know what they say, 'My best pal and my best gal . . . Ha, ha—just don't do anything I wouldn't do—okay kids?"[137] Carolyn seduced Jack—that's the only way it could happen—over a candlelit dinner of pizza and wine, the radio set to KJAZ, the local jazz station. She wistfully recalled dancing with Jack in Denver to the tune of "Too Close for Comfort," and Jack hummed "My Funny Valentine." Years later, Carolyn remembered the consummation of her crush: "When his arms went around me, glints of light sparked in my head as if from a knife sharpening on a wheel, and my veins felt filled with warm, carbonated water."[138] Jack's considerate tenderness provided the romance she missed with her husband, and Kerouac nominated Carolyn "to replace Joan Burroughs as Ideal Mother Image, Madwoman, chick and ignu."[139] For a brief season, Carolyn became the lover of both Jack and Neal, and her two beaus vied for her attention over home-cooked dinners. But by May 1952, when Kerouac left to visit William Burroughs in Mexico, the dynamics among the *ménage à trois* had become strained, and they would never again be the same. Kerouac invited Carolyn to live with him in Mexico, but he returned to his mother just as she was ready to set forth. (Carolyn buried her disappointment in maternal pity and grimly sanguine rationalization: "Poor Jack. He just couldn't be alone for long. Everything had worked out for the best, and his mother would be happier, too."[140])

The male bonds undergirding most of Kerouac's romances reveal that behind each of his women was a man. "He [Neal] always passed on his girlfriends to Jack," Carolyn Cassady observed. "It was a ritual."[141] It is too simple to suggest that Kerouac was vicariously sleeping with his best friends, although he did have sexual relations with men. (Those with Gins-

As to love, who have I ever loved? I am too insane to love anybody else but me, but I have decided to change.
—Jack Kerouac

You and I are in the same boat anyhow no place of our own to call Home.
—Gabrielle Kerouac to Jack Kerouac

I am not a fool! a queer! I am not! He-he! Understand?

—Jack Kerouac

berg grew out of friendship and sympathy, but Kerouac was also known to drunkenly flirt with men, such as Gore Vidal.) Kerouac described his emotional attachments in a 1948 letter to Ginsberg: "I think women are beautiful goddesses and I always want to lay them—Joan, Barbara, all— and I think men are beautiful Gods, including me, and I always want to put my arm around them as we walk somewhere."[142] Taking on his friends' girlfriends allowed him to skip the tortuous first stages of intimacy. Jack was most lively when he was around a human stimulant, like Neal Cassady, or a chemical one, like Benzedrine.

His sexual relationships, however transitory, became subject matter for writing. Although his relationships failed, writing in his small notebooks remained constant. He sketched and then—in very short, very intense bursts—he wrote six novels: *On the Road, Visions of Cody, Dr. Sax, Maggie Cassidy, October in the Railroad Earth, The Subterraneans.* In the closing lines of *The Subterraneans,* Kerouac suggests a link between his failed romances and his novels: "And I go home having lost her love. And write this book."[143]

Go South of the Rio Grande, young man.

—William Burroughs to Allen Ginsberg

BURROUGHS IN MEXICO Fleeing an impending court case for drug possession in New Orleans, William and Joan Burroughs moved to Mexico City in September 1949. He noted a cloudless sky, "that special shade of blue that goes so well with circling vultures, blood and sand—the raw menacing pitiless Mexican blue."[144] He found dingy gay bars, numbers runners, plump brown-skinned men in green gabardine, hennaed whores, leprous street vendors, and boys in white linen and rope sandals, "like exotic animals, of a dazzling sexless beauty."[145] Burroughs felt at home in a land where a policeman held no more status than a street conductor, where anybody could carry a gun, where morphine prescriptions on bright yellow paper were cheap and syringes could be bought over the counter, where corruption was rampant, and where the clap could be cured for $2.40.

Disabusing Jack Kerouac of his romantic illusions about Mexico, Burroughs observed, "It is an Oriental country that reflects 2000 years of disease and poverty and degradation and stupidity and slavery and brutality and psychic and physical terrorism. Mexico is sinister and gloomy and chaotic with the special chaos of a dream. I like it myself, but it isn't everybody's taste."[146]

Going to a cock fight this evening. I like my spectacles brutal, bloody and degrading.
—William Burroughs, in Mexico City

Financial survival posed no problem here; Burroughs' monthly allowance of $200 could sustain middle-class living. William, Joan, and the two children began their odd family life on Cerrada de Medellín, a dead-end residential street in the Colonia Roma section of the city. "I feel like I took off a strait jacket," he wrote Kerouac. "You don't realize how much the U.S. is dragging you until you are out of it and feel the difference."[147] He could install Reichian orgone boxes in his back yard, for example, brandish a .45 in front of a policeman, or carry a small automatic garter. "I have not only the right but the duty to carry a gun and to protect my person against any attack that might deprive my family of support," he wrote.[148]

Burroughs soon ran into an acquaintance who had hung out on the junkies' traffic island at Broadway and 103rd Street. "The group I know here is in no sense Bohemian or intellectual or any segregated group featuring tolerance," he wrote Ginsberg. "They are ex-bartenders, telephone line-men, farmers, cops yet, a sprinkling of inactive criminals, and a large contingent of ex-Army, Navy, Marine, and Merchant Marine."[149] Burroughs hired a lawyer (actress Katy Jurado's brother, Bernabe) who knew exactly who could be paid off at the cheapest prices. In Jurado's office he met a man known as "Old Dave" Tesorero, who sold fake silver crucifixes on the street, and in his manner Burroughs instantly sensed

Jack Kerouac's pencil drawing of Dr. Sax, a figure loosely modeled on William Burroughs

William Burroughs and "Old Dave"
Tesorero, Mexico City, 1950

something familiar: perhaps it was Dave's prematurely wizened face, or the fifty-year-old's cadaverous body. The Mexican turned the lapel of his coat to reveal a hypodermic needle pinned inside. "I've been on junk for twenty-eight years," he said to Burroughs. "Do you want to score?"[150]

The pair worked out a scheme in which Old Dave subscribed to the government's rations for addicts (fifteen grams a month at $2 a gram) and Burroughs bought half of Old Dave's monthly allotment for $30. In this way, he supported his addiction on three grains a day, a more generous dose than at any previous time. Over the next few years in Mexico he would cyclically develop a habit and then go through withdrawal, vowing, "Like I say me and the junk are washed up."[151] When he wasn't using heroin, however, he resorted to cheap liquor. He staggered, bumped into trees, vomited at ten-minute intervals, and developed incipient uremia, an affliction that threatened his health more than heroin. His addiction remained fairly constant; it was merely a matter of picking poisons.

Nowhere in the city could Joan Burroughs buy the Smith, Kline, and French Benzedrine inhalers she enjoyed, so she was forced into withdrawal. The pain of the first three weeks was stanched only by thyroid tablets and indiscriminate faith. "Joan took the loss of her medicine surprisingly well," Burroughs told Ginsberg, "and feels better than in years."[152] But she soon acquired a taste for tequila and began to drink at 8 AM each day. "Evil spirits here sell tequila for forty cents a quart," she wrote Ginsberg, "and I tend to hit the lush rather hard."[153]

It makes things rather difficult for Bill; as for me, I don't care where I live, so long as it's with him.
—Joan Vollmer to Allen Ginsberg, following Burroughs' arrest in Louisiana

JOAN AND BILL Joan and Bill's sexual incompatibility was exacerbated by the different substances they abused. On heroin, Burroughs showed little interest in sex or even in talking. He remained inside his house, making only sporadic contact with Joan. Two days after Bill had established his junk connection with Old Dave, Joan grabbed his spoon and threw the heroin on the floor. Burroughs slapped her twice and she fell onto the bed. "Don't you want to do anything at all?" she asked. "Don't you want to visit some ruins? You know how bored you get when you have a habit. It's like all the lights went out."[154] When Burroughs was off the junk, he was most attracted to young, buyable Mexican men. "The boys are lovely, easy, and cheap (3 pesos = 40 cents) down here," Joan reported to Ginsberg, "but my patience is infinite."[155]

Joan drifted through days in an alcoholic haze that blunted her feelings about her husband's unavailability. Their occasional sex did not alter Burroughs' homosexual feelings. "But laying one woman or a thousand merely *emphasizes* the fact that a woman is not what I want," he wrote Ginsberg. "Better than nothing, of course, like a tortilla is better than no food. But no matter how many tortillas I eat I still want a steak." When his monthly remittance ran low, he resumed sexual relations with Joan. "Around the 20th of the month, things get a bit tight and he lives on tortillas," she appended to Burroughs' letter to Ginsberg.[156] A visit from Lucien Carr in the summer of 1950 helped Joan marshal her diffuse marital discontent, for she and Carr shared romantic feelings (perhaps never acted on sexually), and after he left she petitioned for a divorce in Cuernavaca. (Although the Burroughses had not formally wed, Mexico recognized common-law marriages.) Joan did not follow through on the divorce proceedings, and their sexual incompatibilities remained unresolved. As Burroughs observed in a letter to Ginsberg, "There is, of course, as there was from the beginning, an impasse and cross purposes that are, in all likelihood, not amenable to any solution."[157]

According to Hal Chase—their housemate on West 115th Street who moved to Mexico City and saw the Burroughses there—Joan's level of frustration was higher than it had been in New York. "The struggle between Joan and Bill seemed to be life-and-death," Chase recalled. "She'd describe in detail how he'd be all set to make love and then he'd get a

Joan Vollmer Burroughs, one of the only known pictures of her after living with William

If there's one thing I don't want to be around, and I think no one else particularly wants to be around, it's a drunk with a gun.

—William Burroughs

cramp in his foot."[158] Her accusations of Burroughs' failed masculinity also encompassed his guns. He was at the height of his western gunman phase, and when he brandished his pistols too openly, or got into drunken arguments with political figures, the *policía* disarmed him. He would return home and Joan would taunt him, "So they took your gun away from you, did they?"[159]

The Burroughses nonetheless maintained an extraordinary level of mental understanding, and on his visit Lucien Carr witnessed telepathic connection between them. Bill and Joan played a game in which they sat at opposite ends of their living room, each equipped with pencil and paper. They folded the paper into nine sections and silently drew an image in each square. The correlation of their drawn images hovered around .50—both drew a scorpion, for example, a bottle, a dog. Watching them play, Carr concluded that Joan had the stronger mind, that she was the sender and Burroughs the receiver. One of the last times they played the game, Joan drew a picture of her head surrounded by puffs of smoke, and beneath the image she wrote "troglodyte," a term used by the Mexican press to describe murderers and other heinous criminals.

You've got to put yourself into a state where the projector is on, which is known as inspiration. Or, as Hemingway called it, juice.

—William Burroughs, on the creative process

"WILLY LEE—THE JUNKY WRITING BOY"[160] William Burroughs had made two previous attempts at writing, but each time he had needed a collaborator to help him overcome the feelings his words inspired. "I had a special abhorrence for writing, for my thoughts and feeling put down on a piece of paper," he recalled. "Occasionally I would write a few sentences and then stop, overwhelmed with disgust and a sort of horror."[161] His first serious piece, "Twilight's Last Gleaming," had been written with his boyhood friend and Harvard classmate, Kells Elvins, and the second, "And the Hippos Were Boiled in Their Tanks," with Jack Kerouac. Both his former collaborators encouraged Burroughs' first solo attempt, although they remained strictly behind the scenes. Burroughs was encouraged by the publication of Kerouac's novel *The Town and the City*, and one of Burroughs' first mentions of writing about heroin addiction appeared in the same letter in which he congratulated Kerouac on his novel. ("Frankly it is a lot better than I expected," was Burroughs' compliment.[162])

"There didn't seem to be any strong motivation," Burroughs recalled about beginning to write. "I had nothing else to do. Writing gave me something to do every day."[163] His early reference to the project—doubts about the possibility of publication, plans to let a "professional" turn it into a salable manuscript—reflect Burroughs' diffidence. But he persisted and began recounting his drug experiences in longhand diarylike notes. He hired a young woman to type the manuscript but found that whenever he wrote "junk" she replaced it with "opiates." The manuscript's straightforward chronology and uninflected journalistic style echoed his childhood favorite, *You Can't Win*, Dashiell Hammett, and a style of writing he called Factualism. Using heroin during much of the writing of *Junky* had the effect of removing Burroughs' inner awareness and affect. The narrator's detached voice resembled the hard-boiled tone of a private-eye novel. The pseudonymous character, Bill Lee, is shadowy, unjudging, dryly observant, a shell without inner emotions, hovering between cool existentialism and junk-death. The book closely chronicled his first heroin-using years in New York with Herbert Huncke and Phil White, and it moved through four attempts to kick his addiction, ending with his emigration to Mexico.

During withdrawal from heroin, Burroughs became increasingly sensitive to the links between junk and sex, and he decided to include his observations in the narrative, later separately published as *Queer*. The protagonists of *Junky* and *Queer* are markedly different versions of the same Bill Lee. Burroughs later observed:

> The difference of course is simple: Lee on junk is covered, protected and also severely limited. Not only does junk short-circuit

I don't write from scratch in fact I can't. When I write it is simply a question of putting down in some sequence what is already there.
—William Burroughs

Whenever a true writer gets original, he can't do wrong any more. Like Bill.
—Jack Kerouac, on William Burroughs

While it was I who wrote Junky, *I feel that I was being written in* Queer.
—William Burroughs

the sex drive, it also blunts emotional reactions to the vanishing point. . . . When the cover is removed, everything that has been held in check by junk spills out. The withdrawing addict is subject to the emotional excesses of a child or an adolescent, regardless of his actual age.[164]

Queer painfully recounts Burroughs' relationship with Lewis Marker, a twenty-one-year-old student at Mexico City College. Marker was tall, thin, boyishly disdainful, and heterosexual. He occasionally attended classes on the GI Bill but spent most of his time at the Bounty bar drinking rum and Coke. "Get rich, sleep till noon, and fuck 'em all," was his motto.[165]

"Like a frantic inept Lazarus,"[166] Burroughs pursued this unwinnable romantic object during a period of withdrawal. Sex became a necessary replacement for junk, an element in the equation that he later called "The Algebra of Need." Since junk-starved cells felt disembodied, he felt driven to take over another's body, "straining with a blind worm hunger to enter the other's body, to breathe with his lungs, learn the feel of his viscera and genitals."[167] Burroughs wanted nothing less than a complete merging of himself and Marker. Burroughs remarked in baby talk: "Wouldn't it be booful if we should juth run together into one gweat big blob."[168] Marker declined.

"Usually he selected someone who could not reciprocate," Burroughs observed of himself, "so that he was able—cautiously, like one who tests uncertain ice, though in this case the danger was not that the ice give way but that it might hold his weight—to shift the burden of not loving, of being unable to love, onto the partner."[169] Burroughs staked Marker to meals, got his camera out of hock, did favors; in exchange, Marker occasionally went to bed with him. Marker displayed little physical interest in Burroughs—he once remarked in the middle of sex, "This does

A paper: *from the 1930s and 1940s, the rectangularly folded paper in which heroin was often carried: "Whenever a law needs money for a quick beer, he goes over by Lupita and waits for someone to walk out on the chance he may be holding a paper." [Burroughs] Also called a **deck** or a **junky fold**, a rectangular packet of junk with one end fitting into another and two smaller packets fitted into it: "He opened his fly and extracted a rectangular packet—the junky fold. . . ." [Burroughs] These terms became obsolete when heroin began being sold in #2 capsules, later glassine bags.*

seem to be rather superfluous"[170]—but Burroughs' worldly intelligence and dry wit intrigued him. So long as the raconteur could spin his comic routines, like a hipster Scheherazade, the end would not come, but he sometimes ended up rambling on without an audience. "I'm playing to an empty house now," Burroughs thought at the end of a night at the Bounty. "Now I will ravish my public."[171] He swallowed four Benzedrine tablets and a rum, smoked a marijuana roach in the bathroom, ordered the bus-boy to hold up a mouse he had caught, and, at a distance of three feet, pulled out his old .22 pistol and blasted its head off.

In *Junky*, Burroughs overcame the first hurdle, his disgust at seeing his words on paper, but his writing lacked the peculiar brilliance of his conversation. "Writing must always remain an *attempt*," he wrote Ginsberg. "The Thing itself, the process on sub-verbal level always eludes the writer. A medium suitable for me does not yet exist, unless I invent it."[172] His stories provided the means to connect with what he called "a receiver," and the need intensified during withdrawal. Writing, sex, contact, affirmation became entwined: "Basically the loved one was always and forever an Outsider, a Bystander, an Audience."[173]

Bill was like a mad genius in littered rooms when I walked in. He was writing. He looked wild but his eyes innocent and blue and beautiful.
—Jack Kerouac, on William Burroughs

TWO TRIPS "I have to leave town," Burroughs declared in the summer of 1951.[174] He invited the ever ambivalent Marker to accompany him, with Burroughs paying all expenses. "All I ask is be nice to Papa, say twice a week," he said. "That isn't excessive, is it?"[175] The diffident young man was won over to this proposition one evening after Burroughs delivered an inspired routine about a slave trader. "If I had not achieved the reckless gaiety that charges this fantasy, Marker would have refused to go with me to S.A. [South America]," Burroughs wrote. His scientific curiosity inspired a quest for the hallucinatory drug he had read about in *Argosy* magazine. Scientifically known as *Banisteriopsis caapi*, the herb was called

Carmen: a Mexican prison

William Burroughs' Bookshelf
Oswald Spengler's *Decline of the West*
Wilhelm Reich
Dashiell Hammett
Thomas De Quincey's *Confessions of an English Opium Eater*
The Mayan Codices
Jean Genet
Louis Ferdinand Céline
Joseph Conrad (especially *Lord Jim*)
Count Alfred Habdank Skarbek Korzybski
Philip Wylie
Robert M. Lindner's *Rebel Without a Cause*
Psychoanalytic Quarterly
Jack Black's *You Can't Win*
Denton Welch

Mooch: a robbery victim, someone who "mooches" sleeping time on the subway while drunk, or simply a drunk: "If you get the right rhythm you can work it out even if the mooch is awake." [Burroughs]

ayahuasca by the Indians, and *yage* by gringos. Drinking it was believed to increase telepathic sensitivity. Burroughs had great hope for it; he later wrote to Ginsberg, "Perhaps it will be the final fix."[176]

Burroughs and Marker set out for the high Andes, for the town of Puyo, Ecuador, in the shadow of a 20,561-foot mountain, Chimborazo. They flew to Panama City, hopped a small plane to Quito, endured a fourteen-hour ride in the cold, crowded back quarters of a two-and-a-half-ton truck to Ambato. Finally, after a stretch of narrow road along the edge of a gorge, they reached Puyo, the end of the line. Adversity proved tonic to the junk-sick Burroughs, who calmly registered the discomfort of the trek. Marker felt frightened and tired, his testicles ached, and at one point he became nauseated (Burroughs offered his hat). Ahead of them stretched an unguided trek through the jungle to the camp of an American botanist, Dr. Fuller. Marker pleaded for them to wait until the rain stopped. "Haw haw haw!" Burroughs responded. "They got like a saying down here, like 'I'll pay you what I owe you when it stops raining in Puyo.'"[177]

Carrying a spoiling pork haunch as a gift, the two walked along a muddy donkey trail composed of logs set down crosswise. Sixty-foot crevices and cold streams cut through the trail surrounded by tall, dense hardwood jungle. By the tenth hour Marker felt discouraged, but for Burroughs the trip was a quest. At nightfall, finding a thatched hut in a clearing, they encountered an unlikely pair. Dr. Fuller was a thin, wiry American studying the uses of curare, and Mrs. Fuller was large and red-haired; at the end of the trail, reflected Burroughs, they'd found Jack Sprat and his wife.

Burroughs' hopes of experiencing yage came to nothing. Dr. Fuller grew suspicious, especially after Burroughs' drunken hipster paean to yage. Fuller offered him neither information nor encouragement, only cots for the night's sleep and mosquito netting to keep out the vampire bats. Sleeping in the jungle that night, Burroughs had a prophetic dream. He was standing in front of the Bounty and heard little Billy crying. "The sound of crying came closer," Burroughs recalled, "a wave of sadness, and now he [Burroughs] was crying, his body shaking with sobs."[178] He picked up his child and held him close. They were surrounded by men in convict suits. What were they doing there? Why was he crying? He awoke in deep sadness and tentatively reached over to Marker, then turned his face to the wall.

The first episode in the search for yage was over, and the relationship with Marker was on the wane. But Burroughs' dual quest—for the perfect fix, for the ideal receiver—would continue.

For months, Lucien Carr had been planning to take a vacation from his job with United Press International (UPI) and drive to Mexico City with Jack Kerouac. At the last minute, Kerouac was hospitalized for phlebitis and Allen Ginsberg replaced him. They set off in a battered Chevrolet to visit the Burroughses in mid-August 1951. Ginsberg, fresh from reading the "scroll" version of *On the Road*, was eager to experience the road firsthand. When they arrived, the two men found that Joan's Botticellian looks had coarsened. Her blue eyes looked blankly out from a puffy face, her hair hung lank, and her limp was more pronounced. A bottle of tequila stood on her dresser. When Ginsberg quipped that eight-year-old Julie would soon give her competition, Joan replied matter-of-factly, "Oh, I'm out of the running."[179] She was twenty-seven.

Joan and Lucien shared a go-for-broke impulsiveness and a worldly sense of humor. They went on a week-long drunken spree while Allen remained at home with the children. On their group trips, Allen sat in the back seat, with Lucien at the wheel of the Chevrolet, an open bottle of Oso Negro and Joan at his side, pushing him to the limit, demanding, "How fast can this heap go?"[180] They drunkenly careened along the hairpin turns of the Mexican mountain roads. At one point, too drunk to man-

Stash: *coined in the 1940s, a verb meaning to hide your drugs or other treasured things: "Stash it in a cool spot because it'll mean a whole lot of real gone freebies for you." [Symphony Sid] It can also be a noun, meaning hidden drugs.*

age the wheel, Lucien turned it over to Joan, while he sprawled beneath her manipulating the gas pedal and brake. In the back seat, Ginsberg tried to maintain an air of calm for the sake of Julie and little Billy, who recalled that ride as the first terrifying event in his life. Joan's desperate self-destructive stunts disturbed Allen, and he was terrified by her demonic effect on Lucien. Ginsberg knew they were falling in love.

The quintet somehow arrived safely back in Mexico City. Lucien and Allen deposited Joan and the children at a bus stop near Chapultepec Park and headed north as Joan held Billy in one arm and wistfully waved goodbye. Lucien considered asking her to come with him, he told Ginsberg, but he couldn't steal the wife of a friend, a mother of two. A few days later, about the time Burroughs returned home from his quest for yage, Hal Chase encountered Joan on the street. She told him she had an incurable blood disease and concluded, "I'm not going to make it."[181]

Murder is the national neurosis of Mexico.

            —William Burroughs

THE DEATH OF JOAN BURROUGHS William Burroughs was disappointed to have missed Ginsberg and Carr, and his return to Mexico highlighted the hopelessness of his affair with Marker. But his sense of impending doom hung more heavily than these external circumstances warranted. On Thursday, September 6, a few days after his return, Burroughs planned two mundane tasks. He would sell a gun—a cheap .380 Star automatic that shot low—and he would have sharpened a tarnished Scout knife he had bought in Quito. Around three he heard the tinkling bell of the traveling knife sharpener and he set out with the knife. He later wrote, "As I walked down the street towards his cart a feeling of loss and sadness that had weighed on me all day so I could hardly breathe intensified to such an extent that I found tears streaming down my face. 'What on earth is wrong?' I wondered."[182]

Burroughs returned home and drank heavily with Joan, while a neighbor minded the children. At six, dressed in a beige sport jacket and white shirt, carrying a small overnight bag with the .380 Star automatic, Burroughs set out on foot for 122 Calle Monterrey, John Healy's apartment, where he met Lewis Marker and his recently arrived friend, Eddie Woods. The next arrival was a surprise—Joan. She saw four empty gin bottles lying on the floor and Woods, Healy, and Lewis Marker sprawled on the furniture; Woods described the scene as "just a field of dead soldiers from the running party we always had the first of the month when the checks came in."[183] Joan and Bill sat in stuffed chairs opposite one another, about six feet apart, roughly the same configuration as they assumed for their telepathy games at home. Joan drank gin and *limonada*, and Burroughs recounted his trip to Ecuador in search of yage. The same evening he put forth a new plan for his family—to move to the South American wilderness, where he would shoot game to feed the family. They would starve if they went into the wilderness, Joan retorted, because Burroughs was too shaky to shoot anything. At that point Burroughs drawled, "I guess it's about time for our William Tell act."[184] They had never played such a game before.

Joan balanced a six-ounce water tumbler on her head. She giggled, turned her head aside, and said, "I can't watch this—you know I can't stand the sight of blood."[185] It was only at this point that the others in the room realized that the Burroughses were serious, and it was too late to stop them. "I aimed *carefully at distance of 6 feet for the very top of the glass*," Burroughs recalled four years later.[186] The sound of the .380 Star automatic in the small room was deafening. Joan slumped forward in the chair and the intact glass rolled in concentric circles on the floor. A moment of disbelief hung in the air until Marker said, "Bill I think you hit her."[187] "No!" screamed Burroughs, when he saw the small-caliber wound in Joan's upper left forehead, the bullet going into her brain. He knelt and repeatedly cried, "Joan, Joan, Joan!" and then went into shock.

Put down: *to state or communicate through actions: "He was putting down a little-boy-in-a-foreign-country routine" [Burroughs]. Also means insult, as verb or noun: "It was a typical Beat put-down." [Richards]*

Several people regarded the shooting as portentous. Burroughs' oldest friend, Kells Elvins, had a dream that night of Burroughs and a pot. When Elvins asked what his friend was cooking, Burroughs said, "Brains," and removed the lid to reveal something that looked like white worms.

Hal Chase had seen Joan on the street just a few days before. She looked terrible, he recalled, with thinning hair and open sores on her body. "That William Tell stuff was a sham," Chase believed in hindsight, "a put-up thing to release Bill, to let him commit the ultimate crime."[188]

Many years later, in his introduction to *Queer*, Burroughs described his own interpretation of shooting Joan: he believed that demons had entered his body that day. He held himself responsible for not paying proper respect to the signals: his dream of little Billy and the convict suits, his oppressive tears on the hot afternoon Mexican street. He began to regard writing as the only means to keep the demons at bay:

> I am forced to the appalling conclusion that I would never have become a writer but for Joan's death. . . . I live with the constant threat of possession, and a constant need to escape from possession, from Control. So the death of Joan brought me in contact with the invader, the Ugly Spirit, and maneuvered me into a lifelong struggle, in which I have no choice except to write my way out.[189]

Joan made him great, lives on in him like mad, vibrating.
—Jack Kerouac, after Joan Vollmer's death

AFTER JOAN'S DEATH: THE SECOND QUEST FOR YAGE Joan was interred in the American cemetery in Mexico City; space was rented for seven years, and if her survivor did not renew the lease, the remains would be thrown on the bone heap.

"But don't worry, I, Bernabe Jurado, am going to defend you, and you will not stay in jail," William Burroughs' lawyer promised.[190] He expertly bribed four ballistics experts and coached the witnesses in a synchronized story of Burroughs accidentally firing the gun while pulling back its slide. So effectively did the witnesses perjure themselves, and so corrupt was the judicial system, that Burroughs was sprung from Lecumbere prison in only thirteen days. He was charged with *imprudencia criminal*, which carried a five-year maximum sentence, and he was released on

William Burroughs being interrogated after shooting, Mexico City, September 6, 1951. The headline read: "Heir's Pistol Kills His Wife; He Denies Playing William Tell"

bail of $2,312. When Kells Elvins asked Jurado about the potential for a jail sentence, he exploded, "What! Mr. Burroughs go back to prison? Do you think I want to jeopardize my reputation as a lawyer?"[191] After winning the case, the lawyer used Burroughs as an advertisement for his legal acumen: "There he is! Thirteen days!"[192]

Burroughs' release on bail required a visit every Monday to the prison, where he signed in. Mexico now seemed to impinge on his liberty, and he dreamed of leaving.

Joan Vollmer's mother had said, "I hope Bill Burroughs goes to hell and stays there."[193] Burroughs felt that he had already arrived. Officially classified by the Mexican government as a "pernicious foreigner," he struggled with Joan's death and confronted a season of personal losses. He mourned the desertion of Lewis Marker, who left Mexico, and Old Dave, his regular dealer, who disappeared in November. "He just faded away like an old soldier," Burroughs wrote Ginsberg.[194] A few months after Joan's death, he heard that Phil White, his initiator into the world of junk, had hanged himself in the Tombs after informing on a heroin dealer. ("He used to say: 'I can't understand how a pigeon can live with himself.' I guess Phil couldn't after what he did," Burroughs observed. "Even so, I still haven't changed my opinion of Phil."[195] Burroughs wanted to dedicate *Junky* to White.)

Bill Garver was his only remaining connection to the old gang. The overcoat thief emigrated to Mexico to spend his last years in a country where his remittance money could sustain his expensive taste in drugs and boys. He walked from the plane, his arm bleeding after an attempt to shoot up with a safety pin. "His first words were: 'How do you say enema in Spanish?' Same old Bill."[196]

Shortly before Burroughs left Mexico in the first week of December 1952, he wrote Ginsberg: "Three years in this town and no one I want

Benny, bennies: *Benzedrine, Benzedrine pills; also means overcoat in old Times Square slang*

to say good-bye to when I leave." [197] Jack Kerouac arrived in Mexico City
just in time to see Burroughs depart, and he felt enormously alone as he
wrote this final Mexico snapshot of Burroughs:

> Burroughs is gone at last—3 years in Mexico—lost everything, his
> wife, his children, his patrimony—I saw him pack in his moldy
> room where he'd shot M all the time—Sad moldy leather cases—
> old holsters, old daggers—a snapshot of Huncke—a Derringer pis-
> tol, which he gave to old dying Garver—medicine, drugs—the last
> of Joan's spices, marjoram, new mold since she died & stopped
> cooking—little Willie's shoe—& Julie's moldy school case—all
> lost, dust, & thin tragic Bill hurries off into the night solitaire—ah
> Soul—throwing in his bag, at last, picture of Lucien & Allen—
> Smiled, & left.[198]

Ginsberg received Burroughs' frequent bulletins—written in No. 2
Venus pencil or typed on rented South American typewriters—during his
six-month quest. The first letters arrived from Panama City in January
1953, reporting junk sickness and a case of piles. (Burroughs dripped
blood so regularly that he took to wearing maroon pants.) An early letter,
posted from Bogotá, reported a fortuitous meeting. In a large dim room in
the botany department of the city's university, Burroughs saw a man wearing steel-rimmed glasses and tweeds, and he was attracted by the refined
tone of his muttering: "What have they done with my cocoa speci-
mens?"[199] The speaker, Dr. Richard Evans Schultes, was a prominent authority on hallucinogenic plants, and he had attended Harvard one year
after Burroughs. A few weeks later, the two men headed down the Putu-
mayo River in canoes—one pursuing a scientific investigation, the other
driven by his quest for telepathic consciousness.

Schultes explained yage to Burroughs in scientific and anthropo-
logical terms. It came from a Amazon jungle vine known as *Banisteriopsis*

I must find the Yage.
—William Burroughs to Allen Ginsberg

You have to come to the jungle to get the real kick.
—William Burroughs to Allen Ginsberg

A large dose of Yage is sheer horror.
—William Burroughs

William Burroughs in pursuit of the hallucinogen yage, 1953

caapi. Indians pounded and boiled the bark in water, and after the *brujo* added a few secret ingredients, they drank it. They believed their visions over several hours were communications from the disembodied souls of the spirit world.

Burroughs overdosed on his first experience with yage. He began vomiting every ten minutes, nearly went into convulsions, and remained delirious for four hours. He later found out that this *brujo's* overdose had killed a man a month earlier. During several other trips that summer Burroughs experienced yage's psychoactive properties. "It is the most powerful drug I have ever experienced," he wrote Ginsberg. "That is it produces the most complete derangement of the senses. . . . Like I say it is nothing else. This is not the chemical lift of C, the sexless, horrible sane stasis of junk, the vegetable nightmare of peyote, or the humorous silliness of weed. This is insane overwhelming rape of the senses."[200] Derangement of the senses, central to the New Vision discussed during the Columbia years, had reached its peak in Burroughs' encounter with an "unassuming little witch doctor" in the jungles of high Peru.[201]

In April 1952, Burroughs asked Ginsberg to save his letters, suggesting that they could be collected in a book. Enclosed in the correspondence were self-consciously literary productions, verbal riffs that embellished Burroughs' reports from the drug frontier. Inspired by a request for *Junky* flap copy, for example, he included a biographical note-cum-routine.

> I have worked (but not in the order named) as a towel boy in a Kalamazoo whore house, lavatory attendant, male whore and part-time stool pigeon. Currently living in a remodelled pissoir with a hermaphrodite and a succession of cats. I would rather write than fuck (what a shameless lie). My principal hobby is torturing the cats—we have quite a turnover. Especially in Siameses. That long

silky hair cries aloud for kerosene and a match. I favor kerosene
over gasoline. It burns *slower.* You'd be surprised at the noises a cat
can make when the chips are down. . . .[202]

In May 1953, Burroughs enclosed "Roosevelt After Inauguration,"
calling it "a skit." Reading these five pages of hilarious all-American misan-
thropy, Ginsberg recognized the form as a written variation on Burroughs'
performances in the 115th Street apartment. Where a group of friends had
been the audience for those late-night performances, the audience now
consisted solely of Ginsberg. "I think all writers write for an audience,"
Burroughs confided to Ginsberg. "There is no such thing as writing for
yourself."[203]

After Joan's death and Marker's emigration to Florida, Burroughs
had no one to receive his verbal productions. Through letters, the relationship between Burroughs and Ginsberg moved from that of teacher-student
to author-agent to writer-receiver. For Burroughs, it became intense, one-
way, and absolutely essential.

GETTING PUBLISHED II: *JUNKY* In the early 1950s, Allen Ginsberg
acted as a literary agent for his closest friends. Both William Burroughs
and Jack Kerouac had manuscripts to be peddled—*Junky* and *On the
Road*, respectively. He first submitted *Junky* to Columbia classmates who
had entered publishing—notably Louis Simpson at Bobbs-Merrill and
Jason Epstein at Doubleday. Both editors rejected the manuscripts out of
hand, and Simpson sniffed, "I do think that the novel has a certain form
(check Aristotle)."[204] Ginsberg then turned to Carl Solomon, who became
the unlikely linchpin between the Beats and early publication.

On his release from the psychiatric hospital, Solomon had tried,

*We should get used to calling each
other sweetheart. I understand it is the
standard form of address between agent
and author, but this time I mean it.*
—William Burroughs to Allen Ginsberg

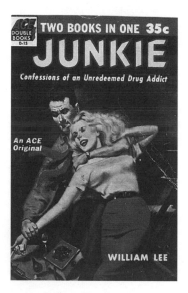

Original jacket for Junkie, *a best-selling Ace original by William Lee, 1953*

like Ginsberg, to go normal: he married a woman named Olive and got a job as an editor for his uncle, A. A. Wyn. Ace Books was the paperback division of Wyn's small publishing company. Typical Ace titles included *Too Hot for Hell*, *The Grinning Gismo*, and *Bloody Hoofs*, but Solomon wanted to supplement this lowbrow list with works by Jean Genet and Louis-Ferdinand Céline. Solomon had met Kerouac, and he knew of Burroughs by legend, so Ginsberg had a leg up on convincing him of their brilliance.

Burroughs' manuscript of *Junky* arrived in chapters, enclosed in his letters to Allen. In April 1952, Ginsberg sold the book to Solomon for $1,000. The publisher distanced the company from *Junky*'s explosive contents by affixing a suitably lurid subtitle—"Confessions of an Unredeemed Drug Addict"—and publishing it back-to-back ("two books in one") with a reprinted 1941 memoir, *Narcotic Agent*. Written by Maurice Helbrandt, a former agent of the Federal Bureau of Narcotics, it was described as "Gripping True Adventures of a T-Man's War Against the Dope Menace."

Junky appeared in 1953. Although it received not a single review, at thirty-five cents a copy it sold an astonishing 113,170 copies in its first year. At the time of publication, Burroughs was searching for yage, and he didn't even acknowledge receipt of the book—"I don't mention it before because I did not feel like talking about it."[205] Burroughs' entry into the world of published authors remained unsung—and it would be nearly a decade before his next book would see publication.

The sanguine editorial relationship between Burroughs and Solomon depended on both Burroughs' geographical distance and Solomon's appreciation of his novel. Neither of these elements was present in the relationship between Carl Solomon and Jack Kerouac, and the dynamics were disastrous. Buoyed by Ginsberg's faith in Kerouac's genius, Solomon offered him a $250 option on his next three novels. The offer, although

Dammit, if these people would only pay me for my genius—hark harock horkc.
—Jack Kerouac

commensurate with the size of the small paperback house, set off friction between such different literary breeds as Solomon and Kerouac.

When Kerouac complained that the advance was puny, Solomon responded that the author was acting like both "a nasty, stupid, worthless, idiot-brat son of a royal house" and "an undertipped head waiter."[206] Solomon described the issue as one of "the classic and absurdly American problem of the Brilliant Young Punk's second book."[207] Ginsberg's response to Solomon reflects both his instrumental role in the Beat movement and his unwavering faith in his friends.

Between incomprehensible *and* incoherent *sits the madhouse. I am not in the madhouse.*
—Jack Kerouac to Carl Solomon

> Are we having the same experience every generation has? Carl called tonight saying the last 9 pages of second version of *On the Road* by Jack was incoherent. He was excited, scared, since he roped Jack into the company at my pushing and advice—and now afraid of having made a wrong move, losing prestige and power at the office. Afraid everybody will blow a gut when they see what Jack's sent in. Carl shook my own self-esteem, threw me into depression. Is there no way we can tell what's good on our own except by personal heart sympathies, going almost against all rational and commercial possibility? I think Jack is the greatest writer alive in America of our own age. . . . Now this second version seems to them a garble of unrelated free associations. I think I will stick by Jack, though I haven't seen the pages yet, only snatches in his letters. He understands me—so he must be great.[208]

Whether conflict with Jack precipitated Solomon's breakdown or whether Carl's state of mind colored his reaction to Kerouac is moot, but Solomon fell apart that spring, following the breakup of his marriage. One afternoon, he attacked the bookcases in his apartment with knives, threw shoes at traffic, smeared paint, and ended up in Bellevue. Ginsberg called

And all you will have succeeded in doing is putting another cookbook on your list to fill the gap I leave. You can spin a thousand neat epigrams to prove that any cookbook is better than the wild visions of Neal Pomeray and the Road. But not when the worms start digesting, brothers and sisters.
—Jack Kerouac to Carl Solomon

*Ginsberg by Burroughs, Burroughs by
Ginsberg, in Ginsberg's apartment, at
the time of the Big Schlupp, fall 1953*

it "Carl's blowtop days."[209] In the midst of this chaos, Ginsberg wrote Burroughs: "This agenting is getting out of hand, with your going off on your own kind of Mobydick, Carl crazy, Jack nutty as a fruitcake. Everybody seems off their heads, blowing tops around me. . . . Why can't everybody calm down, I always say, like the nice people in the boobyhatch."[210]

And so it was that a recent graduate of the boobyhatch led the Beat generation.

Meanwhile, *On the Road* would remained unpublished for another four years. Solomon's final word to Kerouac: "We are interested in getting from you neither a book nor a turd of the month."[211]

BURROUGHS AND GINSBERG: THE BIG SCHLUPP After the South American trip, Burroughs arrived in New York in mid-August 1953, and

taxied to Ginsberg's tenement apartment at 206 East Seventh Street. He carried two suitcases filled with yage and looked visibly displeased to find Gregory Corso visiting. Burroughs glanced at him threateningly, opened his two suitcases of yage, removed a large machete, and began vigorously chopping yage. Corso departed.

At 4:45 each afternoon, Allen would return home from his job as a copy boy at the *World-Telegram,* and the two would talk and edit Burroughs' letters from South America until the morning hours. "His new loquaciousness is something I never had the advantage of," Ginsberg wrote Cassady. "I'm older now and the emotional relationship and conflict of will and mutual digging are very intense, continuous, exhausting and fertile. He creates small usable literary symbolic psychic fantasies daily."[212]

Burroughs thought he had found a loved one capable of returning his feelings; unlike Marker, Allen enjoyed homosexual contact. But Burroughs wanted something more than a sexual relationship; he wanted a complete psychic union of the two men. Sex proved problematic because Ginsberg felt little physical attraction to Burroughs, although he had no trouble tenderly sleeping with him. This experience was familiar—Allen's relationship with Cassady represented its reverse. During sex, Burroughs underwent a transformation, moving from his self-contained masculinity to an effeminate, giggling, passive figure who resembled the English governess he played at the 115th Street apartment. Burroughs was usually the recipient of anal intercourse and frequently ejaculated without a stroke of his hand. Out of bed, Burroughs performed routines for Allen about protoplasmic merging; he called it a "schlupp." As Ginsberg described it, "Bill wanted a relationship where there were no holds barred to achieve an ultimate telepathic union of souls."[213] As Allen wrote, he used the word "schlupp" as "part of an exquisite black-humorous fantasy on Bill B.'s part, hardly the thing to woo a scared lad (I was bodily ungainly anyway), and a parody of his feelings, lest his desire be considered offensive. So he wooed with extravagant self-deprecatory suggestiveness."[214]

Ginsberg's discomfort with Burroughs' intensity increased when the older man asked Allen to live with him. One autumn day, standing on the northeast corner of East Seventh Street and Avenue B, Allen impatiently blurted, "But I don't want your ugly old cock."[215] After rereading Burroughs' letters years later, Ginsberg wrote, "I ever regret the wound I dealt his heart."[216]

The two separated. In December 1953, Ginsberg left for a trip to Mexico. "This is a rare and marvelous trip I need to feed (and free) my soul from ten years of NYC," he wrote Neal Cassady. "So when I see you I'll be able to talk for hours, not only about NYC intellectual beauties, but also many savage solitude of jungles we've never seen—will add to our stores of souls."[217] That same month, Burroughs sailed across the Atlantic for a destination as yet unknown.

Not that Irwin wasn't worthy of him but how on earth could they consummate this great romantic love with Vaseline and K.Y.?

—Jack Kerouac, on Burroughs and Ginsberg's relationship

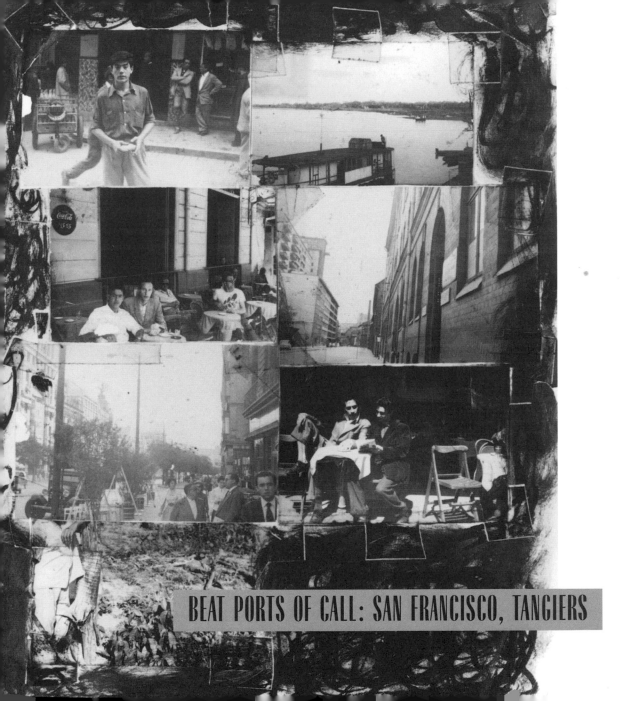

BEAT PORTS OF CALL: SAN FRANCISCO, TANGIERS

*B*URROUGHS IN TANGIERS   William Burroughs was nearing forty when he left New York in December 1953. He didn't know where to go next. He first stopped in Rome to visit his friend Alan Ansen and then decided to go to Tangiers. He knew the city only through Paul Bowles's novels (*The Sheltering Sky* [1949] and *Let It Come Down* [1952]). Through Bowles's words, the city sounded like the utterly marginal, hedonistic, amoral sanctuary that Burroughs had long desired.

From 1946 to 1956, the 225 square miles surrounding Tangiers was an International Zone governed by eight countries that sanctioned smuggling. It quickly became a haven for smugglers and black marketeers, racketeers and chic international low life, the stranded and debauched who washed up on the beach and never left. Burroughs called it "Interzone." It was popularly exclaimed, "My dear, *anything* can happen in Tangiers."[1] The proper members of expatriate society that dominated the city's social life belonged to the diplomatic corps and formed a community of the up-

Quien sabe? Not me. The older I get the less I sabe, the less wisdom, maturity and caution I have.
—William Burroughs, at thirty-nine

I have never seen so many people in one place without money, or any prospects of money.
—William Burroughs, on Tangiers

Members of Tangiers Society and Visitors

Francis Bacon
Herbert and Joella Bayer
Cecil Beaton
Paul and Jane Bowles
William Burroughs
Truman Capote
Alfred Chester
Charles and Phyllis della Faille
Maurice Grosser
Brion Gysin
David Herbert
Barbara Hutton
Gavin Lambert
Tennessee Williams

rooted at Dean's bar and St. Andrew's Church. At another end were the disreputably rich (Barbara Hutton, David Herbert), the literary (Paul and Jane Bowles), and the sexually disgraced. To some of these expatriates, Tangiers embodied exoticism: blue-shadowed faces beneath hooded djellabas, the odor of kif in the medina, the enigmatic Arab calligraphy, the alien barking sound of local speech, and the blank white sun. Burroughs felt the dread beneath Tangiers' brilliant exterior: the city was a trap, built on the lives of people with no prospects. One night at an all-night bar an expatriate leaned over to Burroughs and said, "Life is rotten here, Bill. Rotten. It's the end of the world, Tangiers. Don't you feel it, Bill?"[2]

Burroughs restricted his world to the streets, pharmacies, and, most of all, his room. For fifty cents a day, Burroughs rented a room at the end of a dark alley behind the Socco Chico, which was attached to a male brothel run by a Dutchman who wore full makeup and daily paraded his ensemble of five poodles.

At first, Burroughs considered Tangiers a provincial city that mer-

Tangiers, 1954

ited little more than a good look around. Despite the plethora of Arab boys available for a dollar apiece, Burroughs thought them "an awful-looking people,"[3] scrawny and boringly insistent about their masculinity. ("Oh God!" he wrote Allen. "Such shit I could hear in Clayton, Mo."[4])

The local marijuana (kif) tasted harsh and foul, hurt the throat, and offered no more kick than cornsilk. He quickly tired of watching Arab men hunched over cards and mint tea, and the endless music sounded like a chorus droning out lottery numbers. "And don't ever fall for this inscrutable oriental shit like Bowles puts down (that shameless faker)," Burroughs wrote Ginsberg. "They are just a gabby, gossipy, simple-minded, lazy crew of citizens."[5]

He repeatedly considered leaving—returning to America or to the jungles of South America. The situation brightened after he established himself with a regular boyfriend named Kiki and met the local expatriates ("Junkies, queers, drunks. About like Mexico"[6]) who met after midnight at the Mar Chica bar to discuss their schemes and directionless lives.

Tangiers offered the anonymity and noninterference that Burroughs cherished, and the streetboys began to call him "el hombre invisible." The flip side of the anonymity was Burroughs' utter aloneness. His afternoons with his boyfriend Kiki—an attractive eighteen-year-old Spaniard who was loyal, unconflicted, and sweet—offered respites of physical tenderness, and he repeatedly nursed Burroughs through illness and withdrawal. But when Burroughs embarked on his routines, Kiki's deerlike brown eyes stared at him in vacant confusion.

Sadness about the loss of Ginsberg turned to panic by March 1954, when Burroughs' letters to Ginsberg in Mexico began coming back to him, unclaimed. Burroughs imagined Allen locked in a jail unable to communicate with his friends ("To stupid people, he *looks* like a communist"[7]). "I did not think I was hooked on him like this," he wrote Kerouac. "The withdrawal symptoms are worse than the Marker habit. . . . Tell Allen

Tangiers Hangouts
Diplomatic corps:
    Dean's Bar
    British Library
    St. Andrew's Church
Expatriates:
    Parade Bar
    Thousand and One Nights

All their lives they have drifted with an unlucky current, always taking the wrong turn. Here they are. This is it. Last stop: Socco chico of Tangier.
    —William Burroughs, on Tangiers residents

I have a strange feeling here of being outside any social context.
    —William Burroughs, on Tangiers

I plead guilty to vampirism and other crimes against life. But I love him and nothing cancels love."[8]

When he wasn't just staring at his toe, waiting for the next shot of heroin, Burroughs buried himself in writing, jotting down lines for a novel. He succinctly described his personal dynamics in a letter to Kerouac: "Whenever I encounter the impasse of unrequited affection, my only recourse is in routines. (Really meant for the loved one, to be sure, but in a pinch somebody else be pressed into service.)"[9]

The voices of his characters built up in his head—such as Billy Bradshinkel and Antonio the Portuguese Mooch (whom he privately called "my Portuguese Huncke"[10]). Burroughs implored the unreachable Ginsberg: "I have to have receiver for routine. If there is no one there to receive, routine turns back on me like homeless curse and tears me apart, grows more and more insane (literal growth like cancer) and impossible, and fragmentary like berserk pinball machine and I am screaming: 'Stop it! Stop it!'"[11]

GINSBERG IN MEXICO Allen Ginsberg traveled alone that winter through the Yucatan jungles and ancient Mayan ruins. His five-month Mexican interlude offered respite from his "accommodation to Commercial Society,"[12] but even in the jungle he never stopped trying to sort out "the great garbage pile of the future (which I see as clearly sitting there on the skyline as if it were the Empire State)."[13] Only by standing back from the pressing questions of his vocational future could he see them clearly. As he wrote in his journal, "I left that party in NY for peace—to sit out at nite in front of the thatchroof shelter on a bench sounds of an alien tongue."

The ancient gods, whose divine handiwork he had glimpsed six years ago in the carved cornices of Harlem buildings, once again pre-

sented themselves: "In the bleak flat night of Yucatan/where I come with
my own mad mind to study/alien hieroglyphs of Eternity."[14] The artifacts
of ancient visionary civilizations—Uxmal, Chichén Itzá, Palenque—could
be seen close up, without Blake's poems as a conduit. Ginsberg climbed
the ninety-one steps of Chichén Itzá's temple, slept in a hammock at the
mouth of its central chamber, stared at a carved death's head and thou-
sand-year-old moss-covered stone phalluses, and descended into the priest-
king's crypt. Everywhere he found beckoning images from "our equivalent
Greco-Roman classical ruins of the New World."[15]

    While visiting the ruins, Ginsberg met a scholar named Karena
Shields (known as the "White Goddess"), who invited him to visit her remote plantation. He gladly accepted and remained with her for the next
few months. Since no mail could reach him, Ginsberg was cut off from
his friends. But they appeared in dreams and in the fragmentary movie
scenarios Ginsberg wrote—Burroughs in Europe, disguised with a brush

*Allen Ginsberg at the Finca Tacalpan de
San Leandro, Mexico, spring 1954*

Interest in Buddhism, reflected in this cover of Beatitude

Pah! You, the greatest writer in America, crazy? So was Whitman, so was Thoreau, so was Poe. Burroughs is Poe. He's crazy too. So what.
—Jack Kerouac to Neal Cassady

mustache, fleeing secret agents; Lucien Carr as a golden-haired TV star. One evening, atop an eleventh-century pyramid, high on paracodin, he glimpsed Naomi's face as it had been years ago, beckoning and lively. Near the end of his Mexican trip, Ginsberg sat beneath a huge tree at the foot of Mount Don Juan and wrote "Siesta in Xbalba." Longer than anything he had previously attempted, the eight-page poem represented an advance in his poetry; as he wrote Cassady, "I seem to be back on ball, art *developing* and real serious."[16]

Ginsberg ended his solitary trip in June 1954 and headed north for a visit to the Cassadys, seeking the circle of friends that sustained him: "I want to escape to some great future with Bill Jack Neal Lucien."[17]

BEATIFIC BUDDHISM When Ginsberg was in Mexico, Jack Kerouac was visiting the Cassadys, and there ensued an unlikely battle of the "gods": Buddha vs. Edgar Cayce.

In a parking lot where he worked, Neal had discovered a book about Cayce and had become transfixed by the clairvoyant psychic's belief in karma and reincarnation. The Cassadys named their cocker spaniel after their new guru, attended Cayce group meetings religiously, and found solace in Cayce's belief in past lives. A psychic told Cassady that in previous lives he had been a murderer and an opium addict; as he tearfully listened to the reading, he believed that he had evolved through successive lives, and he saw hope in the future. Carolyn found a new rationalization for their tumultuous marriage. "Reincarnation has to be the explanation of why you and I are together," she said. "That certainly makes me feel better."[18] But Kerouac and Ginsberg regarded Neal's alternating blankness and mania as symptoms of a man grasping at the last straws of sanity. Psychological testing done at this time corroborated their view; Cassady was diagnosed as delusional, on the brink of psychosis.

Riding a bus to visit the Cassadys, Jack Kerouac had spent his trip across America meditating and reading books on Buddhism. His conversion was only a few months old. On his way home from the Richmond Hill Public Library (circa January 1954), he was reading Ashvgosa's *Life of the Buddha* when he came upon a phrase that transfixed him: "REPOSE BEYOND FATE."[19] That evening he meditated for the first time and "saw golden swarms of nothing."[20]

Kerouac's conversion came in the wake of a months-long trough of depression that had delayed his visit to the Cassadys. He felt, not for the first time, that youth had passed and he had touched bottom. "It's all a crrrock, I wanta die," he wrote.[21] In the fall, his girlfriend Alene Lee had left Jack for Gregory Corso. Kerouac tortured himself by spying on her at her waitressing job and showing her his fictional rendition of their affair, *The Subterraneans*. This was the most recent in his string of unpublished novels. When he discovered Buddhism, he was thirty-one, living with his mother, pursued for child support, and unpublished.

Kerouac responded immediately to Buddhism's first two fundamental truths: "All Life Is Sorrowful" and "The Cause of Suffering Is Ignorant Desire."[22] He found in the Mahayana strain of Buddhist thought two model figures with whom he profoundly identified: the Tathagata, who is always en route, moving through life without worldly attachment; and the Bodhisattva, who declines personal salvation on behalf of salvation for all sentient beings. He discovered in Buddhism a charity and forgiveness lacking in Catholicism.

Kerouac desperately tried to surmount his ego and submit to the discipline of Buddhism. After his visit with the Cassadys, he settled into a life of renunciation at Richmond Hill. He grew potatoes and beans in the backyard, swore off drinking and sex, and limited himself to one meal a day. He meditated, studied Buddhism, and even considered writing a new Buddhist-influenced version of *On the Road*. Not always successful in his

I mean you know yourself what Neal may do, how wild he is, even bad sometimes, but you KNOW it and psychiatrists just Measure it and go around smoking pipes.
—Jack Kerouac to Carolyn Casssady

. . . it isn't AS IF it was a dream, it IS a dream . . . see?
—Jack Kerouac to Allen Ginsberg, after studying Buddhism, 1954

So he was a very unique cat—a French Canadian Hinayana Buddhist Beat Catholic savant.
—Allen Ginsberg, on Jack Kerouac

But I am not self-sufficient. I need
audience for my routines. Buddha
doesn't help me a bit. I'm bored and
lonely.
　　—William Burroughs to Jack Kerouac

discipline, he wrote to Ginsberg, "I've been getting sillydrunk again lately in Remo and disgusting myself a la Subterraneans."[23] Burroughs responded to Kerouac's new beliefs by recalling his own experiences with yoga in the early 1940s; as usual, Burroughs had been there first.

> Tibetan Buddhism, and Zen you should look into. Also Tao. Skip Confucius. He is sententious old bore. Most of his sayings are about on the "Confucius say" level. My present orientation is diametrically opposed [to], therefore perhaps progression from, Buddhism. I say we are here in *human form* to learn by the *human* hieroglyphs of love and suffering. There is no intensity of love or feeling that does not involve the risk of crippling hurt. It is a duty to take this risk, to love and feel without defense or reserve. I speak only for myself.[24]

Kerouac's visit with the Cassadys ended after two months in a rancorous fight over the division of some marijuana. Kerouac stormed out and headed for the Cameo Hotel, where he sat in a rocking chair by the window and wrote his first sequence of poems, "San Francisco Blues." The fight over the marijuana had simply focused the difficulties between them, including jealousy over Carolyn, Jack's lack of money, and Neal's increasing withdrawal.

Kerouac found a more receptive disciple in Ginsberg, and their correspondence from this period was dominated by discussions of Buddhism. Appointing himself Ginsberg's teacher, Kerouac wrote a 100-page summary of Buddhism called "Some of the Dharma" and sent Ginsberg detailed suggestions about meditation. The seeds for such spiritualism had been planted during Ginsberg's undergraduate days, when he had read Zen koans in Raymond Weaver's class. At that time he wrote in his journal, "I must find time to spend a season in Tibet."[25] More recently, in

Jack Kerouac's Translations of
Buddhist Terms
Dharma: "truth law"
Nirvana: "Blown-out-ness"
Tathata: "That-Which-Everything-Is"
Tathagata: "Attainer-to-That-Which-
　　Everything-Is"
Bodhisattva-Manasattvas: "Beings of
　　Great Wisdom"

1953, predating Kerouac's conversion, he had immersed himself in books about Chinese painting and "the sublimity and sophistication (meaning learning and experience, not snideness) of the East."[26] He compared Kerouac's conversion to his own visionary experience of 1948: "I am presuming your Buddha experience and my Blake ones are on the same level."[27] Under Kerouac's guidance, Ginsberg's new spiritual search took shape, although he initially objected to Kerouac's emphasis on suffering as "some mean discovery on Jack's part."[28] Years later, after further tutelage with Gary Snyder and Philip Whalen and a trip to Japan, Ginsberg embraced a discipline of daily meditation, took vows, and became an international spokesman, a "Buddhist Jew." But he always credited Kerouac as his first Buddhist guru.

Few accepted Kerouac's Buddhism as serious, some regarded it primarily as a literary conceit, and others thought he simply invented it to suit his own psychological needs. Due to problems with his knees, he never mastered a meditation posture that he could maintain for more than a few minutes, and his version of the Buddhist wise man suspiciously resembled both Jesus Christ and his brother Gerard. But Kerouac discovered in Buddhism explanations for his past and future suffering. In December 1954, he prophetically pondered the two alternatives open to the wise man: "Being famous, he will be hounded to his death; being a nonentity, no one will want to use him."[29]

GINSBERG VISITS THE CASSADYS Allen Ginsberg arrived at the Cassadys', enticed by Neal's promising letters and driven by his eternal hope of renewing their romance. Neal's life seemed utterly changed since Allen had last seen him. Against a backdrop of suburban San Jose, Neal and his family lived in a nine-room house with high ceilings, a bay-windowed dining room, and a roomy porch surrounded by fruit trees and a paved

Shooting gallery: a center for selling drugs and shooting up; used from the 1940s on

Neal Cassady with his three children, Cathleen, John Allen, and Jamie, and his car in San Jose, California, ca. 1954

Pot, pod: *marijuana; entered hipster vocabulary by beginning of the 1950s: "He makes pod but not junk." [Burroughs] Also called, at various times and places,* **muggles, mota** *(around Mexican border towns),* **the weed.**

courtyard and flower beds dotted with marijuana plants. Carolyn had redecorated the house—painting the walls royal blue, sewing tucks in bedsheets to create draperies, burying herself in the lives of the three Cassady children. Neal drove a Rambler station wagon—Kerouac called it "the black & red boat"—and gained financial stability from $16,000 in disability checks he'd received from the Southern Pacific Railroad. Allen observed that Carolyn "lives by this ruinous single-track idea of running the family according to her ideas strictly, ideas which are made copies of *House Beautiful* and are really nowhere."[30] Allen considered Neal's new pathway to salvation a mixture of juvenile flimflammery, crackpot religion, and a desperate attempt to replace his internal emptiness with a prefabricated system of impulse control. Allen's hopes for a renewed relationship were replaced by sexual fantasies about a man who he thought was "suffering from some incipient insanity."[31] He felt "like some nowhere evil beast intruding" on the couple, and it was only through a "Love Poem on Theme by Whitman" that he could create an idealized version of the threesome: "I'll go into the bedroom silently and lie down between the bridegroom and the bride."[32] He occasionally enticed Cassady into bed, enjoying his body when his heart was unavailable. When Carolyn complained to Jack that Allen was making eyes at Neal, Kerouac advised: "Tell Allen to be Myshkin to Neal's Rogozin, not Edouard to Neal's poor Bernard."[33] One morning a month later, Carolyn walked in on them—it was the Denver hotel room scene all over again. She screamed in disgust, forbade Allen ever to see her husband again, lent him $20, and drove him to Berkeley. But this disastrous ending opened the door to another place— perhaps the most instrumental in Ginsberg's life: San Francisco.

Allen and Neal are old buddies and hit the road together and seen visions together, don't be harsh with our Prophets, Miss Virago.
—Jack Kerouac to Carolyn Cassady

Well I guess Carolyn has what she wants, now. What every U.S. bitch of them wants. A man all to herself with no pernicious friends hanging about.
—William Burroughs to Jack Kerouac, following Ginsberg's eviction from the Cassadys'

GINSBERG IN SAN FRANCISCO Arriving in San Francisco in August 1954, Allen Ginsberg made his last stab at middle-class normalcy. He cut his hair, shaved off his beard, wore a tweed suit, and worked for the San Francisco market research firm of Towne-Oller, earning $250 a month. He lived in an elegant Nob Hill apartment with a twenty-two-year-old woman named Sheila Williams Boucher, an ex-roadhouse singer whom he described as hip, pretty, and chic.

At the same time that Ginsberg played the role of Sheila's live-in husband and paternal figure to her four-year-old son, he was importuned by both Neal Cassady—who suddenly, and frantically, wanted to resume sexual relations with Ginsberg—and by William Burroughs, who wanted a more abiding liaison. Burroughs' desires were deeper and less easily satisfied than Cassady's, and the situation grew complicated when Jack Kerouac tried to cheer Burroughs by assuring him that Ginsberg wanted to be with him: "Otherwise, you see, Bill, he wouldn't write and discuss

A pencil portrait of Allen Ginsberg by Carolyn Cassady, 1954

and rehash so much."[34] Knowing that he couldn't meet Burroughs' all-consuming demands, Allen disliked twice rejecting his close friend. When he expressed anger at Kerouac's white lie, Jack responded with a call "for all of us to return to Beat Generation 1947 confessions & honesties."[35]

Sheila Williams Boucher was not ready for confessions, however; when Allen revealed his sexual history with Cassady, she refused to sleep in the same bed. In 1955, even a woman who hung out with black jazzmen and was familiar with marijuana wasn't likely to accept homosexuality. The last of Ginsberg's stabs at middle-class normalcy ended.

I'm Peter Orlovsky. I'm very fine and happy and crazy as a wildflower.
—Peter Orlovsky

A pencil portrait of Peter Orlovsky by Robert LaVigne, 1954

GINSBERG MEETS PETER ORLOVSKY Shortly after Sheila Boucher left Ginsberg, he met the man who would become his domestic partner for several decades. Ginsberg fell in love with the image of a naked blond youth semireclining in a classical pose in a large oil painting by Robert LaVigne. When Ginsberg asked about the model, LaVigne replied, "Oh, that's Peter. He's here."[36] Peter Orlovsky walked into the room.

He was twenty-one, strapping, hawk-nosed, handsome, tall, and pathologically shy. He also seemed too vulnerable to cope with the world. His family included a deaf mother and five siblings, three of whom spent long periods in psychiatric hospitals. Like Kerouac, Orlovsky had been discharged from the Army for mental "disturbance." (When asked to clear the barracks he threw out guns, helmets, and everything he considered ugly, then hung curtains and painted flowers on the soldiers' lockers.) He had experienced a vision of trees bowing to him. Excerpts from Orlovsky's only (1960) autobiographical statement: "Wanted to be a farmer went to high school for that & worked hard, hard, I tell you, very hard, you'd be amazed. Did weight lifting with bus stops. Got to enjoy burnt bacon with mothers help. . . . Enjoy mopping floors, cleaning up cat vommit [sic]. Enjoy swinning [sic] underwater. I want the moon for fun."[37] From the outset Allen and Peter's relationship was tumultuous—Peter's moods were often dark, his periodic demands for solitude were absolute, and his sexual desires were primarily heterosexual.

Ginsberg's ability to cope with Peter's eccentricity and his days of weeping behind locked doors owed a great deal to the emotional training he received from his schizophrenic mother. He had learned the permeable boundaries between reality and hallucination, and he knew how to provide love that was only intermittently returned and to forgive periods of emotional absence. (Shortly after meeting Peter, Allen saw Naomi for the last time; she would live on for another year, never leaving Pilgrim State Hospital.) Allen found in Peter a focus for his devotion. Allen offered his literary talent and his spiritual insight in exchange for Peter's emotional and physical love. Their exchange of vows, performed at 3 AM in the neon and formica milieu of Foster's Coffee Shop, echoed similar vows made seven years earlier on an Oklahoma roadside, and the absolute terms resembled the "schlupp" desired by Burroughs. "At that instant we looked in each other's eyes," Ginsberg recalled, "and there was a kind of celestial cold fire that crept over us and blazed up and illuminated the entire cafeteria and made it an eternal place."[38]

Around this time, taking stock of himself on his twenty-ninth birthday, Allen Ginsberg described his life as a "monstrous nightmare."[39] He had previously despaired about loneliness, personal derailment, and professional dead ends, but the current malaise disturbed him all the more since he had found love, functioned in the respectable world of business, and had enjoyed a live-in heterosexual relationship. Yet he felt dried up. Responding to Ginsberg's own suggestion that an IBM computer could more economically do his work, Towne-Oller had released him, leaving him with $30 a week unemployment. Worst of all, he had suffered from writer's block since settling in San Francisco. All he could do was repeatedly polish his old poems, which had been rejected by Lawrence Fer-

An army is an army against love.
—Peter Orlovsky, asked by
the Army psychiatrist if
he was a Communist

*Peter O sounds very great and I know
that whatever happens, you will know
how to reassure the sad heart therein.*
—Jack Kerouac to Allen Ginsberg

*Allen Ginsberg's apartment,
1010 Montgomery Street,
San Francisco, 1955*

Chinaman: *heroin addiction:
"Chinaman half in and half out of the
door" (I am in the process of kicking).
[Burroughs] "The family jewels is in
hock to the Chinaman" (impotence due
to heroin). [Burroughs]*

linghetti for his City Lights Pocket Poets series. Ginsberg considered publishing his poetry with a mimeograph machine. He even decided to enter graduate school at the University of California in Berkeley, studying Greek and prosody.

A few days after his birthday, Allen dreamed that he talked to Joan Burroughs in Mexico City. With Joan as his touchstone, his writing revived, and he wrote what he considered his best poem to date. "I think it is completely successful," William Burroughs concurred. "I experienced a distinct shock at the end, I could see the picture of her talking and smiling so clear and precise like a telepathic image. I *knew* that I was seeing exactly what you saw."[40] That summer, among the snatches of poetry that appeared in his journal was a line—"I saw the best mind angel-headed hipster damned"[41]—inspired by Carl Solomon. As recounted in Solomon's five-page letter of regressed handwriting wandering in pencil across the page, Solomon had lost his job at A. A. Wyn, abandoned a job selling Eskimo Pies, and coincidentally ended up at Pilgrim State, where Naomi Ginsberg lived. "This is a booby hatch without toilet paper," he reported.[42]

One afternoon during the first week of August, Allen inserted sheets of cheap scratch paper into his secondhand office typewriter, and without intending to write a poem, he improvised in Kerouac style. "As my loves were impractical and my thoughts relatively unworldly, I had nothing to gain," he recalled, "only the pleasure of enjoying on paper those sympathies most intimate to myself and most awkward in the greater world of family, formal education, business and current literature."[43] The poem wasn't confessional, as he had nothing to confess, but purgative.

Ginsberg sounded the overt theme in his opening line: "I saw the best minds of my generation destroyed by madness, starving mystical naked . . ." Ginsberg's format, derived from William Carlos Williams, employed a long line divided into three, each line "a single breath unit" beginning with the fixed base, "Who." Since his breath was as sustained as that of a Jewish cantor, Ginsberg's lines ran longer than Williams', and he described the poem as a chance "to follow my romantic inspiration—Hebraic Melvillian bardic breath."[44]

Writing directly on the typewriter was new to Ginsberg—most of his poems were endlessly reworked in his notebooks—but the combined continuity of fixed structure and latitude of line length provided enormous freedom to improvise. The form derived from Whitman and Williams, but the spirit behind the poem's composition came from Kerouac. "What happened to me was like suddenly being hit with Kerouac's idea that once you wrote something you couldn't really change it," Ginsberg recalled, "because that was the manifestation of the mind's moving in time and the attempt to change and revise and restructure and reorient was, in a sense, a lie."[45] The sound of the poem incorporated the manic verbal drive of a Neal Cassady rap, hipster language, and, as Ginsberg put it, "long saxophone-like chorus lines I knew Kerouac would hear the *sound* of."[46]

Allen Ginsberg's Bookshelf
Walt Whitman
William Blake
William Carlos Williams
Hart Crane
Fyodor Dostoyevsky (especially *The Idiot*)
Franz Kafka (especially *The Trial*)
André Gide (*Lafcadio's Adventures*)
Antonin Artaud
Jean Genet
William Butler Yeats

I want your lingual SPONTANEITY or nothing.
—Jack Kerouac to Allen Ginsberg, after reading "Howl"

Ginsberg crossed a boundary when he typed the line: "who let themselves be fucked in the ass by saintly motorcyclists, and screamed with joy/who blew and were blown by those human seraphim, the sailors, caresses of Atlantic and Caribbean love." At this point mentally declaring the poem unpublishable, Ginsberg felt freed to "write for my own soul's ear and a few other golden ears."[47] He became a channel for the tales of his generation that had courted visions, despair, drugs, and apocalypse. Ginsberg described the first part of the three-part poem as "a lament for the Lamb in America with instances of remarkable lamblike youths,"[48] and the poem chronicled a pantheon of ignus from Ginsberg's life. Here was Herbert Huncke, cruising in Times Square, wandering after release from Riker's Island. Here was Neal Cassady, "secret hero of these poems, cocksman and Adonis of Denver," stealing cars and seducing girls. Here was William Burroughs withdrawing from heroin in Tangiers, Bill Garver stealing overcoats, the denizens of Times Square and the San Remo and the Psychiatric Institute.

Allen Ginsberg writing "Howl" in San Francisco, 1955, by Peter Orlovsky

Before the day ended, Ginsberg finished seven pages, improvising as he went along, and he began a second section, directed specifically to Carl Solomon, who offered a surrogate for his mother, Naomi. Across the top of his manuscript he wrote in pink pencil, "Howl for Carl Solomon," and mailed it to Jack Kerouac in Mexico City, describing it as "nearer to your style than anything."[49] Kerouac recognized the poem's power, but chided Ginsberg for his emendations: "The first spout is the only spout, the rest is time's tired faucet."[50]

The middle section of "Howl," written several days later, was inspired by a paranoiac peyote trip. Wandering through downtown San Francisco, Ginsberg looked up at the ritzy St. Francis Hotel and discerned in its upper regions a robotic death's head, wreathed in smoke, glowing red, emblematic of the materialist evil of the capitalist Metropolis. The clanging of the Powell Street cable car inspired the word "Moloch," the Old Testament god to whom children were sacrificed. Muttering the word, he sat down in a cafeteria off Union Square and sketched out the second section of the poem. By the end of that hellish, hallucinated night, Ginsberg had completed a draft of the long poem that would become better known than any American poem since Eliot's "The Waste Land." "You have to be inspired to write something like that," Ginsberg later observed. "You have to have the right historical situation, the right physical combination, the right mental formulation, the right courage, the right sense of prophecy, and the right information."[51] Ginsberg's impassioned reading of "Howl" two months later would trigger the San Francisco Renaissance.

Fuck Carl Solomon. He's a voyeur in the madhouse. HE'S ALRIGHT
—Jack Kerouac, after reading "Howl"

This poem is undoubtedly the best thing you have done; also, it seems to me, the end of one line of development.
—Williiam Burroughs to Allen Ginsberg, on "Howl"

SIX GALLERY, OCTOBER 13, 1955 Both the Six Gallery and the epochal poetry reading held there on October 13, 1955, were prototypical products of the avant-garde. Every progressive artistic milieu seems to include a cooperative institution like the Six Gallery—situated in a marginal urban area, run by artists and writers with minimal hierarchy—as an open stage and gathering place. The Six Gallery was the reincarnation of an alternative gallery Robert Duncan and Jess (Collins) had founded in 1952 as the King Ubu Gallery, turning an automobile repair shop at 3110 Fillmore Street into an exhibition and performance space. It closed and reopened in 1954 as the Six Gallery, named after six unrecognized artists. The Six Gallery offered the ideal setting for a reading that was organized, as Ginsberg put it, "to defy the system of academic poetry, official reviews, New York publishing machinery, national sobriety and generally accepted standards to good taste."[52]

The reading was initiated by Wally Hedrick, a painter associated with the gallery, who invited the poet Kenneth Rexroth to organize the event. Rexroth enlisted the twenty-three-year-old poet Michael McClure, who, about to become a father, passed the task on to Ginsberg, who became the moving force behind the event. He invited McClure, Philip Lamantia (whom Carl Solomon had introduced to him at the San Remo), and, at Rexroth's suggestion, met and invited both Gary Snyder and Philip Whalen. Kerouac had been invited, too, but he claimed shyness and, after hitchhiking into town from Mexico, warned Ginsberg, "There'll be a lotta typin to be done."[53] As the paterfamilias of an older generation of San Francisco poets, Kenneth Rexroth was invited to emcee the event. Ginsberg mailed out over 100 mimeographed cards and posted announcements in such North Beach bars as The Place, the Co-Existence Bagel Shop, and Gino and Carlo's Bar. As Ginsberg observed, his approach "was purely amateur and goofy."[54]

On the evening of October 13, Ginsberg, Kerouac, and Peter Orlovsky crammed into Lawrence Ferlinghetti's beat-up Austin and arrived at the already crowded gallery shortly before eight o'clock. The intimate 500-square-foot space had white walls and dirt floors, and a makeshift dais had been erected before a backdrop of surrealist furniture forms made

Poet ain't court jester, I say. He, tho, gets up on stage and howls his poems.
—Jack Kerouac, on declining to read at the Six Gallery

PREDICT EARTHQUAKES!
—Jack Kerouac to Allen Ginsberg, upon arriving in the Bay Area

Allen Ginsberg pointing at the St. Francis Hotel, the inspiration for the "Moloch" section of "Howl," by Harry Redl

of orange crates and plaster-dipped muslin. A semicircle of folding chairs was set up for the poets. The crowd of over 100 created a tangible air of excitement, for it was the first time the scattered contingents of San Francisco's poetry intelligentsia-bohemia had come together. The crowd included anarchists, college professors, poets, carpenters, and social leaders. Some wore fur coats, others suits and ties, others jeans and sweaters. At the edge stood Neal Cassady in his Southern Pacific brakeman's uniform, hyperkinetically smiling and bowing to all the guests. He invited the painfully shy Orlovsky to stand beside him, explaining, "Well, I don't know anybody here."[55] Kerouac, at first feeling like a stranger within the large crowd, solicited dimes and quarters for wine and returned with gallon jugs of cheap California burgundy to be passed through the audience for communal chug-a-lugs.

Attired in a secondhand, pin-stripe cutaway jacket and bowtie purchased expressly for the occasion, Kenneth Rexroth stood at a wooden crate and announced, "This is a lectern for a midget who is going to recite the *Iliad* in haiku form."[56] The first three poets—Philip Lamantia, Michael McClure, Philip Whalen—stepped up to read, and a break was declared at 10:30.

Around eleven o'clock, buoyed by red wine, dressed in Levis and a navy sweater, Ginsberg made his way to the lectern, looking like a "horn-rimmed intellectual hepcat."[57] Starting out in a calm and earnest voice that grew in intensity as he fed off the audience's enthusiasm, Ginsberg began to sway rhythmically, waving his arms, taking deep breaths to sustain him through each of the long verse lines. He sounded like a cantor, like a troubadour, and the audience had never heard such rawly extravagant language in public. "I gave a very wild, funny, tearful reading of the first part of 'Howl.'" Ginsberg recalled. "Like I really felt shame and power reading it."[58] Kerouac, eyes closed, began beating rhythmically on a jug of burgundy, scat singing between lines, cheering Ginsberg on—"Go!"

A reading is a kind of communion. The poet articulates the semi-known for the tribe.

—Gary Snyder

"Yeah!" "Correct!"—as he finished each line. (Rexroth was visibly annoyed, but as another audience member observed about Kerouac, "he
kept a kind of chanted, revival-meeting rhythm going . . . the people
gasped and laughed and swayed, they were psychologically had, it was an
orgiastic occasion."[59]) Concluding after about twelve minutes, Ginsberg
recalled, he dissolved in "tears which restored to American poetry the
prophetic consciousness it had lost since the conclusion of Hart Crane's
The Bridge."[60] He looked over to Rexroth, who wiped tears from his eyes
and later recalled, "It just blew up things completely."[61] Philip Lamantia
said the atmosphere was "like bringing two ends of an elecric wire together."[62] The roaring ovation signaled more than drunken excitement.
Michael McClure observed, "So when Ginsberg drew the line with *Howl*
we had to decide whether our toe was on the line too."[63]

   The poets went to Sam Wo's for Chinese food and then on to The
Place to drink. In the late night recall of what had transpired at the Six
Gallery they discerned the transformation of an individual; as McClure
put it, "Howl" was "Allen's metamorphosis from a quiet brilliant burning
bohemian scholar, trapped by his flames and repressions, to epic vocal
bard."[64] That night, Lawrence Ferlinghetti sat down and typed out a
telegram that echoed Ralph Waldo Emerson's message to Walt Whitman
upon receiving *Leaves of Grass*: "I GREET YOU AT THE BEGINNING
OF A GREAT CAREER. WHEN DO I GET THE MANUSCRIPT?"[65]

   The metamorphosis extended beyond the personal advance of
Ginsberg to the communal advance of the San Francisco poetry community. With the cool perspective of hindsight, Gary Snyder described that
evening as "a curious kind of turning point in American poetry."[66] Mc-
Clure recalled, "We had gone beyond a point of no return—and we were
ready for it, for a point of no return. . . . We wanted voice and we wanted
vision."[67]

*Allen Ginsberg reading, San Francisco
State, November 22, 1955, by Walter
Lehrman*

*A latter-day nabi, one of those Hebrew
prophets who came down out of the
hills and cried "Woe! Woe! to the
bloody city of Jerusalem!" in the streets.*
—Kenneth Rexroth, on Allen Ginsberg

No. 2
$1.00

EVERGREEN REVIEW

SAN FRANCISCO SCENE

MILLER   REXROTH   GINSBERG   KEROUAC
DUNCAN   FERLINGHETTI   MILES   RUMAKER

Cover of Evergreen Review's *second issue, devoted to the San Francisco poets, 1957*

SAN FRANCISCO 1950S BOHEMIA MAP

1 Black Cat Café: *710 Montgomery Street. This bar-café, opening in the mid-1930s, was the reigning hangout of San Francisco bohemia for at least a decade, its denizens depicted in a large mural by Cornelius Sampson.*

2 The Cellar: *576 Green Street, North Beach. Known as the Beats' 25-cent-cover nightclub; Lawrence Ferlinghetti, Kenneth Rexroth, Kenneth Patchen, and others read poems to jazz accompaniment. Lenny Bruce performed here.*

3 Foster's Cafeteria: *235 Montgomery Street. This neon-and-formica cafeteria was a cheap hangout for artists and writers, and here, in early 1955, Allen Ginsberg and Peter Orlovsky exchanged vows.*

4 Co-Existence Bagel Shop: *1398 Grant Avenue. A combination delicatessen, eatery, beer joint, hangout, and news center, run by Jay Hoppe. In "Bagel Shop Jazz," Bob Kaufman described its regulars as "shadow people . . . mulberry-eyed girls in black stockings, smelling vaguely of mint jelly . . . turtle-neck angel guys . . . coffee-faced Ivy Leaguers . . . whose Harvard was a Fillmore District step." Plagued by tourists, narcotics agents, and saboteurs (e.g., the man who blew up a toilet bowl with cherry bombs).*

5 The Coffee Gallery: *1353 Grant Avenue. Formerly Miss Smith's Tea Room, subsequently the Lost and Found Saloon. A center for poetry plus jazz plus art; also the site of "Speak-Up" nights and other open forums. Lord Buckley performed here.*

6 Caffè Trieste: *606 Vallejo Street. An archetypal North Beach coffee shop.*

7 the hungry i: *599 Jackson Street. This club was the site of Lenny Bruce's arrest, and of J. F. Goodwin's Beat opera,* The Pizza Pusher.

8 Paper Doll Club: *532 Green Street. A center for painters and poets, later a lesbian meeting place.*

9 The Iron Pot: *639 Montgomery Street. A long-term restaurant-bar hangout for artists and bohemians beginning in the 1940s; paintings hung here, including Hassel Smith's. This setting was used as a scene in Jack Kerouac's* The Subterraneans, *standing in for the San Remo.*

10 Mr. Otis: *532 Green Street. An important meeting place for poets and painters in the late 1950s.*

11 Vesuvio's: *255 Columbus Street (near Broadway). A classic and long-running bohemian bar, across the alley from City Lights, featuring projected postcards instead of television, and paintings collected by owner Henri Lenoir.*

12 Cameo Hotel: *389 Third Street. Jack Kerouac stayed here in 1954 and wrote "San Francisco Blues."*

13 Hotel Wentley: *1214 Polk Street. Allen Ginsberg met Peter Orlovsky in Robert LaVigne's rooms. The hotel gave its name to John Wieners' collection* The Hotel Wentley Poems.

14 Marconi Hotel: *554 Broadway. Allen Ginsberg stayed in this hotel when he arrived in San Francisco in 1954.*

15 City Lights: *261 Columbus Avenue. Founded in June 1953 by Peter D. Martin and Lawrence Ferlinghetti, this was America's first all-paperback bookstore. Its black and yellow awning was designed by Jordan Belson. Shigeyoshi Murao managed the store, while Ferlinghetti ran City Lights Publishing upstairs (later managed by Nancy Peters, wife of Philip Lamantia). It was here that police arrested Murao and Ferlinghetti for selling "Howl."*

16 San Francisco *Art Institute: 800 Chestnut Street. A key influence on San Francisco's art scene; its faculty included Clyfford Still, Mark Rothko, and Elmer Bischoff.*

17 San Francisco State Poetry Center: *1600 Holloway Avenue (off 19th Avenue). Founded by Ruth Witt-Diamant in 1954.*

18 The Place: *1546 Grant Avenue. A bohemian hangout from the 1940s to the 1960s, and a center for underground painting (e.g., Wally Hedrick projected early liquid-light shows on the walls; paintings by Robert LaVigne and Jay DeFeo hung here). It was run by Knute Stiles and Leo Krikorian, both Black Mountain College alumni. What started as Dada Night evolved in the late 1950s into Blabbermouth Night, an open social forum.*

19 Fugazi Hall: *678 Green Street. A setting for poetry readings by James Broughton, Michael Greig, and Michael McClure. The 1958 Poets' Follies was held here.*

20 Bread and Wine Mission: *510 Greenwich Street. Described as "a medieval church to the community," a center for artists, poets, Sunday "agape dinners"; portrayed in the movie* The Subterraneans.

Beatitude *magazine was published here May 1959–July 1960.*

21 Six Gallery: *3119 Fillmore Street. Originally the site of a garage, it was rented for $50 a month and became an alternative space for poets and artists in 1952, when the King Ubu Gallery (named after the Alfred Jarry play) was founded here by Robert Duncan, Jess (Collins), and Harry Jacobus. The gallery was run very informally, with multilith invitations and reluctant guard-artists, until it was shut down in 1953. In October 1954, six people opened the Six Gallery in the same space. The group reading there, culminating in the first reading of "Howl" on October 13, 1955, marks the beginning of the San Francisco Renaissance.*

22 Allen Ginsberg: *1010 Montgomery Street. Ginsberg and Peter Orlovsky lived here beginning February 3, 1955. Ginsberg began writing "Howl" here in August 1955.*

23 Lawrence Ferlinghetti: *1-21 Mission Street. Ferlinghetti lived here from 1950 through 1952.*

24 Lawrence Ferlinghetti: *339 Chestnut, Apt. 20. Ferlinghetti wrote* Coney Island of the Mind *here.*

25 Gary Snyder and Philip Whalen: *corner of Green and Montgomery Streets. Snyder and Whalen lived here in the early 1950s.*

26 Kenneth Rexroth: *702 Wisconsin Street, Potrero Hill. Site of many literary and political gatherings.*

27 Kenneth Rexroth: *250 Scott Street. Scene of Rexroth's Friday literary soirées.*

28 Michael McClure: *707 Scott Street. McClure moved here in 1956 and edited* Ark II–Moby I *with James Harmon.*

29 Neal and Carolyn Cassady: *29 Russell Street, Russian Hill.*

30 2324 Fillmore Street. *This building, with four flats occupied by writers and artists, was the scene of many impromptu jazz parties. During the middle to late 1950s, its residents included Michael and Joanna McClure, with Philip Lamantia visiting frequently; painter Jay DeFeo and her husband, painter Wally Hedrick; Joan Brown and her husband, Bill Brown; and painter Ed Moses.*

31 The Ghost House: *corner of Franklin and Sutter Streets. Named in the early 1950s by a resident, the former Treadwell mansion—a Gothic pile with a large ballroom—was divided into small artists' studios. Among its residents were students of the California School of Fine Arts; poet Philip Lamantia; painters Martin Baer, Wally Hedrick, Harry Jacobus, and Jess (Collins); and poet Robert Duncan. (The last two lived in the ballroom). The building was demolished in the summer of 1953.*

32 Robert Duncan and Jess: *1724 Baker Street. The couple moved here in 1953, taking over the apartment from James Broughton and soon becoming "householders." Stan Brakhage lived in their basement in his late teens. On the walls were murals by Jess and Harry Jacobus.*

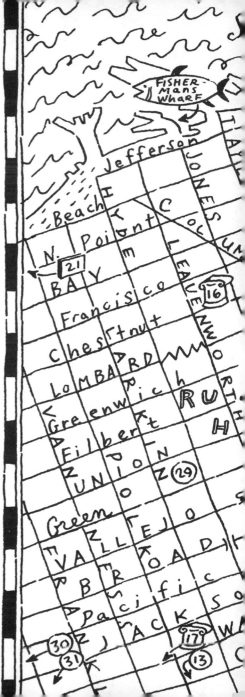

**San Francisco Renaissance
(Those not covered in text, but
associated with the Renaissance)**
Robin Blaser
James Broughton
Kirby Doyle
David Meltzer
Jack Micheline
Harold Norse
Kenneth Patchen
Jack Spicer
Lew Welch
John Wieners

Homer, or the guy who recited Beowulf,
*was show business. We simply want to
make poetry a part of show business.*
—Kenneth Rexroth, on the oral tradition

SAN FRANCISCO RENAISSANCE: AN OVERVIEW Most historians date
the beginning of the San Francisco Renaissance to the Six Gallery reading
in October 1955, and mark its end around 1960, with the demise of *Beatitude* magazine. Such chronological markers are useful, but they neglect
the rich literary background that led to the Renaissance, and they slight
the rich counterculture environment of the 1960s that grew out of the Renaissance. Ascribing a tight set of poetics to the Renaissance is misguided,
for the San Francisco poets were neither doctrinaire nor exclusive—
Michael McClure celebrated poetry's "myriad-mindedness"—but one can
identify several common threads that run through markedly different bodies of poetry.

These poets looked to the first American avant-garde as their forebears. As Robert Duncan said, "We have our origins in a great American
School, a fraternity of poets: Williams, Pound, h. d., Marianne Moore, and
Eliot—and we have, if we write at all, to study their language."[68] The same
publisher who disseminated that generation of poets, James Laughlin,
helped distribute the San Francisco poets through New Directions. But
the San Francisco poets also looked to European forebears—Arthur Rimbaud, Antonin Artaud—and to the East. Artistic allies are often defined by
their foes, and the enemy was quite distinctly the poetry Establishment of
the time, as embodied in such New Critics as Allen Tate and Cleanth
Brooks, and in East Coast literary magazines like the *Sewanee Review*.

The San Francisco poets pursued the experiments of the earlier
American generation in what was called open form poetry. They aspired
in troubadour fashion to revive the spoken voice. This affected not only
poetry's preferred form of presentation—public readings, often accompanied by jazz or simple percussion, rather than printed words—but also
its sound.

Several of the San Francisco poets shared the Beats' interest in confessional poetry, in consciousness-expanding drugs, and in sexual libera-

tion. They also shared the bond of commitment to pacifism and to libertarian anarchism. Interest in Eastern religion, notably Buddhism and Tao-
ism, tied many of the poets together. The natural environment figured
prominently in their poems, depicted as endangered by mid-twentieth-
century civilization and as a beneficent environment for mankind. Poetry
as an expression of the magical can be seen in the shared interest in the occult, Tarot readings, alchemy, automatic writing.

  Aside from shared aesthetic concerns and common themes, the
Renaissance can be best described as overlapping constellations of poets
who chose San Francisco for their home; their tightly knit relationships
mattered as much as their writing. In the East, the Bay Area was dismissed
as an eccentric literary province, but for many Americans it became a
mecca. "In the spiritual and political loneliness of America in the fifties
you'd hitch a thousand miles to meet a friend," wrote Gary Snyder. "Whatever lives needs a habitat, a proper culture of warmth and moisture to
grow. West coast of those days, San Francisco was the only city; and of San
Francisco, North Beach."[69]

  San Francisco prided itself on its tradition of writers, which
stretched back to the nineteenth century—Mark Twain, Bret Harte, Frank
Norris, Joaquin Miller, Mary Elizabeth Parsons, Jack London, George
Sterling. These forefathers were supplemented by such nearby writers as
Robinson Jeffers and Henry Miller. Overlapping with the literary community was what one participant called "the long honorable San Francisco
tradition of Bohemian-Buddhist-Wobbly-mystical-anarchist social involvement."[70] The Bay Area housed a community of philosophical anarchists
and trade unionists whose early-twentieth-century ancestors—such radi-
cals as the Wobblies, Randolph Bourne, and John Reed—made common
cause with America's first avant-garde. Just as the first American avant-
garde had found a sympathetic community in the Italian neighborhood of

San Francisco was a rich network of streams to "trout about" in.
     —Michael McClure

Hot: *emotionally charged, the opposite of cool*

When San Francisco is your home, by birth or adoption, you secretly feel affiliated with a rarity.

—Janet Richards

Greenwich Village, San Francisco had its own supportive Italian community in North Beach, as well as nextdoor Chinatown. Perhaps most crucial, San Francisco provided a literary province that was distinct from the New York Establishment, at the edge of America, looking to the East. "We are a coast people," observed poet Jack Spicer. "There is nothing but ocean behind us."[71]

One of the favorite pastimes of San Francisco's literary pope, Kenneth Rexroth, was reminiscing about the city's literary bohemia of the 1930s, but it was in the wake of World War II that the Bay Area's poets and bohemians mounted an organized effort to initiate little magazines and discussion groups. In the venerable San Francisco tradition, politics as well as poetry shaped these efforts. When he arrived in the city in 1954, Allen Ginsberg was impressed by the foundations laid by earlier generations: "They had prepared a cultural theater in San Francisco, and it was a legitimate community."[72] Instead of recounting the full story of that fertile tradition, a few snapshots can suggest the communal hubs—literary, political, and social—that laid the groundwork for the San Francisco Renaissance.

Joy bang: an occasional shot, not enough to lead to addiction: "Nick also scored for some respectable working people in the Village who indulged in an occasional 'joy bang.'" [Burroughs]

San Francisco's bohemian tradition was embodied in the Black Cat, a café-bar which opened for business in the mid-1930s at 710 Montgomery Street, in North Beach. It offered ten bar stools and a half-dozen tables, a hearty fifty-cent *prix fixe* dinner of heavy soup, salad, and meat, and a convivial, alcoholized atmosphere. Over the bar hung an eight-foot oil-on-plywood painting depicting seventy-six regulars, circa 1938. Here gathered a classic bohemian mix of writers, trade unionists, painters, chess players, models, remittance men, and local characters. Presiding over the establishment was a former butcher named Charlie Haberkern, who drank along with his customers and freely offered drinks and food. (When he died of cirrhosis, the Black Cat regulars were alarmed to discover that he was only thirty-seven.) At the end of World War II, the Black Cat be-

"The Regulars," 1938, the 4 x 8-foot mural by Cornelius Sampson that hung over the bar at the Black Cat Café, San Francisco

came one of San Francisco's most popular gay bars. The evening began with a mixed crowd of artists, writers, and bohemians, to be gradually replaced by homosexual men, and finally by lesbians, who closed the bar in the early hours of the morning. The Alcoholic Beverage Control shut down the Black Cat for infractions on Halloween Night, 1963.

In Waldport, Oregon, a dozen hours north of San Francisco and a universe away from North Beach, stood a camp that, during World War II, became a Civilian Public Service Camp for conscientious objectors. It was isolated and provided little in the way of drink or sex, but its site fronting the Pacific offered transfiguring beauty. "But it's the sea, the sea!" exclaimed resident William Everson. "You cannot live by it and not be touched by what it is, or shaken, made new each time."[73] The Fine Arts Project established at Waldport in 1944—workshops for artists and writers, actors and musicians—drew creative pacifists from all over the country and an enforced artistic camaraderie developed. Theater groups flourished, along with concerts, a brief visiting-artist program with Morris Graves, poetry readings, and the three chief little magazines of the conscientious objector movement (*The Compass*, *Illiterati*, and William Everson's *Untide Press*). Enforced internment in Waldport over several years provided a nucleus for the later, larger community formed in San Francisco, and the motto of Waldport's *Illiterati*—"Creation, Experiment, and Revolution to build a warless, free society"—reflects the West Coast links between the literary avant-garde and the political left. "Actually a good deal of what later happened in the San Francisco scene had its origin right there in Waldport," recalled Everson.[74]

What is not Tide *is* Untide.
—William Everson

In early 1946, the Libertarian Circle formed and met in a huge Victorian house at 1057 Steiner Street. Ranging in number from a dozen to fifty, the participants were dominated by older Europeans who had participated in socialist and pacifist movements. They gathered for discussions about Emma Goldman, mutualist anarchism, or the IWW; they grappled with rethinking revolutionary doctrine in the wake of Stalinist totalitarianism. A few months later, the Libertarian Circle spawned a poetry group that met every Wednesday evening for readings and discussion. Among the local poets who read were Kenneth Rexroth, Robert Duncan, Philip Lamantia, Jack Spicer, Muriel Rukeyser, and William Everson. The poetry in turn spawned both a formal seminar for writers, led by Rexroth and costing a dollar a session, and a little magazine, *The Ark* (1947), which functioned as the literary organ for the branches of libertarian thought. The magazine, edited by Philip Lamantia, included among its twenty contributors not only Bay Area poets but William Carlos Williams, James Laughlin, and Paul Goodman.

Cover of Circle, *designed by Bern Porter, 1945*

Across the Bay, at 2643 Telegraph Avenue in Berkeley, stood Throckmorton Manor, and in its all-black dining room sat Robert Duncan, Jack Spicer, Robin Blaser, and other writers. They modeled their group activities on the Stefan George circle, an early-twentieth-century German cult devoted to art, homosexuality, and beauty. Duncan dominated these weekly discussion groups on such "modern masters" as Sitwell, Stein, Joyce, h.d., Pound, Lawrence. His soliloquies were eloquent and charged, delivered with an impassioned look that was never direct because Duncan was cross-eyed. "It was galvanizing to have someone look at you so penetratingly while neither of his eyes were looking right at you," recalled a participant. "It was almost like a trance phenomenon in which he'd really let himself rip."[75] At other times the group read aloud from *Finnegans Wake*, or listened to visiting Kenneth Rexroth talk about William Carlos Williams.

Finally, unrestricted by geography, was public radio station KPFA. Broadcast from Berkeley, the voices that went out over the airwaves helped unite the Bay Area arts community. Seated at home in his favorite Morris chair, Kenneth Rexroth recorded a weekly half-hour discussion of books and mailed it off for broadcast; he did not restrict himself to poetry, in fact rarely reviewed poetry, but instead offered erudite and impromptu essays on everything from Eastern religion to Byzantine Orthodoxy to contemporary painting. Long before she began programming movie revival houses or writing film criticism for the *New Yorker*, Pauline Kael delivered her opinions on American and foreign movies. Alan Watts delivered Taoist lectures, and Ralph Gleason commented on jazz.

KENNETH REXROTH Throughout the 1940s and most of the 1950s, Kenneth Rexroth reigned as the grand panjandrum of the literary world that some dubbed "the first San Francisco Renaissance." Janet Richards, a

*Subterranean: a variant of **hipster**, coined by Allen Ginsberg in the early 1950s to describe the regulars at the San Remo, and used by Kerouac as the title of* The Subterraneans: *"They [subterraneans] are hip without being corny, they are intellectual as hell and know all about Pound without being pretentious or talking too much about it, they are very quiet, they are very Christlike."*

Kenneth Rexroth, wearing a suit Al Capone gave him in Chicago in the 1920s, San Francisco, 1957, by Jonathan Williams

long-term friend, described the astonishing range of Rexroth's mind: "He was everything: conscientious objector, classical scholar, versed in all sciences, political wiseacre, extreme radical, painter, musician, Orientalist, poet, essayist, and friend of all artists."[76] His role as animator of a nascent avant-garde was pursued with the same unyielding spirit as that of Alfred Stieglitz years earlier—a lone, indefatigable figure gathering like-minded artists, writers, and bohemians in his intimate rooms. His role demanded social skills, but Rexroth was happiest in his solitary cabin among trees or in his bathtub, where he read each evening for two hours.

Born in 1905 and raised in Chicago in the years of that city's poetry renaissance, Kenneth Rexroth moved to San Francisco in 1927. He recognized the city as "a little time pocket" where alternative politics and aesthetics could flourish, and he aspired to develop an alternative to the stultifying East Coast literary Establishment. As William Everson observed, "Rexroth touched the nerve of the future and more than any other voice in the movement called it into being."[77] Rexroth's poetry was widely admired, and two of his collections, *In What Hour* (Macmillan, 1940) and *The Phoenix and the Tortoise* (New Directions, 1944), won the California Literature Silver Award. Most important to the development of San Francisco's literary community, Rexroth was an enterprising organizer, uncompromising radical, and inspiring autodidact.

Marked by a pugnacious bulldog face and sad blue eyes, Rexroth stood ramrod straight, and spoke in a voice that sounded "just like a B gangster pitcher."[78] He cut his own hair, drove a secondhand Willys Knight, which he repaired himself, and dressed in dungaree couture and high-fashion. "It was his mind you noticed about him,"[79] observed a friend, and if he sometimes seemed like an egomaniac pronouncing his opinions ex cathedra, he was also uncannily correct. As William Everson noted, "He delivers his pronouncements with such verve, even aplomb, that you sat there wondering, utterly charmed but rather bedazzled by the pyrotechnics."[80] The fireworks were grounded in encyclopedic knowledge— he knew many languages, the Classical and the avant-garde, the East and the West, the political and the poetic. His personal relations were often strained, he seized conversations and rarely listened, and his mood swings ranged from taciturn silence to maniacal attacks. One friend observed that his feelings were obscure to him, while ideas filled his head. But he was loyal, dependable, supportive of new thought, and noncompetitive. "The

I've never understood why I'm a member of the avant-garde. I write like the great Greeks and Romans and the Chinese and so forth.

—Kenneth Rexroth

Kenneth was like Godwin was to early nineteenth-century England—an anarchist, teacher, political figure, literateur. He was a very brilliant man and put many of us on our feet with a stance we could grow with.
—Michael McClure, on Kenneth Rexroth

We were all brought up on Daddy Rexroth's reading list.
—Robert Duncan

Boy in the boat: *the clitoris*

pain Kenneth inflicted was the price you paid for knowing him," wrote Janet Richards, "but how he changed you was the benefit you got."[81]

In the decades before Rexroth moved from San Francisco to Santa Barbara in 1968, he shaped several generations of writers. Robert Duncan, a member of the older San Francisco generation, captured the in-person magnetism of Rexroth: "He has a truly amazing quantity of knowledge. We learned only last week that he reads the Encyclopedia Britannica from cover to cover yearly. And that is coupled with a high-style in the Johnsonian tradition, a never ceasing to delight and astonishing gift for burlesque, a caustic and affectionate wit. He is, finally, so much the devotee of his own devotees."[82]

ROBERT DUNCAN "In San Francisco Rexroth was our group's *paterfamilias*," recalled poet William Everson, "but on the Berkeley side Duncan was its energy."[83] Robert Duncan was fourteen years younger than Rexroth and altogether different in style—histrionic, effete, in the words of Anaïs Nin, "*l'enfant terrible*, perverse and knowing."[84] But he was, like Rexroth, devoted to independence and to wide-ranging academic learning, and Rexroth observed that the early San Francisco generation "owes more to Duncan than to any other person."[85]

One of the few poets of the Renaissance born in the Bay Area, Robert Duncan was adopted at a young age by two Theosophists who selected him because of his auspicious astrological chart. Duncan grew up within a household that prized myth, esoteric stories, and magical correspondences between everyday incidents and the cosmos. He was an ace student, discovered his poetic vocation during his adolescence, and, at nineteen, began publishing poems in the Berkeley campus literary magazine, *Occident*. His interests ranged from medieval history and romanticism to Gertrude Stein and shamanism. His life during the 1930s and

1940s was peripatetic—moving from Berkeley to Woodstock to New York to San Francisco, living marginally, as he put it, "on the meat market."[86] In 1940 he founded and edited a Woodstock-based little magazine called the *Experimental Review* (1940), and its statement of purpose reflects not only Duncan's heterodoxy but also the "myriad-mindedness" of the San Francisco community: "The *Experimental Review* will investigate the nature of values, objects, dreams, tensions within the social and economic order as well as the more involved states of consciousness—the nature of the primitive, the saint or the mystic."[87] In 1944 he wrote a brave and seminal article, "The Homosexual in Society," for Dwight MacDonald's *Politics*, and against the editor's advice he insisted that his self-identification as a homosexual be signed ("the whole thing has no meaning if it is not signed"[88]). This pioneering piece, critizing the prefabricated marginal world of homosexual camp, earned him the enmity of both homosexuals, such as *View* magazine's Parker Tyler (who considered him a traitor), and heterosexual editors, such as John Crowe Ransom (who rejected a previously accepted poem, "African Elegy," on the basis that it now seemed "to have obvious homosexual advertisement, and for that reason not to be eligible for publication"[89]).

In 1950 Duncan began an enduring domestic relationship with Jess Collins (the artist known as Jess); as Duncan put it, he was no longer "on the meatrack" but had become "a householder." The lovers' partnership provided the domestic base from which he could pursue his protean literary imagination, and they collaborated, exploring the relationship between word and image.

Around the time of the epochal Six Gallery reading, Duncan and Jess were in Mallorca, following a teaching stint at Black Mountain College where Duncan befriended Charles Olson and Robert Creeley. Returning to San Francisco in 1956, Duncan became the assistant director of the San Francisco State Poetry Center; from this position he encouraged

Robert Duncan's Bookshelf
Gertrude Stein
h.d.
Edith Sitwell
Ezra Pound
Henry James
Marcel Proust
Dorothy Richardson
Herman Melville
The Kabbala

When I think of Robert, I see firelight in a hearth and bronze Art Deco women with long hair, and Oz books and cats and San Francisco fog and Jackson Pollock.
—Michael McClure, on Robert Duncan

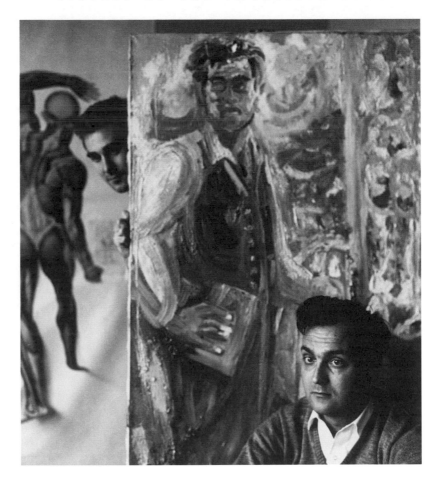

Jess, his "Imaginary Portrait of Robert Duncan," and Duncan in the flesh, San Francisco, 1956, by Harry Redl

cross-fertilization among the Black Mountain and the San Francisco poets. Duncan distanced himself from the poses of San Francisco's Beat era—he eschewed drugs, street language, and public flamboyance. Michael McClure described him as "a time-diver" whose personal aura was charged: "On going to visit Duncan there was the feeling that one was meeting Yeats or Joyce or Nerval or Villon—one felt just before entering, Duncan might have been communing with the troubador Peire Vidal or Emily Dickinson."[90] Long after the Renaissance faded, Duncan maintained his faith in the communion of poets. When Kenneth Rexroth moved to Santa Barbara, Duncan asked a group who would inherit Rexroth's mantle as the grand old man of San Francisco poetry; the answer was Duncan himself. As Janet Richards wrote in the late 1970s, "Now graying, he has become for the San Francisco poetry world a wonderful creature, half Ariel, half Prospero!"[91]

In a Bohemian household you have immediacy to all the arts so that you are going to have some aspect of music, poetry, painting, and also the decoration of things at the same level.
—Robert Duncan

WILLIAM EVERSON / BROTHER ANTONINUS First encountering William Everson in the mid-1940s, on furlough from Waldport, wearing an oversized hat, boots, and green Forest Service uniform. Kenneth Rexroth described Everson as "an autochthon" and quickly added, "Being an autochthon of course is something you don't manage, you are."[92] Born in 1912 to an immigrant Norwegian bandmaster and printer and a Minnesota farm girl, Everson was raised in a small town in California's Fresno County. He briefly attended Fresno State College, experimented with writing, embraced agnosticism, and worked in local canneries and in the Civilian Conservation Corps.

William Everson found his twin vocations—poetry and God—at the age of twenty-three, while reading Big Sur poet Robinson Jeffers. "It was an intellectual awakening and a religious conversion in one," Everson recalled. "Jeffers showed me God. In Jeffers I found my voice."[93] By the 1950s Everson was already a man of accomplishment: he had written a dozen books of poetry; he had been awarded a Guggenheim Fellowship (1949); he had printed and edited Waldport's *Untide Press* (1944); he had founded the Equinox Press (1947). On Christmas Eve 1948, he experienced a religious conversion that inspired him to become a Catholic and

I'm pre-beat.
—William Everson/Brother Antoninus

William Everson/Brother Antoninus' Bookshelf
Robinson Jeffers
D. H. Lawrence
Walt Whitman
Algernon Swinburne
Hart Crane
Ralph Waldo Emerson
Gerard Manley Hopkins

Brother Antoninus at his press, by Harry Redl

enter a Dominican monastery two years later as a lay brother. Given the name Brother Antoninus, "he seemed to have a vision of the monastery as a citadel into which you'd withdraw from the corruption outside,"[94] noted a fellow brother, and Brother Antoninus developed a regimen so severely ascetic that the father superior insisted it be relaxed. He had stopped writing. "It was the crystallized monastic ego that dried the poetry out of me," Everson recalled.[95] But he felt "a psychic break" in the summer of 1956.

Disturbed by the encroachment of the world into the monastery, and aghast when television appeared in the priests' recreation room, Brother Antoninus struggled with depression and the primal and sexual imagery of his dreams. He thought he was throwing out the devil.

Around this same time, Robert Duncan invited him to read his poetry at San Francisco State. Appearing in a white tunic and black scapular, Brother Antoninus developed a possessed, charismatic style that convinced him "that this was my vocation in the Church. People will not read my poems, but when I read to them I can spellbind."[96]

Time magazine dubbed him "The Beat Friar," but his poetic development owed nothing to the Beats, nor did he embrace their rejection of the square world. "I identify with the Beat Generation because of its mystical concerns, its emphasis on the oral as opposed to the academic tradition," said Brother Antoninus.[97] The image of a Catholic poet as a proponent of the Beats upset the Archbishop of San Francisco, who silenced the poet from reading in the Bay Area or giving interviews to the press. Only on the Archbishop's death did Brother Antoninus resume his readings.

Long after the Renaissance was over, until his death in 1994, Everson continued to write the poems—over 800 pages—that collectively comprise the work he called "The Crooked Lines of God." As an apt summation of his life and work, Everson drew his title from the Portuguese proverb "God writes straight with crooked lines."[98]

Lawrence Ferlinghetti Although he never considered himself a Beat—before, during, or after the San Francisco Renaissance—Lawrence Ferlinghetti is invariably linked with the Beats. His life overlapped theirs in style and geography and shared the same pattern of disrupted childhood, connection to Greenwich Village, hitchhiking to Mexico, libertar-

I'm beat to the square, and square to the beat, and that's my vocation.
—William Everson/Brother Antoninus

I was proud to be identified with them, however. I knew it was a revolt needed in American letters.
—William Everson/Brother Antoninus, on the Beat Generation

I remain the solitary poet-utterer that I began.
—William Everson/Brother Antoninus

I lawrence ferlinghetti
wrought from the dark in my mother long
ago
born in a small back bedroom—
. . . .
Someone squeezed my heart
to make it go
I cried and sprang up
Open eye open heart where
do I wander
I cried and ran off
into the heart of the world
                    —Lawrence Ferlinghetti

Lawrence Ferlinghetti's Bookshelf
Gertrude Stein
James Joyce
T. S. Eliot
Ezra Pound
Charles Baudelaire
Thomas Wolfe

ian-pacifist politics, and a scholarly and voracious interest in modern literature. Ferlinghetti's father died five months before he was born (his family shortened the name to Ferling, restored in 1954) and his mother was institutionalized at the state psychiatric hospital in Poughkeepsie, New York. At the age of one, Lawrence began a Dickensian childhood, shuttled between an aunt, an orphanage, and wealthy benefactors, between France and Bronxville, between a street gang called the Parkway Road Pirates and Mount Hermon, a Massachusetts farm school that later became a preparatory school. At the same time that Kerouac, Ginsberg, and Burroughs were congregating in Joan Vollmer's apartment, Ferlinghetti enrolled in Mark Van Doren's and Lionel Trilling's classes at Columbia and pursued a master's degree in literature (awarded in 1947), but his path never crossed theirs. He then moved to Paris for three years of study at the Sorbonne (1947–1950). He wrote a doctoral dissertation on the city as a symbol in modern poetry, and he graduated with distinction.

He returned to America in 1950, married Selden Kirby-Smith (a.k.a. Kirby), and settled in San Francisco, which offered—and continues to offer—him the ideal metropolitan base. Rejecting the academic profession for which he had been trained, Ferlinghetti cobbled together a combination of jobs that allowed him to write and paint. He taught French in night school and Shakespeare at the University of San Francisco, reviewed poetry for the *San Francisco Chronicle*, and covered local exhibitions for *Art Digest*. Through Kenneth Rexroth's soirées, he met the San Francisco literary community. One early acquaintance recalled him as socially unforthcoming, frequently getting lost in fascination with a wine bottle or a verbal juxtaposition or a joke. Then, as if awakening from a deep sleep, "He began taking action. He hasn't stopped taking action since."[99]

One afternoon in 1953 Ferlinghetti saw Peter D. Martin, the son of prominent anarchist Carlo Tresca, erecting a sign that read "Pocket Book Shop." Martin told Ferlinghetti of his desire to promote the incipient

Lawrence Ferlinghetti at City Lights Bookstore, San Francisco, 1956, by Harry Redl

*I was a wind-up toy
someone had dropped wound-up
into a world already
running down*
                    —Lawrence Ferlinghetti

Early City Lights Books
Pictures of the Gone World by Lawrence
    Ferlinghetti (1955)
Thirty Spanish Poems of Love and Exile
    translated by Kenneth Rexroth (1965)
Poems of Humor & Protest by Kenneth
    Patchen (1956)
Howl and Other Poems by Allen
    Ginsberg (1956)
Kora in Hell by William Carlos Williams
    (1957)
Gasoline by Gregory Corso (1958)
Selected Poems by Robert Duncan
    (1959)
Beat Zen, Square Zen, and Zen by Alan
    Watts (1959)
Abomunist Manifesto by Bob Kaufman
    (1959)
Book of Dreams by Jack Kerouac (1960)

paperback revolution, and shortly after that, Ferlinghetti contributed $500 to become Martin's business partner. In June 1953, the two opened America's first paperback bookstore, at 261 Columbus Avenue. In honor of Charlie Chaplin they called it City Lights.

The odd two-story building on the triangular site at the end of an alley offered a humble site to launch the paperback revolution. Greeted by a yellow-and-black-striped awning, one entered a main floor that measured twelve by fifteen feet, presided over by cashier-manager Shigeyoshi Murao. A steep staircase led to a basement four times as large as the first floor. In addition to the warren of shelves, there were round tables, a church pew, and straightback chairs for reading. In 1953 paperbacks consisted mostly of tabloid literature distributed through drugstores and train stations; the only "quality" paperbacks were published by British Penguin and Anchor-Doubleday. City Lights carried a full complement of Penguins and a selection of drugstore paperbacks, as well as small-press magazines and books—such as those published by Bern Porter, Leslie Woolf Hedley, and Jonathan Williams' Jargon Society—and anarchist literature. "I remember the Italian man in a derby who worked on the garbage truck," said Ferlinghetti. "Each week he'd jump off as the truck passed, pick up the Italian anarchist papers *L'Adunata* and *L'Humanità Nova*, and jump back on."[100] City Lights quickly became a hangout for readers, students, and bohemians. The doors stayed open until midnight on weeknights and 2 AM on weekends, and still do.

After buying out Peter Martin in January 1955, Ferlinghetti decided to use City Lights as a base to publish and sell a series devoted to avant-garde literature. He had seen this combination of bookstore-publisher practiced successfully in Paris, and he particularly recalled a paperback series called Poètes d'Aujourd'hui, whose small square format caused it to be known as a *livre de poche*. On August 10, 1955, Ferlinghetti published his first "Pocket Poet" book, his own *Pictures of the Gone World*.

This introduced City Lights' now-classic, nearly square format (4 by 5 inches), printed in black and white, collated and saddle-stitched, and sold for only seventy-five cents to a dollar. Ferlinghetti quickly followed with two other San Francisco–based Pocket Poets: Kenneth Rexroth and Kenneth Patchen. In the summer of 1955, Allen Ginsberg showed Ferlinghetti the sheaf of journal-derived poems of 1951 that William Carlos Williams had liked. Ferlinghetti's funds were very low at the time, but in passing Ginsberg also mentioned his newest work, "Howl." Neither could have imagined that this poem would expose City Lights to international fame and notoriety.

MICHAEL McCLURE When he was a child, Michael McClure wanted to be a naturalist; he later studied anthropology and headed for San Francisco at the age of twenty-one to study the philosophy of postwar art. In his varied vocational interests, and in the disparate groups with which he consorted—writers, rock musicians, painters, later Hell's Angels—he embodied the "myriad-mindedness" of the San Francisco Renaissance. More than any single figure, McClure provided a bridge between the worlds of art, theater, and poetry that so enlivened the San Francisco Renaissance years.

McClure was born on Rimbaud's birthday (October 20, 1932) on the plains of Marysville, Kansas. Due to divorces and remarriages, he was shuttled between Marysville, Seattle, and Wichita. Two abiding loves, poetry and nature, were born during these early years. In his adolescence he discovered old copies of *Transition* and he began reading the modernists—not just the classics (Eliot, Joyce, Pound) but also a younger generation that included Antonin Artaud, Kenneth Patchen, and Kurt Schwitters. In his early teens, McClure began writing free verse, and after his immersion in modernism he grew more interested in perfecting such traditional po-

Non-gun-toting high-schooler Michael McClure pretends to hunt trilobites, Marysville, Kansas, ca. 1950

Michael McClure's Bookshelf
William Blake
William Carlos Williams
Kenneth Patchen
e. e. cummings
William Butler Yeats
Ezra Pound
Antonin Artaud
Charles Olson
Theodore Roethke
Arthur Waley
Kenneth Rexroth
Hans Arp
Percy Shelley
Federico García Lorca
Comic strips: *Smokey Stover* and *The Nutt Brothers: Ches and Wal*
Kurt Schwitters
William Wordsworth

etic forms as villanelles, sonnets, and sestinas. When his high school friend Bruce Conner exposed him to Abstract Expressionist art, McClure began painting in hopes that their gestural style would inspire his poetry. One of

Michael McClure in San Francisco, 1956, by Harry Redl

San Francisco's lures was the distinguished faculty at the California School of Fine Arts (later the San Francisco Art Institute). McClure moved to San Francisco in 1954, and finding that two hoped-for teachers, Clyfford Still and Mark Rothko, no longer taught there, he discovered instead another generation of artists. "I had a sudden feeling that, regarding visual art, I was happy to be in San Francisco and not Paris," recalled McClure. "That was 1954." He enrolled in Robert Duncan's poetry workshop at San Francisco State College and found in the class "a divine milieu."[101]

The dynamic between the adventurous, wild-eyed McClure and the erudite Duncan was perhaps unexpected—the student writing "Petrarchan sonnets in the style of Milton," and the older professor encouraging freer experimentation.[102] McClure met San Francisco's literary community through Duncan and at Kenneth Rexroth's evenings, where he encountered poet Philip Lamantia and was so drawn to his mysticism and surrealism that Lamantia often stayed with McClure. Following a W. H. Auden reading McClure met Allen Ginsberg, and before the evening was out they had shared the visions they had each had of William Blake—he had come to Ginsberg in a Harlem apartment speaking in a voice of stone, and he had appeared to McClure in his adolescence in a dream in which "Blake seemed as real a presence as an automobile."[103] McClure was struck by the difference in their respective visions of Blake. "Allen has a Blake who is a Blake of prophecy, a Blake who speaks out against the dark Satanic Mills," observed McClure. "My Blake is a Blake of Body and of Vision."[104]

It was after this meeting that Michael McClure invited Ginsberg to organize the Six Gallery reading. (McClure couldn't manage it at that moment, for he was about to become a father.) He readied one of his own poems for the reading, the first performance of a work that integrated McClure's interest in tradition, experiment, and biology. "For the Death of 100 Whales" had been written in 1954 as a ballad with a 4-3-4-3 meter and

Turn on: *to get high; to introduce somebody to anything positive: "He turned me on to Zen."*

A-B-C-B rhymes, and then, McClure recalled, "I broke it apart so it was a Cubist poem."[105] When he performed it at the Six Gallery, it reflected his early and continuing interest in forging a poetry of environment and biology.

GARY SNYDER At the beginning of 1950, three Reed College undergraduates—Gary Snyder, Philip Whalen, and Lew Welch—moved into the former coal cellar of a rooming house at 1414 Southeast Lambert Street, a center for Portland's bohemians. Like the student roomers on the floors above, the threesome played guitars and ingested peyote. Each of them wrote poetry in notebooks—mostly lean Imagist lines evoking nature's beauty—with various degrees of seriousness. Snyder published poems in Reed's college literary magazine, Whalen hoped to follow in the footsteps of William Carlos Williams and become a doctor-poet, and Lew Welch immersed himself in an undergraduate thesis on Gertrude Stein. The triumvirate formed the Adelaide Crapsey–Oswald Spengler Mutual Admiration Poetasters Society and played a game of improvising poems around five randomly chosen words. The society was inspired by William Carlos Williams' visit to Reed during the first week of November 1950. When he read his poems aloud, Lew Welch wrote his mother that it was like a good jam session. "These may not sound like poetry to you," Williams had said, "no matter, don't define the damn thing, let 'em come to you—and BESIDES, he said, THEY'RE IN YOUR OWN LANGUAGE."[106] All three members of the Crapsey Society heeded Williams' advice, and would figure prominently in the San Francisco Renaissance. The acknowledged leader of the trio, both at 1414 Southeast Lambert and later in San Francisco, was Gary Snyder.

In his eager embodiment of the American frontier, and in his diligent, nature-savvy manner, Snyder offered an alternative to American

Gary Snyder's Bookshelf
Ezra Pound
T. S. Eliot
Arthur Waley
Jean-Jacques Rousseau
William Blake
Walt Whitman
Henry David Thoreau
D. H. Lawrence
Robinson Jeffers
Kenneth Rexroth
Jaime de Angulo (especially *Indian Tales*)
Black Elk
Franz Boas
John R. Swanton
D. T. Suzuki

Gary Snyder in his rustic retreat north of San Francisco, 1956, by Harry Redl

urban anomie. Raised during the Depression among lumberjacks, Indians, and farmers on a farm outside Seattle, Snyder learned the ways of animals and the rewards of the land, and he read books by Ernest Thompson Seton (the same author who had inspired Burroughs to write his "Autobiography of a Wolf"). He crafted his own moccasins and arrows, mastered archery, camped out, cooked in the middle of a forest. His backwoodsman self-sufficiency and his early interest in the song and story of unlettered societies all found their way into his poetry (Snyder's facile derogators refer to his work as the "bear scat on the trail" school of poetry).[107] One of his mottos during the Reed years foreshadowed the future of Snyder's poetry: "I want to create wilderness out of empire."[108]

Introduced to Asian art at the age of nine, Sndyer found in a Chinese painting of mountains a spiritual dimension that superseded the rugged mountains surrounding him; he was transfixed. His enchantment was reawakened by reading Ezra Pound's and Arthur Waley's translations of Chinese poetry: "I thought, here is a high civilization that has managed to keep in tune with nature . . . that it naturally had an organic, process-oriented view of the world."[109] When Snyder moved to the Bay Area in the fall of 1952, he studied Oriental languages and fashioned an austere life devoted to Zen meditation. When Ginsberg and Kerouac met him in the fall of 1955, Snyder lived in a twelve-by-twelve-foot garden cottage. He owned no chairs and sat cross-legged on a paisley pillow on a straw mat, surrounded by orange crates filled with Zen books and a rucksack supplied with nested metal cookware. He rolled expert Bull Durham cigarettes and cooked on his hibachi a legendary horsemeat sukiyaki with sweet and sour sauce. His slightly slanted green eyes, described by Robert Creeley as "wise old-young eyes,"[110] looked vaguely Oriental, and with his narrow goatee and Japanese pata socks, Snyder looked to Kerouac like "a happy little sage."[111]

To Kerouac, Snyder was not simply an interesting, knowledgeable, and curious young man—he became an icon, "the big hero of the West Coast."[112] Seen as a figure who was spiritual and happily innocent, Snyder fit the niche once reserved for Gerard, more recently for Neal Cassady (who had now become a Cayce-ite "Billy Sunday in a suit"). Snyder actually practiced the self-sufficient life that Kerouac only romanticized. He

Grass: *marijuana, a term from the 1950s. "Grass" had an earlier meaning, in British criminal argot, of squealing, informing. When an acquaintance gave the police information, William Burroughs dubbed him "Grassy Gert."*

entered Kerouac's life shortly after Kerouac had decided he wanted to follow the *dharma*, and Kerouac quickly elevated Snyder to "the number one
Dharma Bum of them all."[113]

Two weeks after the Six Gallery reading, Kerouac and Snyder set
out to climb Yosemite's 12,000-foot Matterhorn Mountain, a few magical
days that became the centerpiece of *The Dharma Bums*, Kerouac's novel
about Gary Snyder. Right off the pages of *Boy's Life*—raisins and nuts and
homemade chocolate pudding frozen in the snow—the trip provided one
of the most stirring vignettes of Kerouac's dream of pure boyhood bonding.
On the trail they composed haiku for one another, and as they neared the
peak, Snyder charged up the mountain in only a jockstrap, reaching the
peak and "letting out his triumphant mountain-conquering Buddha
Mountain Smashing song of joy."[114] Against the chill October majesty of
the midnight Yosemite sky, inspired by the woodsman mate in the sleeping
bag beside him, Kerouac vowed, "I'll tramp with a rucksack and make it
the pure way."[115] The trip provided one of Kerouac's last periods of transcendent happiness. Snyder had warned Kerouac that he was too vexed by
the world, and later reflected that around Jack there circulated "a palpable
aura of fame and death."[116]

PHILIP LAMANTIA "The 'poetic marvelous' and the unconscious are
the true inspirers of rebels and poets!" wrote Philip Lamantia at the age of
sixteen.[117] Although he sounds like other Beat writers, his route bypassed
their Whitmanesque populism for the magic folk tales of his Sicilian
grandmother. On reaching high school, his vision was transformed by seeing exhibitions of paintings by Joan Miró and Salvador Dali. He followed
up by looking through the articles, illustrations, and advertisements in the
Surrealist-oriented magazine *View* (edited by Charles Henri Ford, 1940–
1947); he buried himself in the movement. When he was sixteen, *View*

To rebel! that is the immediate objective of poets! We can not wait and will not be held back . . . the "poetic marvelous" and the unconscious are the true inspirers of rebels and poets.
—Philip Lamantia

Philip Lamantia, San Francisco, 1956,
by Harry Redl

Twisted: *a 1950s term for being busted*
by the police

published several of his poems, prompting André Breton, the Pope of Sur-realism, to call Lamantia "a voice that rises once in a hundred years."[118] Lamantia responded by boarding a train for New York and working for the next year as an assistant editor at *View*. When the war in Europe ended, many Surrealist emigrés returned home, and Lamantia recalled it as "a time of almost immeasurable anguish, and I felt I was absolutely isolated and living in a vacuum."[119]

On his return to San Francisco, Lamantia found fellow spirits at Kenneth Rexroth's gatherings and in the contributors to *Circle* magazine. But by 1949 he had begun a peripatetic existence, with periods of Mexico, Morocco, and France punctuated by returns home to San Francisco. (During a stay in New York, he frequented the San Remo, where he met Carl Solomon, Jack Kerouac, and Allen Ginsberg.) In his travels, Lamantia participated in Washo Indian peyote rituals—a form of derangement of the senses—and felt transfigured by "an extraordinary connectedness with others; with everything."[120] He battled depression and mania and sheer physical burnout. His poems reflected his alienation from the age of nuclear apocalypse and his belief in the transforming powers of magic and eros. On his return to San Francisco in the fall of 1955, he read at the epochal Six Gallery gathering. "Lamantia was the most beautiful and luminous of us all," observed Michael McClure, "and he radiated inspired 'vocal rage' and imagination."[121]

By the end of the 1950s, Lamantia had decided to stop writing and spent the next decade in Europe, studying and choosing poems for publication of his selected *oeuvre* by Penguin and for City Lights. He resumed writing and continues today in his North Beach home.

PHILIP WHALEN The Falstaffian figure of the San Francisco Renaissance was Philip Whalen. Older, larger, and more universally liked than his fellow poets, he managed to balance bawdy humor and easygoing style with strict Zen Buddhist principles and writing discipline. Born October 29, 1923, he grew up in a small town on the Columbia River and wrote his first poem in high school—"something about birds, the stars, and tra-la-la" in free verse.[122] Taking William Carlos Williams as his

Surrealists and Expatriates in New York, 1940s
André Breton
Max Ernst
Charles Henri Ford
Peggy Guggenheim
David Hare
Fernand Léger
Piet Mondrian
Yves Tanguy
Pavel Tchelitchew

I have always dreamed of the ultimate triumph of the sirens . . .
—Philip Lamantia

Philip Whalen's Bookshelf
William Carlos Williams
Gertrude Stein
Thomas Wolfe
D. T. Suzuki

model, he hoped to make a living as a doctor and write as an avocation, but that plan was abandoned when his family couldn't afford medical school. Whalen's post–high school years included jobs as an office boy, a laborer, and an Army Air Corps draftee. The Army gave him the opportunity to sit in the nose of a B-17 while reading Gertrude Stein and writing in his notebook, and the GI Bill gave him the chance to attend Reed College, where he connected with Gary Snyder and Lew Welch.

Like his roommates, Whalen was inspired by Portland's small bohemian community and encouraged by William Carlos Williams' 1950 poetry reading. Whalen had no coherent ideas about his vocational future after college: "I was going to scuffle," he recalled.[123] His pattern over the next few years was to work only when absolutely necessary, depending on friends and spending his summers in a fire lookout station in the Mount Baker National Forest. It was there, in September 1955, that he received a letter from Gary Snyder, inviting him to read at the Six Gallery.

That epochal reading in October brought Whalen into a much larger community of poets, which encouraged him to experiment with his own poetry. He acknowledged the effect of seeing the "Howl" manuscript on his early poem "Sourdough Mountain Lookout," for example, prompting the realization that it was "possible for a poem to be its own shape and size."[124] After a few seasons of the San Francisco Renaissance, he had both deepened his interest in Zen Buddhism and thrown off the strictures of the Imagist-inspired poetry he had written. Perhaps better than anyone else, Whalen captured, in a single running sentence, the impact of the heady San Francisco literary atmosphere:

> Other people's ideas of beauty or conventional notions about beauty in any kind of art were being blasted out of my head by new music and new jazz and new poetry that Allen was actually doing and that Gregory was doing and that Jack was doing and

then there were these fantastic letters coming in at rare intervals from North Africa from Burroughs to Allen and Allen was reading them aloud and I was looking at them and they popped my head in another direction.[125]

Portrait of Philip Whalen, called Buddha Red-Ears, *signed "Jean Louis Kerouac," ca. 1956*

Robert Creeley at the helm, Majorca, 1951, by Jonathan Williams

Swinging: uninhibited: "If you don't swing that thing it don't mean a thing."

ROBERT CREELEY Robert Creeley spent only three months in San Francisco—he arrived in March 1956 and departed for New Mexico in June. However brief his stay, Creeley's involvement in the Renaissance was both instrumental and varied: he typed the stencils for the pre–City Lights, informal publication of "Howl" to be passed around among friends; he organized, with Allen Ginsberg, the first major roundup of the San Francisco poets and the Beats, who appeared alongside the Black Mountain poets in the seventh and final issue of *Black Mountain Review*; he got into several fistfights and spent time in jail; and he contributed to the marital break-up of Kenneth and Marthe Rexroth's marriage. It was a great deal for so little time and for a person of such apparently laconic temperament.

Creeley's background paralleled that of Allen Ginsberg, if one simply substituted Harvard for Columbia, Charles Olson for William Carlos Williams. Born in 1926 in Arlington, Massachusetts, Creeley, like Ginsberg, had gone through a disorienting childhood, had been briefly suspended during his undergraduate years, began smoking marijuana before the age of twenty, and helped edit undergraduate magazines. Creeley dropped out in his final year to drive a truck for the American Field Service in the India–Burma theater of World War II. When he returned in 1946, Creeley married and had three children. He tried living among the Provincetown bohemian community; he struggled with subsistence pigeon and chicken farming in Littleton, New Hampshire. Throughout this period his sense of himself as a writer was minimal—"It was just an imaginative possibility that I really wanted to try to get to"—and in retrospect, he felt he had learned more about poetry from being a pigeon breeder than from all his years at Harvard—he gained a sense of "how to pay attention."[126]

In his undergraduate years, Creeley searched for the usable past in avant-garde poetry. He discovered William Carlos Williams at the age of eighteen, and, as if prophetically, on his twentieth birthday he was given Ezra Pound's *Make It New*. He called the book a "revelation," because Pound "spoke of writing from the point of view of what writing itself was engaged with, not what it was 'about.'"[127] He entered modern poetry's social network in 1950, when he tried to launch a little magazine. The proposal elicited from little-magazine veteran Ezra Pound his classic advice about running a little magazine:

> He suggested I think of the magazine as a center around which, "not a box within which/any item." He proposed that verse con-

Creeley is a genius of the sensorium as Kerouac was and he is a master of the ear as is Miles Davis.
—Michael McClure, on Robert Creeley

Robert Creeley's Bookshelf
William Carlos Williams
Ezra Pound
Hart Crane
André Gide (especially the journals)
Henry Miller
D. H. Lawrence
Wallace Stevens
Paul Valéry
Charles Olson (after 1950)

sisted of a constant and a variant, and then told me to think from that to the context of a magazine. He suggested I get at least four others, on whom I could depend unequivocally for material, and to make the work the mainstay of the magazine's form. But then, he said, let the rest of it, roughly half, be as various and hogwild as possible.[128]

The magazine never got published and Pound reassured "the Creel" that he could wait before "He highflyz as editor."[129] Creeley took the submitted material to Cid Corman, who hosted a weekly radio program called "This Is Poetry"; he used some of Creeley's solicited material to launch *Origin*, which was for several years one of the only non-Establishment poetry outlets. From his attempts to start a magazine he also began correspondences with William Carlos Williams, Denise Levertov, and, most important, Charles Olson, the towering rector of Black Mountain College.

When Creeley initially criticized Olson's poetry as diffusely "looking around for a language," Olson forthrightly replied:

i says, creeley, you're
off yr trolley: a man
god damn well has to come up with his own lang., syntax and song both,
but also each poem under hand has its own language, which is variant of
same[130]

The friendship that began in 1950 continued until Olson's death twenty years later; Olson provided a stimulating mentor. Through Olson, Creeley was invited to teach at Black Mountain College and to edit the *Black Mountain Review*. Founded in 1933, Black Mountain College in North Carolina functioned as America's preeminent school for the avant-garde: its faculty included many expatriates from Nazi Germany and students in the 1950s included Robert Rauschenberg and Cy Twombly. By the mid-1950s, the college was in crisis—enrollment hovered uneasily around fifteen students, the faculty hadn't been paid for a year, and survival depended on raising vegetables and stealing from the local A & P. Paradoxically, this period became one of the most influential times in the college's history. Among the poets involved during the college's final years were not only Olson and Creeley but also Robert Duncan, John Wieners,

Black Mountain Students
Fielding Dawson
Joel Oppenheimer
Robert Rauschenberg
Cy Twombly
Jonathan Williams

Life at Black Mountain College: Dan Rice in the barrel and Robert Creeley on the toilet, 1954, by Jonathan Williams

Jonathan Williams, and Joel Oppenheimer. The Black Mountain community regarded the artist and the poet as holy, and the rest of the world as hopelessly corrupt.

In March 1954, Creeley arrived at the pastoral lakeside setting of Black Mountain College after an all-night drive in a 1940 pickup truck. Creeley had never taught in his life, but that evening he conducted his first class. Teaching seemed disastrous; Creeley was drinking heavily and feeling desperate about the aimless course of his life. He felt in tune with his surroundings, described as "a kind of almost useful desperation of things that gave people a more active context."[131] Students sometimes had to pick him up at the local tavern and bodily force him into the classroom. But Creeley observed after a long career in teaching, "I never found a more useful context for being a teacher than I did there."[132]

As important as his teaching was Creeley's editing of the *Black Mountain Review*. Charles Olson hoped the magazine would revive the school's reputation, but the budget could barely afford the $500 needed for each of its sixty-four-page issues. The print run never exceeded 500 copies, and the poets were unknown to the world at large, but the magazine proved to be the seminal poetry magazine of the mid-1950s; it even gave rise to a historically designated group known as the Black Mountain poets. Creeley included not only poetry and criticism but also images of paintings and photographs by such figures as Franz Kline, Philip Guston, Harry Callahan, and Aaron Siskind. Black Mountain College closed in September 1956, but by then Creeley had been gone for months. "I wanted a new condition and so went west," Creeley wrote, "where I'd never been, to see if that might be an answer."[133]

The San Francisco poetry community embraced Creeley within hours of his arrival; McClure and Whalen elicited reports on Olson, and he grew close to Kerouac and Ginsberg. Feeling depleted and rootless when he arrived in San Francisco, he found in this poetry constellation a

It was our Bible.
—Michael Rumaker, on the
Black Mountain Review

Expelled and imploding . . .
—Charles Olson, on the closing
of Black Mountain College

buoying sense of possibility and freedom. As he later recalled, "For a writer there was really no place that could have been quite like it, just at that time."[134] Kerouac helped free him from the imposition of plot, Snyder offered a mystical potential of hope, Ginsberg gave him permission to include emotions more expansively in his poetry. Before he left in the summer of 1956, Creeley's work had become somewhat looser, freed from the strictures of his laconic purity.

The most concrete result of his visit was the epochal final issue of *Black Mountain Review*. Published in the fall of 1957, it ran 240 pages and conjoined the Beats, the San Francisco poets, and the Black Mountain poets. The issue marked, as Creeley wrote, "unequivocally a shift and opening of the previous center, and finally as good a place as any to end."[135]

BOB KAUFMAN "Bob Kaufman's life is written on mirrors in smoke," observed Jack Kerouac.[136] The poet appeared to be the iconic marginal man—mute, disheveled, wandering the streets of San Francisco's North Beach trailing ZigZag rolling papers and poems, smelling of vodka and orange juice. He was also a revered poet—especially in Europe, where the French called him "the Black American Rimbaud" and the Germans called him "Reisingross" (giant).

From the outset, Bob Kaufman presented an unlikely combination; he was the son of a German Orthodox Jew and an African-American Catholic from Martinique. He had twelve siblings, and he left them all at the age of thirteen to join the merchant marine. Over the next twenty years he circled the world nine times and survived four shipwrecks. A first mate became his shipboard mentor, encouraging the sailor's self-education in the great books, and Kaufman steeped himself in Hart Crane, Walt Whitman, García Lorca, and T. S. Eliot. In 1954 he ended his world travel, set-

Black Mountain Review **#7**
William Burroughs
Robert Creeley
Allen Ginsberg
Jack Kerouac
Denise Levertov
Michael McClure
Charles Olson
Joel Oppenheimer
Gary Snyder
Philip Whalen
Jonathan Williams

Bob Kaufman's Bookshelf
T. S. Eliot
Hart Crane
Federico García Lorca
Nikolai Lenin
Karl Marx
Walt Whitman

Bob Kaufman at twenty-nine, after nine trips around the world, San Francisco, 1954, by Chester Kessler

Bring down: *to depress, from the 1940s: "Don't bring me down." Used as a noun, it means a drag: "If you come right to the point, they [tea heads] say you are a 'bring down.'" [Burroughs]*

tling in San Francisco, where he would live for the remaining thirty-two years of his life.

Kaufman entered the San Francisco scene at a propitious moment, shortly before the poetry explosion at the Six Gallery reading. City Lights first published him—a broadside, *Abomunist Manifesto*, in 1959—and New Directions published his first collection of poems, *Solitude Crowded with Loneliness*, in 1965. Kaufman's central position in the San Francisco Renaissance exceeded his literary output. He played the shaman-like role often found in avant-garde groups—the figure who is most purely dispossessed, most unimpeachably alienated. His commitment to anarchism and freedom of expression was total, and he repeatedly clashed with the police. The most famous of those clashes occurred in August 1959, when the police ripped from the window of the Co-Existence Bagel Shop one of Kaufman's poems; it described the day that Hitler "moved to San Francisco, became an ordinary/policeman, devoted himself to stamping out Beatniks."[137]

Bob Kaufman's importance increased significantly in the years after the poets' exodus from San Francisco began in 1956. With Ginsberg, Corso, Kerouac, Snyder, and Whalen all departed, Kaufman became the movement's guiding force. He helped found *Beatitude* magazine in the spring of 1959. Devoted to undeservedly unpublished poets, the magazine lasted a year. Kaufman, however, became an increasingly iconic figure, both in North Beach and in Europe. In 1963, in the wake of John F. Kennedy's assassination and another battle with the police, Kaufman took a vow of silence that he maintained for ten years. During this period he was sometimes described as the silent "guardian of the center."[138]

When he died of emphysema at sixty, Kaufman left three thin volumes and three poetry broadsides. In honor of his birthplace, he was accorded a New Orleans–style Dixieland band funeral; all the stopping points along the funeral route—the coffee houses and bars where Kaufman had read—evoked the San Francisco Renaissance at its zenith. According to local legend, as Kaufman's ashes were scattered into the San Francisco Bay, to the accompaniment of Charlie Parker's "Just You, Just Me," a seven-color rainbow appeared in an utterly clear sky.

THE RENAISSANCE IN HIGH GEAR The San Francisco Renaissance flourished most intimately in the year after the Six Gallery reading, and in the next year it became a public phenomenon. Just as its beginning would be associated with the first reading of "Howl," its notoriety was associated with City Lights' publication and the Police Department's censorship of the poem. Even Robert Duncan—who had once walked out of a Ginsberg

Frisco is mad, absolutely mad and almost perfect city at the end of the American continent and culture.
—Jack Kerouac

Lawrence Ferlinghetti, Bruce Lipincott, and Kenneth Rexroth at the Cellar, ca. 1957, by Ed Nyberg

reading with hands over his head and had banned him from the home he shared with Jess—acknowledged the poem's embodiment of an era: "When 'Howl' was written and suddenly everyone rightly recognized that that was the age of 'Howl'—like Eliot was the age of 'The Waste Land' from 1920 clear through the end of the thirties."[139]

Just as "Howl" became a literary focal point, North Beach became the Renaissance's geographic center, subject to buses filled with gawking tourists who clogged Grant Avenue. San Francisco bohemia had been around for a few decades, but for the first time San Francisco bohemians were treated like creatures in a zoo. The peripatetic beatnik could wander along Grant Avenue from the Co-Existence Bagel Shop to the Cassadra (for twenty-cent Zen soup) to City Lights Bookstore, and finally to The Place, the archetypal artist-writer-bohemian hangout. Michael McClure called it "the Deux Magots of Frisco."[140] It was not only the locals' community bar but also the setting for music, poetry readings, and informal art exhibitions. On the walls hung Jay DeFeo's postexistential gouaches or Robert LaVigne's paintings of flowers, an "imaginary garden of consciousness,"[141] along with Allen Ginsberg's poetry. The Place provided a forum for amateur poets on Blabbermouth Night—any customer could rise and recite a poem. The denizens of The Place were not only poets but also artists and filmmakers, for the community was sufficiently small and impoverished to be inclusive, an enclave of marginal figures separated from the square world. And the San Francisco Renaissance, like most movements that are described as a "renaissance," encompassed not only poets but painters, filmmakers, performers, and local characters. Most of them worked in straight jobs—as porters, bartenders, proofreaders, typists, models, merchant seamen—which freed their art from the demands of commerce and the straitjacket of profession. Many developed a distinct sartorial style that included faded black pants with loose threads at the cuff, tee-shirts, baggy sweaters, peasant blouses, and long hair. (Outside North Beach, the long-haired men were sometimes greeted with the epithet "queer," whether they were homosexual or not.)

Flourishing at the center of the Renaissance was Allen Ginsberg. At this moment in his life he was surrounded by old friends (Kerouac, Cassady, Corso) and a new fraternity of poets; he enjoyed a domestic life in a rose-covered cottage in Berkeley, a lover, literary recognition, and the chance to write full time. This happy confluence, so long denied, contributed to a period of extraordinary productivity: within six months, Gins-

Everything you tell me about Frisco sounds like U.S. Inferno.
—William Burroughs to Allen Ginsberg

We were all trying to get the exact style of ourselves.
—Michael McClure, on the San Francisco Renaissance

Artists in the Bay Area, 1950s
Wallace Berman
Elmer Bischoff
Joan Brown
Jess [Collins]
Bruce Conner
Jay DeFeo
Richard Diebenkorn
George Herms
Robert LaVigne
Manuel Neri
David Park
Mark Rothko
Clyfford Still

Filmmakers
Jordan Belson
Stan Brakhage
James Broughton
Larry Jordan
Ron Rice
Harry Smith

*I am beginning to think he's a great
saint, a great saint concealed in a
veneer of daemonism.*
——Jack Kerouac, on Allen Ginsberg

berg wrote several of the poems for which he is best known: "Footnote to Howl," "America," "Sunflower Sutra," "A Supermarket in California." In contrast to the intense labor and rewriting of his previous poems, this newest work seemed to roll spontaneously from his mind onto the page. "Sunflower Sutra," for instance, took shape in twenty minutes, as Kerouac and Ginsberg sat beside a littered canal, and Ginsberg almost extemporaneously delivered what Kerouac called "a great sad sutra speech about a grime-covered sunflower."[142]

In addition to Ginsberg's poetic development, his adolescent aspiration to become a labor leader found expression in his new role spearheading the phalanx of West Coast poets. "Maybe I'm too busybody, I don't know," Ginsberg said. "My own view was the old communist thing of 'in unity there is strength,' that we had to fight the whole Western capitalist culture, and the poets all out to be together . . . a certain poets' republic."[143] Two qualities run through Ginsburg's efforts as advanced poetry's booster. First, he was radically inclusive, trying to make common cause with the Black Mountain poets, both generations of San Francisco poets, and the New York School exemplified by Frank O'Hara and John Ashbery. Second, he used his life as an exhibitionistic and apocalyptic platform for the revolution of the word, the politics of sex, the mind-expanding potential of drugs, and the evils of capitalism. Ginsberg promoted younger poets through disparate publication venues. Some of them represented the hip, little-magazine tradition of the avant-garde (he coedited the Beat-related final issue of the *Black Mountain Review* and encouraged a San Francisco issue of the *Evergreen Review*); some of them represented the literary establishment (Ginsberg gave interviews to the *New York Times*, championed poets' work to the editors of the *Partisan Review* and the *Hudson Review*); some represented mass media popular culture (such as *Mademoiselle*). He praised his friends' work to such disparate celebrities as W. H. Auden and John Huston, Edith Sitwell and Louis-Ferdinand Céline, he

Filmmaker Larry Jordan and poets Michael McClure and Philip Lamantia, ca. 1957. Poster by Robert LaVigne, pose by Jordan, shutter snapped by Bruce Conner

read on BBC radio and threw benefit readings in support of such mentors as William Burroughs and William Carlos Williams. Herb Gold derisively called Ginsberg "the greatest publicist for a literary fashion since Ezra Pound made it big with imagism,"[144] and some poets resented Ginsberg's self-appointed leadership. But—as with Pound and the Imagists—they would have been markedly less visible without his promotion, and San Francisco's poetry renaissance might have remained a strictly local phenomenon. For the doors that had been closed to Ginsberg the poet were opened wide to Ginsberg the newly notorious celebrity.

The omelet fell apart, as with such eggs it must.
—Wilfrid Sheed, on the San Francisco Renaissance

THE WANING RENAISSANCE The Six Gallery reading not only catalyzed the Renaissance but destabilized San Francisco's literary community. Its convivial unity had been bolstered by its position somewhere eternally in the wings of the literary Establishment. Now that the spotlight was focused on San Francisco, poets found it more difficult to refrain from competing for the light. Coteries developed. Some poets muttered about Lawrence Ferlinghetti when he rejected their poems for publication by City Lights. When Ginsberg and Snyder read at several colleges in the Northwest, Kerouac exclaimed, "Ginsby boy, he's all over Oregon like horseshit howling his dirty pome."[145] Janet Richards recalled the inevitable jockeying, of "who's really *in* now? Is everybody making a switch from putting down Michael McClure to putting down Gary Snyder instead? Should one be leaning toward Lawrence Ferlinghetti? Jack Spicer? The Black Mountain poets? Kenneth Rexroth? Nobody ever put down Allen Ginsberg, nobody ever put down Jack Kerouac. Even the ignorant-anxious didn't care to put down geniuses."[146]

Success, alas, as it almost always does, led to the worst kind of emotional suicide. Those to whom that kind of success was a temptation have become the trained monkeys, the clowning helots of the enemy.
—Kenneth Rexroth

Some of the forefathers—notably Brother Antoninus, Jack Spicer, and Robert Duncan—expressed misgivings about the young poets' identification with the "Renaissance" label that had once been applied to them.

The different standard of propriety that characterized the older generation is exemplified in these discrepant memories of a visit by Robert Duncan to Allen Ginsberg. Jack Kerouac's handwritten "The Essentials of Spontaneous Prose" was taped to the wall, and Ginsberg was gratified to see how much care Duncan took in reading them. Duncan recalled that he wanted to look at *anything* to avoid looking at Ginsberg, who was in his underwear. "While Allen is blissfully seeing this in angelic dream," Duncan said, "I'm standing like your maiden aunt."[147]

Other San Francisco poets felt that the movement had been taken over by carpetbaggers, simply a new version of the East Coast literary mafia. The Easterners who had lived in San Francisco included Allen Ginsberg, Jack Kerouac, Gregory Corso, Robert Creeley, and John Wieners. Ginsberg recalled resentment of their domination—while thinking, "we were arriving as reinforcements rather than competition at the time."[148] But at their exhilarating best, Michael McClure recalled their conflicts as "once-in-a-lifetime arguments, where everybody basically settles out their individuality, so that you know who you are and always in the future you're going to know why you are. If there's a few bruises you're still going to be friends."[149]

In the wake of Black Mountain College's demise in September 1956, its orphans arrived in town. Many of them were cast in Robert Duncan's evolving work-in-progress, *Medea*, but the effort disintegrated shortly after their arrival in San Francisco. They stayed on, hanging out in a bar run by two former Black Mountain students, Knute Stiles and Leo Krikorian. Both Ginsberg and Corso felt conflict with the newcomers. Ginsberg applauded their openness but considered them "suicidal," "cocksmen," and "hung up on authority like Ezra Pound." Corso was characteristically blunter—he called them "mental gangsters . . . hip squares."[150]

Corso and Kerouac were regarded as exemplars of bad manners. Sometimes it was a matter of loud, surly drunkenness and other times of a

Here we were all being tagged San Francisco or beat poets in 1955, which made no sense, and a lot of people resented it, but it did bring new attention to the scene.
—William Everson/Brother Antoninus

They came to us late, from the slums of Greenwich Village, and they departed early, for the salons of millionairesses.
—Kenneth Rexroth

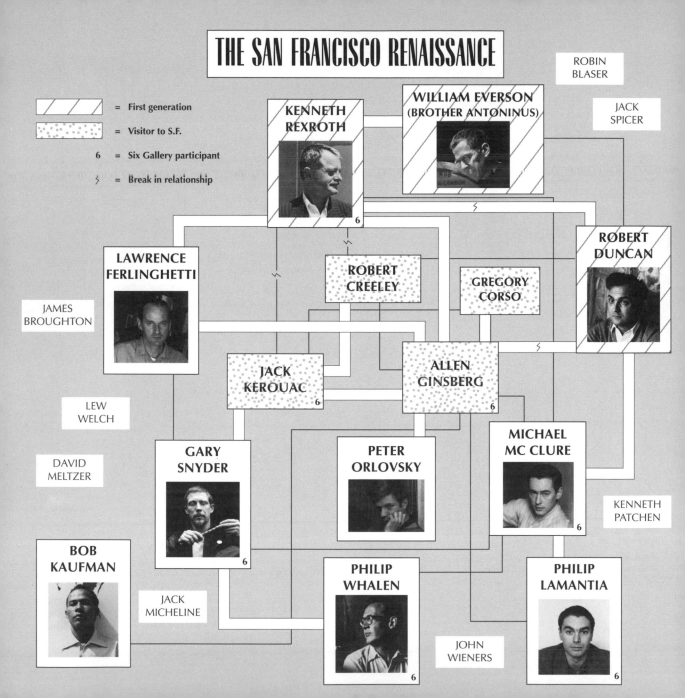

THE SAN FRANCISCO RENAISSANCE

ROBIN BLASER

JACK SPICER

= First generation

= Visitor to S.F.

6 = Six Gallery participant

⌇ = Break in relationship

KENNETH REXROTH 6

WILLIAM EVERSON (BROTHER ANTONINUS)

ROBERT DUNCAN

LAWRENCE FERLINGHETTI

ROBERT CREELEY

GREGORY CORSO

JAMES BROUGHTON

JACK KEROUAC 6

ALLEN GINSBERG 6

LEW WELCH

MICHAEL MC CLURE 6

DAVID MELTZER

GARY SNYDER 6

PETER ORLOVSKY

KENNETH PATCHEN

BOB KAUFMAN

JACK MICHELINE

PHILIP WHALEN 6

PHILIP LAMANTIA 6

JOHN WIENERS

different style that became a fad. "Kerouac was simply naturally rude," observed Janet Richards, "and young people imitated his style, perfectly unaffected in him, and as such quite heroically romantic and seductive, and they debased it."[151] There developed something the older generation dubbed "the Beat putdown," a mixture of churlishness and cool.

Most personally destructive to a sense of Renaissance hegemony was the anguish and vituperation of Kenneth Rexroth. He had been the Beats' sponsor and the master of ceremonies at the Six Gallery reading, but the first cracks in his support could be seen not long after. Rexroth invited Allen Ginsberg, Philip Whalen, Jack Kerouac, and Gary Snyder to dinner. When they arrived, very late and fairly drunk, Kerouac demanded wine, and called Rexroth a "boche."[152] Ginsberg declared that he was a better poet than Rexroth, and furthermore he had youth on his side. Before Marthe Rexroth brought out dinner, Rexroth dismissed the guests.

Rexroth's disenchantment with the Beats took a sharp upturn after Robert Creeley came to San Francisco in March 1956. Creeley and Marthe Rexroth quickly fell in love. The Berkeley orgies Kenneth Rexroth imagined—with his wife, Creeley, Kerouac, and Ginsberg as amorous participants—were fictional, but the romantic feelings between Creeley and Marthe Rexroth, as well as Rexroth's pain, were utterly real. Rexroth became suicidal and soon directed his maniacally agitated paranoia toward the Beats. As he screamed one day when Ginsberg telephoned, "I feel as if I walked into a candystore and got beaten up by a bunch of juvenile delinquents."[153]

Ginsberg would take some of the flak (Rexroth declared that Ginsberg had written himself out), and Rexroth later described the Beat Generation as just a hallucination of the Luce empire. But Rexroth's fury focused on Kerouac, whom he pegged as a panderer in the affair between Marthe Rexroth and Creeley. Before meeting Kerouac, on the basis of his "Jazz of the Beat Generation," Rexroth had ranked him on a par with Cé-

The North Beach hangouts

line and Genet. After the Creeley–Marthe Rexroth affair, his estimation of Kerouac would drop progressively lower, until his reviews became repeated snide putdowns that bespoke something other than literary criticism. (Reviewing Kerouac's poetry, for example, he called Kerouac's version of Buddha "a dimestore incense burner, glowing and glowering sinisterly in the dark corner of a Beatnik pad and just thrilling the wits out of bad little girls."[154])

The most vivid vignette of that era is the long farewell party for Gary Snyder in late April 1956. Snyder, about to sail for Japan on the next stage of his Zen journey, was sharing with Kerouac a small burlap-lined cabin at the end of a hillside horse pasture in Corte Madera, in Marin County. On a Saturday afternoon, about forty guests drove up from the city, and among them were Kenneth Rexroth, Alan Watts, Allen Ginsberg, Peter Orlovsky, Robert Creeley, Philip Lamantia, and Philip Whalen.

Some stayed in the big house listening to Cal Tjader records on

Jack Kerouac and Philip Whalen at Gary Snyder's going-away party, Locke McCorckle's house in Corte Madera, April 1956, by Walter Lehrman

the hi-fi. Kerouac wrote a few days later, "and in the other room wild women are dancing as Creeley of Acton Massachusets and I of Lowell beat."[155] Some sat on long logs around a bonfire, passing marijuana pipes and jugs of California burgundy under the eucalyptus, while Rexroth held forth. Several listened to a recording of Henry Miller, and Ginsberg recalled that it "endeared him to everyone that there was this great literary genius talking in a Brooklyn accent."[156] Creeley recalled "Allen and Peter charmingly dancing naked among a dense pack of clothed bodies, flowers at the prom!"[157] The party continued the next day, beginning with Snyder banging a frying pan and chanting the "Gocchami" chant to announce that pancakes were being served. By the time the dwindling party continued into a third day, it was clear that no one was ready to say goodbye, either to Gary Snyder or to that happy era of the San Francisco Renaissance. To Kerouac, his friends were already becoming phantoms—looking at their sleeping figures he wondered, "Who were all these strange ghosts rooted to the silly little adventure of earth with me?"[158]

Kerouac and Snyder took a last hike together, and Kerouac showed his translations of Buddhist prayers he called "The Diamondcutter of Ideal Wisdom," printed in a notebook just small enough to fit in a rucksack pocket. Snyder departed on May 5, 1956, for Japan, where he would spend most of the next twelve years of his life studying Zen and writing poetry. At the pier, Kerouac handed him a going-away gift, a tiny scrap of paper on which he had carefully printed, "MAY YOU USE THE DIAMOND CUTTER OF MERCY."[159] It was the last time Kerouac ever saw Snyder.

Beatitude magazine, organized by Ginsberg, Bob Kaufman, John Kelly, and William Margolis, was the last publication associated with the San Francisco Renaissance, and many historians mark its end in June 1960 as the final chapter of the Renaissance. The demise of the tightly knit community was vividly felt. The North Beach haunts had been transformed into record stores and sandal-and-jewelry shops. As Ralph J. Glea-

Cover of Beatitude, *September/October 1959*

Liz, Lizzie: *a lesbian: "I was beat that way one time in Marrakesh. Citizen passed a transvestite Jew Lizzie on me as an Abyssinian prince." [Burroughs]*

son recalled, "The great diaspora began like chunks of ice slipping away from an iceberg entering warm waters, a few at a time and then a grand rush."[160] The community fanned out to Big Sur and nearby Bolinas in Northern California, to Venice Beach and New York. Ginsberg and Corso each went abroad, Kerouac returned to his mother, Gary Snyder pursued

Last gathering of the Beat Generation, City Lights Bookstore, 1965, by Larry Keenan. Front row, left to right: Robert LaVigne, Shig Murao, Larry Fagin, Leland Meyezove (lying down), Lew Welch, Peter Orlovsky. Second row, left to right: David Meltzer, Michael McClure, Allen Ginsberg, Daniel Langton, a friend of Ginsberg, Richard Brautigan, Gary Goodrow, Nemi Frost. Back row: Stella Levy, Lawrence Ferlinghetti

his study of Zen Buddhism in Japan, Philip Whalen moved to Oregon. Michael McClure remained in the Bay Area and, with his movie star looks, became a glamorous figure associated with Bob Dylan and the Hell's Angels; he wrote a play, *The Beard* (1965), that fomented several censorship scandals, and he continues to live in the East Bay Hills, writing, teaching, and performing his poetry. Bob Kaufman became an iconic figure of the Renaissance, as much for his saintly, utterly marginal existence and his fights for free speech as for his poetry.

TANGIERS ON JUNK When William Burroughs, still in Tangiers, finally received a letter from Allen Ginsberg in Mexico in May 1954, he'd become addicted to Eukodol, a synthetic form of codeine. Its initial euphoric burst was more like cocaine than heroin and outstripped any heroin in Burroughs' experience. He showed up at the pharmacy each day for a new box of ampules until the druggists no longer extended credit. The vein he hit each day stayed open, "like a red, festering mouth, swollen and obscene."[161] His shooting schedule went from every four hours to every two hours, and his monthly allowance and finally his typewriter went for drugs. Venturing out into the medina, Burroughs experienced paranoid hallucinations. Late one night, after shooting six ampules, he reported, "The ex-captain found me sitting stark naked in the hall on the toilet seat (which I had wrenched from its moorings), playing in a bucket of water and singing 'Deep in the Heart of Texas,' at the same time complaining in clearly enunciated tones, of the high cost of living—'It all goes into razor blades.'"[162] Narratives about addiction follow the classic form of descent, touching bottom, and renunciation or death, and Burroughs' story varied from this scheme only in its details—notably the length of time he bumped along the bottom and his steadfast refusal to renounce the value of his drug experience.

I am getting so far out one day I won't come back at all.
—William Burroughs

M: morphine; M.S.: morphine sulfate, the morphine salt most commonly used in the United States

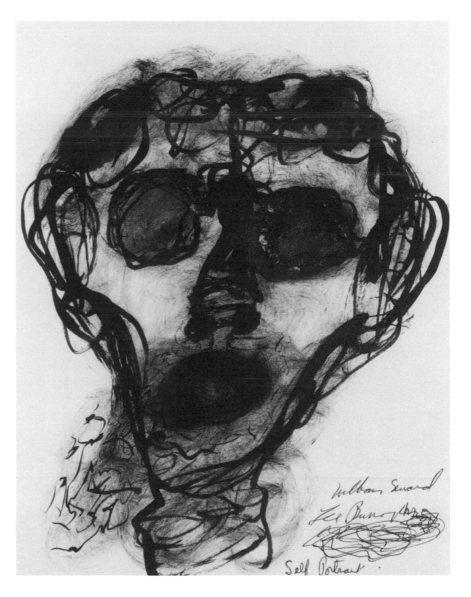

William Burroughs' self-portrait, ca. 1959

Writing became Burroughs' other addiction. Alone in his room, he unloaded his mind onto page after page of yellow foolscap, rolling on the floor and laughing at his production. He could imagine no literary form for his routines, and attempts to organize them into a novel were painful. "What am I trying to do in writing?" he asked himself. "This novel is about transitions, larval forms, emergent telepathic faculty, attempts to control and stifle new forms. . . . I feel there is some hideous new force loose in the world like a creeping sickness, spreading, blighting."[163] A piece he wrote in the 1950s reflects the desperation behind his frenetic activity:

> At the present time writing appears to me as an absolute necessity, and at the same time I have a feeling that my talent is lost and I can accomplish nothing, a feeling like the body's knowledge of disease which the mind tries to evade and deny.
>
> This feeling of horror is always with me now. I had the same feeling the day Joan died, and once when I was a child, I looked out into the hall, and such a feeling of fear and despair came over me for no outward reason, that I burst into tears.
>
> I was looking into the future then. I recognize the feeling, and what I saw has not yet been realized. I can only wait for it to happen. Is it some ghastly occurrence, like Joan's death, or simply deterioration and failure and final loneliness, a dead-end set-up where there is no-one I can contact? I am just a crazy old bore in a bar somewhere with my routines? I don't know but I feel trapped and doomed.[164]

The people in Tangiers who might have appreciated Burroughs' black wit—notably Paul Bowles—avoided the gray, spectral figure, and the expatriates and street characters with whom he associated couldn't understand his writing. Ginsberg offered the only escape from this trap; he was Burroughs' psychological support and link to the outside world. "I always

Tanger is the prognostic pulse of the world, like a dream extending from past into the future, a frontier between dream and reality—the "reality" of both called into question.
—William Burroughs

Chinese cure: a method of drug-use reduction involving distilling decreasing amounts of heroin in Wampole's Tonic, eventually injecting pure Wampole's Tonic

Paul Bowles, author, composer, musicologist, friend of William Burroughs, Tangiers, 1961, by Allen Ginsberg

In short, the intelligentsia of Tangiers has put me in Coventry.
—William Burroughs, on his social expulsion

There is nothing stronger than dream, because dreams are forms of THE LAW.
—William Burroughs to Allen Ginsberg

like keep a letter to you on the stove and put in miscellaneous ideas, a sort of running diary," Burroughs wrote Ginsberg. "Maybe the real novel is letters to you."[165] His correspondence provided the crucible in which Burroughs parlayed and then analyzed the "routines" that seemed to come to him like dictation from his unconscious. Some of them derived from his past—the late Phil White, for example, was resurrected as "Sailor." He distinguished a routine from other literary devices by its ever present potential for danger and its inclusion of the author. "One thing, it is not *completely symbolic*," he wrote, "that is, it is subject to shlup over into 'real' action at any time (like cutting off finger joint and so forth)."[166]

THE CURE   One day, gazing at the empty Eukodol cartons scattered about his room, William Burroughs recalled, "I suddenly realized I was not doing *anything*. I was dying."[167] By 1955, Burroughs had gone through repeated attempts to kick his habit. He had hired his boyfriend Kiki to lock him in his room and hide his clothes away; he had checked into hospitals in Spain and Tangiers; he had undergone prolonged, medicated sleep, quick and slow reductions of morphine, regimens of antihistamines and amorphine. Addiction always resumed. He had heard about an apomorphine treatment devised in England by Dr. John Yerbury Dent—the only treatment that metabolically regulated the cell's physiology. To clear up accumulated debts and provide fare to London, Burroughs solicited $500 from his parents; their delay in supplying money was understandable.

Burroughs checked into Dr. Dent's clinic—only two patients were admitted at a time—in March 1956. Within seven days he reduced from 30 grains of morphine to 0, while receiving apomorphine shots every four hours. The withdrawal was as painful and symptomatic as usual, and for the first four days Burroughs didn't sleep. But the doctor regularly visited him through the wracking hours of the night, from 2 AM to 5 AM. Burroughs described him as "a real croaker, interested in Yage, Mayan archeology every conceivable subject,"[168] who harbored no illusions about the value of "will power." After the treatment was concluded, Burroughs vowed, as he had many times before: "This time I'll make it if it kills me."[169] And this time he did.

He returned to Tangiers to set up a new life at the Villa Muniria— a.k.a. the Villa Delirium and "the original anything goes joint."[170] He rented a single room off a walled garden; it contained a single bed, a $46 typewriter, a small spirit stove, and, in the corner, an orgone box. A taped-together collage of photographs from his yage expedition covered one wall, and another pitted wall was used for target practice.

Burroughs maintained a strict daily regimen. After a simple breakfast of tea and bread, he did situps and then rowed, standing up, Venetian style, in the choppy waters of the Tangiers bay. He returned home about noon. He ate a ball of his homemade *majoun*, washed it down with tea, set out a row of marijuana joints, sat down to his typewriter, and, as he later recalled, "For the first time in my life I began writing full time."[171]

He often prepared by sitting in his orgone box, smoking marijuana,

A shot of Eukodol is like a hot bath that isn't quite hot enough, if you dig me.
—William Burroughs

I'm running out of everything now. Out of veins, out of money.
—William Burroughs

Get off that Junk wagon, boys, it's going down a three mile grade for the junk heap.
—William Burroughs

Recipe for Majoun
Mix finely chopped marijuana with cinnamon, honey, caraway seeds, and ground nutmeg. Cook slowly until it assumes a taffy-like consistency.
—Traditional

and then he began typing at top speed, high for six hours, cackling often. When he finished a page, he tossed it on the floor. "I have entered a period of change more drastic than adolescence or early childhood," he wrote Ginsberg. "I live in a state of constant routine."[172] He moved ever further from the laconic Factualist style of *Junky* toward a form that jettisoned sequence, location, and consistency. Living in Tangiers encouraged his state of mind: "There is no line between 'real world' and 'world of myth and symbol,'" he wrote. "Objects, sensations, hit with the impact of hallucination."[173]

Burroughs' accumulating pages went through many changes of title until Kerouac suggested "Naked Lunch." As Burroughs explained, "The title means exactly what the words say: NAKED Lunch—a frozen moment when everyone sees what is on the end of every fork."[174] The passages evolved spontaneously like spores, unorganized, without center, direction, or narrative. Paul Bowles recalls stepping into Burroughs' room to find "hundreds of pages of yellow foolscap all over the floor, month after month, with heel prints on them, rat droppings, bits of old sandwiches, sardines. It was filthy."[175] When Bowles asked him why the manuscript was so scattered, Burroughs muttered through bites on a candy bar, "Oh, it'll get picked up someday."[176]

Paul Bowles's novels set in Tangiers had lured Burroughs to the city, but he had felt snubbed by Bowles ever since his arrival. As Bowles recalled an early encounter: "His manner was subdued to the point of making his presence in the room seem tentative."[177] A few months after his successful junk cure, while having tea with Bowles, Burroughs so offended a rich American woman that she left the room. Bowles was amused. "I have seen him twice since," Burroughs reported, "and dig him like I never dug anyone that quick before. Our minds similar, telepathy flows like water. I mean there is something portentously familiar about him, like a revelation."[178]

Proposed Titles for Burroughs' Writing
Grand Tour (Hell Is Where Your Ass Is)
Meet Me in Sargasso
Interzone
Word Hoard
On the Road to Sargasso

An addict has little regard for his image.
—William Burroughs

William Burroughs in Tangiers, ca. 1957

*"Jack Kerouac with Burroughs' cat
outside Bill's ground-floor garden room
in the Villa Muniria, Tangiers, 1957."
Caption and photograph (detail) by
Allen Ginsberg*

**ALL TOGETHER: KEROUAC, GINSBERG, BURROUGHS, ORLOVSKY IN
TANGIERS** At this point in his writing, Burroughs craved contact with his
friends. "I needed to work out my method alone," he wrote Ginsberg.
"Now I am badly in need of advice, editing, collaboration."[179] At the moment of Burroughs' greatest need for his old friends, they arrived in Tangiers. Jack Kerouac was the first to sail, booking passage on a Yugoslavian
freighter in February 1957, paying for his ticket with $200 borrowed from
Ginsberg. Burroughs' air of health surprised Kerouac—tanned, toned,
casually dressed in chino pants and a fisherman's cap, Burroughs strode
through the medina, muttering, "Lard assed hipsters, aint [sic] no good for
nothin!"[180] But Burroughs' wildly uncombed hair, his compressed laughter, and his lapses into mad monologues unnerved Kerouac—it was as if
the routines enacted a decade earlier in Joan Vollmer's apartment and
reenacted by the grotesque characters in Burroughs' manuscript had assumed independent life. "I'm shitting out my educated Middlewest background once and for all," Burroughs told him. "By the time I finish this
book I'll be as pure as an angel, my dear."[181] Using his legendary speed-
typing skills, Kerouac put the chaotic manuscript in preliminary order.
Burroughs rewarded him by giving him a small alcohol burner to warm
him through the cold Tangiers nights. But Kerouac's daytime typing inspired nighttime demons: he dreamed of endless strings of bologna emerg-
ing from his mouth, like entrails.

In the two weeks before Allen Ginsberg and Peter Orlovsky arrived,
Kerouac grew homesick. Appalled by the lack of cleanliness in Tangiers,
annoyed by the food, sickened by an overdose of opium, his mind turned
to Wheaties, pine breezes, a kitchen window. Experiencing a "complete
turningabout," he wrote. "Avoid the World, it's just a lot of dust and drag
and means nothing in the end."[182] Following a violent bout of diarrhea,
Kerouac departed on April 5, cutting short his trip, and vowing to himself,
"Jack, this is the end of your world travel—Go home—Make a home in
America."[183]

Peter Orlovsky, Jack Kerouac, and William Burroughs on the beach in Tangiers, taking a break from the Naked Lunch *manuscript, March 1957*

Ginsberg feared facing the intensity of Burroughs' feelings alone, so he invited his boyfriend, Peter Orlovsky, to accompany him to Tangiers. Burroughs assured Allen that he was no longer capable of jealousy and would make no sexual requests. Ginsberg and Orlovsky planned in advance that "the two of us would take him on and do anything he wanted, satisfy him."[184] Peter's manner annoyed Burroughs and tension developed. But the emotional flare-ups were less important than the feelings of camaraderie and the concerted devotion needed to organize Burroughs' vast pile of manuscripts.

Ginsberg and Orlovsky settled in Kerouac's room at the Villa Muniria, one floor above Burroughs. (Kerouac, with characteristic paranoia, accused Ginsberg of pushing him out so he could occupy the room.) Ginsberg adopted his giver-as-receiver mode during this trip, cheering on

Al, I am a fucking saint, that is I been
fucked by the Holy Ghost and knocked
up with Immaculate Woid . . . I'm the
third coming, me, and don't know if I
can do it again . . . so stand by for the
Revelation.
    —William Burroughs to Allen Ginsberg

Burroughs in his monologues and, at the end of the day, cooking up boun-
tiful meals of fish or spaghetti with clam sauce. The heart of each day was
devoted to Burroughs' manuscript. Alan Ansen, visiting from Venice,
helped organize Burroughs' work by joining Ginsberg six hours a day,
spelling each other in tag team fashion at the typewriter. Ansen attacked
the pages with the scrupulous mania of a scholar and former amanuensis of
W. H. Auden. He combed through the hundreds of Burroughs' letters Ginsberg had brought, combined fragments of narrative and routines with the
pages from Burroughs' floor and the notebooks Burroughs had written at
solitary dinners. He indexed the contents and arranged them chronologi-
cally. Ansen and Ginsberg inserted punctuation, set paragraphs, integrated
the routines that popped up in scattered notes and letters, and after two
months of six-hour-a-day work by the two men, the sandwich-trodden pile
spreading across the floor gradually assumed the unlikely form of 200 clean
typed pages. "It's quite a piece of writing—all Bill's energy & prose, plus our
organization & cleanup & structure, so it's continuous and readable, decipherable."[185] Burroughs declared that he was finished with writing.

BEAT TO BEATNIK

THE "HOWL" TRIAL At the time Allen Ginsberg and Jack Kerouac were in Tangiers, Lawrence Ferlinghetti was awaiting trial for obscenity for publishing "Howl," and *On the Road* was readied for publication in the fall.

Howl and Other Poems was published in August 1956, the fourth in the City Lights Pocket Poets series. Eager to spread the revolution of the word, Allen mailed over a hundred review copies to such disparate commentators as W. H. Auden, T. S. Eliot, Marlon Brando, Ezra Pound, Charlie Chaplin, and, of course, Carl Solomon. "Howl" received some favorable reviews from friends and some snide put-downs from poetry Establishment critics, but its initially notorious place in American culture owed most to Captain William Hanrahan of the San Francisco Juvenile Bureau. On May 21, 1957, he ordered the arrest for obscenity of publisher Lawrence Ferlinghetti and Shigeyoshi Murao, the bookstore manager who sold "Howl" to a pair of plainclothes policemen. As William Carlos Williams had observed, "Howl" is "an arresting poem."[1]

How meet it is for Dr. Williams, pediatrician, to introduce "Howl" to the world!
—Donald Justice

The Cops Don't Allow No Renaissance Here.
—Newspaper headline about "Howl" censorship

The "Howl" trial, San Francisco Municipal Court, 1957, with defendants Lawrence Ferlinghetti and Shigeyoshi Murao

Carl Solomon on "Howl"
By the way, my profound thanks for the sentiments expressed in "Howl," an excellent piece of writing and just to my taste. (1957)

I disapprove of "Howl" and everything that was contained therein. (1959)

Feel calmer and take more time.
  —Marianne Moore, on "Howl"

Censorship advocates saw in "Howl" the opportunity to set stringent obscenity guidelines, while the American Civil Liberties Union regarded the matter as a precedent-setting First Amendment case and assembled a formidable set of lawyers to support Ferlinghetti. When the case went to trial in the summer of 1957—in the courtroom of Judge Clayton W. Horn, a Sunday school Bible instructor—the national media dispatched reporters and commentators to San Francisco.

After typing *Naked Lunch*, Ginsberg opted to visit in Europe rather than return for trial, but the team of literary experts assembled on "Howl"'s behalf staunchly defended the work's literary merit. Whitman and Dada were invoked as forebears, "Howl" was called "The Waste Land" of the younger generation, and Ginsberg's inclusion of "language of the street" and homosexuality in a poem were deemed necessary, as Mark Schorer testified, to "this picture which the author is trying to give us of modern life as a state of hell."[2] The most unequivocal and unapologetic support

came from Kenneth Rexroth, who called the poem "probably the most remarkable single poem published by a young man since the second war."[3]

Announcing his verdict on October 3, 1957, Judge Horn declared
Ferlinghetti and Murao not guilty. The trial provided not only a beacon of
light for free expression but a spotlight trained on the Beat Generation.
The other, even brighter spotlight of that fall season of 1957 was Viking's
publication of *On the Road*.

"Howl" is the confession of faith of the generation that is going to be running the world in 1965 and 1975—if it's still there to run.

—Kenneth Rexroth

ON THE ROAD IS PUBLISHED On the afternoon of September 4,
1957, Jack Kerouac arrived in New York on a Greyhound bus from
Florida, and at midnight he walked to a newsstand at Broadway and West
Sixty-Sixth Street to buy a *New York Times*. Opening to page 27, he read
Gilbert Millstein's review of *On the Road*. "Just as, more than any other
novel of the Twenties, *The Sun Also Rises* came to be regarded as the testament of the Lost Generation," Kerouac read, "so it seems certain that *On
the Road* will come to be known as that of the Beat Generation."[4] He
awoke to a phone call the next morning from a Viking editor who was
bringing over a case of champagne; before noon, three bottles were empty.

Thus began an episode in Jack Kerouac's life that was both a dream
and a nightmare. There were endless calls from journalists and television
producers seeking interviews. Soon *On the Road* climbed onto the bestseller list, where it stayed for five weeks, peaking at number eleven. German and Italian rights were quickly sold, the Book Find Club featured the
novel, and it went into a second printing within two weeks of publication.
Off-Broadway producers begged him to write a play (which he did, in the
course of a single night, and called it *The Beat Generation*), and he was be-
sieged with lucrative offers to write for *Pageant*, *Esquire*, and *Playboy*. The
downtown Village Vanguard engaged him to read, backed by jazz musicians. Warner Brothers offered $110,000 for the film rights (although Ker-

Well, Kerouac has come off the road in high gear . . . I hope he has a good set of snow tires.

—Viewer watching Kerouac at Village Vanguard

ouac's agent unsuccessfully held out for $150,000), and Marlon Brando expressed interest in playing Dean Moriarty. Gabrielle basked in her son's new celebrity, receiving letters from branches of the Kerouac family who had long been out of touch, but for Jack the experience of fame was harder to handle. As he wrote Neal Cassady, "Everything exploded."[5]

The media were less drawn to Kerouac the person than to the Beat avatar he conveniently represented. He was new fodder for the rebel-without-a-cause trend in the tradition of *The Wild One* and mythic martyr James Dean (another instance in which the movies established the arche-type before literature). Had *On the Road* been published shortly after it was written, it might have died, but six years later, America had tuned into the commercial potential of youth culture. "Howl" had prepared the way, but the publication of *On the Road* marked the beginning of the popular culture blitz. The media big guns took aim at a life style that threatened the Eisenhower era and domestic tranquility à la Ozzie and Harriet.

Kerouac's handsome brooding face, his strong jaw, generous lips, blue eyes, and dark hair were striking when seen in the tabloid newsprint, on the glossy paper of *Mademoiselle* and *Life*, or on television screens. An audience of 40 million viewers tuned in to WOR-TV for John Wingate's popular talk show, *Nightbeat*. They saw Kerouac on a swivel stool—his hair tousled and a wild look in his eye—telling his host "I'm waiting for God to show me His face."[6] Letters arrived from yearning nonconformists everywhere who declared their empathy ("Will meet you soon in neon mi-rages & night & desolate rivers"[7]). Women wanted to sleep with him, and a group of nuns petitioned the Franciscan fathers to perform a mass on his behalf. His girlfriend, Joyce Johnson, noted that men wanted to fight her boyfriend, while women telephoned imploringly: "You're young. I'm twenty-nine, and I've got to fuck him now!"[8]

At the outset of the media blitz, Kerouac dreamed of police chas-ing him through Lowell and endless ranks of children chanting his name.

Nobody knows whether we were catalysts or invented something, or just the froth riding on a wave of its own. We were all three, I suppose.
—Allen Ginsberg

He went on a five-week drunken spree in New York, fueled by Schenley's instead of Thunderbird, populated with "girls girls girls"[9] who threw themselves at him and whom Kerouac passively obliged. As Kerouac's first season of fame drew to a close, the strain on him became overwhelming. With Burroughs in Tangiers, Cassady in California, and Ginsberg in Paris, Kerouac faced the publicity glare alone. He barely maneuvered the blitz with alcohol, "my liquid suit of armor, my shield which not even Flash Gordon's super ray gun could penetrate."[10]

Jack Kerouac listening to himself on the radio, 1959, by John Cohen

Too much adulation is worse than non-recognition, I see now.
— Jack Kerouac

He is prince of the hips, being accepted in the court of the rich kings. . . . He must have hated himself in the morning—not for the drinks he had, but because he ate it all up the way he really never wanted to.
—Howard Smith, on Jack Kerouac

[I] don't know how to drive, just typewrite.
—Jack Kerouac

Funky: from 1920s African-American slang, the stench associated with too many people at a jook-joint function; later used by jazz musicians in the 1940s to suggest fundamental soulfulness.

Kerouac experienced not just the inevitable strain of being a public figure but also psychological dissonance. His ravenous audience—critics and fans alike—identified Kerouac with the manic protagonist Dean Moriarty rather than the observer Sal Paradise. The public saw Kerouac as an ecstatic, virile, latter-day cowboy, relentlessly and expertly driving fast cars across the broad face of America, a Lothario whose sexual drive and appetite for drugs were limitless, an iconoclastic hipster with radical values. Kerouac embodied an icon so remote from his personality, his friend John Clellon Holmes observed, "he no longer knew who the hell he was supposed to be."[11] A passenger rather a driver, Kerouac was notoriously unsure behind the wheel of a car. He didn't talk in manic bursts or media-friendly soundbites but in shy, religious paeans. His politics were paranoid and conservative: he thought McCarthy had "all the dope on the Jews and the fairies."[12] His sexual relations with women were insecure, brotherly, and passive; he worried that his penis was small, and he sometimes needed a combination of alcohol, fellatio, and masturbation to arouse him from impotence. His sweetheart was not a hot, gone chick but his stocky mother, and it was to her that he returned after the New York blitzkrieg.

After the rave in the *New York Times*, the positive reviews were more temperate, and the negative reviews outdid one another in bile. Kerouac became a Beat whipping boy. Derision from the mainstream press—attacking the novel as an apologia for a Dionysian, criminal life style—was predictable. But many intellectuals, including Columbia graduates Herbert Gold and Norman Podhoretz, also attacked the book and fueled Kerouac's anti-Semitism.

Malcolm Cowley had urged him to follow *On the Road* with a novel marketable to the burgeoning paperback trade. He wanted a book that chronicled further adventures of Kerouac's friends, but he cautioned against the driven, personal prose of his earlier works. Kerouac would have

preferred to see in print one of his Proustian epics—*Maggie Cassidy*, or
what Kerouac considered his spontaneous prose masterpiece, *Visions of
Cody*. But he compliantly sat down to write a novel that employed straightforward sentences and a coherent narrative. Equipped with Benzedrine
and a long roll of teletype paper, Kerouac sat down to ten Olympian writing sessions in November 1958, typing some 15,000–20,000 words each
time. He completed the novel with relative ease and called it *The Dharma
Bums*. At the novel's center was the character of Japhy Ryder, based on
Gary Snyder, who had replaced Neal Cassady's Dean Moriarty in Kerouac's pantheon. (The Kerouac-based character was named Ray Smith, as
he had been in early versions of *On the Road*.) Japhy Ryder offered a
highly sympathetic figure who espoused Buddhism, lived in tune with nature, and put the "beatific" in "Beat." Cowley edited the novel into more
conventional form, but Kerouac staunchly resisted; after the struggle to get
his work published, he didn't want to become a commercial commodity
whose words were dictated by publishers. When *The Dharma Bums* was
published in October 1958, the critical response was derisive, with the exception of Ginsberg's review in the *Village Voice* and praise in the *American Buddhist*. It nonetheless sold well, and long after Kerouac's other
books had gone out of print, it became in the 1960s a bible for "the rucksack revolution" it prophesied. At the time of publication, however, Kerouac felt discouraged. "That's my last potboiler!" he declared.[13] Four years
would pass before he would write another novel.

BEATNIK The confluence of *On the Road*'s publication and the
"Howl" trial not only launched Jack Kerouac and Allen Ginsberg into
media stardom but announced the arrival of a new social type in American
popular culture. After San Francisco columnist Herb Caen coined a clever
word for it—"beatnik"—the phenomenon became an American industry

A parody ad in Mad, *a real ad in the*
Village Voice

Mad *looks at the Beat Generation, September 1960, cover by George Woodbridge*

The beatnik is the torchbearer of those all-but-lost values of freedom, self-expression, and equality.
—Norman Mailer

The Beat Generation may once have been human beings—today they are simply comical bogies conjured up by the Luce publications.
—Kenneth Rexroth

I'm such a myth in the Village, every time I go in a bar people rush up and talk to some idealized image they have of me. . . . I hardly exist and talk as simple Allen any more.
—Allen Ginsberg

virtually without precedent. Vogue and commerce had popularized previous avant-gardes in art and literature (such as the Surrealists and the fashion industry, the Harlem Renaissance and Harlemania). But none had been regarded with equivalent sociological fascination by such a mainstream youth audience; the Beats were greeted as something akin to American literature's first rock stars.

The media projection of the beatniks as "angry young men" and juvenile delinquents reflected America's rebellious urges in the midst of the supposedly sunny Eisenhower era. The beatnik archetype offered a slightly more adult alternative to rock-and-roll, hot rods, and Associated Press syndicated columns like "What Young People Think." The beatnik became the odd psychic juncture for existential anomie, classic bohemianism, and youth culture, for it seemed to provide a conveniently sweeping rejection of everything from Pat Boone and TV dinners to Disneyland and the Organization Man. Media co-optation of the Beat Generation proved to be so effective that by the end of the decade Gregory Corso declared to Art Buchwald, "Every face you see is a beatnik face."[14]

Becoming a commodified simulacrum, the beatnik, proved unsettling for the participants. In *Time*-speak, Ginsberg became "the discount-house Whitman of the Beat Generation," and Kerouac was the "latrine laureate of Hobohemia."[15] As Kerouac wrote Ginsberg, "This fame shot makes you gripe more than blow, doesn't it."[16] Their identities were reduced to soundbites by the Luce publishing empire, which—far more than the San Francisco Renaissance and the Beat Generation combined—created the beatnik. Ginsberg compared it to the birth of Frankenstein.

As constructed by the media in paint-by-numbers fashion, the male beatnik (the "cat") sported a goatee, the thinner and scragglier the better, and long hair hanging loose over the collar. He wore no earrings but sometimes a free-form crucifix pendant, a black beret, black jeans with a black turtleneck sweater, or, in summer, a white tee-shirt. His favorite activities were smoking reefers, playing bongo drums, and chanting poetry with a cool jazz backup. The female beatnik (the "chick") was thin, wore long straight hair and pale makeup, and aspired to look like the Charles Addams character Morticia. She dressed in dark leotards and sandals. Her favorite activities were drinking espresso, attending poetry readings, and dating black jazz musicians. The indigenous habitats of the beatnik were a dark North Beach coffee house and a spare garret-like "pad" equipped with naked light bulbs, a hot plate for warming espresso coffee, and Mexican cow bells.

Within the literary world, only a few critics—among them Norman Mailer and Kenneth Rexroth—supported the Beats. More typical were the responses of Ginsberg's Columbia classmates Herbert Gold and Norman Podhoretz, who led the attack in the highbrow journals. Most striking about the contemporary critical response to *On the Road* and "Howl" was its utter lack of actual *literary* criticism. The writing was instead treated as a social phenomenon that threatened morality, literature, and Western civilization itself. "Kerouac has appointed himself prose celebrant to a pack of unleashed zazous," wrote Gold in *The Nation*.[17] In the *Partisan Review*, Norman Podhoretz described Kerouac's motto: "Kill the intellectuals who can talk coherently, kill the people who can sit still for five minutes at a time, kill those incomprehensible characters who are capable of getting seriously involved with a woman, a job, a cause."[18] Rather than treating Kerouac and Ginsberg as writers who transformed their life experience into literature, the critics considered the works symptoms of psychological and sociological pathology. Examined under the same lens were not only Kerouac and Ginsberg but England's Angry Young Men and James Dean, leading the highbrow critics to issue jeremiads against juvenile delinquents, jazz, homosexuality, drugs, and adolescence.

Kenneth Rexroth's response cut both ways. He prophesied that Ginsberg would be "the first genuinely popular, genuine poet in over a

I get called a beatnik sometime. Do I look like one?

—Carl Solomon

Anti-Beat Critics
John Ciardi
Benjamin DeMott
James Dickey
Herbert Gold
John Hollander
Norman Podhoretz
John Updike

The "Archetypal" Beatnik
Male:
  Goatees
  Berets
  Smokes marijuana
  Jeans
  Second-hand clothes
  Free-form silver crucifix pendants
  Dark glasses
  Plays bongo drums
  Paints large expressionist canvases
  Chants poetry to jazz back-up
  Verges on the sexually ambiguous
  Hair over the collar
  Appreciates Method acting
Female:
  Jeans
  Black leotards
  Waxy eye make-up
  Morticia-like complexion
  Svelte
  Drinks dark espresso coffee
  Cooks with garlic
  Dates black jazz players

When you take dehydrated Hipster and add watery words to make Instant Beatnik, the flavor is gone but the lack of taste lingers on.
—Herbert Gold

The revolt of the spiritually underprivileged and the crippled of the soul—young men who can't think straight and so hate anyone who can.
—Norman Podhoretz, on the Beat Generation

Communists, Beatniks, Eggheads.
—America's Three Menaces, according to J. Edgar Hoover, at the 1960 Republican Convention

Mr. Beatnik Goes to Washington

generation."[19] But Kerouac, perhaps for extraliterary reasons, was ridiculed: Rexroth described *On the Road* as the work of a "furious square," filled with characters who possessed the sense of "May flies and little children," and he predicted the Beat fad would quickly be "as dead as Davy Crockett caps."[20]

The beatnik phase, prepared for by the San Francisco Renaissance, continued in full force from the fall of 1957 to 1960. Its popularity can be measured by such cultural phenomena as a successful "Rent-A-Beatnik" business in Greenwich Village, the thriving commerce in army surplus stores, the get-photographed-with-a-beatnik booths in North Beach, a spate of beatnik exploitation novels, and shops selling "sandals for beatnik dogs."

THE BEAT GENERATION ON SCREEN By 1959, the beatnik phenomenon had spread beyond literature, clothes, and coffee houses. Atlantic Records advertised its product as "the label in tune with the Beat Generation,"[21] for example, the soap opera *Helen Trent* added a Beat character to its cast, and the popular television series, *The Many Loves of Dobie Gillis*, featured aspiring beatnik Maynard G. Krebs, who wore a sweatshirt, grew a goatee, carried bongos, and quailed at the prospect of working. Two films released in 1959 vied for *The Beat Generation* title, while a third film, never finished, was to have been called *The Beatniks*. The two completed films dramatically reflect the difference between the Beat Generation and its ersatz media offshoot.

The winner in its claim to the title, *The Beat Generation*, was a ninety-five-minute M-G-M Cinemascope film produced by B-movie schlockmeister Albert Zugsmith. The film's melodramatic plot featured a sociopathic rapist and a police sergeant in pursuit. When he's not haunting housewives, the villain drinks espresso with a beatnik crowd, who are depicted, in *Variety*'s words, as "Freudian cases who impersonate statues and gaze moronically at Vampira reading a jingle on how to loathe one's parents."[22] Used as lurid wallpaper against which the melodrama is played, beatniks embody what has come to be known as "the Other," reinforcing American fear of the burgeoning subculture.

Jack Kerouac wrote the film that lost its claim to the *Beat Generation* title, released in 1959 as *Pull My Daisy*. It offered the most authentic version of the Beat Generation on film, casting several of the original participants in episodes from their personal history, shot in a style that offered a cinematic analogy to spontaneous prose. The film also exemplifies the collaborative process. The title came from the first line of the doggerel poem "Fie My Fum," which Ginsberg, Cassady, and Kerouac jointly composed over several months in 1949—shortly after Kerouac had made his first cross-country trip with Cassady, at the time Ginsberg entered the psychiatric hospital. The movie's improbable narrative was actually a fairly direct rendition of a 1955 evening at the Cassadys' Los Gatos household. Carolyn Cassady had invited a local bishop over, and his arrival with his mother and aunt in tow coincided with an unexpected visit from Kerouac, Ginsberg, Orlovsky, and other friends. Before the evening ended, Kerouac had repeatedly said to the bishop, "I love you," while Ginsberg had discussed sex with the bishop's bewildered family.

Two years later, Kerouac used this anecdote as the basis for the third act of his play, hastily written over a weekend and called *The Beat Generation*. A year later, painter Alfred Leslie and photographer Robert Frank spawned the idea to form a limited movie partnership called G-String Enterprises and film the play's last act. They cast a mixture of friends from the art and literary world (the only professional performer was French actress Delphine Seyrig, recruited at the last minute), and paid them each about $20 a day. They rented an Arriflex 16 mm camera, evoked a minimalist version of the Cassady home in Alfred Leslie's loft at 108 Fourth Avenue, and raised the necessary $15,000. Leslie appeared

Beat Exploitation Novels

Bang a Beatnik by Ira Staver
Beat Girl by Bonni Golightly
Beatnik Wanton by Don Elliott
Bongo Gum by Richard E. Geis
Jesus Was a Beatnik by Jim Oaks Bryan
Lust Pad by Andrew Shaw
Pads Are for Passion by Sheldon Lord
Sintime Beatniks by D. S. Froeman

Cast of *Pull My Daisy*

Allen Ginsberg as Allen Ginsberg
Peter Orlovsky as Peter Orlovsky
Gregory Corso as Jack Kerouac
Larry Rivers as Neal Cassady
Delphine Seyrig as Carolyn Cassady
Richard Bellamy as the Bishop
Alice Neel as the Bishop's mother
David Amram as the musician

The Beat Generation is no longer about poetry. The Beat Generation is now about everything.

—Gregory Corso

with a megaphone labeled "The Director," and for fourteen days at the end of 1958 they filmed for eight hours a day. Robert Frank set the camera on a tripod and shot three takes of most scenes, and no sound was recorded. "No one was thinking about, 'We're gonna make the classic, underground, out-of-focus, beatnik epic, twenty minutes long,'" recalled participant David Amram. "Everybody was thinking it might be fun to get together and have kind of a home movie."[23] One of the issues to be solved was creating a coherent movie narrative without giving up immediacy and spontaneity. Although the film has been subsequently characterized as an improvised cinematic skit, the production was actually carefully thought out, and the cast rehearsed the seemingly spontaneous action. *Pull My Daisy* was not a home movie, as Leslie observed, but a facsimile of a home movie.

Beatniks on screen: a scene from Albert Zugsmith's The Beat Generation, *1959*

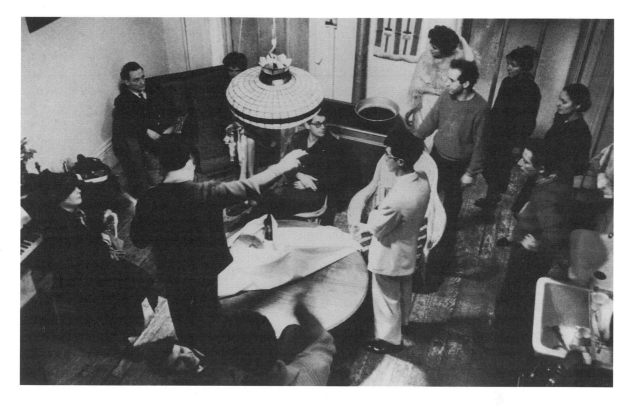

Leslie and Frank were discouraged after viewing the soundless rushes, and their spirits were not brightened by Kerouac's drunken recording of the film's narration. After the first recording, Kerouac insisted that once was enough, that he believed in spontaneous prose, and that he was "touched by the hand of God."[24] Although Kerouac was persuaded to record his narration two more times, the filmmakers still feared they had produced a shapeless disaster. The spontaneous spirit of the final twenty-eight-minute film was created largely after the fact, as sound and image were edited together. The cuts jumped from one take to another, with only

Beat Generation on screen: on the set of Pull My Daisy, *made by Alfred Leslie and Robert Frank, with (left to right) Larry Rivers, Gregory Corso, Alfred Leslie, Delphine Seyrig Youngerman, David Amram, Allen Ginsberg, Dick Bellamy, Robert Frank, Denise Parker, Sally and Gert Berliner, New York, 1959, by John Cohen*

casual concern for strict continuity, and the sound editors closely looped together different versions of Kerouac's narration, backed by David Amram's vibrant jazz score.

The film premiered November 11, 1959, at Amos Vogel's downtown *cinémathèque*, Cinema 16, and later played commercially at the New Yorker Theater (although the promotional strategy of distributing daisies along Fifth Avenue backfired, since many pedestrians thought the stunt advertised Doris Day's latest vehicle, *Please Don't Eat the Daisies*). In the decades since its release, long after *The Beat Generation* dropped from circulation, *Pull My Daisy* continues to play regularly on campuses and at film societies. With Robert Frank's richly saturated black-and-white images and David Amram's jazzy score complementing Kerouac's narration, the film now looks like an inside view of Beat friendship, and it has become a classic of American independent film.

BEAT WOMEN To the charismatic men at the center of their lives, women of the Beat Generation played roles as girlfriends, supports, and mother figures. They appear in the Beat *romans à clef* as amalgams or types rather than protagonists with distinct personalities. A similar anonymity encompassed many of the more recently minted beatnik women, but the new generation also included more substantial figures like Hettie (Mrs. LeRoi) Jones, Diane DiPrima, Helen (Mrs. Edward) Dorn, Joyce Johnson, and Elise Cowen. Greenwich Village and North Beach provided them a coming-of-age crucible. Chief among their hangouts were jazz clubs—especially the Five Spot, home of Thelonius Monk—and coffee houses. When they came to the Village from Long Island (like Hettie Cohen Jones) or the Upper West Side (like Joyce Glassman Johnson), they wore Downtown outfits: black tights from Goldin Dance Supply on Eighth Street, belts with brass spiral fasteners, sandals that laced up the

Beatnik: Coined after "Sputnik," this word was first publicly used by columnist Herb Caen in the April 2, 1958, San Francisco Chronicle: "Look Magazine, preparing a picture spread on San Francisco's Beat Generation (oh, no, not AGAIN!), hosted a party in a North Beach house for 50 Beatniks, and by the time word got out around the sour grapevine, over 250 bearded cats and kits were on hand. . . ." The word became the popular media term to describe a camp follower of the Beat Generation.

ankle, and dangling beaten-copper earrings. (To understand the radical nature of such an outfit, one must remember that the dress code for working women required nylons and high-necked dresses, even in summer.) Lionel Trilling's wife Diana didn't like the look of the Beat girls—"So many blackest black stockings," she sniffed after seeing them at a 1959 Columbia reading by Allen Ginsberg, Gregory Corso, and Peter Orlovsky.[25]

"In the 1950s, sex—if you achieved it—was a serious and anxious act," wrote Joyce Johnson.[26] "Real Life was sexual,"[27] she believed, and sex became a primary arena of development in three women—Hettie Jones, Diane DiPrima, and Joyce Johnson—associated with the Beats. For Joyce Johnson, that revolt meant losing her virginity before marrying and getting an illegal abortion in Canarsie; for Hettie Jones it meant marrying an African-American man, bearing him two children, and proudly raising them; for Diane DiPrima it meant pursuing affairs with both men and women and writing explicit, joyful erotica. To call them "feminist" would be anachronistic, but they did conduct lives that were not subservient to their men, and they looked to other women for support and identity.

JOYCE JOHNSON Joyce Johnson (née Glassman) grew up a block away from Joan Vollmer's commune apartment on 115th Street, and the two probably passed one another on Broadway sometime in 1945 or 1946. Joan was learning to use inhalers, Joyce was about to enter adolescence, learning to be a Jewish girl with Gentile inflections, a music student who practiced on the family's Steck baby grand, groomed for the professional niche that her mother never occupied. Sex was an uncomfortable subject in the family—the genital area was referred to as "down below," and her father, on first imagining his only daughter's deflowering, walked into the bathroom and vomited. The precocious daughter entered Barnard, just around the corner, before her sixteenth birthday and soon began to know

The truth of the matter is we don't understand our women; we blame them and it's all our fault.
—Jack Kerouac, On the Road

Field: *a field of marijuana: "That's what everybody used to say about me, man, that year: 'The trouble with Ervie is he found a field.'" [Kerouac, 1950, imitating a hipster]*

Jack Kerouac and Joyce Johnson in Greenwich Village, by Jerome Yulsman

not only college life but also the lures of Greenwich Village. Her chief guide was fellow Barnard student Elise Cowen, who was infatuated with an unpublished poet named Allen Ginsberg, wrote him constant postcards (and later typed his manuscript of "Kaddish" and jumped out of a window). In December 1956, Elise Cowen introduced Joyce Johnson to Ginsberg.

One Saturday night a month later, Johnson answered the phone to hear Jack Kerouac inviting her to meet him, on Allen Ginsberg's suggestion, at the Eighth Street Howard Johnson's. To join an unknown man in the Village was a daring act, and the twenty-one-year-old student applied extra eye shadow before hopping the subway to Astor Place. When she saw a figure at the counter, tanned after sixty-three days alone on a mountaintop, wearing a flannel lumberjack shirt, she thought, "He's the only person in Howard Johnson's in color."[28] Kerouac wolfed down frankfurters, home fries, and baked beans, and, since he had no money, Johnson paid the bill (a first for her). In his blue eyes she saw "the look of a man needing love" and believed she could cure his tender melancholy.[29] She helped him weather the nightmare of fame that struck full force in the fall of 1957, and she listened to his endless stories. She offered him sex, although his behavior in bed wasn't fierce but "oddly brotherly and somewhat reticent."[30] In its outlines, Kerouac's relationship with her resembled that with his other girlfriends, but several things distinguished it: the relationship lasted longer, Johnson was more intellectual, and the intensity of her infatuation reflected the hunger of the coming generation that lionized *On the Road.* "The 'looking for something' Jack had seen in me was the psychic hunger of my generation," she wrote. "Thousands were waiting for a prophet to liberate them from the cautious middle-class lives they had been reared to inherit."[31] Over their two years of sporadic living together and dating, Joyce Johnson put up with everything from alcoholism and emotional withdrawal to buddyism and mother love. Kerouac told her, "Always do what you want," and the prospect of freedom confused her.[32]

Chucks: *excessive hunger, often for sweets, after kicking a heroin addiction: "I have seen addicts who did not eat for a month. Then he gets the 'chucks' and eats everything in sight." [Burroughs]*

Their final parting scene on a street corner in the fall of 1959 consisted of this stylized repartee: "You're nothing but a big bag of wind!" said Johnson. "Unrequited love's a bore!" replied Kerouac.[33] Joyce Johnson carried on her life after the breakup, married, raised a son, divorced, wrote two novels, and worked as an editor for Dial Press. The fruit of her relationship with Kerouac came many years later. At age forty-seven, Joyce Johnson set down those early years, and her memoir, *Minor Characters*, provided an inside view of a woman coming of age in the Beat era, with one foot in the respectable middle-class literary world and the other in Greenwich Village.

HETTIE JONES Hettie Cohen met LeRoi Jones in March 1957, when he applied for a job at the *Record Changer*. He was happily surprised to find his interviewer reading Kafka's *Amerika*, and she was pleased to encounter someone so smart and direct, stabbing the air with his middle finger, the angular V of his hairline accentuating his expression. "But his movements were easy, those of a man at home not only in skin but in muscle and bone," wrote Hettie. "And he led with his head. What had started with Kafka just went on going."[34] LeRoi Jones had been raised in a middle-class Newark family, attended Rutgers and Howard University, and served as a gunner in the U. S. Air Force. Profoundly alienated from all these milieus, he felt a surge of identification when he read "Howl"; he later called it the most important poetic influence of the period.

Hettie Jones, worker on The Record Changer *and* Yūgen, *wife of LeRoi Jones, New York, 1959, by James O. Mitchell*

When Hettie Cohen married LeRoi Jones on October 13, 1958, her family was appalled. She described the decision to marry Jones as inevitable and simple because she loved him. It was nevertheless a daring decision, for even in the Village's accepting milieu, there were only a half-dozen interracial couples. So offended was the Italian community just south of Washington Square that bands of male toughs sometimes threat-

LeRoi Jones in New York, ca. 1959, by James O. Mitchell

Joint: a marijuana cigarette; began in the 1950s, following **stick**: "Don't Bogart that joint."

ened them. The difference between this and other Beat liaisons was that, as Hettie Jones observed, they "made acquaintance *through work* rather than simply *as wife.*"[35]

The Joneses' work together played an important role in the Beat movement—both their founding of a little magazine and their establishment of an informal salon in the large flat they shared at 402 West Twentieth Street. In 1958, LeRoi hatched the idea for a little magazine that would publish the work of young writers. Inspired by "Howl," he wrote a letter to Allen Ginsberg on toilet paper, asking him if he were for real and soliciting contributors to the new magazine. Ginsberg encouraged the magazine by drawing from his broad network of friends; soon the Joneses' widening circle included Frank O'Hara, Jack Kerouac, Diane DiPrima, Gregory Corso, Robert Creeley, and Joel Oppenheimer. The pool of po-

THE BIRTH OF THE BEAT GENERATION

tential contributors to the magazine was rich. Hettie drew on her magazine expertise—she had been the subscription manager on the *Record Changer* and the business manager of the *Partisan Review*—to run the office. They decided to call the magazine *Yūgen, a new consciousness in arts and letters*, and on the ochre cover appeared a Japanese ideogram that meant "elegance, beauty, grace, transcendence of these things, and also nothing at all."[36] Hettie typed up the twenty-four-page first issue on a rented IBM and laid it out on the Joneses' kitchen table with a T-square and triangle. In March 1958, the first issue appeared. Both the magazine and the Joneses' flat became a meeting point for the Beats' New York contingent. In its eight issues, which appeared irregularly until December 1962, *Yūgen* published not only the Beats but the San Francisco poets, the New York poets, and the Black Mountain poets.

The Joneses' party guests included the habitués of the Cedar Bar, the painters who showed in the new storefront galleries that appeared on East Tenth Street, jazz musicians, and writers. Hettie cooked up spaghetti for a hundred and got kegs from A&M Beer Distributors, and the bashes became regular events. Ginsberg described them as "an acme of good feeling. A lot of mixing, black white hip classic."[37]

The Joneses separated in the early 1960s, and when LeRoi asked for a divorce in 1965, many regarded the breakup as a symbol of the crumbling civil rights coalition of blacks and whites. After the murder of Malcolm X, in February of that year, LeRoi became increasingly involved in the politics of black separatism and soon changed his name to Amiri Baraka. His ex-wife, now "Mrs. Hettie Jones," pursued her literary and activist life. In addition to raising her two daughters, she wrote a dozen children's books, directed a day-care program on the Lower East Side, and helped to write a history of an antipoverty agency. At the end of the 1980s, she wrote her memoir, *How I Became Hettie Jones*, and provided an unsparing, affectionate, and bittersweet perspective on her earlier years in Greenwich Village.

List of Contributors to *Yūgen*
Ray Bremser
Gregory Corso
Allen Ginsberg
Jack Kerouac
Frank O'Hara
Charles Olson
Joel Oppenheimer
Gary Snyder
Philip Whalen
John Wieners

Bugged: *bothered, unstrung; also used as a verb, meaning to bother: "Don't bug me."*

DIANE DIPRIMA While still working at *Partisan Review*, Hettie Jones had hired Diane DiPrima to stuff envelopes, but she soon played a larger role in the Joneses' life. She became LeRoi's lover and gave birth to his daughter. Although their affair did not continue, DiPrima continued to be a literary colleague in running a monthly poetry newsletter called *Floating Bear*. Hettie admired DiPrima's self-direction, her infectious laughter, and her pluck, but she also observed that DiPrima "tended to wear lovers like chevrons."[38]

Diane DiPrima is sometimes called the archetypal Beat woman, a description that reflected both her enormous drive and her key organizational role in Beat-related activities. She provided an apt combination of Beat qualities: absolute independence, wide sexual experience from mid-teens on, familiarity with drugs, the Village, jazz, and bohemian style. And she resolutely pursued literature as her vocation; after flirting with the idea of becoming a theoretical physicist, she decided at the age of fourteen that she would live the life of a poet.

In the mid-1950s, just before the Beats became known, her friends were called the "new bohemians." They affected much the same style (Levis, sweatshirts, sandals) as later beatnik garb, although their couture was less studied. The conglomeration of friends—Actors Studio members, Ayn Rand addicts, jazz fiends, leftover Poundians, homosexual Ballet Theater dancers, and macho painters—reflected the bohemian mix of the 1950s. Her various "pads" were filled with friends, who often slept together on a fold-out couch or a double bed. ("The bed would hold up to four of us comfortably," DiPrima wrote, "and out of this fact grew nuances of relationship most delicate in their shading."[39]) Before the Beats ever came into her life, DiPrima fraternized with the new bohemian community:

> As far as we knew, there was only a small handful of us—perhaps forty or fifty in the city—who knew what we knew: who raced about in Levis and work shirts, made art, smoked dope, dug the

Diane DiPrima, New York City, 1959,
by James O. Mitchell

new jazz, and spoke a bastardization of the black argot. We surmised that there might be another fifty living in San Francisco,
and perhaps a hundred more scattered throughout the country:
Chicago, New Orleans, etc., but our isolation was total and impenetrable, and we did not try to communicate with even this
small handful of our confreres.[40]

DiPrima was ladling beef stew at a communal dinner when a
friend handed her the recently published *Howl and Other Poems*. So taken
was she by the first lines that she set down her ladle, walked to the Hudson
piers, and read the whole poem through, then returned to the group and
read it aloud. "I knew that this Allen Ginsberg, whoever he was, had broken ground for all of us—all few hundred of us—simply by getting this
published."[41]

Over the next decade, DiPrima would further settle that once for-
bidden territory—with her own poetry and with her activities in the poetry
community. In 1958, Totem Press published her first book of poetry, *This
Kind of Bird Flies Backward*, and many others followed. A list of DiPrima's
publishers suggests the constellation of little presses that were alive in the
late 1950s and 1960s: Totem Press, Auerhahn Press, Poets Press, Capra
Press, City Lights Books. Young poets depended entirely on this alternative
network, in whose development DiPrima played a prominent and continuing role.

In the late 1960s, Maurice Girodias of Olympia Press (the publisher of *Naked Lunch* and assorted erotica) invited DiPrima to write her
life story as erotica. DiPrima needed money and quickly wrote enough for
an advance: "It was the first and only time I'd ever written a 'potboiler,' and
it was clearly the course to take."[42] Girodias invariably returned her install-
ments requesting "MORE SEX." Conceived as a potboiler, DiPrima's
Memoirs of a Beatnik nonetheless became her most-read work. Among

Cop out: *to settle into conventionality, to "sell out" or "cop a plea." One could cop out by shaving a beard, wearing button-down collars, or getting a straight job.*

other things she described how it felt to participate in a Beat orgy—being in bed with Ginsberg, Kerouac, and two others was "warm and friendly and very unsexy—like being in a bathtub with four other people."[43] DiPrima's memoir not only provided a vivid picture of bohemian New York life in the mid-1950s but restored to erotica real bodies, lived-in humor, and a canny comfort about sex surpassing that of the Beat males.

BEAT HOTEL The publication of *Naked Lunch*, Ginsberg's composition of "Kaddish," and Burroughs' discovery of cut-ups took place against the background of a Left Bank hotel at 9 rue Git-le-Coeur. One walked up the stairs to find on the sloping landing a squat toilet hole and peeling walls, and a look into the rooms revealed bare floors, leaky ceilings, and shabby furnishings dimly lit by a 40-watt bulb, all scented with stale Gauloise cigarettes. Municipal officials gave it the lowest of thirteen ratings, *Time* called it "the fleabag shrine," and Gregory Corso gave it the name that stuck: the Beat Hotel. Madame Rachou, the aged and formidable proprietress, charged $30 a month and didn't care what went on in her rooms, from sex to drugs to drawing on the walls. She was highly selective about her clientele, and her forty-two rooms were always full. Its residents at various times included Allen Ginsberg and Peter Orlovsky, Gregory Corso (who lived in the tiny garret), painter-restaurateur Brion Gysin, William Burroughs, poet Harold Norse, along with jazz musicians and prostitutes. Calling it the ideal artists' community, Norse observed, "Not until it was all over, years later, did we realize how unique it was."[44]

When Ginsberg and Orlovsky moved into room 25 of the Beat Hotel in October 1957, Allen pulled from his backpack the dog-eared *Naked Lunch* manuscript that he had carried through Spain and Italy. Only one publisher in Paris would be interested in it—Maurice Girodias, whose Olympia Press provided the sort of publishing venture that has

It was like a Marx Brothers movie directed by Madame Blavatsky.
—Ted Morgan, on the Beat Hotel

Cat: *Derived from African-American slang of the 1930s for a jazz player, the term can mean any man, but more often one with pizzazz: "a cool cat."*

"Gregory Corso, Paris 1957, his attic 9 rue Git-le-Coeur with magic wand, Louvre postcards tacked to wall left, wooden angel kid on wire right, window on courtyard." Photograph and caption by Allen Ginsberg

proved essential to the avant-garde. Founded in 1953, it carried on the formula his father, Jack Kahane, had pioneered in 1931 with the Obelisk Press: publish a mixed list of erotica and avant-garde literature. Girodias published a line of "d.b.s" (dirty books) called the Traveler's Companion, directed to the tourist trade who in Paris could buy books banned in their own countries. The titles offered in his mail-order catalogue were farmed out to writers for $500 a book, set in type, and quickly distributed; Girodias worked fast because he always operated one step ahead of bankruptcy and the law. This line financed his publication of serious literature, beginning in 1954 with Samuel Beckett's *Watt*, continuing with three other Beckett novels, Vladimir Nabokov's *Lolita*, and J. P. Donleavy's *The Ginger Man*. (Many of the series' usual patrons were unpleasantly surprised to find that they had unwittingly purchased Literature: "You're giving yourself a bad name," wrote one irate customer.[45]) The time-honored and successful combination of erotica and literature worked in New York as well as in France, and these economically marginal publishers have historically (and necessarily) manned the front lines in the struggle for free speech. Only by coming through such a back door was *Naked Lunch* likely to be published.

Allen Ginsberg burst into the offices of the Olympia Press and announced to Girodias, "I have this manuscript that I've brought back from

Traveler's Companions

With Open Mouth by Carmencita de las Lunas
I've Got a Whip in My Suitcase by Beauregard de Farniente
White Thighs by Count Palmiro Vicarion
Sin for Breakfast by Faustino Perez
Love on a Trampoline by Sybah Darrich
Of Sheep and Girls by Robert M. Duffy

Peter Orlovsky and Allen Ginsberg in room 25 of the Beat Hotel, 1957, by Harold Chapman

That is the usual novel has happened.
This novel is happening.
　　—William Burroughs, on *Naked Lunch*

Tangier and it's by Bill Burroughs and it's the masterpiece of the century."[46] Girodias, however, instinctively recoiled from the look of the manuscript, which he later described as rat-nibbled and chaotic, the outward manifestation of an unstable character. Girodias declared that it was not a book.

Girodias would change his mind two years later, but only after *Naked Lunch* had become a *cause célèbre* due to censorship.

KADDISH Shortly after his experience with Girodias, Allen Ginsberg began to emotionally confront his mother's death over a year before. He had mailed her a dittoed copy of "Howl," and on the eve of her death, on June 9, 1956, she wrote her son a caring and fairly lucid letter. "Don't take chances with your life!" she cautioned. "I wish you get married. Do you like farming? It's as good a job as any. . . . I wish I were out of here and home at the time you were young; then I would be young. I'm in the prime of life now. . . . I hope you are not taking drugs as suggested by your poetry. That would hurt me. Don't go in for ridiculous things."[47]

The letter had been mailed from Pilgrim State mental hospital two days after Naomi's death, and by the time it reached Allen he had read his brother's account of "the smallest funeral on record": seven people showed up at the Beth Moses Cemetery graveside, and the functionary who led the brief service didn't get Naomi's name right. Worst of all, in the absence of a minyan—the required quorum of ten men—*kaddish* could not be read. "[A]s Lou said, Naomi (mother) was 'let down' for the last time," Allen's brother reported.[48] Shortly after that, while walking with Kerouac and Orlovsky, Ginsberg entered a San Francisco synagogue and asked them to say a prayer for his mother; again there was no minyan. It was up to him, Allen decided; in his journal of July 1956 he noted, "Write Kaddish."[49] But he couldn't confront the task for another sixteen months.

S: schizophrenia: "I have thought a great deal about Schizophrenia (S in the trade)." [Burroughs]

On November 13, 1957, seated in the legendary 1920s hub, the
Café Select, he began to write and weep as he set down the first lines of a
formal elegy. He sent them to Kerouac. He couldn't continue that day, but
his Paris journals contained pages called "Elegy for mamma." The next
concerted attempt was over a year later in his Lower East Side apartment.
He had just returned from his friend Zev Putterman chanting sections of
the book of Jewish prayer. At 6 AM on a Saturday morning he embarked on
a marathon writing session. He took a few Benzedrine pills and Peter
Orlovsky sustained him with coffee and hard-boiled eggs. By Sunday night
he had completed fifty-eight tear-stained pages that resonated with the
rhythms of mourning, tinged by the metaphysical, dominated by his long-
remembered emotions for his mother.

*Naomi Ginsberg in a field of flowers,
before the onslaught of schizophrenic
breaks, Milltown, New Jersey*

He didn't put the manuscript in order for another eighteen months, after a thirty-hour Benzedrine-driven editing session. When he sent it to Lawrence Ferlinghetti, he still doubted whether it should be published: "I don't know what it'll look like to you, poetry or not—huge white elephant maybe—you figure out what to do with it."[50] Ferlinghetti also had doubts and suggested he cut it. After further editing and cutting five pages, Ginsberg read it aloud to Kerouac and decided, "It sounded foursquare and right what I want."[51] Only now was he ready to see it published.

"Kaddish" is Ginsberg's most moving work. After he had written this elegy for his mother and for his own lost childhood, Naomi could finally be mourned.

GINSBERG AND BURROUGHS AT THE BEAT HOTEL William Burroughs moved into room 15 of the Beat Hotel on January 16, 1958. Allen felt wary, but he found Burroughs in a state of tender lucidity. He had stopped drinking and writing, and Ginsberg noticed that, after years of keeping age at bay, Burroughs suddenly looked older. He spent his afternoons seated on his bed mentally surveying the traumatic and demonic experiences of his life until he reached the state of a clear, impersonal observer. As Ginsberg described it, "Rather than trying to combat and still and shut up his fantasies which fill his mind and shut out bliss, he plunges into his fantasies, fills them out and feels them as much as he can."[52] These sessions offered a self-administered extension of his twice-a-week psychoanalysis, and more than at any previous time, he approached serenity.

Burroughs responded to Allen without possessive longing, and he shared with Ginsberg a vision of "a benevolent sentient center to the whole Creation."[53] They sat up late at night in the Beat Hotel and came to an intuitive rapprochement that reached moments of quivering sensitivity before settling into the rhythms of benevolent domesticity. Ginsberg

Angel, saint, holy: Retaining their customary meaning, these words were used by the Beats to celebrate the sanctity of their lives: "Lucien is his Angel." [Kerouac, on Ginsberg] "The bum's as holy as the seraphim!" [Ginsberg, "Footnote to Howl"]

cooked, Burroughs went out each afternoon to his psychoanalyst and to
pick up paregoric, and the day ended with an evening walk on the boule-
vard St. Germain. For the first time in years there was a feeling of uncom-
plicated reconciliation. When Ginsberg left Paris for New York in July
1958, Burroughs was in tears.

CUT-UPS A year after Ginsberg had left, Burroughs was still living
in the Beat Hotel. He had met a new lover—a brilliant English mathe-
matician named Ian Sommerville, who looked uncannily like a young
Burroughs. He would continue, off and on, as Burroughs' boyfriend for
the next decade. More important to his writing, Burroughs developed a
close friendship with his neighbor at the Beat Hotel, Brion Gysin, the artist
and former Tangiers restaurateur who introduced him to a revolutionary
means of producing literature.

   After slicing through a stack of *New York Herald Tribune*'s one October afternoon in 1959, Gysin read through the sections randomly joined
together from different layers of newsprint and he was so vastly amused
that several denizens of the Beat Hotel thought he was having an attack of
hysteria. "Cut-ups," as he called them, offered a verbal counterpart to the
Surrealist parlor game, the exquisite corpse (*cadavre exquise*), but Burroughs regarded cut-ups as far more important than a parlor game. The
juxtaposition of lines introduced wholesale randomness into his writing,
and he likened the result to the modernist collage that had been accepted
in the art world forty years earlier. Armed with a Stanley knife instead of a
typewriter, Burroughs and Gysin enlisted the help of Gregory Corso and
Sinclair Beiles and began slicing pages and depositing them in four bas-
kets. Burroughs described the process: "Pages of text are cut and rearranged to form new combinations of word and image, that is, the page is
actually cut with scissors, usually into four sections, and the order is re-

Shake: *a drug shakedown, a search by the law: "I had asked him to keep the grass . . . out of the apartment in case of a shake, except what he was using."* [Burroughs]

William Burroughs in room 15 on the fifth floor of the Beat Hotel (the wire trays contain manuscripts), ca. 1959, by Harold Chapman

arranged. . . . I take a page of text, my own or someone else's . . . lining up the lines. The composite text is then read across, half one text and half the other. Perhaps one of ten works out and I use it."[54]

Burroughs not only cherished the felicitous accidents of one line bleeding into another but saw cut-ups as a revolutionary means of breaking down the control dictated by linear narrative, a means of composition that more accurately represented his associational mind-state and deranged the senses without drugs. He later began to discern in the juxtapositions prophetic announcements, as if his foreknowledge were now set before him in type; he simply had to be receptive to their signals. Burroughs' fascination with cut-ups continued despite the fact that his friends regarded them as highly dubious (even Gregory Corso disassociated himself from the selection in *Minutes to Go*, the first cut-up book). Burroughs believed, as he informed Paul Bowles, that "it works in the hands of a master."[55]

NAKED LUNCH: CENSORSHIP—PUBLICATION—CENSORSHIP Allen Ginsberg continued his campaign to get *Naked Lunch* published. At City Lights, Lawrence Ferlinghetti rejected the manuscript, and the only possibilities for publication were the little magazines where Ginsberg had both connections and influence. The first excerpt from *Naked Lunch* to see publication appeared in the last issue of the *Black Mountain Review* (fall 1957), and the scabrous language aroused little comment. But a year later, when Irving Rosenthal published a nine-page excerpt in the University of Chicago–sponsored monthly *Chicago Review*, a battle between censors and writers was joined that would be frequently repeated over the next eight years. The conflict opened with a *Chicago Daily News* columnist denouncing the excerpt as "one of the foulest collections of printed filth I've seen publicly circulated,"[56] and embarrassed university officials soon joined in, suppressing the publication of further excerpts by Burroughs in the next issue. Rosenthal and six staff members resigned and started their own magazine—named *Big Table* at Kerouac's suggestion, and partly supported by a benefit reading by Ginsberg, Corso, and Orlovsky—to publish the banned contents of the *Chicago Review*.

Big Table's first issue, March 1959, contained ten episodes of *Naked Lunch* and was impounded by the Chicago Post Office. Over a year later, Judge Julius J. Hoffman absolved the *Naked Lunch* episodes as "not akin to lustful thoughts." (Hoffman would, a decade later, preside over the

That's not writing, it's plumbing.
—Samuel Beckett, on cut-ups

In order to earn my reputation I may have to start drinking my tea from a skull since this is the only vice remaining to me.
—William Burroughs, on his notoriety

"The book grabs you by the throat," says L. Marland, distinguished critic. "It leaps in bed with you, and performs unmentionable acts. . . . This book is a must for anyone who would understand the sick soul, sick unto death, of the atomic age."

—William Burroughs' fantasized review of his work-in-progress, *Naked Lunch*

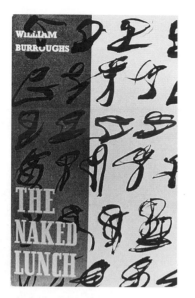

The first jacket for Olympia Press's Naked Lunch, *designed in purple and yellow by Burroughs, 1959*

We do not feature masochism this season in Hell, psychic or any other kind.

—William Burroughs

Chicago Seven trial.) As a result of the trial, Maurice Girodias whiffed the scent of literary notoriety, and in June 1960 he reconsidered publishing *Naked Lunch*. He quickly wrote up a contract that gave Burroughs an $800 advance and retained for himself one-third of all English-language rights. Having witnessed the five-year circuitous route to publication of *On the Road*, Burroughs gamely entrusted his manuscript to Girodias: "O.K. for better or for worse, in sickness or on the nod."[57] The scattered routines that eluded any form of organization now had to be prepared for the printers in ten days, and Burroughs found that "pressure welded the whole book together into a real organic continuity which it never had before."[58] When the galleys were returned from the printer in random order, Burroughs declared the sequence as good as any other; *Naked Lunch* was sent to the printer with minor changes and a Burroughs-designed cover of thick marks against a purple and yellow ground. By late July 1959, the unpublishable had been published as number 76 of the Traveler's Companion series in an edition of 10,000. In the anonymous tradition of Burroughs' first book, *Junky*, it received not a single review.

Rights were quickly sold to Germany and Italy and, in the United States, for $3,000 to Barney Rosset's Grove Press. But *Naked Lunch* would undergo several trials—both literal and metaphorical—before finally being published in Burroughs' native America three years later.

In the 1950s, Grove Press occupied a niche similar to Olympia Press, publishing such avant-garde writers as Genet and Beckett as well as erotica. At the time publisher Barney Rosset bought the rights to *Naked Lunch* he was engaged with censorship trials in fourteen localities over Henry Miller's *Tropic of Cancer*. Only after Miller's novel was cleared of obscenity charges in June 1964 were legal precedents set that created a safer climate for the publication of *Naked Lunch*.

By the time it hit American bookstores on November 20, 1962, *Naked Lunch* had become a legendary unseen work. A prestigious critical foundation was laid earlier that year by Burroughs' participation in a literary conference in Scotland. Along with Henry Miller, Norman Mailer, and Mary McCarthy, Burroughs represented the United States. Mailer and McCarthy described Burroughs as the current writer who most influenced the literary cognoscenti (a declaration met largely by bewildered silence from the audience, since most of them had never heard of William Burroughs). Before the international community of writers who collectively wielded enormous clout in the rarefied world of literary quarterlies and advance-guard writing, Burroughs set the framework for his novel, "In writing I am acting as a mapmaker, an explorer of psychic areas," Burroughs said. "And I see no point in exploring areas that have already been thoroughly surveyed."[59]

Even admiring critics found it difficult to describe the novel— Mary McCarthy compared it to Action Painting, others described it as an existential, absurdist parable, as a Swiftian satire, or as modern confessional literature. Herbert Gold summed it up as "less a novel than a series of essays, fantasies, prose poems, dramatic fragments, bitter arguments, jokes, puns, epigrams—all hovering about the explicit subject matter of making out on drugs while not making out in either work or sex."[60] Only a few magazines, notably *Time*, dragged in Burroughs' personal life. (Burroughs successfully sued *Time* for defamation of character, but the court determined his reputation was worth only a few dollars.) Perhaps the most striking thing about *Naked Lunch*'s critical reception among serious, reputation-making journals was the speed with which this profoundly subversive and difficult work was granted a place in the literary canon as a grotesque masterpiece of the twentieth century.

Naked Lunch underwent one final censorship trial; it was literally "banned in Boston." The city that had suppressed Theodore Dreiser's *An American Tragedy* and Lillian Smith's *Strange Fruit* brought its charges of obscenity to the Massachusetts Superior Court. Citing *Jacobellis* v. *Ohio*—

Grove Press Authors
Simone de Beauvoir
Samuel Beckett
Jean Genet
Eugene Ionesco
D. H. Lawrence
Alain Robbe-Grillet
Marquis de Sade
Hugh Selby

What we are all trying for is to get as much freedom, as much liberty of expression, not only in writing, not on paper, not in talk, but in action, and the whole world today is in my mind strangled.

—Henry Miller, at a 1962 literary conference

If Saint Augustine were writing today he might well write something like Naked Lunch.

—Norman Holland, testifying on behalf of *Naked Lunch*

Cover of Evergreen Review, *1960:*
Barney Rosset's warning

in which the judge had ruled about pornography, "I know it when I see it"—presiding Judge Eugene A. Hudson declared *Naked Lunch* obscene.[61] Grove Press's lawyer, First Amendment expert Edward de Grazia, appealed to the Massachusetts Supreme Court. After arguing the case on October 8, 1965, the court delayed decision pending outcomes of trials before the Supreme Court. On March 21, 1966, Justice William Brennan stipulated three criteria for obscenity, all of which must be met:

1. The dominant theme of the material taken as a whole appeals to a prurient interest in sex.

2. The material is patently offensive because it affronts contemporary community standards relating to the description or representation of sexual matters.

3. The material is utterly without redeeming social value.

In the first application of Brennan's criteria, five of the seven judges ruled that *Naked Lunch* was not obscene.

This was not only the final chapter in the publication of *Naked Lunch* but also a landmark in publishing history. It was the last literary work to be suppressed by U. S. Customs, the U. S. Post Office, or a state government; and the decision about *Naked Lunch* marked an end to literary censorship in America (although censorship in other arts still flourishes). If *Naked Lunch* did not qualify as obscene—with its scenes of brutal homosexuality, cannibalism, hanging-ejaculations, and every known four-letter word—an enforceable standard of obscenity became difficult to imagine. As Allen Ginsberg put it, the word had been liberated.

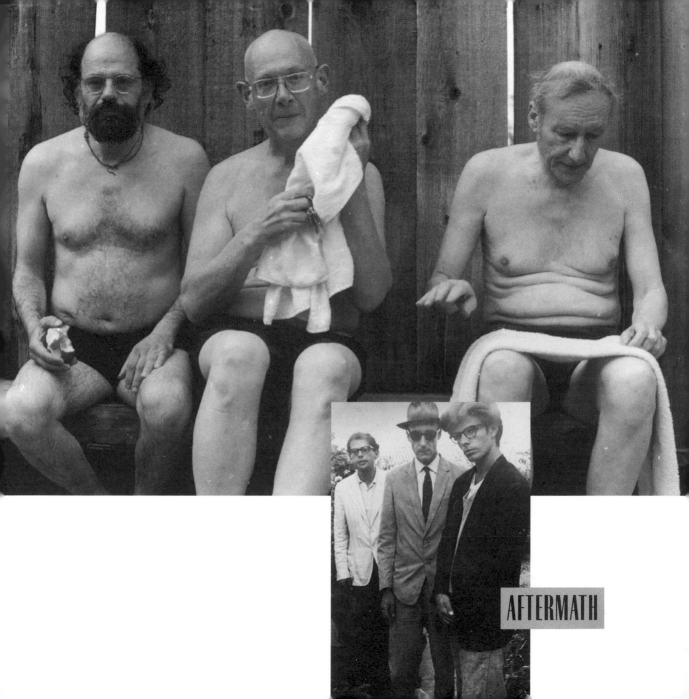

AFTERMATH

Overleaf:
Allen Ginsberg, Philip Whalen, and
William Burroughs at the Naropa
Institute in Boulder, Colorado, 1976,
by Gordon Ball (top)

Allen Ginsberg, William Burroughs, and
Peter Orlovsky at the Villa Muniria,
Tangiers, 1961 (bottom)

*N*EAL CASSADY: AFTERMATH In the wake of *On the Road*'s publication, Neal Cassady became a local celebrity as the model for the novel's protagonist. The police felt his open use of marijuana and his North Beach reputation as Johnny Potseed posed a threat. He was arrested in April 1958 for possession of marijuana and sentenced to five years in prison. For possession of three "offbrand cigarettes" of marijuana Neal Cassady (officially known as A-47667) spent 787 days in San Quentin. When he wasn't sweeping flug from the prison textile mill, he lay in a sagging bunk in a $4^1/_2$ by $7^1/_2$ by $9^1/_2$ foot cell. He wrote his wife that the isolation inspired him to "ponder past mistakes, present agonies & future defeats in light of whatever insights your thus disturbed condition allows."[1] He was annoyed that the prison library's copy of *On the Road* was constantly checked out, and he resented the prison newspaper's column on the exiled "Prime Minister" of the "Beatnuts." After a few months, Neal began to thrive within the viselike strictures of the prison routine. He

How this beat beatster beats a beat bastille.
—Neal Cassady, in San Quentin

You well know we both consider imprisonment an unparalleled opportunity to attain greater grace & I'm sensing this purging in even greater amounts as I persevere in prayer & meditation.
　　　—Neal Cassady to Carolyn Cassady, from San Quentin

Neal Cassady in San Quentin for possession of marijuana, ca. 1959, by Harry Redl

buried himself in religious reading, memorizing all the Popes' tenures, digesting Mary Baker Eddy, and attending every available church service (confession, mass, a Protestant service, and a Negro fundamentalist service). He memorized prayers, which he repeated in mantra-like fashion. "This ex-beatster beats a beat bastille: Rule: blank mind desire proportionately to each bodily nullification."[2] He was inspired by a course on religion taught by fifty-nine-year-old Gavin Arthur, who became his mentor, and later, in the days outside prison, his support. (When Cassady later slept with Arthur, he completed a distinguished intergenerational homosexual daisy chain: Cassady slept with Arthur, who'd slept with Edward Carpenter, who'd slept with Walt Whitman.)

In his letters to Carolyn, Neal vowed that he would never again run afoul of the law, and he meant it at the time. On his release from San Quentin on June 3, 1960, he and Carolyn drove directly to a North Beach jewelry shop and chose matching new gold rings to mark their new beginning. But the perennial complications in Neal's life flooded back soon enough: Carolyn and the three kids living in Los Gatos, his mistress Jacky Gibson demanding he divorce Carolyn (Kerouac offered to solve the problem by marrying Jacky), the boredom of his nightshift job changing truck tires in San Jose, the mounting losses at the horse track, the revoked driver's license, the short jail stints for driving infractions. Ginsberg and Kerouac encouraged him to revise his memoirs, *The First Third*, and Ferlinghetti offered to publish them. But even with Ginsberg taking dictation, Neal couldn't revise or write, and the fragments wouldn't appear until after Cassady's death. When his drug use increased—primarily speed and marijuana, and later LSD—all semblance of order disappeared. Carolyn considered him "just a charge to me—like the children—I'm just a haven."[3] The Cassadys finally divorced in 1963.

Cassady's life had a final, brilliant chapter as "Speed Limit," the commander of the Merry Pranksters' psychedelic bus. When Neal met

Ken Kesey in late 1962, Kesey was a Stanford graduate student in creative writing. He and his writing cohorts lived at Perry Lane—described by Malcolm Cowley as "the Left Bank of Stanford"[4]—where Kesey soon ate his first marijuana brownie. In 1959 he had volunteered to be a paid ($100) guinea pig at the Menlo Park Veterans Hospital, where, over a few weeks, he ingested a variety of psychoactive drugs—psilocybin, mescaline, LSD, amphetamine IT-290. After consuming eight peyote buttons, Kesey transformed his hospital experiences into *One Flew Over the Cuckoo's Nest*. On the heels of the novel's publication in 1962, Neal Cassady entered the picture one afternoon, shirtless, weaving into a living room where Larry McMurtry was reading from *Leaving Cheyenne*. As one onlooker recalled, Neal "sort of danced over them and just came to the front of the room," rapping all the way.[5] Since *On the Road* had figured as a guidepost in Kesey's life, he was very pleased to meet Dean Moriarty in the flesh. Cassady was, in turn, impressed with *One Flew Over the Cuckoo's Nest*, and he began calling Kesey "Chief."

At that time, Kesey championed a collection of creators he called "The Neon Revolution," and he soon formed his own group, dubbed the Merry Pranksters. They were part of the generation that succeeded the Beats, joyously conspiring to disrupt the Establishment with the "bravado of an elite military unit,"[6] thriving on psychedelics, risk, and games. They had no platform, but, as Kesey said, "What we hoped was that we could stop the coming end of the world."[7]

Contemplating a trip across the continent for the 1964 publication of Kesey's second novel, *Sometimes a Great Notion*, the Pranksters bought a 1939 International Harvester school bus, cut a hole in the roof, installed microphones and PA systems, and painted mandalas and Day-Glo patterns on the exterior. The sign above the windshield said "FURTHER," the spray-painted slogan running along the side said "A VOTE FOR BARRY IS A VOTE FOR FUN," and the legend in the rear read "CAUTION:

The Revolution Has Begun—Stop giving your authority to Christ & the Void & the Imagination—you are it, now, the God . . . you are needed—stop hiding yr. light in a bushel.
—Allen Ginsberg to Neal Cassady, December 1960

The Neon Revolution, According to Ken Kesey
Lenny Bruce
William Burroughs
Ornette Coleman
Günter Grass
Anna Halprin
Wally Hedrick
Joseph Heller
New Wave filmmakers
John Rechy

When you went riding with [Cassady], it was to be as afraid as you could be, to be in fear for your life.
—Jerry Garcia, on Neal Cassady's driving

The Merry Pranksters' bus, "Further," 1964: "A Vote For Barry Is A Vote for Fun"

At his purest, Cassady was a tool of the cosmos.
—Jerry Garcia

WEIRD LOAD." (The passengers themselves had none of the long-hair, tie-dyed look one might expect, for the trip occurred before hippie regalia had come into being.) A dozen Pranksters set out on June 14, 1964, with Neal Cassady at the wheel. It was *On the Road* for a new generation.

"We are actually fourth-dimensional beings in a third-dimensional world and happening in a second-dimensional world," rapped Cassady into the microphone above his head, as he fiddled with the radio dial, beat time on the steering wheel, and fingered a joint. One associate described his free-associating, psychic commentary as "making sense yet no sense . . . talking nonstop under waterfalls."[8] His driving and his rap embodied the Pranksters' euphoric, go-for-broke attitude, and Cassady quickly became an icon among the Pranksters. He was part Beat mentor, part erotic pyrotechnician, and part guru—or, as his girlfriend, Ann Murphy, put it, "muscles, meat, and metaphysics."[9] Ginsberg described Cassady's role to Herbert Huncke: "He's become a sort of fantastic continuously talking (on 7 or 8 levels of simultaneous association) teacher."[10]

When the Pranksters reached the East Coast in July, Neal steered the bus to Jack Kerouac's house in Northport, Long Island. The two hadn't seen one another for four years. That night Cassady lured Jack to the Merry Pranksters' Madison Avenue party. Entering the room drinking whiskey from a paper bag, Kerouac was disoriented to find cameras, floodlights, tape recorders, a six-man band, and a room filled with people tripping on acid. "Dig this, Jack," exclaimed Neal, "the tape recorders and the cameras, just like we used to do, only this time professionally!"[11] Kerouac made his way to a sofa draped with an American flag. He carefully and mutely folded it, Boy Scout fashion, in a neat triangle, and glumly sat down while Allen Ginsberg led the group in a chant. Cassady, speeding on amphetamines and acid, was poor company. The Pranksters manically tried to perform for Kerouac; as one recalled, "They tried to make him join their big party."[12] Only Kesey had the sensitivity to treat him as an elder, quietly telling Kerouac that his place in history was solid. Jack replied, "I know."[13] It was the last time Kerouac saw Cassady—although by the end of his life, conflating his real identity and his media identity, Cassady would sometimes refer to himself as "Kerouassady."

In January 1966, Kesey was apprehended for marijuana possession and the Merry Pranksters disbanded, some remaining in California, some following Kesey to Mexico. Cassady headed south of the border. He felt cut off from his old Beat associates and his marriage, although he periodically telephoned Carolyn to say, "I'm coming home."[14] He sent several desperate letters to Ginsberg, and they had a final meeting in 1967. "His skin was cold, chill, sweaty & corpselike," Ginsberg remembered. "I think it was the first time I ever got out of bed with Neal voluntarily."[15]

On February 3, 1968, shortly before his forty-second birthday, Cas-

Merry Pranksters
Ken Babbs
Neal Cassady
Paul Foster
Jerry Garcia
Ken Kesey
Mountain Girl

Old red face W. C. Fields Toad Guru trembling shy hungover sick pot bellied Master . . . afraid to drink himself to death.

—Allen Ginsberg, describing Jack Kerouac at the Pranksters' party

All along the roadside, you see the smattered and charred and twisted remains of people who had fairly loose heads and who, in an effort to emulate Cassady, burned themselves. I'm not talking about ten or twenty people.

—Wavy Gravy

sady set out from the small town of Celaya, Mexico, to retrieve the "magic bag" he had left behind in the San Miguel de Allende railway station. It contained a Bible, letters from Ginsberg and Kerouac, and personal touchstones of his life. He stopped at a Mexican wedding party, where he consumed enormous quantities of *pulque* after downing Seconals all day. He knew the danger of combining "cankers and lush," but perhaps it no longer mattered to him. He vowed to make good on his promise to walk

Neal Cassady, right, as "Speed Limit," at the wheel of the Pranksters' bus

Neal Cassady shaving at Allen Ginsberg's apartment, San Francisco, ca. 1962, by Larry Keenan

along the fifteen miles of railroad track between San Miguel de Allende and Celaya, counting aloud each tie as he crossed it. As legend goes, he said, "64,928" and dropped over. He was discovered the next morning by *campesinos* and died later that day of congestion and overexposure. His cremated remains arrived at Carolyn's house in a box with the typed message: "Contiene Cenizas Del Sr. Neal Cassady Jr."[16]

JACK KEROUAC: AFTERMATH Jack Kerouac had always desired recognition of his literary stature alongside Melville and Shakespeare; in its stead he got a niche in the pantheon of American pop culture alongside James Dean and Maynard G. Krebs. His media fame brought him neither

After *On the Road*
The Subterraneans (Grove, 1958)
The Dharma Bums (Viking, 1958)
Doctor Sax (Grove, 1959)
Maggie Cassady (Avon, 1959)
Mexico City Blues (Grove, 1959)
Tristessa (Avon, 1960)
Book of Dreams (City Lights, 1961)
Big Sur (Farrar, Straus, & Cudahy, 1962)
Visions of Gerard (Farrar, Straus, 1963)
Desolation Angels (Coward-McCann, 1965)
Vanity of Duluoz (Coward-McCann, 1968)
Visions of Cody (McGraw-Hill, 1973)

Fame makes you stop writing.
        —Jack Kerouac to Allen Ginsberg

I see nothing ahead for me but ease and joy and yet my mind is so dark, and so lonesome sometimes I could cry on your shoulder or Bill's or Neal's any minute.
        —Jack Kerouac to Allen Ginsberg

joy nor satisfaction, but perhaps nothing could alter his deeply ingrained rhythms of loneliness and increasing dependence on mother and alcohol.

At least the now famous Kerouac could get his previously scorned manuscripts published. By the time Kerouac died at the age of forty-seven, most of the episodes in the mythic Duluoz legend had been published, like a capacious Proustian epic of an adventurous working-class American life. But the ubiquity of newly published Kerouac titles didn't signal a burst of creativity—most of them were the manuscripts he had written during the early and mid-1950s. And the book that Kerouac considered his best, *Visions of Cody*, remained unpublished during his lifetime.

The satisfaction of seeing his books finally in print was mitigated by the scurrilous reviews they inspired. At first the critics took potshots at Kerouac as "the King of the Beats," and subsequently they derided him as a Beat has-been, repeatedly urging him to grow up and to discipline his prose. Kerouac began to discern a Jewish-intellectual conspiracy. But negative reviews were preferable to being ignored; when *Book of Dreams* was published in 1960, it received no reviews at all.

Despite the publication of his novels, Kerouac found no place in either the literary Establishment (which considered him puerile and anti-intellectual) or among popular publishers (who considered him a threat to their own middle-class values), so Kerouac's writing during the last ten years of his life appeared mostly in such sex-oriented magazines as *Nugget, Escapade,* and *Playboy.* The most money he ever made was $15,000 for the movie rights to *The Subterraneans*, which featured George Peppard in the Kerouac role. (The much-vaunted movie rights to *On the Road* were not sold until after Kerouac's death, when Francis Ford Coppola paid more money to the Kerouac estate than the author had made from all his books combined.) Kerouac's first experience with financial solvency brought him the chance to clear up old debts and to live out his lifelong dream of supporting his mother, but the writing time it bought him was now dissipated in alcohol, television watching, and diffuse depression.

Kerouac's circle of friends grew increasingly circumscribed. Whether he lived in Northport, Long Island, his boyhood town, Lowell, Massachusetts, Hyannis, Massachusetts, or Orlando, Florida, his chief companion was Gabrielle. There were sporadic affairs, but Gabrielle always rejected Jack's women as not being good enough for her son: they were witches, they didn't wash dishes properly, or their hair was too long. (Jack's perennial romance, Carolyn Cassady, became available when she divorced Neal in 1963, but Jack decided that she would belong to Neal until he died.) Gabrielle controlled Jack's money through their joint bank account, and she enforced Jack's vow at his father's deathbed that he would always care for his mother. Gabrielle was able at last to be a housewife, fixing snacks for her son, drinking whiskey and lo-cal gingerale as she watched television, religious medals pinned to her slip, reciting her rosary. Gabrielle effectively kept her son away from his old friends. She wrote Ginsberg a letter threatening to report him to the FBI as a homosexual if he ever came near her son, for example, discouraged contact with Neal Cassady, and wrote Burroughs hectoring letters (which he burned). "My God!" Burroughs concluded. "She really has him sewed up like an incision."[17]

Jack married Stella Sampas, the older sister of his close childhood friend Alex Sampas, in November 1966—Gabrielle had suffered a stroke two months earlier and needed a capable caretaker. "Who says you can't go home again?" Kerouac rhetorically asked, as the newlyweds returned to Lowell, where Jack tried to buy the two-story house on Beaulieu Street in which Gerard had died. It wasn't for sale. Kerouac's boyhood friends were disturbed by his unbathed stench, by his nonstop rambling, and especially by his alcoholism. He drank over a quart a day of Johnny Walker Red, washed down with Falstaff beer and Colt .45 malt liquor. His new wife tried to prevent his drunken escapades by hiding his shoes, but Jack was nonetheless thrown out of most of Lowell's bars, sometimes barefoot.

"To break through the barrier of language with WORDS, you have to be in orbit around your mind," he wrote shortly after he returned to

A page from Jack Kerouac's journal, April 18, 1960—the cost of Beat fame

I keep falling in love
with my mother.
                    —Jack Kerouac

I'm not about to throw my mother to the dogs of eternity.
                    —Jack Kerouac to Allen Ginsberg

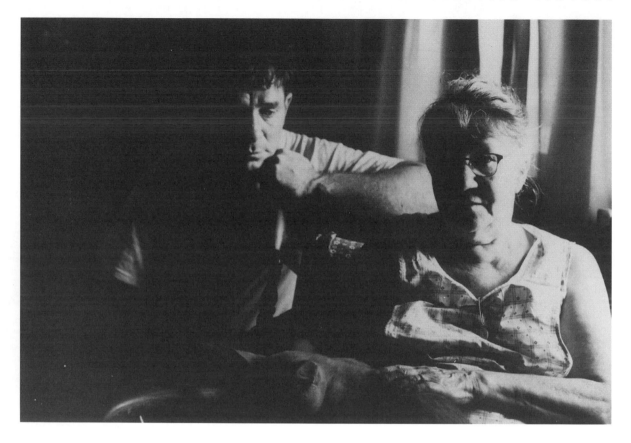

Jack Kerouac and his mother, Hyannis, 1965, by Ann Charters

Lowell, "and I may go up again if I regain my strength."[18] The secure combination of his mother, a vigilant wife, and his hometown helped him to settle down to composing the novel that would be his last. His writing room was set in order, the teletype roll in the electric typewriter lit by a Woolworth lamp embellished with a "Genius at Work" sign, a mirror arranged so that he could watch himself writing, and presiding over it all, a crucifix. He could no longer write in the marathon bursts of earlier days, so his daily output varied from a few pages to a single paragraph, but he stuck to his ethos of spontaneity and complete honesty, and by mid-May 1967 he had completed a ninety-three-foot teletype roll. He called it *Vanity of Duluoz*, read it into a tape recorder, listened to its sound, and judged the prose less poetic than his earlier work. But, he reflected, "Now there's no time for poetry anyway."[19]

Vanity of Duluoz was the final episode in his endless epic, the Legend of Duluoz. Subtitled "An Adventurous Education," the novel's narrative harked back to the first days of the Beat triumvirate in New York. Much of the same material had been covered in his first novel, *The Town and the City*. Those early days of promise were now evoked, not in fevered expectation, but from the vantage point of one ready to allow the vanity of personal and artistic ambitions to be replaced by peaceful indifference: "It just didn't matter what I did any time, anywhere, and with anyone; life is funny like I said."[20] It was the tone of a man ready to depart this earth.

Published two days after Neal Cassady's death, the novel received support from unlikely quarters (*Time*, for example, called it his best novel) mixed with more critical reviews. It was a commercial failure and wasn't published in paperback until twenty-five years after Kerouac's death. More than ever, Kerouac felt cut off from the friends depicted in his novel, although he sometimes carried on garrulous drunken telephone conversations with them until the bills ran so high that his wife tore the phone out of the wall. He alternately refused to believe that Cassady had died and brooded about others blaming him for Cassady's death. He had written off Ginsberg as "a hairy loss," and Burroughs lived mostly on another continent. Before Kerouac appeared on William Buckley's television show, *Firing Line*, in 1968, he had a final reunion with his friends. Always the wise elder, Burroughs corrected Jack's memory of past events and warned him not to participate in Buckley's show, to no avail. Ginsberg sat in the studio audience, however, and watched his old friend, drunk on Teacher's

Keep running after a dog, and he will never bite you; drink always before the thirst, and it will never come upon you.
—Jack Kerouac

*When you and me and Bill have ALL
our work published they'll be no more
talk about Nabokovs and Silones. What
a long time it will take, and when it
comes, it never matters anymore, and
then we go into eternity and don't care
anyway.*
    —Jack Kerouac to Allen Ginsberg

Scotch, make anti-Semitic remarks and declare that he shouldn't be
linked with Ginsberg. After the show, Allen tenderly grasped Jack and bid
him farewell for the last time: "Goodbye, drunken ghost."[21]

Buckley had invited Kerouac to comment on the post-Beat generation of hippies, who regarded him as a progenitor. One day during his last
years, Kerouac and a friend picked up a long-haired hippie hitchhiker,
who exclaimed, "Man, this is the life on the road!"[22] Kerouac thus witnessed the rise of the 1960s generation for whom he was both a reluctant
forefather and a nostalgic icon. Although he granted that the flower children were pursuing spiritual enlightenment, he distrusted the instant ex-
pansion of consciousness through drugs such as LSD, declaring, "Walking
on water wasn't made in a day."[23] Kerouac reviled Abbie Hoffman and
Jerry Rubin and opposed their leftist politics. About the 1968 riots he observed, "There are people who make a rule of creating chaos so that once
the chaos is under way they can then be elected as the people who take
care of the chaos."[24] Kerouac's last piece of writing, commissioned for
newspaper syndication, was a screed against hippies and the antiwar movement, and it bore the title, "After Me, the Deluge."

By the time Kerouac died on the morning of October 21, 1969, he
was paunchy, a victim of Johnny Walker Red mixed with Dexedrine pills.
Just before he began hemorrhaging, he was sitting before the television set,
watching *The Galloping Gourmet* with a notebook in hand and thoughts
for a new novel in his head. The next book would cover the years after the
publication of *On the Road*, and in homage to his father's small Lowell
paper, *The Spotlight*, it would be titled *The Beat Spotlight*.

Services were held in Lowell's St. Jean Baptiste Church, where
Jack had served as an altar boy thirty-five years earlier. The crowd included
hippies, Lowell associates, and old friends: John Clellon Holmes, Robert
Creeley, and agent Sterling Lord. Edie Parker entered the room and
yelled, "I'm Mrs. Jack Kerouac!"[25] Allen Ginsberg, Peter Orlovsky, and

*When I die, Neal, my face in the grave
will be a bony mask with holes . . .
SO WHAT AM I SUPPOSED TO DO?*
    —Jack Kerouac to Neal Cassady, 1951

Gregory Corso linked arms as they mutely approached the open casket. Corso had the impulse to remove the corpse from the casket and toss it across the room, "Because he wasn't there, this was the body."[26] (Corso restrained himself.) Ginsberg looked down at his friend in a black-and-white-checked sport jacket and red bowtie, holding a rosary in his hands, and observed that it was a "shock first seeing him there in theatric-lit coffin room as if a Buddha in *Parinirvana* pose, come here left his message of illusion-wink & left the body behind."[27] Before interring Kerouac in an unmarked grave, Father "Spike" Morissette delivered the final words: "Our hope and our prayer is that Jack has now found complete liberation, sharing the visions of Gerard. Amen. Alleluia."[28]

When the universe fails to see Jack, then Jack will die . . .
—Gregory Corso to Allen Ginsberg

ALLEN GINSBERG: AFTERMATH Allen Ginsberg pursued, literally to the ends of the earth, his vision from the summer of 1948. He tried to recapture that transfiguring moment when Blake spoke to him, through drugs and through spiritual quests in India and Japan. "The remarkable thing is that I stupefied myself from 1948 to 1963," Ginsberg reflected. "A long time—that's fifteen years preoccupied with one single thought."[29]

In his pursuit of altered consciousness Ginsberg tried many drugs, and the two most vividly recalled were yage (ayahuasca) and LSD-25. He first experienced LSD in 1959, as part of Gregory Bateson's experiments at the Mental Research Institute in Palo Alto, and described it to his father: "This drug seems to automatically produce a mystical experience. Science is getting very hip."[30]

In January 1960, Ginsberg went to Peru, climbed to the top of Machu Picchu, and later imbibed yage. He again found himself on a spiritual journey, as he wrote in his notebook: "I have come home, I am God, and I demand admittance thru the door."[31] He continued his quest, following the jungle path of William Burroughs to the *curanderos* of Pucallpa.

I have spent about as many hours high as I have spent in movie theaters—sometimes three hours a week, sometimes twelve or twenty or more, as at a film festival.
—Allen Ginsberg

"The Vomiter" by Allen Ginsberg, drawn under the influence of yage

Yen: to get sick because of a lack of heroin-related drugs (opium, morphine, Dilaudid, pantopon, codeine, dionine): "You know yourself when a guy is yenning, he doesn't look behind him. He's running." [Burroughs]

This beerlike brew of *Banisteriopsis caapi* was stronger than previous potions, and the cosmos threatened to split apart as he witnessed the "great squid of Eternity opening and closing its mouth in vast slow motion in the inner phantasmal recesses of imagination during hallucinated state—with undersea fringed labia."[32] Facing death and madness, it was the most potent experience he had ever had. "The LSD was perfection," he wrote, "but didn't get me so deep in, nor so horribly in."[33] Unsure whether he dared to continue, he sought the wise counsel of Burroughs. "There is nothing to fear," Burroughs replied. "Your Ayahuasca consciousness is more valid than your Normal consciousness."[34] Ginsberg returned for a final experience, where he again experienced the inevitable duality of God and death and confronted "a self condemned to worry about its extinction."[35] But he recorded in his journal a momentary resolution to his yage-induced feelings of mortality: "Widen the area of consciousness till it becomes so wide it includes its own death. This is the purpose of life."[36]

Ginsberg conducted his next major drug experiment—with psilocybin mushrooms—on November 26, 1960, at Harvard under the aegis of Professor Timothy Leary, then beginning his experiments with consciousness-expanding drugs. Under the influence of 36 milligrams of psilocybin, listening to Wagner's *Götterdämmerung*, Ginsberg felt that he was the Messiah, destined to lead a revolution. He wandered downstairs naked, determined to let the world know the importance of his experience by calling Nikita Khrushchev, William Carlos Williams, and Norman Mailer. Identifying himself to the operator as God ("G-O-D," he spelled it out for her), he was connected to Jack Kerouac, whom he exhorted to come immediately to Boston: "I am high and naked and I am King of the Universe. Get on the plane. It is time!"[37] Ginsberg and Leary agreed that world leaders should take psilocybin: "Everyone plugged in at once announce the Coming Union of All Consciousness."[38] Allen's epiphany was not unlike his previous messianic experiences, but in the company of Leary it proved a portentous forerunner of the 1960s widespread drug experimentation. As Leary looked back on that evening: "And then we started planning the psychedelic revolution."[39]

Before further pursuing this psychedelic revolution, Ginsberg tried to expand his consciousness through spiritual means. At the beginning of 1962, accompanied by Peter Orlovsky, he set out for India, where he met Gary Snyder and Joanne Kyger and remained for a year. Going from one ashram to another, he repeatedly asked gurus the way to spiritual enlightenment. One advised him to take William Blake as his guru; others told him, "Your own heart is your guru."[40] The words he would longest remember were those of Dudjom Rinpoche, whom Allen met on June 3, 1962, his thirty-sixth birthday. "If you see anything horrible, don't cling to it. If you see anything beautiful, don't cling to it."[41] He was repeatedly instructed to turn away from the metaphysical and live in his body, as that was the form he was born for.

Near the end of his trip, on July 17, 1962, Ginsberg was sitting on the Kyoto–Tokyo express, reviewing not only this advice but all the sights of his year in India—the burning bodies on funeral pyres, the scenes of poverty. As the Japanese landscape quickly passed by he had an ecstatic experience. Echoing the old vision in the Columbia bookstore, when he had seen beyond the masks of mortal vulnerability, he now surveyed his fellow passengers and "saw how exquisitely dear they all were—we all were. . . . I suddenly didn't want to be *dominated* by that nonhuman any more, or even be dominated by the moral obligation to enlarge my consciousness any more," he recalled. "Or do anything any more except *be* my heart—which just desired to be and be alive now."[42] Ginsberg wept.

Shortly after he returned to the United States, Ginsberg participated in his first political demonstration, on the occasion of Madame Nhu's visit to San Francisco, and expressed his unique perspective in words that his biographer Barry Miles called "pure hippie rhetoric, enun-

Everybody who hears my voice try the chemical LSD at least once, every man, woman, and child in good health over the age of fourteen.
—Allen Ginsberg

Just taking acid's not yoga. Yoga is getting through acid, knowing what to do with acid. Yoga is knowing how to be neat when you're high.
—Allen Ginsberg

Allen Ginsberg in India, 1962, by Peter Orlovsky

ciated for the first time—the direct result of his experience on the train in Japan."[43] Ginsberg's presence in a public demonstration signaled his coming decades in the spotlight, as he shifted energies from his private search for spirituality to the public stage of countercultural politics. Training his sensitive eye on the world around him, Ginsberg foresaw the hippies, the sexual revolution, and the influence of Zen. He soon became a forefather to the 1960s Love Generation, and in his ubiquitous poster guise as an underground Uncle Sam, he became its most iconic figure.

The Whitman-like expansiveness of Ginsberg's extraliterary career during the 1960s and after defies summary here. For years he simply seemed to appear everywhere as the spokesman for, in Jane Kramer's words, "an amalgamated hippie-pacifist-activist-visionary-orgiastic-anarchist-orientalist-psychedelic underground."[44] He kissed on behalf of gay rights; he testified in freedom-of-expression trials such as the censorship of Jack Smith's *Flaming Creatures*; he marched to protest the Vietnam War; he spoke out for the legalization of marijuana; he chanted and played his harmonium on behalf of religious freedom. At virtually every key gathering of the 1960s counterculture, Ginsberg was a notable presence: the 1967 March on Washington, the Francisco Be-In, the 1968 Chicago Democratic Convention riots, and the late 1960s Warhol Factory. His activity was not simply national but global, and he intractably purveyed his vision even when doctrinaire politicians, right and left, evicted him from their countries.

All the while he continued writing poetry and receiving accolades for his work: a Pulitzer Prize, a Guggenheim Fellowship, induction into the American Academy of Arts and Letters (1974). Even *Time* magazine called him "a national treasure." He is widely considered the best living American poet in the bardic tradition.

Perhaps as remarkable as Ginsberg's widespread celebrity is the modest equanimity with which he has borne it. Over the past decades, many elements of Ginsberg's style have remained constant: his warm avuncular presence, owlish eyes behind large glasses, a toothy grin, and an eternally game slouch. After traveling globally and speaking before crowds, he would return to the corner of a friend's borrowed room, where he had created his makeshift home from a sleeping bag and mattress, or to his own apartment, which became a long-running residence for friends. Ginsberg initially read for free and later—to avoid paying taxes that supported the Vietnam War—founded the Committee on Poetry (which gave support to poets who helped in "altering the consciousness of the Nation toward a more humane spirit of Adhesiveness prophesied by Whitman"[45]). He has remained equally active backstage, networking, encouraging publications, and promoting poets. Gregory Corso once remarked that Ginsberg operated like a Jewish businessman, and another friend called him the casting office of the underground. He has become the torchbearer of

Gary Snyder, Michael McClure, Allen Ginsberg, and others celebrate Peace and Love at the "Gathering of the Tribes for a Human Be-in," San Francisco, January 14, 1967, by Lisa Law

the Beat Generation's legacy—without his archival zeal, his panache for
the group's publicity, and his generosity to scholars, the study of the Beat
Generation would be considerably diminished. In his role as Beat historian, Ginsberg outlined the broad effects of the Beat Generation, and the
activities that became linked to it, directly or indirectly. The Beat heritage,
in Ginsberg's eye:

- Spiritual liberation; sexual revolution of liberation i.e. gay libera-
  tion, catalyzing black liberation, women's liberation, gray pan-
  ther liberation
- Liberation of the Word from censorship
- Demystification and/or decriminalization of some laws against
  marijuana and other drugs
- Spread of ecological consciousness emphasized early by Snyder
  and McClure
- Opposition to the military-industrial machine civilization
- Return to appreciation of idiosyncrasy as against state regimenta-
  tion
- Respect for land and indigenous peoples.
- Less rich conspicuous consumption
- Eastern thought (and meditation)
- Non-theism, no cosmic fascism, or thus, cosmic antifascism
- Candor/frankness: end of secrecy and paranoia fear from CIA,
  KGB, nuclear secrecy, through to sexual secrecy, on a contin-
  uum[46]

As much as he cherishes that past, Ginsberg's life is directed
toward future travels, future books, future readings. As his old friend
Philip Whalen recently commented, shaking his head, "Allen, he's
irrepressible."[47]

Allen Ginsberg's New York kitchen, featuring Arthur Rimbaud, Chögyam Trungpa, Walt Whitman, by Gordon Ball

WILLIAM BURROUGHS: AFTERMATH William Burroughs has said that all his life has been devoted to a single connected work, "several novels all interlocking and taking place simultaneously in a *majoun* dream."[48] The hundreds of manuscript pages, notes, and routines that remained after *Naked Lunch* was published—what he called his "Word Hoard"— would overflow into subsequent novels. What he initially called his sequel, *Naked Free Lunch*, eventually fueled three novels, *The Soft Machine, The Ticket That Exploded*, and *Nova Express*. When Burroughs exhausted his word hoard, he developed new routines, and in the thirty-five years since *Naked Lunch* he has obsessively turned out manuscript after manuscript. Characters have been recycled, phrases reused, and earlier works later cut up and folded in upon one another to yield new works, while old books were rewritten and republished in new versions. Burroughs has occasionally found himself hobbled and depressed by writer's block, or wondering whether there is anything more to say, but year after year he has persisted. He has created a nonlinear map of his personal consciousness and a

I think all writers write for an audience. There is no such things as writing for yourself. Only they never find out who the audience is. When you find out who you are writing for I think you stop writing.
—William Burroughs to Allen Ginsberg

*What are you rewriting? A lifelong
preoccupation with Control and Virus.
Having gained access the virus uses the
host's energy, blood, flesh and bones to
make copies of itself.*
                        —William Burroughs

prophetic vision of a corrupt, despoiled world, each episode contributing
to a large, nightmarish mosaic.

Burroughs describes himself as simply "a recording instrument,"
but that instrument is strikingly different from Christopher Isherwood's "I
am a camera." He might rise from a light sleep to jot down a dream, or recall childhood memories or psychological traumas, or follow his drug-
fueled interior visions. "All my writing comes from the psychic thing,"
Burroughs said. "You sit down and a light turns on and you see a set or
character. In other words, writing a novel is like watching a film. I tran-
scribe it."[49] Fending off the Ugly Spirit by writing has been a therapeutic
process without catharsis, a continuous exorcism.

The themes and characters that ran through his first books reap-
pear in altered guises. *The Soft Machine* opens with an episode of Burroughs and "Sailor" (Phil White) drunk-rolling in New York in 1946, for
example, and *The Ticket That Exploded* harks back to Burroughs and
Marker in South America on the first quest for yage. The literal addiction
recounted in *Junky* was transformed into a more encompassing metaphor
that has assumed many guises throughout his books: the cast of characters
fight agents of control (by the state, church, drugs, love, and, above all, the
Ugly Spirit), combatting their inexorable, internal "algebra of need." Burroughs' Trak Enterprises, for example, operates on the motto: "Invade,
Damage, Occupy."[50]

I am the cat that walks alone.
                        —William Burroughs

Although his early writing depended on the support and collaboration of his close friends, Ginsberg and Kerouac, the years since *Naked
Lunch* have seen Burroughs' associations widen and his writing identified
with something broader than the Beat Generation. He has, indeed, been
acknowledged by the literary community and, beginning in the 1970s, embraced by successive generations as a New Wave pop star and the godfa-
ther of the counterculture. As singer Patti Smith put it: "He's up there with
the Pope."[51] Burroughs' growing celebrity hasn't been reflected in growing
literary income—advances on his books hovered around $25,000, and he

earned far more by public reading, occasional movie roles (*Drugstore Cowboy*), and selling his old letters and manuscripts to university archives.

Two distinctly different ceremonies honoring Burroughs reflect his odd celebrity. The first of these, the Nova Convention, took place over three days in December 1978 on New York's Lower East Side. Emceed by performance artist Laurie Anderson, it consisted of academic panels interspersed with performers ranging from John Cage and Merce Cunningham to Patti Smith and Frank Zappa. At the center—as the linchpin between America's old avant-garde and the new age of punks—was Burroughs, who proclaimed in the keynote speech: "This is the Space Age and we're here to go."[52] Many of his new generation of fans had never read any Burroughs but knew him as one of the figures on the cover of *Sergeant Pepper's Lonely Hearts Club Band*. Musicians drew from Burroughs' words—"heavy metal" originated in *Naked Lunch*'s "heavy metal thunder," for example, and Steely Dan was named after a dildo in *Naked Lunch*; David Bowie used Burroughs' cut-up technique to create the lyrics of *Diamond Dogs*.

The second ceremony took place five years later. The setting—the American Academy and Institute of Arts and Letters—was more august, and the *escargots en croûte*–munching, Beaujolais–drinking participants were several generations older. They had gathered to induct new members, and—as a result of Allen Ginsberg's energetic politicking and the support of Norman Mailer, John Ashbery, Christopher Isherwood, Peter Matthiessen, and Hortense Calisher—Burroughs became one of them. (That he was not fully "one of them" was suggested by the work he submitted for an exhibition of work by new members—a painting called *Gun Door*, created by firing a shotgun at a wooden panel covered with bags of paint; it was not hung.) Hortense Calisher told the assembled: "William Burroughs' *Naked Lunch* marked him as an innovator in the form and content of the novel, and as a cultural symbol." Burroughs gave a polite bow and accepted the institute's purple and gold rosette, henceforth to be worn on his lapel. "These people, twenty years ago, they were saying I be-

No one in his senses would want to be God, and certainly not me. I don't have the qualifications.
—William Burroughs

longed in jail," Burroughs observed. "Now they're saying I belong in their club. I didn't listen to them then, and I don't listen to them now."[53]

In the early 1980s—after decades spent in Mexico, Tangiers, Paris, London, and New York—Burroughs bought a two-bedroom, white clapboard home on a shady acre of land next to a drainage creek, 270 miles west of the St. Louis neighborhood in which he had grown up. Lawrence, Kansas, had its own unlikely literary pedigree—both Langston Hughes and Frank Harris had lived there—but a major attraction for Burroughs was the presence of his Kansas-born secretary-editor-companion, James Grauerholz. (Beginning at age twenty-one and continuing to the present, Grauerholz has proved invaluable to what is called "William Burroughs Communications." Grauerholz does everything from editing and anthologizing to lecture booking and movie script rewriting.) "Time was every creative person had to be in Paris, London, New York, etc.," Burroughs wrote his friend Brion Gysin. "That's all over and done with. Went out when the jets came in."[54] He exchanged the stimulus of urban living—"the continual stream of second attention awareness"[55]—for a town environment that cost half as much as city living, and he furnished his house with garage-sale furniture and an electric typewriter. Here he could fish, he could commune with his six cats, and he could shoot his collection of handguns, shotguns, and rifles.

In *The Western Lands*, then seventy-three-year-old Burroughs wrote what sounded like a valedictory: "The old writer couldn't write anymore because he had reached the end of words, the end of what can be done with words. And then?"[56] But the valedictory tone was only momentary, and Burroughs continued writing. He wrote the libretto to *The Black Rider*, an operatic collaboration with Robert Wilson and Tom Waits, for example, and has begun work on a subsequent opera. Shortly after his eightieth birthday, Viking published Burroughs' collection of dreams, *My Education*. Much of his time is now devoted to painting, some of it accomplished with a shotgun, some with a spray can.

William would make a greater prisoner. You know, in solitary.
—James Grauerholz, on William Burroughs

I have never regretted my experience with drugs. When you stop growing you start dying. An addict never stops growing.
—William Burroughs

*William Burroughs at home in
Lawrence, Kansas, March 19, 1992,
by Allen Ginsberg*

Burroughs has repeatedly stated that his life has been a continual effort to keep the evil force at bay—through writing, psychoanalysis, and Scientology. On April 16, 1992, he made an attempt to exorcise the Ugly Spirit. Burroughs, Ginsberg, and five friends drove to the old stone house outside Lawrence where Burroughs had once lived, and there they descended into a hole over which arched a bower of twigs and branches sheathed in black plastic, with a fire pit in the middle. The heat and smoke in the sweat lodge were almost unbearable. Melvin Betsellie, a big-bellied Navajo shaman, presided over the exorcism of Burroughs' evil spirit. The assembled listened as the shaman invited them to share his grandfathers' medicine, blew on a shrill bone whistle, and prayed to the elements. All the while, more hot stones, water, and cedar shavings were added to the fire pit, and the air became unbearably smoky. The shaman took coals from the fire and put them in his mouth, lighting up his throat's gorge, swallowed the evil spirit in the embers, retched them up again, and then touched Burroughs with a burning coal. Burroughs felt nothing. Finally captured, the spirit was jiggled in the bone whistle and blown into the fire. The assembled sent Burroughs their best healing thoughts, while Ginsberg felt in touch with all the generations who had "appreciated his adventurous spirit and his insight and lonely courage and the beauty of his stubborn realism."[57]

Burroughs thought the Ugly Spirit was a product of his capitalist forebears. "It's very much related to the American Tycoon. To William Randolph Hearst, Vanderbilt, Rockefeller, that whole stratum of American acquisitive evil. . . . The ugly American at his ugly worst. That's exactly what it is."[58] The shaman later told him that he had been overconfident, that Burroughs' evil entity was stronger than any he had ever met and that he had been deeply frightened. But he had finally seen it and been able to gain control: the Ugly Spirit was a faceless white skull with winglike protuberances and no eyes.

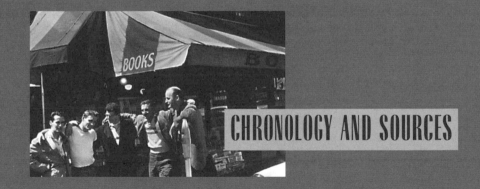

CHRONOLOGY AND SOURCES

CHRONOLOGY:
THE BEAT GENERATION, 1943–1960

1943

Early 1943: Jack Kerouac works on a novel entitled "The Sea Is My Brother" while at home in Lowell, Massachusetts.

Spring: Following a suicide attempt, Lucien Carr is hospitalized in Cook County Hospital, Chicago. After discharge, he moves to New York and enrolls at Columbia as a second-quarter freshman. David Kammerer follows.

Spring: William Burroughs moves to New York.

May: Jack Kerouac is granted an honorable discharge from the Navy, with a diagnosis of "indifferent character."

June: Kerouac ships out to Liverpool on the *George Weems*.

Ca. December: Through his girlfriend Edie Parker, Kerouac meets Lucien Carr and begins a friendship.

December: Allen Ginsberg meets Lucien Carr, who soon introduces him to William Burroughs and David Kammerer.

1944

Lucien Carr, Jack Kerouac, and Allen Ginsberg theorize about the New Vision; centrally important are three concepts: (1) Naked self-expression is the seed of creativity.

GENERAL CHRONOLOGY:
1943–1960

1943

The Casablanca Conference is convened to coordinate military strategy against the Axis powers.

A danceable form of jazz called jive emerges, and the most popular dance is the Jitterbug.

Owing to the lack of wartime access to Paris, American women's fashions become newly independent of Continental influence.

Dwight D. Eisenhower is named Supreme Commander of Allied forces in Europe.

The Supreme Court rules that schoolchildren should not be compelled to salute the American flag if doing so poses a religious conflict.

Richard Rodgers and Oscar Hammerstein's musical *Oklahoma!* marks an advance in the integration of music and narrative.

The young Communist League declares itself dissolved

1944

Franklin Delano Roosevelt becomes the first president to be elected to a fourth term.

THE BEAT GENERATION

(2) The artist's consciousness is expanded by derangement of the senses. (3) Art eludes conventional morality.

Sixteen-year-old Philip Lamantia works as assistant editor at *View* magazine.

February: William Burroughs meets Kerouac via David Kammerer.

Circle, edited by George Leite, is published in San Francisco. It includes works by Henry Miller, Robert Duncan, William Everson, and Kenneth Rexroth, and marks the beginning of the first San Francisco Renaissance.

Spring: Lucien Carr introduces Jack Kerouac and Allen Ginsberg.

Late April: *The Illiterati* is published, including poems by William Everson.

Summer: Men at the Civilian Public Service Camp for conscientous objectors in Waldport, Oregon, establish a fine arts project; it includes artists, writers, actors, and musicians and becomes a seedbed for the San Francisco Renaissance.

August 14: Lucien Carr mortally stabs his amorous pursuer, David Kammerer, and involves Kerouac and Burroughs in the aftermath of the manslaughter; they are arrested and charged as material witnesses.

August 22: As a means of raising bail bond to get out of jail, Kerouac marries Edie Parker, and they soon move to her family home in Grosse Pointe, Michigan. The marriage will be annulled in September 1946.

GENERAL

Meat rationing ends and production of consumer goods resumes.

The Communist Party disbands and reforms as a nonparty group, the Communist Political Association.

Appalachian Spring, choreographed by Martha Graham and composed by Aaron Copland, premieres.

Allied forces carry out coordinated landings in Normandy.

The Supreme Court rules that race cannot be used to deny voting rights.

Paris and Brussels are liberated from German occupation.

Top box-office stars: Bing Crosby, Gary Cooper, Bob Hope, Betty Grable, Spencer Tracy, Greer Garson, Humphrey Bogart, Abbott and Costello, Cary Grant, Bette Davis.

Two best-selling novels wage censorship battles: Lillian Smith's *Strange Fruit*, and Kathleen Winsor's *Forever Amber*. A New York judge declares D. H. Lawrence's *Lady Chatterley's Lover* obscene; the decision is overturned by a higher court.

An automatic, sequence-controlled computer with a 50-foot control panel is created at Harvard.

Both men's and women's fashions emphasize big shoulders and pointed lapels, known as the "football player" look.

THE BEAT GENERATION

October 6: Lucien Carr's manslaughter trial is held; he is sentenced to one to twenty years at the Elmira Reformatory; he is released in 1946.

December: Edie Parker moves with her former roommate, Joan Vollmer, into a large communal apartment at 419 West 115th Street, and Kerouac soon joins them.

1945

Under pseudonyms Burroughs (a.k.a. Will Dennison) and Kerouac (a.k.a. Mike Ryko) collaborate on a novel, "And the Hippos Were Boiled in Their Tanks," that recounts the events leading up to the death of David Kammerer; it is never published.

January: Allen Ginsberg starts writing his first serious poems.

March 16: Ginsberg is apprehended by Columbia University officials for writing "Fuck the Jews" and "[Columbia President] Butler has no balls" in the dust on his windowsill. He is suspended for a year and in June moves into Joan Vollmer's apartment on 115th Street.

May 1, 1945: Kerouac conceives of writing a novel that contrasts his New England upbringing with his experiences in New York; this is the seed for his first published novel, *The Town and the City*.

GENERAL

Lt. John F. Kennedy displays "extreme heroism" when his PT-109 is cut in half by a Japanese destroyer.

The Germans develop the first large missile, 1,600 pounds, with a 200-mile range.

Wartime paper shortages stimulate experimentation with soft-cover books.

"Kilroy was here" becomes a popular graffiti slogan, valorizing American GIs.

1945

U.S. Armed Forces total 7.2 million. War casualties: 292,000 killed or missing; 613,611 wounded.

Earl S. Tupper develops polyethylene containers, calls them Tupperware.

Iwo Jima falls to U.S. Marines after thirty-six days of fighting.

Victory in Europe is declared on May 8, known as V-E Day.

The United Nations opens in San Francisco; the U.S. Senate ratifies the UN charter by a vote of 89 to 2.

Paperback books help spur a boom in publishing.

"Bebop" jazz becomes popular.

THE BEAT GENERATION

August 1, 1945: Neal Cassady marries LuAnne Henderson.

August: Burroughs returns to New York from St. Louis.

Fall: A seminal discussion, known as "The Night of the Wolfeans," takes place at Joan Vollmer's communal apartment. Kerouac and Hal Chase are the Wolfeans, Ginsberg and Burroughs are the non-Wolfeans.

1946

Ca. January: William Burroughs is introduced to heroin by Herbert Huncke and Phil White. Around the same time Burroughs moves into Joan Vollmer's apartment.

April: Burroughs is arrested for forging a prescription slip, and in June he is given a four-month suspended sentence and remanded to St. Louis.

Spring: While his father is dying, Jack Kerouac begins writing *The Town and the City*.

Summer: The Joan Vollmer communal apartment disintegrates; Burroughs is in St. Louis, Ginsberg at sea, Kerouac in his family's home, and Vollmer increasingly suffers from amphetamine-induced delusions.

September: Allen Ginsberg reviews William Carlos Williams' *Paterson* (1) for the *Passaic Valley Examiner* and concludes, "The book and I have little in common." This is his first contact with Williams.

GENERAL

The United States drops atomic bombs on Hiroshima and Nagasaki.

Roberto Rosselini's *Open City* establishes neorealism in film.

1946

The Atomic Energy Commission is established.

Mother Frances X. Cabrini is canonized; she is the first U.S. citizen to become a saint in the Catholic Church.

The "ranch-type" house becomes popular and leads to construction of split-level homes.

The United Nations accepts a John D. Rockefeller gift for construction of a permanent home in New York.

The French war in Vietnam begins.

Ezra Pound is confined to St. Elizabeth's mental hospital on charges of treason; he remains there until 1958.

The Nuremburg trials end in the conviction of fourteen Nazi war criminals.

Winston Churchill, in a speech in Fulton, Missouri, coins the term "Iron Curtain" in reference to the Soviet Union.

THE BEAT GENERATION

October: Joan Vollmer is hospitalized in Bellevue's psychiatric ward.

December: Burroughs drives to New York to bail Joan Vollmer out of Bellevue; they conceive William Burroughs III in a Times Square hotel room and plan to move to Texas and raise marijuana.

December: Neal Cassady and his wife, LuAnne, take a trip to New York and meet Kerouac and Ginsberg. Neal's relationships with both Kerouac and Ginsberg will prove significant, as a literary model and as a sexual initiator.

1947

The San Remo begins to be the hangout for hipsters, writers, artists, and bohemians; it remains a center until the mid-1950s.

Gregory Corso begins a three-year stay at Clinton State Prison, where he educates himself in the prison library and begins writing poetry.

January: William Burroughs and Joan Vollmer move to a farm near New Waverly, Texas, to raise vegetables and marijuana. Herbert Huncke joins them a month later.

January 10: Allen Ginsberg has his first significant interaction with Neal Cassady, and they soon have sexual relations and form an intense relationship.

March 4: Cassady ends his first season in New York, seen off at the Greyhound bus station by Kerouac and Ginsberg.

GENERAL

Bugsy Siegel opens the Flamingo, marking the beginning of Las Vegas' aspiration to become the "entertainment capital of America."

Dr. Benjamin Spock's *The Common Sense Book of Baby and Child Care* is published and revolutionizes child-rearing.

African Americans vote in the Mississippi Democratic primary for the first time.

1947

President Harry S Truman states the principle of Soviet containment (the Truman Doctrine).

Pan-American Airways inaugurates the first globe-circling airline (round-the-world fare is $1,700).

Secretary of State George Marshall proposes the European Recovery Program (the Marshall Plan) to give economic aid to certain war-torn European nations.

Bubble-gum-blowing contests become popular.

The Taft-Hartley Bill is enacted to curb unions' alleged abuses of power.

The Polaroid camera is developed.

Tennessee Williams' A *Streetcar Named Desire* is produced on Broadway; it wins the Pulitzer Prize.

THE BEAT GENERATION

Spring: Cassady begins an affair with Carolyn Robinson.

July: Ginsberg goes to Denver to be with Cassady and finds him involved in an affair with Carolyn Robinson.

July 17: Kerouac takes a bus to Denver to be with Cassady and Ginsberg, finds them preoccupied with each other, and in August takes a bus to San Francisco.

July 21: William Burroughs III is born in New Waverly, Texas.

August 29: Ginsberg and Cassady arrive at the Burroughses' farm in New Waverly, Texas.

September: Gary Snyder matriculates at Reed College, where he studies literature and anthropology and graduates in 1950.

September 7: Following a break-up with Cassady, Ginsberg ships out on the *John Blair*, bound for Dakar.

September 30: Burroughs, Huncke, and Cassady transport a car full of marijuana to New York to sell; the deal turns out disastrously, and Burroughs abandons plans to raise marijuana.

1948

April 1: Neal Cassady marries Carolyn Robinson.

May: Jack Kerouac finishes the first draft of *The Town and the City*.

GENERAL

The "New Look" dominates female fashion, emphasizing a tiny waist and pointed bosom.

Jackie Robinson becomes the first African American to sign a contract with a major baseball club.

Oral Roberts gains a following as a God-assisted healer.

The sharp rise in sales of cheeses advertised on the *Kraft Television Theater* demonstrates television's marketing potential.

The House Un-American Activities Committee begins hearings and indicts the "Hollywood Ten" for contempt, leading to a blacklist of alleged Communist sympathizers.

Chrysler, Pepsi-Cola, Gimbels, and the *Encyclopaedia Britannica* lead in a trend toward business patronage of the arts.

The Spring Grove Hospital in Maryland announces that schizophrenia can be cured by prefrontal lobotomy.

Howdy Doody and *Meet the Press* premiere on television.

Thor Heyderdal sets sail from Peru on the *Kon-Tiki*.

1948

Goldmark develops the long-playing phonograph record (LP).

The New York City Ballet is founded under the leadership of Lincoln Kirstein and George Balanchine.

THE BEAT GENERATION

Summer: Allen Ginsberg experiences a vision in an East Harlem apartment: William Blake speaks to him. This experience becomes his guiding force for the next fifteen years.

June: Burroughs reads Wilhelm Reich and becomes interested in orgone boxes.

November: Kerouac meets John Clellon Holmes, who will write the first novel about the Beat Generation.

November: Kerouac begins an account of his travel experiences in 1947, and by Thanksgiving he has finished the first version of *On the Road*.

December 24: William Everson experiences a visionary conversion, leading him to become a Dominican lay monk and to adopt the name Brother Antoninus.

December 29: Neal Cassady, LuAnne Henderson, and Al Hinkle arrive at Kerouac's home in North Carolina.

1949

Barney Rosset begins Grove Press.

January 28: Jack Kerouac, Neal Cassady, LuAnne Henderson, and Al Hinkle depart New York, beginning the trip that will be fictionalized in *On the Road*. En route they stay with William Burroughs in Louisiana.

February: In San Francisco, Cassady dumps Kerouac and LuAnne; after a few days Kerouac takes a bus back to his mother's.

GENERAL

When Jean Genet is sentenced to life imprisonment, influential writers intercede on his behalf and he is released.

Mahatma Gandhi is assassinated in India.

Alger Hiss is indicted on two counts of perjury for reportedly giving secrets to Communist spies.

The first Supreme Court hearing on a state obscenity law (New York's) upholds the state's suppression of Edmund Wilson's *Memoirs of Hecate County*.

The State of Israel is founded.

The Supreme Court declares religious education in public schools a violation of the First Amendment.

"The Cold War" becomes common parlance to describe East-West relations.

1949

George Orwell's *1984* is published.

The American Cancer Society and the National Cancer Institute warn that cigarette smoking may cause cancer.

Sixteen attend the last gathering of Civil War veterans.

American women begin wearing bikini bathing suits.

THE BEAT GENERATION

February: Herbert Huncke turns up at Allen Ginsberg's apartment in desperate straits, and begins to take over the apartment and stock it with "hot goods" stolen by Vicki Russell and Little Jack Melody.

March 29, 1949: Kerouac's novel *The Town and the City* is accepted by Robert Giroux of Harcourt, Brace with an advance of $1,000.

April: William Burroughs is arrested on a drug charge in Louisiana.

April 21: Ginsberg rides with Vicki Russell and Little Jack Melody in a car filled with stolen goods; all three are apprehended and arrested.

May: On the strength of the advance for his novel, Kerouac "retires" to Denver; his mother soon joins him but will return in July.

June 29: Ginsberg is admitted as an inpatient to the Columbia Psychiatric Institute, a condition of his sentencing for his arrest in April. On his first day he meets fellow inmate Carl Solomon.

Fall: Kerouac first uses the term "beat generation" in conversation with John Clellon Holmes.

September: Burroughs and Joan Vollmer move to Mexico City.

December: Carl Solomon is discharged from the Columbia Psychiatric Institute.

GENERAL

Arthur Miller's *Death of a Salesman* opens on Broadway, wins the Pulitzer Prize, and becomes the first play to be a Book-of-the-Month Club selection.

The North Atlantic Treaty Organization (NATO) is established.

Cortisone is discovered, to be used for pain relief in rheumatoid arthritis.

South Africa enacts apartheid laws.

The Emmy Awards are founded to recognize achievement in television.

Television's first situation comedies (*I Remember Mama*, *The Goldbergs*) premiere.

The postwar baby boom levels off.

Fads include: lady wrestlers, Canasta, short straight hair, Caesar salads, mother-daughter matching playsuits, plastic erector sets.

"Cool jazz" becomes popular, as performed by Miles Davis, the Modern Jazz Quartet, and others.

THE BEAT GENERATION

1950

Robert Duncan meets painter and collagist Jess Collins; they soon begin living together, and form an enduring domestic partnership.

Lawrence Ferling (who will restore his name to Ferlinghetti in 1954) moves from Paris to San Francisco, where he remains to the present day.

Three Reed College students, Gary Snyder, Philip Whalen, and Lew Welch, live together. Gary Snyder publishes his first poems in a Reed College student publication.

February 27: Allen Ginsberg is discharged from the Columbia Psychiatric Institute and begins a campaign to lead a "normal" life.

March: Ginsberg hears William Carlos Williams at the Guggenheim Museum, and a few days later writes the older poet a letter that will initiate an instrumental literary relationship.

March 2: Jack Kerouac's novel *The Town and the City* is published and released to mixed reviews and poor sales; sales virtually end by April.

Ca. March: Allen Ginsberg and Gregory Corso meet at the Pony Stable, a Greenwich Village lesbian bar, and begin a long-term friendship.

Spring: Carl Solomon's article "Report from the Asylum—Afterthoughts of a Shock Patient" is published (under the pseudonym Carl Goy) in *Neurotica*.

GENERAL

1950

Senator Joseph R. McCarthy of Wisconsin charges that the State Department has been infiltrated by Communists.

Congress passes the McCarran Act (Internal Security Act) over President Truman's veto. It provides for the registration of Communists and Communist-front organizations.

Jackson Pollock paints *Lavender Mist*, the first "action painting."

Prefabricated fallout shelters grow in popularity.

Charles Schulz creates the *Peanuts* comic strip.

Dresses become more natural and wearable; young people wear their hair short and dress in dungarees and ballet shoes.

American forces, under the command of Douglas MacArthur, cross the 38th parallel to invade North Korea.

President Truman authorizes the Atomic Energy Commission to produce the hydrogen bomb.

The Dave Brubeck Quartet is formed and soon becomes the most popular jazz combo in the world.

Illiteracy in the United States reaches a new low of 3.2 percent.

The United Nations reports that of the 800 million children in the world, 480 million are undernourished.

THE BEAT GENERATION

Spring: William Burroughs begins writing an autobiographical narrative called "Junk," later published as *Junky*.

July 10: Neal Cassady bigamously marries Diana Hansen, pregnant with his child; he is still married to Carolyn Cassady and returns to her on the day of the wedding.

August: Lucien Carr visits the Burroughses in Mexico; soon after, Joan takes action to divorce Burroughs.

November 17: Kerouac marries Joan Haverty, an ex-girlfriend of Bill Cannastra, a friend who was beheaded on October 12 in a subway accident.

December 27: Kerouac receives a 23,000-word confessional letter from Cassady, known as the "Joan Letter." Kerouac proclaims it "a masterpiece," and is inspired to write in a no-holds-barred prose style.

December: Burroughs completes a first draft of *Junky*.

1951

Winter to spring: Neal Cassady works on his autobiographical memoir, published in 1971 as *The First Third*.

March: John Clellon Holmes shows Kerouac his novel *Go*, about members of "The Beat Generation," including thinly disguised portraits of Ginsberg, Kerouac, Cassady, and Huncke.

Spring: Cid Corman's *Origin* begins publication.

Spring: William Burroughs begins writing *Queer*.

GENERAL

The Lonely Crowd by David Riesman is published.

The first American homosexual-rights group for men, the Mattachine Society, is founded in Los Angeles.

Herblock coins the term "McCarthyism," and among those on the Hollywood blacklist are Gypsy Rose Lee, Arthur Miller, Pete Seeger, Zero Mostel, Howard K. Smith, and Orson Welles.

The first successful aorta and kidney transplants are performed.

A *Life* survey yields the most popular teen idols: Louisa May Alcott, Joe DiMaggio, Vera-Ellen, Franklin Delano Roosevelt, Abraham Lincoln, Roy Rogers, General Douglas MacArthur, Clara Barton, Doris Day, Sister Elizabeth Kenny, Babe Ruth, and Florence Nightingale.

Alger Hiss is found guilty of perjury.

1951

Julius and Ethel Rosenberg are found guilty of conspiring to transmit classified military documents to the Soviet Union; they are executed in 1953.

American Telephone and Telegraph becomes the first corporation to exceed one million stockholders.

UNIVAC I is the first mass-produced computer.

A video camera is developed that records both pictures and sound on magnetic tape.

THE BEAT GENERATION

April: Kerouac types, at great and continuous speed on a taped-together scroll, a new version of *On the Road,* which is essentially the version published in 1957.

June: Gary Snyder graduates from Reed College with a degree in anthropology and literature.

Early July: Burroughs and Lewis Marker take a trip to Ecuador in search of yage, returning in early September.

August: Allen Ginsberg and Lucien Carr visit Joan Burroughs in Mexico City.

September 6: Burroughs shoots Joan during a drunken William Tell routine. She dies; he spends thirteen days in jail.

October 25: Kerouac discovers "spontaneous prose," also known as "wild form" and "bop prosody."

December: At the urging of editor Carl Solomon and agent Ginsberg, Ace Books gives Kerouac a $250 advance for *On the Road.*

1952

Robert Duncan, Jess Collins, and Harry Jacobus found the King Ubu Gallery at 3110 Fillmore Street; after its demise it will be reincarnated as the Six Gallery.

January: Jack Kerouac arrives in San Francisco to stay with the Cassadys, and remains until May; during this visit Kerouac and Carolyn Cassady begin an affair.

GENERAL

Truce talks are held between the United Nations and Korea.

Color television is introduced in the United States.

Teenage girls wear poodle skirts with saddle shoes.

The first transcontinental television is broadcast between San Francisco and New York.

The United States explodes the first hydrogen bomb.

Carl Rogers popularizes nondirective client-centered therapy.

The market for casual at-home wear grows with the popularity of television.

First appearance of: push-button garage doors, college credit via television, infrared stoves, Dacron suits, power steering, vibrating mattresses.

1952

The architectural firm of Skidmore, Owings, and Merrill designs the Lever House (New York).

Samuel Beckett's *Waiting for Godot* becomes the most famous play in the "theater of the absurd."

Research shows that the genetic material of viruses is DNA.

THE BEAT GENERATION

January: Allen Ginsberg sends William Carlos Williams a group of poems adapted from his journal fragments. Williams is enthusiastic and declares that Ginsberg's poems merit publication.

February 16: Janet Michelle Kerouac is born in Albany, New York; Kerouac denies paternity and avoids support payments.

April: Kerouac completes an alternative version of *On the Road* (published in 1973 as *Visions of Cody*); it reflects his interest in "bop prosody" and "vertical form."

April: Ginsberg takes his first peyote.

May: Carl Solomon rejects *Visions of Cody* and suffers a psychotic break.

July: While visiting William Burroughs, Jack Kerouac writes *Doctor Sax* over two months of afternoons smoking marijuana in Burroughs' bathroom.

July: A. A. Wyn, publisher of Ace Books, pays Burroughs a $1,000 advance for *Junky*.

Fall: Gary Snyder moves to San Francisco and Philip Whalen moves in as a roommate.

Fall: Scribner's publishes John Clellon Holmes's novel *Go*, which becomes a bestseller.

November 16: Holmes's article "This Is the Beat Generation" is published in the *New York Times Magazine*.

GENERAL

The Supreme Court rules that teachers considered subversive can be barred from the public schools.

Ralph Ellison's *Invisible Man* is published.

Panty raids are carried on at college campuses throughout the country.

Dwight David Eisenhower and Richard Milhous Nixon are elected president and vice-president on the Republican ticket; Republicans gain control of Congress.

Popular songs include "Cry," "Kiss of Fire," "Wish You Were Here," "I Went to Your Wedding," and "Wheel of Fortune."

Hollywood develops 3-D movies, to be viewed through special glasses; after a brief success the novelty wears off.

By presidential order, United States steel mills are seized in order to prevent a strike; the Supreme Court declares the seizure unconstitutional.

Twenty-six-year-old Dane George Jorgensen is surgically transformed into Christine Jorgensen.

New vocabulary: hot rod, miniaturization, globalist, Pentagonese, telethon, psycholinguistics, hack.

Mad comics begins publication.

Television premieres include: *I've Got a Secret*, *The Adventures of Ozzie and Harriet*, *Dragnet*, and *The Today Show*.

THE BEAT GENERATION

December 8: Burroughs leaves Mexico and cannot return without threat of arrest.

1953

January to June: William Burroughs embarks on his second search for yage.

Ca. May: Burroughs' *Junky: Confessions of an Unredeemed Drug Addict* is published in a 35-cent Ace paperback that also contains *Narcotics Agent* by Maurice Helbrant; it receives no reviews but sells 113,170 copies in its first year. At the same time Burroughs writes his first "routines."

June: City Lights, America's first paperback book store, is founded by Peter D. Martin and Lawrence Ferlinghetti at 261 Columbus Avenue.

Summer: Gary Snyder leaves San Francisco to work as a lookout on Sourdough Mountain, then enters University of California at Berkeley to study Oriental languages.

Mid-August: Burroughs arrives in New York, intending to stay a month with Allen Ginsberg coediting *The Yage Letters*. He falls in love with Ginsberg and they have an intense affair, which is cut off by Ginsberg.

December: Burroughs leaves for Europe, first Venice and in January Tangiers, where he will remain until 1958.

July: Malcolm Cowley, an adviser at Viking, expresses interest in publishing the April 1951 *On the Road*, and calls Jack Kerouac "the most interesting writer who is not being published today."

GENERAL

1953

Hugh Hefner begins publishing *Playboy*.

The United States Communist Party is ordered to register with the Justice Department as an organization controlled by the USSR.

Fashion designers focus on men's clothes. Bermuda shorts for the businessman are promoted for the summer months, while women adopt a gamine hairstyle known as the Italian haircut.

The Department of Health, Education, and Welfare is created.

The General Electric Company declares that all Communist employees will be discharged.

Alfred Charles Kinsey publishes the controversial *Sexual Behavior in the Human Female*.

The Korean War ends; 25,604 Americans are dead.

Swanson's TV dinners are introduced, premiering with turkey and gravy.

Popular songs include "I Believe," "Doggie in the Window," "Till I Waltz with You," and "I'm Walking Behind You."

THE BEAT GENERATION

Fall: Kerouac writes "Essentials of Spontaneous Prose."

October: After his girlfriend Alene Lee rejects Kerouac, he writes *The Subterraneans* in a seventy-two-hour burst.

1954

Bob Kaufman moves to San Francisco, where he stays for the remaining twenty-two years of his life.

Michael McClure moves to San Francisco, where he meets Robert Duncan at The Poetry Center in San Francisco State University.

January: William Burroughs settles in Tangiers.

January: Jack Kerouac begins a serious study of Buddhism and helps teach Allen Ginsberg, who nearly simultaneously had become interested in Buddhism.

Early January: Carolyn and Neal Cassady discover the writings of Edgar Cayce, who becomes their guru.

January: Ginsberg travels in Mexico until June.

February 8: Kerouac arrives in San Jose to visit the Cassadys.

GENERAL

Edmund Hillary and Tenzing Norkay climb Mount Everest.

The comic-book market expands to 650 titles.

Earl Warren becomes Chief Justice of the Supreme Court.

New vocabulary: drag-strip, cookout, split-level, discount house, egghead, girlie magazine, jet stream.

1954

Plastic contact lenses are developed.

The United Steelworkers of America bans Communists, fascists, and members of the Ku Klux Klan from membership.

Antipolio inoculation begins, using a serum developed by Dr. Jonas Salk.

The publishing industry thrives on books about the Cold War, subversion, and the A-bomb.

The average American's favorite meal is fruit cup, vegetable soup, steak and potatoes, peas, rolls and butter, pie à la mode.

The U.S. Supreme Court rules that segregation by race in public schools is unconstitutional.

Davy Crockett debuts, garners the highest TV ratings of the decade, and spawns a $100 million industry.

THE BEAT GENERATION

March: Robert Creeley moves to Black Mountain College in North Carolina to teach and edit the *Black Mountain Review*.

Spring: The first *Black Mountain Review* is published; it is 64 pages long, and the print run is 500 copies. It will last for seven issues, ending in 1957.

June: Ginsberg stays with the Cassadys until August, when he moves to San Francisco.

December: Ginsberg meets Peter Orlovsky at Robert LaVigne's apartment and quickly falls in love, first with LaVigne's painting of Orlovsky and then with the man.

1955

Gregory Corso's *The Vestal Lady on Brattle and Other Poems* is published.

"The Mexican Girl" section of Kerouac's *On the Road* is published in *Paris Review*.

Spring: John Wieners enrolls at Black Mountain College.

Spring: Robert Duncan teaches at Black Mountain, leaves, and returns in the summer of 1956.

Early August: In a marathon session Allen Ginsberg writes the first and last sections of "Howl for Carl Solomon."

GENERAL

New York Stock Exchange prices reach the highest point since 1929.

The Army-McCarthy hearings begin, are televised, and result in a censure of Senator Joseph McCarthy for conduct unbecoming a senator.

Disneyland begins on TV.

National concern about juvenile delinquency rises; its causes are attributed to lurid comic books and pulp magazines.

Ninety percent of adult Americans drink 3–4 cups of coffee per day; 64 percent drink beer, wine, or liquor; 45 percent smoke at least a pack of cigarettes a day.

1955

Blacks boycott segregated city bus lines in Montgomery, Alabama; Dr. Martin Luther King, Jr., the boycott leader, gains national prominence for advocating passive resistance.

Affordable transistor radios become popular.

Lawrence Welk, bandleader, begins a weekly TV show with a completely musical format.

James Dean dies in an automobile accident.

Pizza becomes popular.

THE BEAT GENERATION

August 10: City Lights Press publishes its first book, Pocket Poet Number 1: Lawrence Ferlinghetti's *Pictures of the Gone World*.

September 9: Kerouac travels from Mexico City to Berkeley, where he meets up with Ginsberg and soon after with Gary Snyder and Philip Whalen.

October: The seventh issue of *New World Writing* publishes Kerouac's "Jazz of the Beat Generation."

October 13: A poetry reading is held at the Six Gallery; organized by Ginsberg and emceed by Kenneth Rexroth, it features readings by Philip Lamantia, Michael McClure, Gary Snyder, Philip Whalen, and Ginsberg, whose first reading of "Howl" (though incomplete) galvanizes the crowd. This event marks the beginning of the San Francisco Poetry Renaissance.

1956

January: Jack Kerouac completes *Visions of Gerard* in twelve days.

March: *Ark II-Moby I*, edited by James Harmon and Michael McClure, is published.

March: Robert Creeley arrives in San Francisco, becomes friends with Ginsberg and Kerouac, has an affair with Kenneth Rexroth's wife, and coedits the final issue of

GENERAL

Marian Anderson, contralto, becomes the first black to sing with the Metropolitan Opera; Arthur Mitchell, dancer and choreographer, becomes the first black to dance with a major company (the New York City Ballet).

Rock-and-roll music is attacked as "immoral" and as contributing to juvenile delinquency.

Television viewers watch the first filmed presidential press conference.

Thorazine and reserpine are introduced to combat the symptoms of schizophrenia.

Disneyland opens in Anaheim, California.

The first American lesbian-rights organization, the Daughters of Bilitis, is founded in San Francisco.

The Presbyterian Church approves the ordination of women ministers.

1956

Elvis Presley debuts on Ed Sullivan's weekly TV show, achieves national fame with the song "Heartbreak Hotel." For the next sixteen months, Elvis has at least one song on the Top Ten, including "Hound Dog," "Don't Be Cruel," and "Love Me Tender."

Automobile production is high; about 1 in 8 cars is a station wagon.

THE BEAT GENERATION

the *Black Mountain Review*. He leaves San Francisco in June.

March: In London William Burroughs undergoes a successful apomorphine withdrawal from heroin addiction.

Spring: The epochal Six Gallery poetry reading is repeated in Berkeley, and Allen Ginsberg reads the complete "Howl."

May 5: Gary Snyder leaves for Japan, where he studies Zen.

Summer: John Wieners returns to Boston after his final semester at Black Mountain College and publishes the first issue of *Measure*, dominated by poets affiliated with Black Mountain and San Francisco.

June: Kerouac hitchhikes north from San Francisco to Desolation Peak and stays there "sixty-three days and nights, to be exact."

June 9: Naomi Ginsberg dies. Because there is not a minyan at her burial, *kaddish*, the prayer for the dead, cannot be said.

Fall: Black Mountain College closes.

Fall: Brother Antoninus/William Everson decides that public reading is his vocation.

September 2: The first "enthusiastic report" about the "Pacific Coast upstarts" by Richard Eberhart appears in

GENERAL

Dizzy Gillespie and his band are sent by the U.S. State Department on a good-will tour, the first jazz musicians to be subsidized by the government.

John Osborne's play *Look Back in Anger* marks the debut of Britain's "angry young men."

Southdale, the first indoor shopping mall, opens in Minnesota.

Dwight David Eisenhower is reelected president by a landslide.

Maria Callas debuts at the Metropolitan Opera.

The first transatlantic telephone cable system begins operation.

The Methodist Church abolishes racial discrimination.

Three days of campus violence at the University of Alabama follow the suspension of Autherine Lucy, the first black student enrolled; she is soon expelled.

Frank Lloyd Wright begins construction on the Guggenheim Museum (completed 1959).

The Salk vaccine for polio enters the open market.

The Broadway success of *My Fair Lady* makes the Edwardian look fashionable among women, while more men adopt the buttoned-down "Madison Avenue look."

The Beat Generation

the *New York Times Book Review*; this is the first East Coast recognition of the San Francisco Renaissance.

October 30: Responding to a heckler at a poetry reading in Los Angeles, Ginsberg challenges the man to strip and takes off all his own clothes.

October: City Lights publishes Ginsberg's *Howl and Other Poems* as part of its Pocket Poet series; the book sells briskly and soon goes into another printing.

December: Viking agrees to publish Kerouac's *On the Road* (an agreement brokered by Malcolm Cowley and literary agent Sterling Lord); publication is slated for fall 1957.

Late 1956: The original nucleus of San Francisco writers has mostly dispersed.

1957

Early 1957: Barney Rosset begins publishing the *Evergreen Review*. The second issue focuses on the "San Francisco Scene."

LeRoi Jones (later Imamu Amiri Baraka) and his wife, Hettie Cohen, move to Greenwich Village. Jones becomes an "outspoken promoter and defender" of the Beat writers.

February: *Mademoiselle* publishes an article on the San Francisco Renaissance, marking the beginning of unlikely connections between the literary movement and popular culture.

General

Teenage fashion is divided between the "weenies" (white bucks, crew cuts, pants with buckles in back) and the "greasers" (leather jackets, ducktails, tee-shirts).

Eleven African Americans are arrested in the Montgomery, Alabama, bus boycott.

Drive-in theaters multiply.

Members of the lower middle class move to the suburbs in greater numbers.

New vocabulary: headshrinker, fuzz, cop-out, hero sandwich, the most.

1957

West Side Story opens on Broadway, featuring juvenile delinquents as protagonists.

The sack dress is introduced by Balenciaga and popularized by Dior; it consists of an unfitted waistline and a hemline one inch below the knee.

The Wolfenden Report on homosexuality and prostitution is published in Britain.

President Eisenhower sends troops to Little Rock, Arkansas, to enforce desegregation.

THE BEAT GENERATION

February 15: Jack Kerouac departs for Tangiers, where he types William Burroughs' manuscript of *Naked Lunch* and stays until April.

Early March: Allen Ginsberg, Peter Orlovsky, and Alan Ansen arrive in Tangiers to help edit *Naked Lunch*.

March 25: Chester McPhee, from the U.S. Customs Office in San Francisco, confiscates 520 copies of Ginsberg's *Howl and Other Poems* and declares it "obscene." Customs releases the books May 29, following a challenge by the ACLU. Three days later Lawrence Ferlinghetti and Shigeyoshi Murao, manager of the City Lights Bookshop, are arrested for publishing and selling obscene literature.

Spring: At The Cellar, Rexroth and Ferlinghetti experiment in reciting poetry to jazz music; this marks the beginning of a trend.

Summer: Norman Mailer's essay "The White Negro: Superficial Reflections on the Hipster" is published in *Dissent*.

August: The final issue of the *Black Mountain Review* (No. 7), coedited by Robert Creeley and Allen Ginsberg, is published; its contributors include Ginsberg, Corso, Burroughs, Kerouac, Snyder, Duncan, Whalen, Lamantia, Louis Zukofsky, Denise Levertov, and Hugh Selby, Jr.

September 5: Viking publishes Kerouac's *On the Road*, the *New York Times* gives it a rave review, and the book soon rises to number 7 on the bestseller list.

GENERAL

A firm link between cigarette smoking and lung cancer is established.

James Hoffa and his Teamsters Union are expelled from the CIO.

The world's longest suspension bridge opens in Michigan.

The Supreme Court rules against Michigan's conviction of a bookseller for selling John Howard Griffith's *The Devil Outside*, stating that the state's law would reduce adults to reading only what might be deemed fit for children.

Popular songs include "Love Letters in the Sand," "Tammy," "Fascination," "Young Love," and "Round and Round."

The USSR launches *Sputnik I* and *II*, the first manmade satellites.

The first nationally televised videotaped production, *Truth or Consequences*, is broadcast.

Bouffant hairdos become popular.

Elvis Presley buys Graceland.

Fads: Silly putty, Dick Clark's *American Bandstand*, Bloody Mary jokes, Dogpatch costumes.

Charles Van Doren wins $129,000 as a quiz-show contestant on *21* and becomes a national intellectual hero.

THE BEAT GENERATION

October: Ginsberg and Peter Orlovsky take up residence at the Beat Hotel, 9 rue Git-le-Coeur, in Paris.

October 3: Judge Clayton Horn declares *Howl* "not obscene" and offers a criterion for obscenity.

November 13: Ginsberg, in a Paris café, begins writing "Kaddish."

December 9: Kerouac finishes *The Dharma Bums*.

1958

Kerouac, Philip Lamantia, Howard Hart, and Dave Amram do a jazz-poetry reading in New York at the Brata Galley.

John Wieners' first book, *The Hotel Wentley Poems*, is published in San Francisco.

Mid-January: William Burroughs takes up residence at the Beat Hotel, where he begins an important literary collaboration with Brion Gysin, called "cut-ups."

February: Grove Press publishes Kerouac's *The Subterraneans*.

March: LeRoi Jones and Hettie Cohen publish the first issue of *Yugen*, which lasts eight issues, until December 1962.

April 2: In his column in the *San Francisco Chronicle*, Herb Caen coins the term "beatnik," which becomes widely used.

GENERAL

The number of long-term patients in mental hospitals decreases sharply due to new psychotropic medications.

Congress passes the first civil rights legislation since 1872.

Top box-office stars: Rock Hudson, John Wayne, Pat Boone, Elvis Presley, Frank Sinatra, Gary Cooper, William Holden, James Stewart, Jerry Lewis, Yul Brynner.

The venereal disease rate increases for the first time since 1948.

1958

Joseph Welch's *The Blue Book of the John Birch Society* sets forth the basic tenets of the ultraconservative organization.

Xcrox produces the first commercial copying machine.

Barbie dolls are first marketed.

Charles Starkweather and his fifteen-year-old girlfriend, Caril Fugate, are arrested after a string of eleven murders.

U.S. churches report large increases in membership since 1950. Largest gains are by the Roman Catholic Church, Southern Baptist Convention, Churches of Christ, and Methodist Church.

Hula hoops become the biggest toy fad in history; they are outlawed in Japan.

Explorer I, America's first satellite, is launched.

THE BEAT GENERATION

April 8: Neal Cassady is arrested in San Francisco for possession of three marijuana cigarettes.

June 14: Cassady is sentenced to five years to life in San Quentin, where he is transferred on July 4.

October 13: Hettie Cohen and LeRoi Jones marry.

October 15: Viking publishes Kerouac's *The Dharma Bums*.

Winter: An excerpt from Burroughs' *Naked Lunch* is featured in the fourth issue of *Chicago Review*, later censored.

1959

Beatnik publicity reaches its peak in national magazines, in B-movies such as Albert Zugsmith's *The Beat Generation*, and in the appearance of a beatnik character, Maynard G. Krebs, on the television series *The Many Loves of Dobie Gillis*.

Broadsides by Bob Kaufman, *Abomunist Manifest* and *Second April*, are published by City Lights Books.

January 2: *Pull My Daisy* begins production (completed six weeks later) in Alfred Leslie's Bowery loft, under the direction of Alfred Leslie and cinematographer Robert Frank.

January 29: Ginsberg and Corso participate in a fundraiser to support the censored *Chicago Review*.

GENERAL

Vladimir Nabokov's *Lolita* is published and becomes a notorious bestseller.

Lawrence Alloway first uses the term "pop art" in print.

The Edsel is introduced and soon flops.

Popular songs include "Purple People Eater," "Bird Dog," "A Certain Smile," and "Your Precious Love."

The Communist Party's *Daily Worker* suspends publication.

Elvis Presley reports to the draft board.

1959

Lorraine Hansberry's *Raisin in the Sun* becomes the first drama by a black woman to be produced on Broadway.

D. H. Lawrence's *Lady Chatterley's Lover* is published after a thirty-year ban due to obscenity rulings.

Berry Gordy, Jr., founds Motown Records, the company that produces many of the great soul groups of the 1960s.

French New Wave cinema becomes a force in international film.

Popular songs include "Stagger Lee," "Tom Dooley," "He's Got the Whole World in His Hands," and "The Battle of New Orleans."

The first seven U.S. astronauts are selected.

THE BEAT GENERATION

March: The first issue of *Big Table* is published, as a result of the censorship of the *Chicago Review*. The U.S. Post Office bans the mailing and impounds 499 copies.

May 9: *Beatitude* magazine begins publication, printed at the Bread and Wine Mission in San Francisco; its final issue appears July 1960.

July: Olympia Press publishes Burroughs' *Naked Lunch* in an edition of 10,000 copies.

September: Brion Gysin and William Burroughs discover the possibilities of cut-ups.

December: An excerpt of Kerouac's *Visions of Cody* is published by New Directions in an edition of 750 copies.

1960

Minutes to Go, a book of cut-ups by Burroughs, Brion Gysin, Gregory Corso, and Sinclair Beiles, is published.

Donald M. Allen's anthology *The New American Poetry: 1945–1960* is published; it is the first time that the Beats, Black Mountain, and San Francisco poets are given a prominent place in a "mainstream" anthology.

Bob Kaufman's *Does the Secret Mind Whisper?* is published by City Lights Books.

GENERAL

The Grammy Awards are created to honor recording achievements; the Best Album of the Year award goes to *The Music from Peter Gunn.*

Winning contestant Charles Van Doren reveals that the *21* quiz show is a fake.

Rock-and-roll stars Buddy Holly, Ritchie Valens, and the Big Bopper die in an airplane crash.

To compete with television, movies become racier (e.g., *Some Like It Hot, Anatomy of a Murder*).

Nikita Khrushchev tours the United States, and is denied entrance to Disneyland because security cannot be guaranteed.

Eighty-six percent of American families own a television set, and the average person spends 42 hours watching television.

1960

African Americans stage sit-ins in the South to force desegregation of lunch counters and other public places.

Chubby Checker causes an international dance craze with his recording of "The Twist."

The Nixon-Kennedy debates demonstrate the importance of television in politics.

The Southern Presbyterian Church declares marital sexual relations without procreative intentions not sinful.

THE BEAT GENERATION

May 23: Allen Ginsberg first tries yage in Peru.

June: A movie version of *The Subterraneans* opens, featuring George Peppard as the Jack Kerouac character.

July 5: Judge Julius J. Hoffman sets aside the ban on the issue of *Big Table* that features excerpts from *Naked Lunch*.

July 4: Neal Cassady is released from prison.

August: Jack Kerouac stays in Lawrence Ferlinghetti's cabin in Bixby Canyon and undergoes nightmarish visions and delerium tremens, recounted in *Big Sur*.

November 26: Under Timothy Leary's guidance, Ginsberg tries psilocybin mushrooms, and the two consider the psychedelic revolution.

GENERAL

The automobile industry begins to shift to compact cars to meet falling sales and imports of foreign economy and sports models.

John Fitzgerald Kennedy and Lyndon Baines Johnson are elected president and vice-president on the Democratic ticket; at forty-three, Kennedy becomes the youngest president and the first Roman Catholic elected.

Alan Freed, promoter of rock-and-roll, and seven others are arrested on charges of commercial bribery, known as the "payola" scandals.

ACKNOWLEDGMENTS

Of the many people who contributed to the creation of this book, I wish to first acknowledge the scholars of the Beat Generation and the San Francisco Renaissance. Without their work my own would have been impossible; their specific contributions are cited in the book's endnotes.

Allen Ginsberg and his associates—Bob Rosenthal, Peter Hale, Althea Crawford, and Jacqueline Gens—were key supports, providing contacts, encouragement, suggestions for photographs. Without Ginsberg's prescient archival instincts and continuing energy and good will, any study of the Beat Generation would be severely diminished. John Sampas, executor of the Jack Kerouac Estate, was gracious and encouraging throughout, not only granting permission but helping identify previously unpublished photographs. James Grauerholz, director of William Burroughs Communications, offered astute and encouraging direction beyond the call of duty.

Several people read the entire manuscript and provided valuable suggestions—Ann Charters, James Grauerholz, Bill Morgan, Frances Somerman Soond, Robert L. Caserio, and Mason Cooley. In addition, Michael McClure and Lawrence Ferlinghetti each provided a sharp-eyed reading of the San Francisco sections. I especially want to thank Robert Atkins, who read the manuscript several times and endured life with the author through its many stages; neither was easy and both are lovingly appreciated.

Herbert Huncke was an invaluable consultant on the language of the hipsters and their cohorts; he provided information on their rich oral tradition that could not be found in print. William Schuyler provided a verbal snapshot of William Burroughs as a childhood playmate. In addition to reading the manuscript, Bill Morgan provided helpful bibliographic information. Robert E. Johnson was a model of generosity in sharing his vast knowledge of the San Francisco Renaissance. Two assistants, Andrew Harmon and Jesse Levitt, helped coordinate information, dates, and sources, and the latter single-handedly plotted the map of Kerouac's cross-country trips. Lisa Phillips shared valuable insights from her exhibition, "Beat Culture and the New America," at the Whitney Museum.

For help in assembling images for the book I want to thank the indefatigable Althea Crawford for her guidance to the Allen Ginsberg Archive, Ann Schneider for her heroic job of researching the beatnik era, and Kate Bernhardt and Ralph Lombreglia, colleagues in *A Jack Kerouac ROMnibus*, for directing me to unknown photographs. I also want to thank Robert LaVigne, Jonathan Williams, Michael Schumacher, Geoff Smith and Elva Griffith at Ohio State University, Bernard Crystal, Jean Ashton, Brenda Hearing and Patrick Lawlor of the Columbia University Special Collections, Harry Redl, Carolyn Cassady, Robert Soond and Frances Somerman Soond, Gordon Ball, Walter Lehrman, John Cohen, Deborah Bell, Charles Campbell, Bernie Mindich, Michael Kohler, and Raymond Foye.

For assistance too varied to categorize I thank my agent, the late, sorely missed Diane Cleaver, and my new agent, Joy Harris, as well as Bill Berkson, Theresa Luisotti, Hitosako Motoo, Rita Bottoms, Salleigh Rothrock, Fiona Paulus, Sara Barrett, Tom Blewitt, Rudy Lemcke, Michael deLisio, Emile Bedriomo, Athena Angelus, Mic Sweeney, Jane Hammond, Bill Corbett, Saun Ellis, Albert Gelpi, and Francisco Drohojowski.

At Pantheon, several people were especially helpful: Shelley Wanger, my editor, displayed infectious enthusiasm and a commitment to stylishness; Lan Nhat Nguyen offered much-needed and tireless organization; Altie Karper, Jo Metsch, Fearn Cutler, Kathy Grasso, Jeanne Morton, and Elizabeth Lipp helped realize, in production and design, the ever-tricky integration of text and image. I am grateful to Pantheon for giving its support and resources to this promising series, *Circles of the Twentieth Century*.

NOTES

Foreword

1. W. E. B. Du Bois, "The Conservation of Races," cited in Wilson J. Moses, *The Golden Age of Black Nationalism, 1850–1925* (Hamden, Conn.: Archon, 1978), p. 134.
2. James, cited in Ann Charters, "Introduction," *The Portable Beat Reader* (New York: Viking, 1992), p. xv.

Beats All

1. John Tytell, "An Interview with Herbert Huncke," in Arthur and Kit Knight, eds., *unspeakable visions of the individual* 3, nos. 1–2 (1973): 9.
2. Ginsberg, in William Plummer, *The Holy Goof: A Biography of Neal Cassady* (New York: Paragon House, 1981), p. 46.
3. Herb Caen, *San Francisco Chronicle*, April 2, 1958.
4. Kerouac, in Charters, *Portable Beat Reader*, p. xxxiv.
5. Dennis McNally, *Desolate Angel: Jack Kerouac, the Beat Generation, and America* (New York: Random House, 1979), p. 116.
6. Allen Ginsberg, interview with the author, New York, April 10, 1995.
7. William S. Schuyler, interview with the author, Palo Alto, Calif., January 28, 1994.
8. Barry Miles, *William Burroughs: El Hombre Invisible* (New York: Hyperion, 1993), p. 21.
9. Ibid., p. 24.
10. Ted Morgan, *Literary Outlaw: The Life and Times of William S. Burroughs* (New York: Holt, 1988), p. 26.
11. Ibid., p. 31.
12. William Burroughs, *The Letters of William S. Burroughs, 1945–1959*, ed. Oliver Harris (New York: Viking, 1993), p. 393.
13. Morgan, *Literary Outlaw*, p. 35.
14. William Burroughs, "Foreword," in Jack Black, *You Can't Win* (New York: Amok Press, 1988), p. vi.
15. Morgan, *Literary Outlaw*, p. 40.
16. Ibid., pp. 49, 48.
17. William Burroughs, "The Name Is Burroughs," in *The Adding Machine* (New York: Seaver Books, 1986), p. 8.
18. Morgan, *Literary Outlaw*, p. 52.
19. Ibid., p. 57.
20. Ibid., p. 62.
21. Burroughs to Allen Ginsberg and Peter Orlovsky, October 27, 1959, in Burroughs, *Letters*, p. 433.
22. I thank Peter Swales for sharing his unpublished work on this period, given as a lecture, "Burroughs in the Bewilderness," at the Institute of Contemporary Art, London, February 4, 1994.
23. Burroughs, "The Names is Burroughs," in *The Adding Machine*, p. 9.
24. George Plimpton, ed., *Writers at Work: The "Paris Review" Interviews*, 3rd series (New York: Penguin, 1977), p. 285.
25. Burroughs, "Twilight's Last Gleaming" in *Interzone*, ed. James Grauerholz (New York: Penguin, 1990), p. 3.
26. Ibid., p. 17.
27. Ibid., p. 15.
28. Tytell, "Interview with Herbert Huncke," p. 7.
29. Morgan, *Literary Outlaw*, p. 84.
30. William Burroughs, "Lee's Journals," in *Interzone*, p. 64.
31. Kerouac to Neal Cassady, December 28, 1950, in Jack Kerouac, *Selected Letters 1940–1956*, ed. Ann Charters (New York: Viking, 1995), p. 247.
32. Jack Kerouac, *Visions of Gerard* (New York: Penguin, 1963), p. 2.
33. Ibid.
34. Gerald Nicosia, *Memory Babe: A Critical Biography of Jack Kerouac* (New York: Grove Press, 1983), p. 26.
35. Kerouac, *Visions of Gerard*, p. 109.

36. McNally, *Desolate Angel*, p. 15.
37. Tom Clark, *Jack Kerouac* (New York: Paragon House, 1990), p. 21.
38. Ibid., p. 25.
39. Ann Charters, *Jack Kerouac: A Life* (New York: Warner, 1973), p. 30.
40. Barry Miles, *Ginsberg: A Biography* (New York: Simon & Schuster, 1989), p. 27.
41. Allen Ginsberg, Journals, Ginsberg Collection, Stanford University.
42. Miles, *Ginsberg*, p. 29.
43. Ginsberg, Journals, Ginsberg Collection, Stanford University.
44. Miles, *Ginsberg*, p. 29.
45. Allen Ginsberg, "Kaddish," in *Collected Poems 1947–1980* (New York: Harper & Row, 1984), p. 223.
46. Ginsberg, Journals, Ginsberg Collection, Stanford University.
47. Ibid.
48. Allen Ginsberg, "Confrontation with Louis Ginsberg's Poems," in *Collected Poems of Louis Ginsberg*, Michael Fournier, ed (Orono, Me.: Northern Lights, 1992), p. 416.
49. Michael Schumacher, *Dharma Lion: A Biography of Allen Ginsberg* (New York: St. Martin's Press, 1992), p. 11.
50. Louis Ginsberg to Allen Ginsberg, quoted in Louis Ginsberg, *Collected Poems*, p. 30.
51. Ginsberg, Journals, Ginsberg Collection, Stanford University.
52. Allen Ginsberg, opening quotation for Journal, "The Book of Martifice," October 1943, Ginsberg Collection, Stanford University.
53. Schumacher, *Dharma Lion*, p. 10.
54. Ibid., p. 15.
55. Miles, *Ginsberg*, p. 26.
56. Ibid., p. 24.
57. Ibid., p. 35.
58. Allen Ginsberg, "Interview with Allen Ginsberg," *Playboy*, April 1969, p. 86.
59. Ginsberg, "Kaddish," in *Collected Poems*, p. 214.
60. Miles, *Ginsberg*, p. 35.
61. Charters, *Kerouac*, p. 37.
62. Kerouac to Cornelius Murphy, n.d., 1943, in Kerouac, *Selected Letters*, p. 63.
63. Kerouac to George J. Apostolos, April 7, 1943, ibid., p. 60.
64. Clark, *Kerouac*, p. 59.
65. Miles, *Ginsberg*, p. 37.
66. Schumacher, *Dharma Lion*, p. 25.
67. Miles, *Ginsberg*, p. 36.
68. Ibid., pp. 41–42.
69. Ginsberg's quotation of Yeats, ibid., p. 36.
70. Ginsberg, Journals, Ginsberg Collection, Stanford University.
71. Ginsberg to Neal Cassady, May 1949, in *As Ever: The Collected Correspondence of Allen Ginsberg and Neal Cassady*, ed. Barry Gifford (Berkeley: Creative Arts, 1977), p. 56.
72. Ginsberg, Journals, Ginsberg Collection, Stanford University.
73. Barry Gifford and Lawrence Lee, *Jack's Book* (New York: St. Martin's Press, 1978), p. 36.
74. Schumacher, *Dharma Lion*, p. 29.
75. Morgan, *Literary Outlaw*, p. 90.
76. Charters, *Kerouac*, p. 42.
77. Jack Kerouac, "Claude," n.d., Ginsberg Collection, Special Collections, Columbia University.
78. Nicosia, *Memory Babe*, p. 115.
79. Ibid.
80. Miles, *Ginsberg*, p. 44.
81. Nicosia, *Memory Babe*, p. 116.
82. Clark, *Kerouac*, p. 61.
83. Allen Ginsberg, interviewed by Allen Young, in Winston Leyland, ed., *Gay Sunshine Interviews*, vol. 1 (San Francisco: Gay Sunshine Press, 1978), p. 98.

84. Ibid.
85. Morgan, *Literary Outlaw*, p. 91.
86. Jack Kerouac, *Vanity of Duluoz* (New York: Coward-McCann, 1968), p. 207.
87. Morgan, *Literary Outlaw*, p. 112.
88. Kerouac to Neal Cassady, September 13, 1947, in Kerouac, *Selected Letters*, p. 126.
89. Ginsberg, Journals, Ginsberg Collection, Stanford University.
90. Kerouac to Allen Ginsberg, November 13, 1945, in Kerouac, *Selected Letters*, p. 100.
91. Allen Ginsberg, interview with the author, New York, March 27, 1995.
92. Allen Ginsberg, "Dialogue on Morality," June 23, 1944, in Journals, Ginsberg Collection, Stanford University.
93. Ibid.
94. Allen Ginsberg, "The New Vision," in Journals, Ginsberg Collection, Stanford University.
95. Ginsberg, Journals, Ginsberg Collection, Stanford University.
96. Morgan, *Literary Outlaw*, p. 88.
97. Ibid., p. 98.
98. Allen Ginsberg, "Essay in Character Analysis: Lucien Carr," 1944, in Journals, Ginsberg Collection, Stanford University.
99. Allen Ginsberg, "A Romanticized Version of a Tragedy," ca. 1944, in Journals, Ginsberg Collection, Stanford University.
100. Morgan, *Literary Outlaw*, p. 103.
101. Ginsberg, "A Romanticized Version of a Tragedy."
102. Morgan, *Literary Outlaw*, p. 104.
103. Ibid.
104. Ibid.
105. "Student Murders Friend, Sinks Body," *New York Times*, August 17, 1944, p. 13.
106. Kerouac to Mrs. Parker, September 1, 1944, in Kerouac, *Selected Letters*, p. 76.
107. Nicosia, *Memory Babe*, p. 130.
108. Ginsberg, Journals, Ginsberg Collection, Stanford University.
109. Ibid.
110. Morgan, *Literary Outlaw*, p. 113; Ginsberg, Journals, Ginsberg Collection, Stanford University.
111. Kerouac to Caroline Kerouac Blake, March 14, 1945, in Kerouac, *Selected Letters*, p. 87.
112. Ibid.
113. Ginsberg, interview with the author, New York, March 27, 1995.
114. N. M. McKnight to Louis Ginsberg, March 17, 1945, in Schumacher, *Dharma Lion*, p. 54.
115. Gifford and Lee, *Jack's Book*, p. 41.
116. Ibid.
117. Morgan, *Literary Outlaw*, p. 112.
118. Kerouac to Caroline Kerouac Blake, March 14, 1945, in Kerouac, *Selected Letters*, p. 87.
119. Kerouac to Allen Ginsberg, November 13, 1945, ibid., p. 100.
120. Ibid., p. 112.
121. *William Burroughs*, documentary film by Howard Brookner, 1984.
122. Ginsberg, Journals, Ginsberg Collection, Stanford University.
123. Ginsberg, interview with the author, New York, March 27, 1995.
124. McNally, *Desolate Angel*, p. 80.
125. Miles, *Ginsberg*, p. 69.
126. Hal Chase, interview with Ted Morgan, Paso Robles, Calif., March 15, 1985, in Morgan Archives, Arizona State University.
127. Herbert Huncke, *Guilty of Everything* (New York: Paragon House, 1990), p. 69.
128. Huncke, in Brookner, *William Burroughs*.
129. Huncke, *Guilty*, p. 70.
130. Ibid., p. 71.
131. William Burroughs, *Junky* (New York: Penguin, 1977), p. 8.
132. Huncke, *Guilty*, p. 70.

133. Burroughs, *Junky*, p. xv.
134. Ibid., p. xvi.
135. Allen Ginsberg, recording a "dream letter" from John Clellon Holmes, Journal, 1954; quoted in Joyce Johnson, *Minor Characters* (Boston: Houghton Mifflin, 1983), p. 79.
136. Huncke, *Guilty*, p. 74.
137. Miles, *Ginsberg*, p. 73.
138. Burroughs in Brookner, *William Burroughs*.
139. Ginsberg, "The New Vision."
140. Morgan's notes, Ted Morgan Collection, University of Arizona.
141. Huncke, *Guilty*, p. 74.
142. Allen Ginsberg, introduction to "Birthday Ode," ca. 1949, in Journals, Ginsberg Collection, Stanford University.
143. Morgan, *Literary Outlaw*, p. 115.
144. Brookner, *William Burroughs*.
145. Morgan, *Literary Outlaw*, p. 124.
146. Brookner, *William Burroughs*.
147. Ginsberg, Journals, Ginsberg Collection, Stanford University.
148. Morgan, *Literary Outlaw*, p. 126.
149. Ginsberg, Journals, Ginsberg Collection, Stanford University.
150. Ibid.
151. Nicosia, *Memory Babe*, p. 134.
152. Kerouac to Allen Ginsberg, October 1944, in Kerouac, *Selected Letters*, p. 81.
153. Nicosia, *Memory Babe*, p. 134.
154. McNally, *Desolate Angel*, p. 74.
155. Brookner, *William Burroughs*.
156. Nicosia, *Memory Babe*, p. 163.
157. Ginsberg, Journals, Ginsberg Collection, Stanford University.
158. Ibid.
159. Schumacher, *Dharma Lion*, p. 50.
160. Leyland, *Gay Sunshine Interviews*, p. 107.
161. Morgan's notes, Ted Morgan Collection, University of Arizona.
162. Ginsberg, Journals, Ginsberg Collection, Stanford University.
163. Morgan, *Literary Outlaw*, p. 125.
164. Ibid., p. 127.
165. Ginsberg, interview with the author, New York, March 27, 1995.
166. Morgan, *Literary Outlaw*, p. 132.
167. Joan Vollmer to Edie Parker, January 1, 1947, ibid., p. 133.
168. Ginsberg, Journals, Ginsberg Collection, Stanford University.

Beat Icons

1. Allen Ginsberg, "Footnote to Howl," in *Collected Poems*, p. 134.
2. Nicosia, *Memory Babe*, p. 253.
3. Jack Kerouac, *On the Road* (New York: Viking, 1957), p. 8.
4. Nicosia, *Memory Babe*, p. 371.
5. Herbert Huncke, interview with the author, New York, February 25, 1995.
6. Huncke, *Guilty*, p. 17.
7. William Burroughs, "Foreword," in Huncke, *Guilty*, p. vii.
8. Huncke, interview with the author, New York, March 12, 1995.
9. Huncke, interview with the author, New York, February 25, 1995.
10. Ibid.
11. Ibid.
12. Huncke, *Guilty*, p. 43.
13. Ginsberg, Journals, Ginsberg Collection, Stanford University.
14. Ginsberg, interview with the author, New York, March 27, 1995.
15. Allen Ginsberg, "On Huncke's Book," in Arthur and Kit Knight, eds., *unspeakable visions of the individual* 3, nos. 1–2 (1973): 21.
16. Gifford and Lee, *Jack's Book*, p. 39.

17. Huncke, *Guilty*, p. 77.
18. Carl Solomon, *Emergency Messages: An Autobiographical Miscellany*, ed. John Tytell (New York: Paragon House, 1989), p. 48.
19. Ibid., p. 54.
20. Solomon to Allen Ginsberg, July 15, 1950, Ginsberg Collection, Special Collections, Columbia University.
21. Solomon, *Emergency Messages*, p. 60.
22. Solomon to Ginsberg, n.d., Ginsberg Collection, Special Collections, Columbia University.
23. Neal Cassady, *The First Third and Other Writings* (San Francisco: City Lights, 1971; expanded ed., 1981), p. 47.
24. Ibid., p. 100.
25. Ibid., p. 112.
26. Ibid., p. 170.
27. Ibid.
28. Kerouac, *On the Road*, p. 4.
29. Ibid., p. 10.
30. John Clellon Holmes, "The Gandy Dancer," in *Representative Men: The Biographical Essays* (Fayetteville: University of Arkansas Press, 1988), p. 202.
31. Cassady, *First Third*, p. 26.
32. Nicosia, *Memory Babe*, p. 172.
33. Kerouac, *On the Road*, p. 10.
34. Ibid., p. 39.
35. Ibid., p. 10.
36. Ibid., p. 7.
37. Ginsberg, Journals, Ginsberg Collection, Stanford University.
38. Miles, *Ginsberg*, p. 84.
39. Ginsberg, Journals, Ginsberg Collection, Stanford University.
40. Ibid.
41. Ibid.
42. Ibid.
43. Cassady to Ginsberg, March 30, 1947, in Ginsberg and Cassady, *As Ever*, p. 11.
44. Cassady to Ginsberg, June 1947, ibid., p. 23.
45. Carolyn Cassady, *Off the Road: My Years with Kerouac, Cassady, and Ginsberg* (New York: Morrow, 1990), p. 19.
46. Allen Ginsberg, "The Visions of the Great Rememberer," in Jack Kerouac, *Visions of Cody* (1972; New York: Penguin, 1993), p. 403.
47. Ginsberg, Journals, Ginsberg Collection, Stanford University.
48. Cassady, *Off the Road*, p. 29.
49. Kerouac to Neal Cassady, August 26, 1947, in Kerouac, *Selected Letters*, pp. 118–19.
50. Ginsberg to Cassady, n.d., Ginsberg Collection, Stanford University.
51. Ginsberg, Journals, Ginsberg Collection, Stanford University.
52. Cassady, *Off the Road*, p. 21.
53. Ginsberg, Journal, quoted in Miles, *Ginsberg*, p. 91.
54. Burroughs to Allen Ginsberg, October 10, 1946, in Burroughs, *Letters*, p. 8.
55. Kerouac, *Visions of Cody*, p. 125.
56. Huncke, interview with the author, New York, March 12, 1995.
57. Huncke, interview with the author, New York, February 26, 1995.
58. Morgan, *Literary Outlaw*, p. 137.
59. Ginsberg to Lionel Trilling, August 1947, Ginsberg Collection, Stanford University.
60. Tytell, "Interview with Herbert Huncke," p. 7.
61. Morgan, *Literary Outlaw*, p. 137.
62. Ginsberg, Journals, Ginsberg Collection, Stanford University.
63. Kerouac, *Visions of Cody*, pp. 139, 140.
64. Morgan, *Literary Outlaw*, p. 144.
65. Kerouac, *Visions of Cody*, p. 141.
66. Ginsberg, Journal, September 1, 1947, quoted in Miles, *Ginsberg*, p. 91.
67. Cassady to Ginsberg, March 15, 1949, in Ginsberg and Cassady, *As Ever*, p. 55.

68. Kerouac, *Visions of Cody*, p. 124.
69. Morgan, *Literary Outlaw*, p. 146.
70. Ibid., p. 148
71. Burroughs to Jack Kerouac, April 1952, in Burroughs, *Letters*, p. 113.
72. Morgan, *Literary Outlaw*, p. 149.

Beat Lives, Beat Literature

1. Kerouac to Ginsberg, September 6, 1945, in Kerouac, *Selected Letters*, p. 98.
2. Charters, *Kerouac*, p. 60.
3. Kerouac to Allen Ginsberg, n.d., Ginsberg Collection, Special Collections, Columbia University.
4. Charters, *Kerouac*, p. 62.
5. Ginsberg, Journals, Ginsberg Collection, Stanford University.
6. Miles, *Ginsberg*, p. 98.
7. Cassady to Ginsberg, May 1948, in Ginsberg and Cassady, *As Ever*, p. 35.
8. Plimpton, *Writers at Work*, p. 302.
9. Ginsberg to Bertrand Russell, September 27, 1952, Ginsberg Collection, Stanford University.
10. Plimpton, *Writers at Work*, p. 302.
11. Ibid., p. 303.
12. Ibid.
13. Ibid., p. 308.
14. Ginsberg to Bertrand Russell, September 27, 1952, Ginsberg Collection, Stanford University.
15. Plimpton, *Writers at Work*, p. 309.
16. Ibid., pp. 303–4.
17. Miles, *Ginsberg*, p. 105.
18. Morgan, *Literary Outlaw*, p. 173.
19. Plimpton, *Writers at Work*, p. 310.
20. Paul Portuges, *The Visionary Poetics of Allen Ginsberg* (Santa Barbara, Calif.: Ross-Erikson, 1978), p. 27.
21. Cassady, *Off the Road*, p. 63.
22. Ibid., p. 64.
23. Ibid., p. 143.
24. Ibid., p. 141.
25. Kerouac to Allen Ginsberg, December 15, 1948, Ginsberg Collection, Special Collections, Columbia University.
26. Kerouac to Hal Chase, October 19, 1948, in Kerouac, *Selected Letters*, p. 169.
27. Nicosia, *Memory Babe*, p. 239.
28. Ibid., p. 238.
29. Ibid., p. 240.
30. Kerouac to Allen Ginsberg, December 15, 1948, in Kerouac, *Selected Letters*, pp. 176–77
31. Gifford and Lee, *Jack's Book*, p. 124.
32. Ibid., p. 125.
33. Ibid.
34. Burroughs to Allen Ginsberg, January 16, 1949, in Burroughs, *Letters*, p. 35.
35. Kerouac, *On the Road*, p. 134.
36. Ibid., p. 140.
37. Burroughs to Allen Ginsberg, January 10, 1949, in Burroughs, *Letters*, p. 33.
38. Kerouac, *On the Road*, p. 143.
39. Ibid., p. 146.
40. Ibid.
41. Burroughs to Ginsberg, January 30, 1949, in Burroughs, *Letters*, p. 37.
42. Kerouac, *On the Road*, p. 156.
43. Ibid., p. 170.
44. Ibid.
45. Schumacher, *Dharma Lion*, p. 107.
46. Ginsberg, Journals, Ginsberg Collection, Stanford University.
47. Ibid.
48. Ibid.
49. Schumacher, *Dharma Lion*, p. 108.
50. Ginsberg, Journals, Ginsberg Collection, Stanford University.
51. Jane Kramer, *Allen Ginsberg in America* (New York: Random House, 1969), p. 126.

52. Ginsberg, Journals, Ginsberg Collection, Stanford University.
53. Schumacher, *Dharma Lion*, p. 111.
54. Ginsberg, Journals, Ginsberg Collection, Stanford University.
55. Ibid.
56. Carl Solomon, *Mishaps, Perhaps* (San Francisco: Beach Books, Texts & Documents, 1968), p. 40.
57. Miles, *Ginsberg*, p. 117.
58. Ibid., p. 119.
59. Kerouac to Allen Ginsberg, June 10, 1949, in Kerouac, *Selected Letters*, p. 191.
60. Ginsberg, Journals, Ginsberg Collection, Stanford University.
61. Kramer, *Ginsberg in America*, p. 41.
62. Miles, *Ginsberg*, p. 122.
63. Ginsberg, Journals, Ginsberg Collection, Stanford University.
64. Solomon, *Mishaps, Perhaps*, p. 45.
65. Solomon to Ginsberg, n.d., Ginsberg Collection, Stanford University.
66. Solomon and Ginsberg, draft of letter to T. S. Eliot, December 19, 1949, Ginsberg Collection, Stanford University.
67. Solomon, *Emergency Messages*, p. 33.
68. Solomon to Ginsberg, July 15, 1950, Ginsberg Collection, Stanford University.
69. Miles, *Ginsberg*, p. 125.
70. Ginsberg, Journals, Ginsberg Collection, Stanford University.
71. Ibid.
72. Miles, *Ginsberg*, p. 129.
73. Ginsberg to Cassady, summer 1950, in Ginsberg and Cassady, *As Ever*, p. 67.
74. Ginsberg to Cassady, January 1952, ibid., p. 115.
75. Ginsberg, Journals, Ginsberg Collection, Stanford University.
76. Ginsberg to Lionel Trilling, December 1948, Ginsberg Collection, Stanford University.
77. Ginsberg to Cassady, October 31, 1950, in Ginsberg and Cassady, *As Ever*, p. 73.
78. Chandler Brossard, "Tentative Visits to the Cemetery: Reflections on My Beat Generation," *Review of Contemporary Literature* 7 (1987): 13.
79. Gloria Sukenick, in Ronald Sukenick, *Down and In: Life in the Underground* (New York: Macmillan, 1987), p. 19.
80. Judith Malina, *The Diaries of Judith Malina 1947–1957* (New York: Grove Press, 1984), p. 172.
81. Ibid., p. 181.
82. Anatole Broyard, "Portrait of a Hipster," *Partisan Review* 15, no. 6 (June 1948): 721.
83. Norman Mailer, "Mailer's Reply," in *Advertisements for Myself* (New York: Putnam, 1959), p. 363.
84. Ned Polsky, in ibid., p. 366.
85. Milton Klonsky, "Greenwich Village: Decline and Fall," in Chandler Brossard, *The Scene Before You: A New Approach to American Culture* (New York: Rinehart, 1955), p. 26.
86. Mailer, "Mailer's Reply," p. 363.
87. Shelley, "A Defence of Poetry," quoted in Thomas McClanahan, "Gregory Corso," *Dictionary of Literary Biography*, vol. 5, *American Poets Since World War II* (Detroit: Gale Research, 1980), p. 142.
88. Ibid., p. 143.
89. Miles, *Ginsberg*, p. 133.
90. Gifford and Lee, *Jack's Book*, p. 178.
91. Gregory Corso, "Elegiac Feelings American," in *Elegiac Feelings American* (New York: New Directions, 1970), p. 24.
92. Ginsberg, interview with the author, New York, March 27, 1995.
93. Kramer, *Ginsberg in America*, p. 174.
94. Ginsberg, Journals, Ginsberg Collection, Stanford University.
95. Paul Mariani, *William Carlos Williams: A New World Naked* (New York: McGraw-Hill, 1981), p. 607.

96. Schumacher, *Dharma Lion*, p. 123.
97. Mariani, *William Carlos Williams*, p. 605.
98. Schumacher, *Dharma Lion*, p. 123.
99. Williams to Harriet Monroe, March 5, 1913, in *The Selected Letters of William Carlos Williams*, ed. John C. Thirlwall (New York: Obolensky, 1957), p. 25.
100. Pound, quoted in Michael Reck, *Ezra Pound: A Close-up* (New York: McGraw-Hill, 1967), p. 95.
101. Williams to Lowell, March 11, 1952, in Williams, *Selected Letters*, p. 312.
102. Schumacher, *Dharma Lion*, p. 124.
103. Miles, *Ginsberg*, p. 146.
104. Allen Ginsberg, "The Bricklayer's Lunch Hour," in *Collected Poems*, p. 4.
105. Williams to Ginsberg, February 27, 1952, in Miles, *Ginsberg*, p. 145.
106. Ibid., p. 146.
107. Ginsberg to Cassady, June 23, 1953, in Ginsberg and Cassady, *As Ever*, p. 147.
108. Miles, *Ginsberg*, p. 153.
109. Ibid.
110. Ginsberg to Cassady, September 4, 1953, in Ginsberg and Cassady, *As Ever*, p. 153.
111. Allen Ginsberg, "The Green Automobile," in *Collected Poems*, p. 86.
112. Nicosia, *Memory Babe*, p. 279.
113. Ibid., p. 287.
114. Ginsberg to Lionel Trilling, n.d., Ginsberg Collection, Stanford University.
115. Nicosia, *Memory Babe*, p. 301.
116. Plummer, *The Holy Goof*, p. 87.
117. Nicosia, *Memory Babe*, p. 337.
118. Plummer, *The Holy Goof*, p. 86.
119. Ginsberg to Cassady, February 1951, in Ginsberg and Cassady, *As Ever*, p. 101.
120. Cassady to Ginsberg, May 17, 1951, ibid., p. 104.
121. Kerouac to Cassady, December 27, 1950, in Kerouac, *Selected Letters*, p. 243.
122. Nicosia, *Memory Babe*, p. 337.
123. Charters, *Kerouac*, p. 127.
124. Kerouac to Neal Cassady, April 15, 1955, in Kerouac, *Selected Letters*, p. 473.
125. Kerouac to Cassady, May 22, 1951, ibid., p. 315.
126. Nicosia, *Memory Babe*, p. 343.
127. Kerouac, *Visions of Cody*, p. 93.
128. Kerouac, "Essentials of Spontaneous Prose" in Charters, *Portable Beat Reader*, p. 58.
129. Ibid., p. 57.
130. Ibid.
131. Kerouac to Allen Ginsberg, May 18, 1952, in Kerouac, *Selected Letters*, p. 356.
132. Tim Hunt, *Kerouac's Crooked Road: Development of a Fiction* (Hamden, Conn.: Archon Books, 1981), p. 145.
133. Kerouac to Carolyn Cassady, August 10, 1953, in Kerouac, *Selected Letters*, p. 358.
134. Nicosia, *Memory Babe*, p. 371.
135. Cassady, *Off the Road*, p. 218.
136. Kerouac, *Visions of Cody*, p. 398.
137. Cassady, *Off the Road*, p. 163.
138. Ibid., p. 167.
139. Allen Ginsberg to Carolyn Cassady, late 1952; in Ginsberg and Cassady, *As Ever*, p. 135.
140. Cassady, *Off the Road*, p. 204.
141. Gina Berriault, "Neal's Ashes," *Rolling Stone*, October 12, 1972, p. 32.
142. Kerouac to Ginsberg, December 15, 1948, Ginsberg Collection, Special Collections, Columbia University.
143. Nicosia, *Memory Babe*, p. 445.
144. William Burroughs, "Introduction," in *Queer* (New York: Viking Penguin, 1985), p. v.
145. Ibid., p. x.
146. Burroughs to Kerouac, May 1951, in Burroughs, *Letters*, p. 91.
147. Burroughs to Kerouac, April 1952, ibid., p. 114.

148. Burroughs to Ginsberg, January 11, 1951, ibid., p. 79.
149. Burroughs to Ginsberg, December 20, 1951, ibid., p. 97.
150. Morgan, *Literary Outlaw*, p. 175.
151. Burroughs to Ginsberg, May 5, 1951, in Burroughs, *Letters*, p. 87.
152. Burroughs to Ginsberg, October 13, 1949, ibid., p. 54.
153. Morgan, *Literary Outlaw*, p. 173.
154. Ibid., p. 176.
155. Ibid., p. 157.
156. Burroughs to Ginsberg, May 1951, in Burroughs, *Letters*, p. 89.
157. Burroughs to Ginsberg, March 18, 1949, ibid., p. 45.
158. Chase, interview with Morgan, Paso Robles, Calif., March 15, 1985, in Morgan Archives, Arizona State University.
159. Ibid.
160. William Burroughs' signature in Burroughs to Allen Ginsberg, April 22, 1952, in Burroughs, *Letters*, p. 121.
161. Burroughs, *Interzone*, p. 70.
162. Burroughs to Kerouac, March 10, 1950, in Burroughs, *Letters*, p. 65.
163. Plimpton, *Writers at Work*, p. 145.
164. Burroughs, *Queer*, pp. xii–xiii.
165. Morgan, *Literary Outlaw*, p. 185.
166. Burroughs, *Queer*, p. xiv.
167. Morgan, *Literary Outlaw*, p. 187.
168. Burroughs, *Queer*, p. 100.
169. Burroughs, *Interzone*, p. 64.
170. Morgan, *Literary Outlaw*, p. 187.
171. Burroughs, *Queer*, p. 73.
172. Burroughs to Ginsberg, May 23, 1952, in Burroughs, *Letters*, p. 126.
173. Burroughs, *Interzone*, p. 64.
174. Burroughs, *Queer*, p. 61.
175. Morgan, *Literary Outlaw*, p. 187.
176. Burroughs, *Junky*, p. 156..
177. Burroughs, *Queer*, p. 114.
178. Ibid., p. 118.
179. Morgan, *Literary Outlaw*, p. 191.
180. Ibid., p. 192.
181. Ibid., p. 193.
182. Burroughs, *Queer*, p. xxi.
183. Morgan, *Literary Outlaw*, p. 195.
184. Ibid., p. 194.
185. Ibid., p. 196.
186. Burroughs to Allen Ginsberg, February 7, 1955, in Burroughs, *Letters*, p. 263.
187. Ibid., p. 196.
188. Chase, interview with Morgan, Paso Robles, Calif., March 15, 1985, in Morgan Archives, Arizona State University.
189. Burroughs, *Queer*, p. xxii.
190. Morgan, *Literary Outlaw*, p. 201.
191. Ibid., p. 202.
192. Burroughs to Allen Ginsberg, February 20, 1948, in Burroughs, *Letters*, p. 18.
193. Morgan, *Literary Outlaw*, p. 215.
194. Burroughs to Ginsberg, January 19, 1952, in Burroughs, *Letters*, p. 101.
195. Ibid.
196. Burroughs to Ginsberg, July 1952, ibid., p. 134.
197. Burroughs to Ginsberg, November 5, 1952, ibid., p. 140.
198. Kerouac to John Clellon Holmes, December 9, 1952, in Kerouac, *Selected Letters*, pp. 388–89.
199. Morgan, *Literary Outlaw*, p. 218.
200. Burroughs to Ginsberg, July 3, 1953, in Burroughs, *Letters*, pp. 179, 180.
201. Burroughs to Ginsberg, January 19, 1952, ibid., p. 101.
202. Burroughs to Ginsberg, April 22, 1952, ibid., p. 121.
203. Burroughs to Ginsberg, October 6, 1952, ibid., p. 138.

204. Louis Simpson to Allen Ginsberg, May 29, 1952, in Ginsberg Collection, Stanford University.
205. Burroughs to Ginsberg, August 3, 1953, in Burroughs, *Letters*, p. 187.
206. Morgan, *Literary Outlaw*, p. 206.
207. Ibid.
208. Ginsberg, Journals, Ginsberg Collection, Stanford University.
209. Ibid.
210. Schumacher, *Dharma Lion*, p. 148.
211. Morgan, *Literary Outlaw*, p. 206.
212. Ginsberg to Neal Cassady, September 4, 1953, in Ginsberg and Cassady, *As Ever*, p. 154.
213. Miles, *Burroughs*, p. 66.
214. Allen Ginsberg, "Recollections of Burroughs Letters," in William S. Burroughs, *Letters to Allen Ginsberg, 1953–1957* (New York: Full Court Press, 1982), p. 5.
215. Schumacher, *Dharma Lion*, p. 157.
216. Ginsberg, "Recollections of Burroughs Letters," p. 6.
217. Miles, *Ginsberg*, p. 156.

Beat Ports of Call: San Francisco, Tangiers

1. Miles, *Burroughs*, p. 74.
2. Burroughs to Allen Ginsberg, March 1, 1954, in Burroughs, *Letters*, p. 198.
3. Ibid., p. 199.
4. Burroughs to Ginsberg, January 26, 1954, ibid., p. 195.
5. Burroughs to Ginsberg, February 9, 1954, ibid., p. 195.
6. Burroughs to Ginsberg, March 1, 1954, ibid., p. 198.
7. Burroughs to Jack Kerouac, May 4, 1954, ibid., p. 209.
8. Burroughs to Kerouac, April 22, 1954, ibid., p. 205.
9. Ibid., p. 204.
10. Ibid., p. 205.
11. Burroughs to Ginsberg, April 7, 1954, ibid., p. 201.
12. Ginsberg, "Recollections of Burroughs Letters," p. 7.
13. Allen Ginsberg, *Journals: Early Fifties Early Sixties*, ed. Gordon Ball (New York: Grove Press, 1977), p. 55.
14. Allen Ginsberg, "Siesta in Xbalba," in *Collected Poems*, p. 101.
15. Kerouac to John Clellon Holmes, February 19, 1954, in Kerouac, *Selected Letters*, pp. 407–8
16. Ginsberg to Cassady, May 12, 1954, in Ginsberg and Cassady, *As Ever*, p. 182.
17. Ginsberg, *Journals: Early Fifties Early Sixties*, p. 34.
18. Cassady, *Off the Road*, p. 233.
19. Clark, *Kerouac*, p. 131.
20. Jack Kerouac, "The Last Word," *Escapade* 4, no. 2 (October 1959): 72.
21. Clark, *Kerouac*, p. 131.
22. Nicosia, *Memory Babe*, p. 458.
23. Kerouac To Ginsberg, early May 1954, in Kerouac, *Selected Letters*, p. 410.
24. Burroughs to Jack Kerouac, May 24, 1954, in Burroughs, *Letters*, p. 213.
25. Ginsberg, Journals, Ginsberg Collection, Stanford University.
26. Schumacher, *Dharma Lion*, p. 153.
27. Ginsberg to Kerouac, ca. fall 1954, quoted in Schumacher, *Dharma Lion*, p. 195.
28. Gifford and Lee, *Jack's Book*, p. 215.
29. Jack Kerouac, "Some of the Dharma," quoted in Nicosia, *Memory Babe*, p. 471.
30. Ginsberg to Kerouac, quoted in Miles, *Ginsberg*, p. 168.
31. Ibid., p. 167.
32. Allen Ginsberg, "Love Poem on Theme by Whitman," *Collected Poems*, p. 115.
33. Kerouac to Carolyn Cassady, July 2, 1954, in Kerouac, *Selected Letters*, p. 427.
34. Morgan, *Literary Outlaw*, p. 251.

35. Schumacher, *Dharma Lion*, p. 186.
36. Miles, *Ginsberg*, p. 177.
37. Kramer, *Ginsberg in America*, p. 42.
38. Schumacher, *Dharma Lion*, p. 193.
39. Ibid., p. 199.
40. Miles, *Ginsberg*, p. 186.
41. Schumacher, *Dharma Lion*, p. 200.
42. Carl Solomon to Allen Ginsberg, 1955, Ginsberg Collection, Stanford University.
43. Schumacher, *Dharma Lion*, p. 200.
44. Allen Ginsberg, "Notes Written on Finally Recording Howl," liner notes to *Allen Ginsberg Reads Howl and Other Poems* (Fantasy Records 7006, 1959).
45. Kramer, *Ginsberg in America*, p. 140.
46. Schumacher, *Dharma Lion*, p. 201.
47. Ginsberg, "Notes Written on Finally Recording Howl."
48. Ibid.
49. Schumacher, *Dharma Lion*, p. 204.
50. Kerouac to Ginsberg, August 19, 1955, in Kerouac, *Selected Letters*, p. 508.
51. Schumacher, *Dharma Lion*, p. 207.
52. Barry Miles, ed., *Howl: Original Draft Facsimile, Transcript and Variant Versions, Fully Annotated by Author, with Contemporaneous Correspondence, Account of First Public Reading, Legal Skirmishes, Precursor Texts and Bibliography* (New York: Harper & Row, 1986), p. 165.
53. Kerouac to Ginsberg, September 1–6, 1955, in Kerouac, *Selected Letters*, p. 511.
54. Miles, *Howl*, p. 165.
55. James McKenzie, interview with Peter Orlovsky, North Dakota, 1975, in Knight and Knight, *unspeakable visions of the individual* 9, no. 1 (1979): 23.
56. Linda Hamalian, *A Life of Kenneth Rexroth* (New York: Norton, 1991), p. 244.
57. Jack Kerouac, *The Dharma Bums* (New York: Viking, 1958), p. 10.
58. Kramer, *Ginsberg in America*, p. 48.
59. John Allen Ryan, quoted in Rebecca Solnit, *Secret Exhibition: Six California Artists of the Cold War Era* (San Francisco: City Lights, 1990), p. 48.
60. Miles, *Howl*, p. 165.
61. Bruce Cook, *The Beat Generation*, (Westport, Conn.: Greenwood Press, 1983), p. 165.
62. Glen Burns, *Great Poets Howl: A Study of Allen Ginsberg's Poetry, 1943–1955* (New York: P. Lang, 1983), p. 332.
63. Michael McClure, "Allen for Real: Allen Ginsberg," in Michael McClure, *Lighting the Corners: On Art, Nature, and the Visionary: Essays and Interviews* (Albuquerque: University of New Mexico Press, 1993), p. 163.
64. Miles, *Ginsberg*, p. 196.
65. Ibid., p. 197.
66. Schumacher, *Dharma Lion*, p. 216.
67. Ibid., p. 215.
68. Ekbert Faas, *Young Robert Duncan: Portrait of the Homosexual in Society* (Santa Barbara, Calif.: Black Sparrow Press, 1983), p. 278.
69. Gary Snyder, "North Beach," in *The Old Ways* (San Francisco: City Lights, 1977), p. 45.
70. William Everson, "Shaker and Maker," in Geoffrey Gardner, ed., *For Rexroth: The Ark 14* (New York: The Ark, 1980), pp. 25–26.
71. Jack Spicer, in McClure, *Lighting the Corners*, p. 44.
72. Gifford and Lee, *Jack's Book*, p. 224.
73. Everson to Duncan, in Faas, *Young Robert Duncan*, p. 168.
74. David Meltzer, ed., *The San Francisco Poets* (New York: Ballantine, 1971), p. 76.
75. Hilda Burton, in Faas, *Young Robert Duncan*, p. 211.
76. Janet Richards, *Common Soldiers* (San Francisco: Archer, 1979), p. 274.
77. Lee Bartlett, *William Everson: The Life of Brother*

Antoninus (New York: New Directions, 1988), p. 95.

78. Hamalian, *Rexroth*, p. 221.
79. Richards, *Common Soldiers*, p. 274.
80. Linda Hamalian, "Everson on Rexroth: An Interview," *Literary Review* 26, no. 3 (Spring 1988): 424.
81. Richards, *Common Soldiers*, p. 311.
82. Faas, *Young Robert Duncan*, p. 191.
83. Bartlett, *William Everson*, p. 94.
84. Faas, *Young Robert Duncan*, p. 9.
85. Kenneth Rexroth, *American Poetry in the Twentieth Century* (New York: Seabury Press, 1971), p. 165.
86. Richards, *Common Soldiers*, p. 222.
87. Faas, *Young Robert Duncan*, p. 87.
88. Ibid., p. 150.
89. Ibid., p. 151.
90. Michael McClure, "Robert Duncan: A Modern Romantic," in *Lighting the Corners*, p. 92.
91. Richards, *Common Soldiers*, p. 222.
92. Hamalian, "Everson on Rexroth," p. 426.
93. James A. Powell, "Brother Antoninus," in Ann Charters, ed., *Dictionary of Literary Biography*, vol. 16 (Detroit: Gale Research, 1983), pp. 190–91.
94. Bartlett, *William Everson*, p. 162.
95. Meltzer, *San Francisco Poets*, p. 99.
96. Bartlett, *William Everson*, p. 170.
97. Ibid., p. 169.
98. Powell, "William Everson," p. 191.
99. Richards, *Common Soldiers*, p. 316.
100. Lawrence Ferlinghetti, interview with the author, January 27, 1994, San Francisco.
101. Robert I. Bertholf and Ian Reid, eds., *Robert Duncan: Scales of the Marvelous* (New York: New Directions, 1979), p. 19.
102. Mick McAllister, "An Interview with Michael McClure," in Arthur and Kit Knight, eds., *Kerouac and the Beats* (New York: Paragon House, 1988), p. 211.

103. Michael McClure, *Scratching the Beat Surface* (San Francisco: North Point Press, 1982), p. 138.
104. McClure, "Allen for Real: Allen Ginsberg," in *Lighting the Corners*, p. 170.
105. McClure, "The Beat Journey: An Interview," ibid., p. 133.
106. Lew Welch, *I Remain: The Letters of Lew Welch and Correspondence of His Friends*, ed. Donald Allen (Bolinas, Calif.: Grey Fox Press, 1980), p. 41.
107. Dan MacLeod, "Gary Snyder," in Charters, *Dictionary of Literary Biography*, p. 490.
108. Carol Baker, "1414 S. E. Lambert Street," in John Halper, ed., *Gary Snyder: Dimensions of a Life* (San Francisco: Sierra Club Books, 1991), p. 26.
109. MacLeod, "Gary Snyder," p. 489.
110. Ekbert Faas, "Robert Creeley," in Charters, *Dictionary of Literary Biography*, p. 145.
111. Kerouac, *Dharma Bums*, p. 11.
112. Alvah Goldbook, the Ginsberg-based character, in ibid., p. 32. The Kerouac character agrees.
113. Ibid., p. 9.
114. Ibid., p. 84.
115. Ibid., p. 77.
116. Nicosia, *Memory Babe*, p. 495.
117. Nancy J. Peters, "Philip Lamantia," in Charters, *Dictionary of Literary Biography*, p. 330.
118. Ibid., p. 330.
119. Ibid., p. 331.
120. Ibid., p. 332.
121. McClure to Steven Watson, March 1, 1995.
122. Paul Christensen, "Philip Whalen," in Charters, *Dictionary of Literary Biography*, p. 554.
123. Ibid., p. 556.
124. Ibid., p. 558.
125. Ibid.
126. Martin Duberman, *Black Mountain: An Exploration in Community* (Garden City, N.Y.: Anchor Press/Doubleday, 1973), pp. 408, 409.
127. Ibid., p. 144.

128. Robert Creeley, "Introduction," in *Black Mountain Review* (reprint ed.; New York: AMS Press, 1969), p. iv.
129. Ibid.
130. Ibid., p. 144.
131. Duberman, *Black Mountain*, p. 419.
132. Ibid.
133. Creeley, "Introduction," p. xii.
134. Ibid.
135. Ibid., p. xiii.
136. Mel Clay, *Jazz—Jail and God: Bob Kaufman* (San Francisco: Androgyne Books, 1987), p. vi.
137. "Legendary Beat Poet Bob Kaufman Dies," *San Francisco Chronicle*, January 13, 1986.
138. Clay, *Jazz—Jail and God*, p. 63.
139. "Talking with Duncan," in McClure, *Lighting the Corners*, p. 84.
140. Michael McClure, "Ninety-One Things About Richard Brautigan," ibid., p. 43.
141. Michael McClure, "Allen for Real," ibid., p. 161.
142. Kerouac to Stella Sampas, November 9, 1955, in Kerouac, *Selected Letters*, p. 528.
143. Gifford and Lee, *Jack's Book*, p. 224.
144. Herbert Gold, "How to Tell the Beatniks from the Hipsters," *Noble Savage* 1 (Spring 1960): 132.
145. Kerouac to Lucien Carr, February 24, 1956, in Kerouac, *Selected Letters*, p. 562.
146. Richards, *Common Soldiers*, pp. 325–26.
147. Faas, *Young Robert Duncan*, p. 279.
148. Gifford and Lee, *Jack's Book*, p. 222.
149. Ibid., p. 221.
150. Duberman, *Black Mountain*, pp. 438–39.
151. Richards, *Common Soldiers*, p. 323.
152. Hamalian, *Rexroth*, p. 246.
153. Ibid., p. 259.
154. Ibid., p. 271.
155. Kerouac to John Clellon Holmes, May 27, 1956, in Kerouac, *Selected Letters*, p. 580.
156. Ginsberg, interview with the author, New York, March 27, 1995.
157. Faas, "Robert Creeley," p. 145.
158. Kerouac, *Dharma Bums*, p. 199.
159. Ibid., p. 215.
160. Ralph J. Gleason, "Begone, Dull Beats," *New Statesman*, June 2, 1961, p. 94.
161. Burroughs to Ginsberg, June 16, 1954, in Burroughs, *Letters*, p. 215.
162. Burroughs to Ginsberg, September 21, 1955, ibid., p. 280.
163. Burroughs, *Interzone*, p. 69.
164. Ibid., p. 70.
165. Burroughs to Ginsberg, June 24, 1954, in Burroughs, *Letters*, pp. 216–17.
166. Ibid., p. 216.
167. Plimpton, *Writers at Work*, p. 147.
168. Burroughs to Ginsberg, May 8, 1956, in Burroughs, *Letters*, p. 317.
169. Ibid.
170. Burroughs to Ginsberg, September 16,1956, ibid., p. 326.
171. Miles, *Burroughs*, p. 77.
172. Burroughs to Ginsberg, October 13, 1956, in Burroughs, *Letters*, p. 329.
173. Burroughs, *Interzone*, p. 128.
174. William Burroughs, "Deposition: Testimony Concerning a Sickness," in *Naked Lunch* (New York: Grove Press, 1961), p. v.
175. Miles, *Burroughs*, p. 78.
176. Ibid.
177. Paul Bowles, *Without Stopping: An Autobiography* (New York: Putnam, 1992), p. 323.
178. Burroughs to Ginsberg, October 29, 1956, in Burroughs, *Letters*, p. 337.
179. Ibid., p. 356.
180. Jack Kerouac, *Desolation Angels* (New York: Coward-McCann, 1965), p. 307.
181. Ibid., p. 311.

182. Ibid., p. 301.
183. Ibid., p. 315.
184. Miles, *Burroughs*, p. 79.
185. Ibid., p. 81.

Beat to Beatnik

1. William Carlos Williams, "Introduction," in Allen Ginsberg, *Howl and Other Poems* (San Francisco: City Lights, 1956), p. vi.
2. Schumacher, *Dharma Lion*, p. 261.
3. Ibid., p. 262.
4. Gilbert Millstein, *New York Times*, September 5, 1957.
5. Clark, *Kerouac*, p. 161.
6. Johnson, *Minor Characters*, p. 190.
7. Jack Kerouac to Allen Ginsberg, August 11, 1958, Ginsberg Collection, Special Collections, Columbia University.
8. McNally, *Desolate Angel*, p. 243.
9. Clark, *Kerouac*, p. 165.
10. McNally, *Desolate Angel*, p. 242.
11. Clark, *Kerouac*, p. 166.
12. Plummer, *The Holy Goof*, p. 104.
13. John Montgomery, *Kerouac West Coast* (Palo Alto, Calif.: Fels & Firn, 1976), n.p.
14. Art Buchwald, "The Upbeat Beatnik," *New York Herald Tribune*, January 4, 1960.
15. Fred McDarrah, ed., *Kerouac and Friends* (New York: Morrow, 1985), p. 19.
16. Kerouac to Ginsberg, August 28, 1958, Ginsberg Collection, Special Collections, Columbia University.
17. Herbert Gold, "Hip, Cool, Beat—and Frantic," *Nation*, November 6, 1957, p. 349.
18. Nicosia, *Memory Babe*, p. 567.
19. Kenneth Rexroth, "San Francisco Letter," *Evergreen Review* 1, no. 2 (Summer 1957): 10.
20. Clark, *Kerouac*, pp. 165, 167.

21. Lionel Trilling, in Hettie Jones, *How I Became Hettie Jones* (New York: Penguin, 1991), p. 129.
22. "Ron," review of *The Beat Generation*, *Variety*, July 1, 1959.
23. Blaine Allan, "The Making (and Unmaking) of *Pull My Daisy*," *Film History* 2, no. 3 (September–October 1988): 189.
24. Ibid., p. 197.
25. Jones, *How I Became Hettie Jones*, p. 129.
26. Johnson, *Minor Characters*, p. 89.
27. Ibid., p. 30.
28. Ibid., p. 127.
29. Ibid.
30. Ibid., p. 132.
31. Ibid., p. 137.
32. Ibid., p. 154.
33. Ibid., p. 253.
34. Jones, *How I Became Hettie Jones*, p. 2.
35. Ibid., p. 129.
36. Title page of *Yūgen*, quoted in Jones, *How I Became Hettie Jones*, p. 54.
37. Miles, *Ginsberg*, p. 252.
38. Jones, *How I Became Hettie Jones*, p. 98.
39. Diane DiPrima, *Memoirs of a Beatnik* (Paris: Olympia Press/Traveler's Companion, 1969), p. 63.
40. Ibid., p. 126.
41. Ibid., p. 127.
42. Ibid., p. 137.
43. Ibid., p. 131.
44. Harold Norse, *Memoirs of a Bastard Angel: A Fifty-Year Literary and Erotic Odyssey* (New York: Morrow, 1989), p. 347.
45. Morgan, *Literary Outlaw*, p. 278.
46. Ibid., p. 280.
47. Naomi Ginsberg to Allen Ginsberg, written June 8, postmarked June 11, 1956, in Miles, *Ginsberg*, p. 208.
48. Eugene Brooks to Allen Ginsberg, June 11, 1956, Ginsberg Collection, Stanford University.

49. "Allen Ginsberg Reads 'Kaddish,' a Twentieth-Century Ecstatic Poem," liner notes, Atlantic Records #4001, 1966.
50. Ibid.
51. Ginsberg to Lawrence Ferlinghetti, October 11, 1960, ibid.
52. Schumacher, *Dharma Lion*, p. 274.
53. Miles, *Burroughs*, p. 86.
54. Ibid., p. 113.
55. Morgan, *Literary Outlaw*, p. 407.
56. Ibid., p. 296.
57. Burroughs to Allen Ginsberg, August 24, 1959, in Burroughs, *Letters*, p. 421.
58. Burroughs to Ginsberg, July 1959, ibid., p. 418.
59. Morgan, *Literary Outlaw*, p. 338.
60. Miles, *Burroughs*, p. 106.
61. Jonathon Green, ed., *The Encyclopedia of Censorship* (New York: Facts on File, 1990), p. 221.

Aftermath

1. Neal Cassady to Carolyn Cassady, in Knight and Knight, *Beat Angels*, p. 8.
2. Ibid., p. 6.
3. Carolyn Cassady to Allen Ginsberg, October 31, 1962, Ginsberg Collection, Special Collections, Columbia University.
4. Paul Perry and Ken Babbs, *On the Bus: The Complete Guide to the Legendary Trip of Ken Kesey and the Merry Pranksters* (New York: Thunder's Mouth Press, 1990), p. 108.
5. Ed McClanahan, ibid., p. 33.
6. Stewart Brand's phrase, in Plummer, *The Holy Goof*, p. 122.
7. Perry and Babbs, *On the Bus*, p. 43.
8. "L.," "My Visions of Neal," in Rudi Horemans, ed., *Beat Indeed!* (Antwerp, Belgium: EXA, 1985), p. 95.
9. Plummer, *The Holy Goof*, p. 143.
10. Miles, *Ginsberg*, p. 376.
11. Perry and Babbs, *On the Bus*, p. 84.
12. Ron Bivert, ibid., p. 86.
13. Nicosia, *Memory Babe*, p. 653.
14. Berriault, "Neal's Ashes," p. 36.
15. Plummer, *The Holy Goof*, p. 153.
16. Berriault, "Neal's Ashes," p. 36.
17. Burroughs to Ginsberg, July 24, 1958, in Burroughs, *Letters*, p. 392.
18. Kerouac, "The First Word," *Escapade* 12, no. 1 (January 1967): 33.
19. Clark, *Kerouac*, p. 204.
20. Nicosia, *Memory Babe*, p. 675.
21. McNally, *Desolate Angel*, p. 338.
22. Nicosia, *Memory Babe*, p. 684.
23. Miles, *Ginsberg*, p. 286.
24. McNally, *Desolate Angel*, p. 338.
25. Nicosia, *Memory Babe*, p. 698.
26. Gifford and Lee, *Jack's Book*, p. 315.
27. Ibid., p. 316.
28. Charters, *Kerouac*, p. 367.
29. Miles, *Ginsberg*, p. 327.
30. Ibid., p. 260.
31. Ibid., p. 269.
32. Ibid., p. 270.
33. Ibid., p. 271.
34. Ibid., p. 272.
35. Ibid., p. 273.
36. Schumacher, *Dharma Lion*, p. 332.
37. Miles, *Ginsberg*, p. 279.
38. Schumacher, *Dharma Lion*, p. 347.
39. Ibid.
40. Swami Shivananda, in Plimpton, *Writers at Work*, p. 315.
41. Miles, *Ginsberg*, p. 309.
42. Plimpton, *Writers at Work*, p. 316.
43. Miles, *Ginsberg*, p. 331.
44. Kramer, *Ginsberg in America*, p. 13.
45. Ibid., p. 100.

46. Allen Ginsberg, "A Definition of the Beat Genera-
    tion," *Friction* 1, nos. 2–3 (1982): 50. Also Ginsberg,
    telephone interview with the author, New York, July
    14, 1995.
47. Philip Whalen, interview with the author, San Fran-
    cisco, February 1, 1994.
48. Burroughs to Ginsberg, September 20, 1957, in Bur-
    roughs, *Letters*, p. 367.
49. Morgan, *Literary Outlaw*, p. 595.
50. William Burroughs, *The Soft Machine* (New York:
    Grove Press, 1966), quoted in Miles, *Burroughs*,
    p. 122.

51. Brookner, *William Burroughs*.
52. Morgan, *Literary Outlaw*, p. 548.
53. Ibid., p. 13.
54. Ibid., p. 571.
55. Ibid.
56. William Burroughs, *The Western Lands* (New York:
    Penguin, 1987), p. 258.
57. Allen Ginsberg, "Account of Purification of Spirit of
    William S. Burroughs," March 17–22, 1992, Gins-
    berg Collection, Stanford University.
58. Ibid.

Sources for Marginal Quotations

Page ix   "Complex works of art": Paul Rosenfeld, "When New York Became Central," *Modern Music*, summer 1946, p. 84.

Page x   "Artists to my mind": Burroughs to Allen Ginsberg, in Ann Charters, ed., *The Portable Beat Reader* (New York: Viking Penguin, 1992), p. xxxi.

Page 3   "Humility is indeed beatness": Burroughs to Allen Ginsberg, May 30, 1953, in William Burroughs, *The Letters of William S. Burroughs 1945–1959*, ed. Oliver Harris (New York: Viking, 1993,), p. 166.

Page 4   "It's time we thought": Holmes to Kerouac, April 28, 1950, in Jack Kerouac, *Selected Letters 1940–1956*, ed. Ann Charters (New York: Viking, 1995), p. 226, n. 1.

Page 4   "The essence of the phrase": Allen Ginsberg, "A Definition of the Beat Generation," *Friction* 1, nos. 2–3 (1982): 52.

Page 4   "What have we done": Paul O'Neill, "The Only Rebellion Around," *Life*, November 30, 1959, p. 130.

Page 4   "Kerouac opened a million": William Burroughs, "Remembering Jack Kerouac," in *The Adding Machine* (New York: Seaver Books, 1986), p. 180.

Page 5   "By avoiding society you": Gregory Corso, "Variations on a Generation," in Charters, *The Portable Beat Reader*, p. 183.

Page 5   "Neal: His names were long": Allen Ginsberg, Journals, Ginsberg Collection, Stanford University.

Page 6   "In the U.S. you have": Burroughs to Allen Ginsberg, July 10, 1953, in Burroughs, *Letters*, p. 185.

Page 6   "We are now contending": Kerouac to Neal Cassady, December 28, 1950, in Kerouac, *Selected Letters*, p. 247.

Page 6   "But listen . . . do you realize": Kerouac to Neal Cassady, October 3, 1948, ibid., p. 167.

Page 7   "Here once the kindly dope": Beginning of Kerouac's poem "A Remembrance of Walking Past the Hotel Wilson," in Gerald Nicosia, *Memory Babe: A Critical Biography of Jack Kerouac* (Berkeley: University of California Press, 1994), p. 162.

Page 8   "To re-edit the world": Anatole Broyard, "Portrait of a Hipster," *Partisan Review* 15, no. 6 (June 1948): 721.

Page 9   "When we get where": William Burroughs, *Queer* (New York: Viking Penguin, 1985), p. 76.

Page 9   "Hip is the affirmation": Norman Mailer, in Nicosia, *Memory Babe*, p. 206.

Page 9   "In the 1940s pre-med students": Herbert Huncke, interview with the author, New York, February 26, 1995.

Page 10   "If God made anything better": William Burroughs, *Junky* (New York: Penguin, 1977), p. 142.

Page 10   "Just when you think": Burroughs, *Queer*, p. x.

Page 10   "'Get ready to cop'": Burroughs, *Junky*, p. 50.

Page 11   "Capable boy": Ted Morgan, *Literary Outlaw: The Life and Times of William S. Burroughs* (New York: Holt, 1988), p. 41.

Page 12   "If Harvard doesn't": Ibid., p. 57.

Page 13   "The only *possible* ethic is": Burroughs to Jack Kerouac, March 15, 1949, in Burroughs, *Letters*, p. 42.

Page 13   "I could have been a successful": William Burroughs, "Lee's Journals," in *Interzone*, ed. James Grauerholz (New York: Penguin, 1989), p. 66.

Page 13   "A sucker is": Burroughs, *Junky*, pp. 15–16.

Page 14   "The most dangerous thing": Burroughs to Ginsberg, 1953, in William Plummer, *The Holy Goof: A Biography of Neal Cassady* (New York: Paragon House, 1981), p.94.

Page 14   "My affections, being concentrated": Burroughs, "Lee's Journals," in *Interzone*, p. 90.

Page 15   "Get with those technicolor": Burroughs to Allen Ginsberg, April 22, 1925, in Burroughs, *Letters*, p. 121.

Page 16   "Safety lies in exterminating": Burroughs, "Lee's Journals," *Interzone*, pp. 67–68.

Page 16   "The waiter nodded": Burroughs, *Junky*, p. 47.

Page 16   "Everything was solid that year": Kerouac to Neal Cassady, October 6, 1950, in Kerouac, *Selected Letters*, p. 234.

Page 17   "I was born, my damned sin": Kerouac to Neal Cassady, December 28, 1950, ibid., p. 250.

Page 20   "I believe my brother": Ibid., p. 253.

Page 21   "Judas is me": Kerouac to Neal Cassady, January 9, 1951, ibid., p. 282.

Page 21   "How I loved my mother": Kerouac to Neal Cassady, December 28, 1950, ibid., p. 252.

Page 21   "He was an angel": Kerouac to Neal Cassady, January 9, 1951, ibid., p. 282.

Page 21   "You are destined to be": Joe Kerouac to Jack Kerouac, in Tom Clark, *Jack Kerouac* (New York: Paragon House, 1990), p. 19.

Page 22   "I believe that memories": Kerouac to Neal Cassady, January 3, 1951, in Kerouac, *Selected Letters*, p. 268.

Page 23   "Forget this writing": Leo Kerouac to Jack Kerouac, in Dennis McNally, *Desolate Angel: Jack Kerouac, the Beat Generation, and America* (New York: Random House, 1979), p. 15.

Page 23   "Either I'm a genius": Ginsberg, in Michael Schumacher, *Dharma Lion: A Biography of Allen Ginsberg* (New York: St. Martin's Press, 1992), p. 16.

Page 26   "He laid a C-note": Huncke, interview with the author, New York, February 26, 1995.

Page 27   "If at first": Louis Ginsberg, "Keep an O'Pun Mind" (newspaper column).

Page 28   "Sure, man, that cat's": John Clellon Holmes, *Go*, in Charters, *The Portable Beat Reader*, p. 159.

Page 29   "Brains and brawn": Horace Mann yearbook entry for Jack Kerouac, in McNally, *Desolate Angel*, p. 40.

Page 30   "Go into the American night": Jack Kerouac, *Vanity of Duluoz* (New York: Coward-McCann, 1968), p. 94.

Page 32   "My life is like a sea": Kerouac to Neal Cassady, January 9, 1951, in Kerouac, *Selected Letters*, p. 285.

Page 33   "A man of letters": Kerouac to Navy psychiatrist, 1943, in Nicosia, *Memory Babe*, p. 106.

Page 33   "All girls go fruit": Kerouac to John Clellon Holmes, February 8, 1952, in Kerouac, *Selected Letters*, p. 338.

Page 34   "Know these words": Ginsberg, in Barry Miles, *Ginsberg: A Biography* (New York: Simon & Schuster, 1989), p. 43.

Page 35   "Lucien Carr's Fetishes": Ginsberg, Journals, Ginsberg Collection, Stanford University.

Page 35   "Huge apocalyptic novels": Allen Ginsberg to Jack Kerouac, July 13, 1949, in Kerouac, *Selected Letters*, p. 210, n. 5.

Page 36   "Do you realize Hubbard": Irwin Garden, in Jack Kerouac, *Desolation Angels* (New York: Coward-McCann, 1965), p. 312.

Page 37   "Nobody can actually *like* Burroughs": Kerouac to Caroline Kerouac Blake, March 14, 1945, in Kerouac, *Selected Letters*, p. 89.

Page 37   "It's a finkish world": Burroughs to Kerouac, in Nicosia, *Memory Babe*, p. 119.

Page 38   "Eddify yer mind": Burroughs to Kerouac, in McNally, *Desolate Angel*, p. 77.

Page 38   "Like Proust be an old": Jack Kerouac, "Belief & Technique for Modern Prose," in Charters, *The Portable Beat Reader*, p. 59.

Page 39   "When will we go": Arthur Rimbaud, in Kerouac, *Selected Letters*, p. 79.

Page 41   "Let's buy some tubes": Burroughs, *Junky*, pp. 14–15.

Page 44   "'See? See?'": Jack Kerouac, *On the Road* (New York: Viking, 1957), p. 137.

Page 46   "Flaming Cool Youth": Kerouac to Sterling Lord, September 17, 1956, in Kerouac, *Selected Letters*, p. 586.

Page 46   "A raw mind": Kerouac to Neal Cassady, October 6, 1950, ibid., p. 234.

Page 48   "And now, this curtain": Ginsberg, in Miles, *Ginsberg*, p. 54.

Page 49   "We are all sealed": Kerouac to Ginsberg, August 23, 1945, in Kerouac, *Selected Letters*, p. 92.

Page 49   "Joan is the nicest woman": Ginsberg, Journals, Ginsberg Collection, Stanford University.

Page 50   "I never seen such": Jack Kerouac, *The Subterraneans* (New York: Grove Press, 1958), p. 40.

Page 50   "Every time I hit Panama": Burroughs, *Queer*, p. 123.

Page 51   "He tried unsuccessfully": Ginsberg, Journals, Ginsberg Collection, Stanford University.

Page 51   "She's a whole lot": Kerouac, *The Subterraneans*, p. 15.

Page 52   "Whom I love most": Ginsberg, Journals, Ginsberg Collection, Stanford University.

Page 53   "I take a bang": Burroughs to Allen Ginsberg, December 20, 1951, in Burroughs, *Letters*, p. 98.

Page 53   "At present I have": Burroughs to Allen Ginsberg, January 11, 1951, ibid., p. 77.

Page 54   "We long ago realized our flesh": Kerouac to Ginsberg, December 15, 1948, in Kerouac, *Selected Letters*, p. 176.

Page 54   "You could dip into": Chase, in Nicosia, *Memory Babe*, pp. 151–52.

Page 54   "They didn't want to learn": Chase, interview with Ted Morgan, Paso Robles, Calif., March 15, 1985, in Morgan Archives, Arizona State University.

Page 54   "Both chippying": Burroughs to Allen Ginsberg, March 1, 1954, in Burroughs, *Letters*, p. 198.

Page 56   "A junky spends half": Burroughs, *Junky*, p. 123.

Page 56   "I think it no exaggeration": Ibid., p. xv.

Page 57   "Only my mother": Kerouac to Neal Cassady, July 28, 1949, in Kerouac, *Selected Letters*, p. 215.

Page 59   "She had an inner beauty": Huncke, in Barry Gifford and Lawrence Lee, *Jack's Book* (New York: St. Martin's Press, 1978), p. 55.

Page 59   Allen Ginsberg's lists of bars: Ginsberg, Journals, Ginsberg Collection, Stanford University.

Page 60   "Then we picked up": Allen Ginsberg to Kerouac, January 2, 1947, in Kerouac, *Selected Letters*, p. 108.

Page 61   "I am of course": Kerouac to Neal and Carolyn Cassady, May 27, 1952, ibid., p. 358.

Page 61   "A curious illusion": Burroughs to Allen Ginsberg, September 16, 1956, in Burroughs, *Letters*, p. 327.

Page 62   "But I was off": Burroughs, *Junky*, p. 140.

Page 63   "I wouldn't let them": Burroughs to Allen Ginsberg, June 24, 1949, in Burroughs, *Letters*, p. 51.

Page 64   "I wish you, Jack": Ginsberg, "To Kerouac in the Hospital," Journals, Ginsberg Collection, Stanford University.

Page 64   "Artist shmartist": Leo Kerouac, in McNally, *Desolate Angel*, p. 22.

Page 64   "Now he peddled": Burroughs, *Junky*, p. 29.

Page 65   "Well, about five nights ago": Burroughs, *Queer*, p. 34.

Page 66   "Like when I was the cheapest thief": Burroughs to Allen Ginsberg, June 6, 1953, in Burroughs, *Letters*, p. 169.

Page 66   "I have a little": Huncke, interview with the author, New York, February 26, 1995.

Page 67   "I saw Joan last week-end": Kingsland to Ginsberg, October 1946, Ginsberg Collection, Special Collections, Columbia University.

Page 67   "Despite the temptations": Burroughs to Allen Ginsberg, April 16, 1949, in Burroughs, *Letters*, p. 53.

Page 67   "I Regal up": Burroughs, *Junky*, p. 91.

Page 71   "'He's mad,' I said": Jack Kerouac, *On the Road*, p. 226.

Page 72   "The hip-bohemian criminal": Solomon to Kerouac, early 1952, in Nicosia, *Memory Babe*, p. 368.

Page 72   "Tell me of Huncke": Kerouac to Allen Ginsberg, April 1948, in Kerouac, *Selected Letters*, p. 147.

Page 73   "Alas—such is the luck": Huncke to Allen Ginsberg, 1947, Ginsberg Collection, Special Collections, Columbia University.

Page 74   "Huncke is always the same": Kerouac to Neal Cassady, September 13, 1947, in Kerouac, *Selected Letters*, p. 127.

Page 74   "We went to [Herbert]": Holmes, in Plummer, *The Holy Goof*, p. 35.

Page 76   "Dig, now, out": Neal Cassady, ibid., p. 67.

Page 76   "How right you are": Allen Ginsberg to Kerouac, August 25, 1955, in Kerouac, *Selected Letters*, p. 508.

Page 77   "For a real bum kick": Burroughs, "Lee's Journal," in *Interzone*, p. 82.

Page 78   "We are all guttersnipes": Carl Solomon, "Pilgrim State Hospital," in *Mishaps, Perhaps* (San Francisco: City Lights Books, 1966).

Page 78   "A western kinsman": Kerouac, *On the Road*, p. 10.

Page 79   "I became the unnatural son": Neal Cassady, *The First Third and Other Writings* (San Francisco: City Lights Books, 1971; expanded ed., 1981), p. 47.

Page 79   "I was a nannybeater": Kerouac, *The Subterraneans*, p. 11.

Page 80   "I see no greatness": Cassady to Allen Ginsberg, in Plummer, *The Holy Goof*, p. 48.

Page 80   "I have thought of Neal": Holmes to Ginsberg, n.d., Ginsberg Collection, Stanford University.

Page 82   "But you must also stop": Kerouac to Cassady, July 28, 1949, in Kerouac, *Selected Letters*, p. 213.

Page 82   "He came to the door stark naked": Kerouac, *On the Road*, p. 182.

Page 83   "What is all the holy feeling": Kerouac to Cassady, ca. April 15, 1955, in Kerouac, *Selected Letters*, p. 472.

Page 83   "Perhaps you are a temptation": Ginsberg to Cassady, August 1948, in Plummer, *The Holy Goof*, p. 31.

Page 84   "Don't you remember": Ginsberg to Cassady, fall 1947, ibid., p. 45.

Page 84   "Neal is his God-bone": Kerouac to John Clellon Holmes, June 24, 1949, in Kerouac, *Selected Letters*, p. 200.

Page 85   "He laid claims": Broyard, "Portrait of a Hipster," pp. 726–27.

Page 85   "To pick up means": Huncke, interview with the author, New York, February 26, 1995.

Page 85   "If you asked me": Ibid.

Page 86   "If you can't boogie": Kerouac, *On the Road*, p. 87.

Page 87   "I was out all of junk": Burroughs, *Junky*, p. 25.

Page 88   "I thought it": Herbert Huncke, interview with the author, New York, March 12, 1995.

Page 89   "Shooting is my principal": Burroughs to Jack Kerouac, November 30, 1948, in Burroughs, *Letters*, p. 27.

Page 91   "Naturally, I thought": Herbert Huncke, according to Neal Cassady, in Jack Kerouac, *Visions of Cody* (1972; New York: Penguin, 1993), p. 139.

Page 91   "It was a house": Huncke, interview with the author, New York, March 12, 1995.

Page 91   "When you shoot": Burroughs, *Junky*, p. 87.

Page 92   "But no such happy forest": Ginsberg, in Texas, 1947, Ginsberg Collection, Stanford University.

Page 92   "It may be kind of": Huncke, interview with the author, New York, February 26, 1995.

Page 93   "Elitch is bad for muscles": Kerouac to Neal Cassady, December 3, 1950, in Kerouac, *Selected Letters*, p. 239.

Page 97   "I am going to marry": Kerouac, ca. 1947, Ginsberg Collection, Stanford University.

Page 98   "Death hovers over": Kerouac, in McNally, *Desolate Angel*, p. 53.

Page 98   "My subject as a writer": Kerouac to Hal Chase, April 19, 1947, in Kerouac, *Selected Letters*, p. 107.

Page 98   "Art is the highest": Nietzsche, quoted in ibid., p. 81, n. 5.

Page 98   "Read Jack's Novel last week": Ginsberg, Journals, Ginsberg Collection, Stanford University.

Page 99   "I feel like writing a huge novel": Kerouac to Neal Cassady, September 13, 1947, in Kerouac, *Selected Letters*, p. 130.

Page 99   "Just a little boy": Alan Ansen, in Nicosia, *Memory Babe*, p. 456.

Page 100   "I was so sick": Ginsberg, quoted in Kerouac to Ginsberg, September 6, 1945, in Kerouac, *Selected Letters*, p. 94.

Page 100   "The use of mixtures": Gregory Corso, "Variations on a Generation," in Charters, *The Portable Beat Reader*, p. 182.

Page 101   "I want to be a saint": Ginsberg to Van Doren, n.d., in Plummer, *The Holy Goof*, p. 41.

Page 101   "A couple of steeazicks": Kerouac to William Burroughs, July 14, 1947, in Kerouac, *Selected Letters*, p. 108.

Page 102   "Wherever I go I see myself": Ginsberg, Journals, Ginsberg Collection, Stanford University.

Page 102   "As a habit takes hold": Burroughs, *Junky*, p. 22.

Page 103   "That initial difference": Kerouac to Cassady, June 27, 1948, in Kerouac, *Selected Letters*, p. 154.

Page 103   "Don't worry": Cassady to Jack Kerouac, October 5, 1947, ibid., p. 134.

Page 103   "Suffice to say I just": Cassady, in Plummer, *The Holy Goof*, p. 84.

Page 105   "What's your road, man?": Kerouac, *On the Road*, p. 251.

Page 105   "I have almost real reason": Kerouac to Allen Ginsberg, December 15, 1948, in Kerouac, *Selected Letters*, p. 177.

Page 105   "I went with him": Kerouac, in Clark, *Kerouac*, p. 80.

Page 105   "Lucien in New York": Kerouac to Allen Ginsberg, ca. May 1954, Ginsberg Collection, Special Collections, Columbia University.

Page 107   "The only thing to do": Kerouac, *On the Road*, p. 119.

Page 107   "We were all delighted": Ibid., p. 133.

Page 108   "She loved that man": Ibid., p. 146.

Page 108   "'[Bull] seems to me'": Ibid., p. 147.

Page 109   "'Oh, smell the people!'": Ibid., p. 140.

Page 109 "I mean, man, whither": Ibid., p. 119.

Page 109 "Drive your Chevrolet": Dinah Shore, in Karal Ann Marling, *As Seen on TV: The Visual Culture of Everyday Life in the 1950s* (Cambridge, Mass.: Harvard University Press, 1994), p. 148.

Page 110 "In all probability": Huncke, journal, 1946, in Herbert Huncke, *Huncke's Journal* (New York: Poets' Press, 1965), p. 5.

Page 110 "I also look forward": Kerouac to Allen Ginsberg, July 14, 1955, in Kerouac, *Selected Letters*, p. 500.

Page 110 "What's with you": Burroughs to Allen Ginsberg, December 20, 1956, in Burroughs, *Letters*, p. 345.

Page 111 "The more obligation Huncke is under": Burroughs to Allen Ginsberg, January 30, 1949, ibid., p. 39.

Page 111 "Sooner or later": Burroughs, *Junky*, p. 52.

Page 112 "All my geniuses are in jail": Kerouac to Alan Harrington, April 23, 1949, in Kerouac, *Selected Letters*, p. 187.

Page 112 "I admire you for delivering": Kerouac to Ginsberg, July 5, 1949, Ginsberg Collection, Special Collections, Columbia University.

Page 113 "When I came out of": Carl Solomon, "Electric Shock," in *Mishaps, Perhaps*, p. 24.

Page 113 "I am now become": Ginsberg, quoted in Jack Kerouac to Neal Cassady, July 28, 1949, in Kerouac, *Selected Letters*, p. 217.

Page 114 "There are no intellectuals": Solomon, in Nicosia, *Memory Babe*, p. 284.

Page 114 "*Madness is confusion of levels*": Burroughs to Ginsberg, June 4, 1952, in Burroughs, *Letters*, p. 128.

Page 116 "Bliazasted a moment ago": Kerouac to Neal Cassady, December 3, 1950, in Kerouac, *Selected Letters*, p. 238.

Page 118 "You say you have found out": Burroughs to Ginsberg, May 1, 1950, in Burroughs, *Letters*, p. 68.

Page 118 "A square is some guy": Corso, "Variations on a Generation," in Charters, *The Portable Beat Reader*, p. 184.

Page 119 "By the way what ever became": Burroughs to Jack Kerouac, April 1952, in Burroughs, *Letters*, p. 115.

Page 119 "In such places as Greenwich Village": Norman Mailer, "The White Negro," *Dissent*, Summer 1957; reprinted in Norman Mailer, *Advertisements for Myself* (New York: Putnam, 1959), p. 339.

Page 120 "Do the sad souls": Judith Malina, March 2, 1957, in *The Diaries of Judith Malina 1947–1957* (New York: Grove Press, 1984), p. 214.

Page 122 "Wild mad eastside funny Gregory": Kerouac to Philip Whalen, December 31, 1956, in Kerouac, *Selected Letters*, p. 597.

Page 122 "The weed available": Burroughs, *Junky*, p. 19.

Page 123 "If you believe you're a poet": Corso, in Ronald Sukenick, *Down and In: Life in the Underground* (New York: Macmillan, 1987), p. 13.

Page 124 "Because Jack, like me": Ibid., p. 24.

Page 125   "If you have a choice": Corso, in Barry Miles, ed., *Howl: Original Draft Facsimile, Transcript and Variant Versions, Fully Annotated by Author, with Contemporaneous Correspondence, Account of First Public Reading, Legal Skirmishes, Precursor Texts and Bibliography* (New York: Harper & Row, 1986), p. 174

Page 128   "Paste this in yr. hat": Kerouac, May 11, 1955, Ginsberg Collection, Special Collections, Columbia University.

Page 128   "Let's sip some tea": Huncke, interview with the author, New York, February 26, 1995.

Page 129   The Three Imagist Rules: Ezra Pound, in Steven Watson, *Strange Bedfellows: The First American Avant-Garde* (New York: Abbeville Press, 1991), p. 194.

Page 129   "I'll have seen 41 states": Kerouac to Caroline Kerouac Blake, September 25, 1947, in Kerouac, *Selected Letters*, p. 131.

Page 130   Proposed titles for *On the Road*: Kerouac to Neal Cassady, December 3, 1950, ibid., p. 238 and n. 1.

Page 130   "Americans should know": Whitman, in Morgan, *Literary Outlaw*, p. 288.

Page 131   "Let's you and I revolutionize": Kerouac to Cassady, July 28, 1949, in Kerouac, *Selected Letters*, p. 215.

Page 132   "I want us all together": Kerouac to Ginsberg, July 26, 1949, ibid., p. 210.

Page 134   "My book has not sold": Kerouac to Yvonne Le Maitre, September 8, 1950, ibid., p. 229.

Page 134   "I know literature": Kerouac to Cassady, July 28, 1949, ibid., p. 215.

Page 135   "Rather, I think one should write": Cassady to Kerouac, December 1947, ibid., p. 136.

Page 136   "John Holmes is a latecomer": Kerouac to Allen Ginsberg, March or April 1952, ibid., p. 345.

Page 136   "The charging restless mute": Kerouac to Allen Ginsberg, May 18, 1952, ibid., p. 357.

Page 136   ". . . *wild form*, man": Kerouac to John Clellon Holmes, June 5, 1952, ibid., p. 369.

Page 137   "I've told all the road now": Kerouac to Neal Cassady, May 22, 1951, ibid., p. 315.

Page 138   "I'm the bop writer": Kerouac, in Clark, *Kerouac*, p. 123.

Page 138   "It's the *only way to write*": Kerouac to Allen Ginsberg, May 18, 1952, in Kerouac, *Selected Letters*, p. 356.

Page 138   "Strip your psyche to the bare bones": Burroughs, "Ginsberg's Notes," in *Interzone*, p. 129.

Page 139   "Blow as deep": Kerouac, in Clark, *Kerouac*, p. 103.

Page 141   "As to love, who have I ever loved?": Kerouac to Neal Cassady, October 3, 1948, in Kerouac, *Selected Letters*, p. 168.

Page 141   "You and I are in the same boat": Gabrielle Kerouac to Jack Kerouac, April 1, 1956, ibid., p. 574.

Page 142   "I am *not* a fool!" Kerouac to Neal Cassady, October 3, 1948, ibid., p. 167.

Page 142   "Go South of the Rio Grande": Burroughs to Ginsberg, January 11, 1951, in Burroughs, *Letters*, p. 78.

Page 143   "Going to a cock fight": Burroughs to Jack Kerouac, April 3, 1952, ibid., p. 109.

Page 144   "It makes things rather difficult": Vollmer to Ginsberg, April 13, 1948, in Ginsberg

Collection, Special Collections, Columbia University.

Page 146   "If there's one thing": Burroughs, *Junky*, p. 132.

Page 146   "You've got to put yourself": Burroughs, in Morgan, *Literary Outlaw*, p. 595.

Page 147   "I don't write from scratch": Burroughs to Jack Kerouac, April 3, 1952, in Kerouac, *Selected Letters*, p. 340.

Page 147   "Whenever a true": Kerouac, May 11, 1955, in Ginsberg Collection, Special Collections, Columbia University.

Page 147   "While it was I": Burroughs, *Queer*, p. xiv.

Page 148   "Whenever a law": Burroughs, *Junky*, p. 116.

Page 148   "He opened his fly": Ibid., p. 141.

Page 149   "Bill was like a mad genius": Kerouac to Allen Ginsberg, May 10, 1952, in Kerouac, *Selected Letters*, p. 352.

Page 150   "If you get the right": Burroughs, *Junky*, p. 35.

Page 151   "Stash it in a cool spot": From Symphony Sid's bebop radio program, late 1940s.

Page 152   "Murder is the national": Burroughs, *Queer*, p. 21.

Page 153   "He was putting down": Ibid., p. 5.

Page 153   "It was a typical Beat": Janet Richards, *Common Soldiers* (San Francisco: Archer, 1979), p. 323.

Page 154   "Joan made him great": Kerouac to Allen Ginsberg, May 10, 1952, in Kerouac, *Selected Letters*, p. 353.

Page 157   "*I must find the Yage*": Burroughs to Allen Ginsberg, May 23, 1952, in Burroughs, *Letters*, p. 126.

Page 157   "You have to come to the jungle": Burroughs to Ginsberg, July 10, 1953, ibid., p. 186.

Page 157   "A large dose of Yage": Burroughs to Ginsberg, ibid., p. 155.

Page 158   "That is it produces": Burroughs to Ginsberg, July 8, 1953, ibid., pp. 179–80.

Page 159   "We should get used to calling": Burroughs to Ginsberg, April 5, 1952, ibid., p. 111.

Page 160   "Dammit, if these people": Kerouac to William Burroughs, May 1955, in Kerouac, *Selected Letters*, p. 481.

Page 161   "Between *incomprehensible*": Kerouac to Solomon, August 5, 1952, ibid., p. 376.

Page 161   "And all you will have": Ibid., p. 377.

Page 164   "Not that Irwin wasn't": Kerouac, *Desolation Angels*, p. 314.

Page 167   "*Quien sabe?* Not me": Burroughs to Allen Ginsberg, May 30, 1953, in Burroughs, *Letters*, p. 166.

Page 167   "I have never seen so many people": Burroughs, "International Zone," in *Interzone*, p. 52.

Page 169   "All their lives they have drifted": Ibid., p. 49.

Page 169   "I have a strange feeling here": Burroughs to Allen Ginsberg, October 29, 1956, in Burroughs, *Letters*, p. 337.

Page 170   "There is an end-of-the-world feeling": Burroughs to Allen Ginsberg, June 16, 1954, ibid., p. 215.

Page 170   "I need you so much": Burroughs to Ginsberg, January 12, 1955, ibid., p. 255.

Page 172   "Pah! You, the greatest writer": Kerouac to Cassady, April 15, 1955, in Kerouac, *Selected Letters*, p. 472.

Page 173   "I mean you know yourself": Kerouac to Carolyn Cassady, August 26, 1954, ibid., p. 441.

Page 173   ". . . it isn't AS IF": Kerouac to Ginsberg, May 1954, ibid., p. 413.

Page 173   "So he was a very unique": Ginsberg, in Jane Kramer, *Allen Ginsberg in America* (New York: Random House, 1969), p. 47.

Page 174   "But I am not self-sufficient": Burroughs to Kerouac, September 3, 1954, in Burroughs, *Letters*, p. 233.

Page 174   List of Buddhist definitions by Kerouac, in Kerouac, *Selected Letters*, p. 567.

Page 176   "He makes pod": Burroughs to Allen Ginsberg, February 19, 1955, in Burroughs, *Letters*, p. 270.

Page 177   "Allen and Neal are old buddies": Kerouac to Carolyn Cassady, August 26, 1954, in Kerouac, *Selected Letters*, p. 441.

Page 177   "Well I guess Carolyn has what she wants": Burroughs to Kerouac, September 3, 1954, in Burroughs, *Letters*, p. 232.

Page 178   "I'm Peter Orlovsky": Orlovsky, in Schumacher, *Dharma Lion*, p. 306.

Page 179   "An army is an army": Orlovsky, in Miles, *Ginsberg*, p. 182.

Page 179   "Peter O sounds very great": Kerouac to Ginsberg, January 18, 1955, in Kerouac, *Selected Letters*, p. 459.

Page 180   "Chinaman half in": Burroughs to Allen Ginsberg, November 5, 1952, in Burroughs, *Letters*, p. 140.

Page 180   "The family jewels": Burroughs, "Lee's Journals," in *Interzone*, p. 73.

Page 181   "I want your lingual": Kerouac to Ginsberg, August 19, 1955, in Kerouac, *Selected Letters*, p. 508.

Page 183   "Fuck Carl Solomon": Ibid.

Page 183   "This poem is undoubtedly the best": Burroughs to Ginsberg, March 14, 1956, in Burroughs, *Letters*, p. 315.

Page 184   "Poet ain't court jester": Kerouac to Malcolm Cowley, September 20, 1955, in Kerouac, *Selected Letters*, p. 519.

Page 184   "PREDICT EARTHQUAKES!": Kerouac to Ginsberg, in Glen Burns, *Great Poets Howl: A Study of Allen Ginsberg's Poetry, 1943–1955* (New York: Peter Lang, 1983), p. 331.

Page 186   "A reading is a kind of": Gary Snyder, *The Real Work: Interviews and Talks, 1964–1979* (New York: New Directions, 1980), p. 5.

Page 187   "A latter-day nabi": Rexroth, in Brown Miller and Ann Charters, "Kenneth Rexroth," in Ann Charters, ed., *Dictionary of Literary Biography*, vol. 16 (Detroit: Gale Research, 1983), p. 463.

Page 192   "Homer, or the guy": Ibid., p. 460.

Page 193   "San Francisco was a rich network": Michael McClure, *Lighting the Corners: On Art, Nature, and the Visionary: Essays and Interviews* (Albuquerque: University of New Mexico Press, 1993), p. 44.

Page 194   "When San Francisco is your home": Richards, *Common Soldiers*, p. 317.

Page 194   "Nick also scored": Burroughs, *Junky*, p. 56.

Page 196   "What is not *Tide*": Everson, in Lee Bartlett, *William Everson: The Life of Brother Anto-*

ninus (New York: New Directions, 1988), p. 45.

Page 197   "They are hip without": Kerouac, *The Subterraneans*, p. 2.

Page 199   "I've never understood": Rexroth, in Miller and Charters, "Kenneth Rexroth," in Charters, *Dictionary of Literary Biography*, p. 463.

Page 200   "Kenneth was like Godwin": Michael McClure, in Barry Silesky, *Ferlinghetti: The Artist in His Time* (New York: Warner, 1990), p. 47.

Page 200   "We were all brought up": Robert Duncan, in Linda Hamalian, *A Life of Kenneth Rexroth* (New York: Norton, 1991), p. 154.

Page 201   "When I think of Robert": McClure, *Lighting the Corners*, p. 90.

Page 203   "In a Bohemian household": Robert Duncan, in Richard Candida Smith, *Utopia and Dissent: Art, Poetry, and Politics in California* (Berkeley: University of California Press, 1995), p. 169.

Page 203   "I'm pre-beat": Everson/Brother Antoninus, in Lee Bartlett, *Benchmark & Blaze* (Metuchen, N.J.: Scarecrow Press, 1979), p. 12.

Page 205   "I'm beat to the square": Ibid., p. 11.

Page 205   "I was proud to be": Everson/Brother Antoninus, in Bartlett, *William Everson,* p. 172.

Page 205   "I remain the solitary poet-utterer": Ibid., p. 169.

Page 206   "I lawrence ferlinghetti": Ferlinghetti, in Larry Smith, "Lawrence Ferlinghetti," in Charters, *Dictionary of Literary Biography*, p. 201.

Page 208   "I was a wind-up toy": Ibid., p. 201.

Page 208   Early City Lights Books: Adapted from Ralph Cook, *City Lights Books: A Descriptive Bibliography* (Metuchen, N.J.: Scarecrow Press, 1992).

Page 215   "To rebel! that is the immediate objective": Philip Lamantia, in Nancy Peters, "Philip Lamantia," in Charters, *Dictionary of Literary Biography*, p. 330.

Page 217   "I have always dreamed": Ibid., p. 329.

Page 221   "Creeley is a genius": McClure, *Lighting the Corners*, p. 173

Page 224   "It was our Bible": Michael Rumaker, in Martin Duberman, *Black Mountain: An Exploration in Community* (Garden City, N.Y.: Anchor Press/Doubleday, 1973), p. 416.

Page 224   "Expelled and imploding": Charles Olson, ibid., p. 438.

Page 226   "If you come right": Burroughs, *Junky*, p. 17.

Page 227   "Frisco is mad": Kerouac to John Clellon Holmes, February 8, 1952, in Kerouac, *Selected Letters*, p. 338.

Page 229   "Everything you tell me about Frisco": Burroughs to Ginsberg, November 12, 1954, in Burroughs, *Letters*, p. 239.

Page 229   "We were all trying": McClure, *Lighting the Corners*, p. 37.

Page 230   "I am beginning to think": Kerouac to John Clellon Holmes, May 27, 1956, in Kerouac, *Selected Letters*, p. 579.

Page 232   "The omelet fell apart": Wilfrid Sheed, "Beat Down and Beautific," in *The Good Word* (New York: Dutton, 1978), p. 111.

Page 232 "Success, alas, as it almost always does": Rexroth, in Miller and Charters, "Kenneth Rexroth," in Charters, *Dictionary of Literary Biography*, p. 462.

Page 233 "Here we were all being": Everson/Brother Antoninus, in Bartlett, *William Everson*, p. 168.

Page 233 "They came to us late": Rexroth, in Miller and Charters, "Kenneth Rexroth," in Charters, *Dictionary of Literary Biography*, p. 462.

Page 236 "As for Rexroth": Kerouac to Gary Snyder, January 15, 1956, in Kerouac, *Selected Letters*, p. 539.

Page 237 "I was beat that way": Burroughs, *Queer*, p. 69.

Page 239 "I am getting so far out": Burroughs to Allen Ginsberg, October 13, 1956, in Burroughs, *Letters*, p. 329.

Page 241 "Tanger is the prognostic pulse": Burroughs to Jack Kerouac and Allen Ginsberg, November 2, 1955, ibid., p. 302.

Page 242 "In short, the intelligentsia": Burroughs to Allen Ginsberg, July 15, 1954, ibid., p. 223.

Page 242 "There is nothing stronger": Burroughs to Ginsberg, September 28, 1958, ibid., p. 397.

Page 243 "A shot of Eukodol": Burroughs to Ginsberg, April 20, 1955, ibid., p. 271.

Page 243 "I am running out": Burroughs, "Lee's Journals," in *Interzone*, p. 68.

Page 243 "Get off that Junk wagon": Burroughs to Allen Ginsberg, September 11, 1959, in Burroughs, *Letters*, p. 424.

Page 244 "An addict has little regard": Burroughs, *Queer*, p. xii.

Page 246 "Most secure form of security": Burroughs to Ginsberg, June 24, 1954, in Burroughs, *Letters*, p. 217.

Page 248 "Al, I am a fucking saint": Burroughs to Ginsberg, October 13, 1956, ibid., p. 331.

Page 251 "How sweet It Is": Donald Justice, in Lewis Hyde, ed., *On the Poetry of Allen Ginsberg* (Ann Arbor: University of Michigan Press, 1984), p. 41.

Page 251 "The Cops Don't Allow No Renaissance Here": Newspaper headline quoted in Lawrence Ferlinghetti, "Horn on 'Howl,'" in Charters, *The Portable Beat Reader*, p. 256.

Page 252 "By the way, my profound thanks": Solomon to Allen Ginsberg, December 29, 1957, in Ginsberg Collection, Stanford University.

Page 252 "I disapprove of 'Howl'": Solomon to Allen Ginsberg, July 7, 1959, ibid.

Page 252 "Feel calmer and take": Marianne Moore, in James E. B. Breslin, "Introduction: The Presence of Williams in Contemporary Poetry," in Breslin, ed., *Something to Say: William Carlos Williams on Younger Poets* (New York: New Directions, 1985), p. 16.

Page 253 "'Howl' is the confession": Kenneth Rexroth, "San Francisco Letter," *Evergreen Review* 1, no. 2 (Summer 1957): 11.

Page 253 "Well, Kerouac has come off": Nicosia, *Memory Babe*, p. 565.

Page 254 "Nobody knows whether": Ginsberg, in Burns, *Great Poets Howl*, p. 404.

Page 255 "Too much adulation": Kerouac to Carolyn Cassady, early 1959, in Clark, *Kerouac*, p. 173.

Page 256   "He is prince of the hips": Howard Smith, originally in *Village Voice*, 1957; quoted in Sukenick, *Down and In*, p. 38.

Page 256   "[I] don't know how to drive": Kerouac to Neal and Carolyn Cassady, January 10, 1953, in Kerouac, *Selected Letters*, p. 396.

Page 258   "The beatnik is the torchbearer": Norman Mailer, "Hipster and Beatnik," in *Advertisements for Myself*, p. 374.

Page 258   "The Beat Generation may once": Rexroth, in Miller and Charters, "Kenneth Rexroth," in Charters, *Dictionary of Literary Biography*, p. 462.

Page 258   "I'm such a myth": Ginsberg, in Morgan, *Literary Outlaw*, p. 310.

Page 259   "I get called a beatnik": Carl Solomon, ca. 1967, in Kramer, *Ginsberg in America*, p. 70.

Page 260   "When you take dehydrated Hipster": Herbert Gold, in Burns, *Great Poets Howl*, p. 35.

Page 260   "The revolt of the spiritually": Norman Podhoretz, in Morgan, *Literary Outlaw*, p. 289.

Page 260   "Communists, Beatniks, Eggheads": J. Edgar Hoover, ibid., p. 289.

Page 261   Beat Exploitation Novels: Adapted from notes to CD *The Beat Generation* (Rhino Records #R2/R4 70281,1992).

Page 262   "The Beat Generation is no longer": Gregory Corso, "Variations on a Generation," in Charters, *The Portable Beat Reader*, p. 183.

Page 265   "The truth of the matter": Kerouac, *On the Road*, p. 122.

Page 265   "That's what everybody": Kerouac to Neal Cassady, October 6, 1950, in Kerouac, *Selected Letters*, p. 234.

Page 266   "I have seen addicts": Burroughs, *Junky*, p. 28.

Page 273   "It was like a Marx Brothers movie": Morgan, *Literary Outlaw*, p. 308.

Page 276   "That is the usual novel": Burroughs to Allen Ginsberg, October 28, 1957, in Burroughs, *Letters*, p. 375.

Page 276   "I have thought": Burroughs to Allen Ginsberg, June 18, 1956, ibid., p. 321.

Page 278   "Lucien is his Angel": Kerouac to John Clellon Holmes, June 24, 1949, in Kerouac, *Selected Letters*, p. 200.

Page 278   "The bum's as holy": Allen Ginsberg, *Collected Poems, 1947–1980* (New York: Harper, 1984), p. 134.

Page 279   "I had asked him": Burroughs to Allen Ginsberg, July 13, 1952, in Burroughs, *Letters*, p. 136.

Page 281   "That's not writing": Samuel Beckett, in Morgan, *Literary Outlaw*, p. 323.

Page 281   "In order to earn my reputation": Burroughs, ibid., p. 320.

Page 281   "'The book grabs you by the throat'": Burroughs to Allen Ginsberg, January 12, 1955, in Burroughs, *Letters*, p. 255.

Page 282   "We do not feature masochism": Burroughs to Allen Ginsberg, July 1959, ibid., p. 418.

Page 283   "What we are all trying": Miller, in Morgan, *Literary Outlaw*, p. 337.

Page 283   "If Saint Augustine were writing": Holland, ibid., p. 345.

Page 287   "How this beat beatster": Cassady, in Plummer, *The Holy Goof*, p. 110.

Page 288   "You well know we both": Cassady to Carolyn, n.d., ibid., p. 107.

Page 289   "The Revolution Has Begun": Ginsberg to Cassady, December 4, 1960, ibid., p. 115.

Page 289   "The Neon Revolution, According to Ken Kesey," ibid., p. 122.

Page 289   "When you went riding": Jerry Garcia, ibid., p. 132.

Page 290   "At his purest": Ibid., p. 127.

Page 291   "Old red face W. C. Fields": Ginsberg, in Clark, *Kerouac*, p. 201.

Page 291   "All along the roadside": Wavy Gravy, in Plummer, *The Holy Goof*, p. 146.

Page 294   "Fame makes you stop writing": Kerouac to Ginsberg, n.d., in Nicosia, *Memory Babe*, p. 564.

Page 294   "I see nothing ahead for me": Kerouac to Ginsberg, June 29, 1963, Ginsberg Collection, Special Collections, Columbia University.

Page 295   "I keep falling in love": Kerouac, in Clark, *Kerouac*, p. 175.

Page 295   "I'm not about to throw": Kerouac to Ginsberg, n.d., ibid., p. 200.

Page 297   "Keep running after a dog": Kerouac to Allen Ginsberg, July 14, 1955, in Kerouac, *Selected Letters*, p. 500.

Page 298   "When you and me and Bill": Kerouac to Ginsberg, August 28, 1958, Ginsberg Collection, Special Collections, Columbia University.

Page 298   "When I die, Neal": Kerouac to Cassady, January 3, 1951, in Kerouac, *Selected Letters*, p. 273.

Page 299   "When the universe fails": Corso to Ginsberg, n.d., in Nicosia, *Memory Babe*, p. 555.

Page 299   "I have spent about": Allen Ginsberg, "The Great Marijuana Hoax," *Atlantic Monthly*, November 1966, p. 107.

Page 300   "You know yourself": Burroughs, *Junky*, p. 50.

Page 301   "Everybody who hears my voice": Ginsberg, in *East Village Other*, January 1967; quoted in Morgan, *Literary Outlaw*, p. 385.

Page 301   "Just taking acid's not yoga": Ginsberg, in Kramer, *Ginsberg in America*, p. xvi.

Page 302   "In a country that has never": Ibid., p. 9.

Page 302   "He made life too messy": Diana Trilling, in McNally, *Desolate Angel*, p. 75.

Page 305   "I think all writers write for an audience": Burroughs to Ginsberg, October 1952, in Burroughs, *Letters*, p. 138.

Page 306   "What are you rewriting?": Burroughs, *Queer*, p. xxiii.

Page 306   "I am the cat": Burroughs, in Morgan, *Literary Outlaw*, p. 571.

Page 307   "No one in his senses": Ibid., p. 293.

Page 308   "William would make": James Grauerholz, in *William Burroughs*, documentary film by Howard Brookner.

Page 308   "I have never regretted my experience": Burroughs, *Junky*, p. xv.

Introductory Nonfiction Bibliography

Burroughs, William. *The Letters of William S. Burroughs, 1945–1959*. Edited by Oliver Harris. New York: Viking, 1993. Burroughs' pre-fame letters.

Cassady, Carolyn. *Off the Road: My Years with Kerouac, Cassady, and Ginsberg*. New York: Morrow, 1990. The memoirs of Cassady's wife.

Cassady, Neal. *The First Third and Other Writings*. San Francisco: City Lights Books, 1971; expanded ed., 1981. Fragments of early autobiography.

Charters, Ann. *Kerouac: A Biography*. San Francisco: Straight Arrow Books, 1973. The first Kerouac biography.

———, ed. *The Beats: Literary Bohemians in Postwar America*. 2 vols. Vol. 16 of *Dictionary of Literary Biography*. Detroit: Gale Research, 1983. The best single source for the writers connected with the Beats and the San Francisco Renaissance.

Clark, Tom. *Jack Kerouac*. New York: Harcourt Brace Jovanovich, 1984. A readable introductory biography.

DiPrima, Diane. *Memoirs of a Beatnik*. Paris: Olympia Press/Traveler's Companion, 1969. Early, erotic memoirs.

Gifford, Barry, and Lee, Lawrence. *Jack's Book*. New York: St. Martin's Press, 1978. An oral history of Kerouac and friends.

Huncke, Herbert. *Guilty of Everything*. New York: Paragon House, 1990. Huncke's memoirs.

Johnson, Joyce. *Minor Characters*. Boston: Houghton Mifflin, 1983. Memoirs of the period by Kerouac's girlfriend.

Jones, Hettie. *How I Became Hettie Jones*. New York: Dutton, 1990. Clear-eyed memoirs of the period.

Kerouac, Jack. *Selected Letters 1940–1956*. Edited by Ann Charters. New York: Viking, 1995. Annotated letters from Kerouac's pre-fame period.

McNally, Dennis. *Desolate Angel: Jack Kerouac, the Beat Generation, and America*. New York: Random House, 1979.

Miles, Barry. *Ginsberg: A Biography*. New York: Simon & Schuster, 1989. The first, highly readable biography of Ginsberg.

———. *William Burroughs: El Hombre Invisible*. New York: Hyperion, 1993. The most recent Burroughs biography.

Morgan, Ted. *Literary Outlaw: The Life and Times of William S. Burroughs*. New York: Holt, 1988. The most thorough biography of Burroughs.

Nicosia, Gerald. *Memory Babe: A Critical Biography of Jack Kerouac*. New York: Grove Press, 1983. The most exhaustive Kerouac biography.

Plummer, William. *The Holy Goof: A Biography of Neal Cassady*. New York: Paragon House, 1981. A biography of Cassady.

Schumacher, Michael. *Dharma Lion: A Biography of Allen Ginsberg*. New York: St. Martin's Press, 1992. The most comprehensive Ginsberg biography.

Solomon, Carl. *Mishaps, Perhaps*. San Francisco: Beach Books, Texts & Documents, 1968. A selection of pieces by Solomon.

Tytell, John. *Naked Angels: The Lives and Literature of the Beat Generation*. New York: McGraw-Hill, 1976. An overview of Burroughs, Kerouac, and Ginsberg.

INDEX

Page numbers in *italics* refer to illustrations.

CREDITS

PERMISSIONS ACKNOWLEDGMENTS

Grateful acknowledgment is made to the following for permission to reprint previously published and unpublished material:

Eugene Brooks: Excerpt from a June 1956 letter to Allen Ginsberg. Reprinted by permission of Eugene Brooks.

Ann Charters: Excerpts from "Kenneth Rexroth" by Ann Charters, from *The Dictionary of Literary Biography,* vol. 16, edited by Ann Charters (Gale Research, Detroit, 1983), copyright © 1983 by Gale Research Company. Reprinted by permission of Ann Charters.

Paul Christensen: Excerpts from "Philip Whelan" by Paul Christensen, from *The Dictionary of Literary Biography,* vol. 16, edited by Ann Charters (Gale Research, Detroit, 1983), copyright © 1983 by Gale Research Company. Reprinted by permission of Paul Christensen.

Columbia University: Excerpt from an April 13, 1948, letter from Joan Vollmer to Allen Ginsberg; excerpts from unpublished letters from Jack Kerouac, Carolyn Cassady, John Kingsland, Gary Snyder, and Herbert Huncke; excerpts from Allen Ginsberg's journal entries. Allen Ginsberg Papers, Rare Book and Manuscript Library, Columbia University. Reprinted by permission of Columbia University.

Creative Arts Book Company: Excerpts from *As Ever: The Collected Correspondence of Allen Ginsberg and Neal Cassady,* edited by Barry Gifford. Reprinted by permission of Creative Arts Book Company, Berkeley, CA, Donald S. Ellis, publisher.

The Estate of Carl Solomon: Excerpts from "Electric Shock" from *Mishaps, Perhaps* by Carl Solomon; excerpts from unpublished letters by Carl Solomon. Reprinted by permission of The Estate of Carl Solomon, Elaine Friedman, executrix.

Allen Ginsberg: Excerpts from liner notes from "Howl" (Fantasy Records) by Allen Ginsberg, copyright © Allen Ginsberg; excerpt from "A Definition of the Beat Generation" by Allen Ginsberg (*Friction,* vol. 1, nos. 2–3, 1982, and an interview granted July 14, 1995). Reprinted by permission of Allen Ginsberg.

HarperCollins Publishers, Inc., and Penguin Books Ltd.: Excerpts from "The Bricklayer's Lunch Hour," "The Green Automobile," "Howl," "Kaddish," and "Siesta in Xbalba," from *Collected Poems 1947–1980* by Allen Ginsberg, copyright © 1947, 1953, 1954, 1955, 1959 by Allen Ginsberg. Copyright renewed. Rights in the United Kingdom administered by Penguin Books Ltd, London. Reprinted by permission of HarperCollins Publishers, Inc., and Penguin Books Ltd.

Henry Holt and Company, Inc., The Bodley Head, and International Creative Management, Inc.: Excerpts from *Literary Outlaw* by Ted Morgan, copyright © 1985 by Ted Morgan. Rights in the United Kingdom administered by The Bodley Head, London. Reprinted by permission of Henry Holt and Company, Inc., The Bodley Head, and International Creative Management, Inc.

Hyperion and Virgin Publishing Limited: Excerpts from *William Burroughs: El Hombre Invisible* by Barry Miles, copyright © 1993 by Barry Miles. Rights in the United Kingdom controlled by Virgin Publishing Limited, London. Reprinted by permission of Hyperion and Virgin Publishing Limited.

Marlowe & Company: Excerpts from *The Holy Goof* by William Plummer, copyright © 1989 by William Plummer. Reprinted by permission of Marlowe & Company.

New Directions Publishing Corporation: Excerpts from "True Confessional" from *Endless Life* by Lawrence Ferlinghetti, copyright © 1973 by Lawrence Ferlinghetti.

ILLUSTRATION CREDITS

Page 1 Courtesy of the Archive of Allen Ginsberg. Copyright © 1994 NYC. All rights reserved.

Page 7 Courtesy of the Ohio State University Libraries, Rarebooks and Manuscripts, and William S. Burroughs.

Page 11 Courtesy of Los Alamos Historical Museum Photo Archives.

Page 12 Courtesy of Harvard Yearbook Publications, Inc.

Page 15 Courtesy of *Burroughs: Eine bild-Biographie* by Michael Kohler.

Page 18 © John Sampas, literary executor of the Jack and Stella Kerouac Estate.

Page 19 © John Sampas, literary executor of the Jack and Stella Kerouac Estate.

Page 20 © John Sampas, literary executor of the Jack and Stella Kerouac Estate.

Page 22 Courtesy of the Archive of Allen Ginsberg. Copyright © 1994 NYC. All rights reserved.

Page 24 Courtesy of Michael Schumacher and the Archive of Allen Ginsberg.

Page 25 Courtesy of the Archive of Allen Ginsberg. Copyright © 1994 NYC. All rights reserved.

Page 26 Courtesy of the Archive of Allen Ginsberg. Copyright © 1994 NYC. All rights reserved.

Page 27 Courtesy of the Archive of Allen Ginsberg. Copyright © 1994 NYC. All rights reserved.

Page 28 Courtesy of the Archive of Allen Ginsberg. Copyright © 1994 NYC. All rights reserved.

Page 31 © John Sampas, literary executor of the Jack and Stella Kerouac Estate.

Page 34 © John Sampas, literary executor of the Jack and Stella Kerouac Estate.

Page 43 Courtesy of the Archive of Allen Ginsberg. Copyright © 1994 NYC. All rights reserved.

Page 47 Courtesy of the Historic Newspaper Archives.

Page 55 © 1995, Collection of Richard Lorenz, Berkeley, California.

Page 58 Courtesy of the Ohio State University Libraries, Rarebooks and Manuscripts.

Page 63 © John Sampas, literary executor of the Jack and Stella Kerouac Estate.

Page 69 (left) Courtesy of the Archive of Allen Ginsberg. Copyright © 1994 NYC. All rights reserved.

Page 69 (right) Photograph by Allen Ginsberg. Copyright © 1994 NYC. All rights reserved.

Page 75 Courtesy of Culver Pictures.

Page 81 Photograph by Edward D. White, Jr. Courtesy of the Archive of Allen Ginsberg.

Page 82 Courtesy of the Archive of Allen Ginsberg. Copyright © 1994 NYC. All rights reserved.

Page 90 Photograph by Allen Ginsberg. Copyright © 1994 NYC. All rights reserved.

Page 95 (left) Photograph by Allen Ginsberg.

Page 95 (right) Drawing by Robert LaVigne. Courtesy of the Robert LaVigne Papers, Rare Book and Manuscript Library, Columbia University.

Page 104 Courtesy of Carolyn Cassady.

Page 106 Courtesy of Carolyn Cassady.

Page 115 Photograph by Allen Ginsberg. Copyright © 1994 NYC. All rights reserved.

Page 123 Photograph by Harold Chapman. Courtesy of the Archive of Allen Ginsberg.

Page 126 Photograph by Eve Arnold/Magnum Photos.

Page 133 Photograph by Elliott Erwitt/Magnum Photos.

Page 137 © John Sampas, literary executor of the Jack and Stella Kerouac Estate.

Page 139 Courtesy of Carolyn Cassady.

Page 143 Copyright © 1995 by The Estate of Jack Kerouac, John Sampas, Literary Representative. Reprinted by permission of Sterling Lord Literistic, Inc.

Page 144 Courtesy of William S. Burroughs.
Page 145 Courtesy of the Archive of Allen Ginsberg.
Page 155 Courtesy of the Archive of Allen Ginsberg.
Page 158 Courtesy of the Ohio State University Libraries, Rarebooks and Manuscripts, and William S. Burroughs.
Page 160 Courtesy of Mr. and Mrs. Soond.
Page 162 Courtesy of the Archive of Allen Ginsberg.
Page 163 Photograph by Allen Ginsberg. Copyright © 1994 NYC. All rights reserved.
Page 165 Photographs by William S. Burroughs. Courtesy of the Ohio State University Libraries, Rarebooks and Manuscripts.
Page 168 Courtesy of the Ohio State University Libraries, Rarebooks and Manuscripts.
Page 171 Camera in hands of Peter Orlovsky. Photograph by Allen Ginsberg. Copyright © 1994 NYC. All rights reserved.
Page 172 Courtesy of Am Here Books.
Page 176 Courtesy of Carolyn Cassady.
Page 177 Courtesy of Carolyn Cassady.
Page 178 Drawing by Robert LaVigne. Courtesy of the Robert LaVigne Papers, Rare Book and Manuscript Library, Columbia University.
Page 180 Photograph by Allen Ginsberg. Copyright © 1994 NYC. All rights reserved.
Page 182 Camera in hands of Peter Orlovsky. Photograph by Allen Ginsberg. Copyright © 1994 NYC. All rights reserved.
Page 185 © Harry Redl, 1994
Page 187 Photograph by Walter Lehrman.
Page 188 © 1957, by Evergreen Review, Inc. Courtesy of Barney Rosset.
Pages 190–91. Map illustration © 1995 by Eric Hanson.
Page 195 Painting by Cornelius Sampson. Courtesy of the Collection of Robert E. Johnson.
Page 196 Design by Bern Porter. Copyright 1945 by Circle. Courtesy of Am Here Books.
Page 198 Photograph by Jonathan Williams.
Page 202 © Harry Redl, 1994.

Page 204 © Harry Redl, 1994.
Page 207 © Harry Redl, 1994.
Page 209 Photograph by Jack Morrison. Courtesy of Michael McClure.
Page 210 © Harry Redl, 1994.
Page 213 © Harry Redl, 1994.
Page 216 © Harry Redl, 1994.
Page 219 Portrait by Jack Kerouac, signed Jean Louis Kerouac. Copyright © 1995 by The Estate of Jack Kerouac, Inc., John Sampas, Literary Representative. Reprinted by permission of Sterling Lord Literistic, Inc. Courtesy of the Collection of Philip Whalen.
Page 220 Photograph by Jonathan Williams.
Page 223 Photograph by Jonathan Williams.
Page 226 Photograph by Chester Kessler. Courtesy of the Collection of Robert E. Johnson.
Page 228 Photograph by Ed Nyberg. Courtesy of the Ed Nyberg Photographs, 1957, Archives of American Art, Smithsonian Institution.
Page 231 Photograph by Larry Jordan. Courtesy of Michael McClure.
Page 235 Both illustrations courtesy of the Collection of Janice Belmont.
Page 236 Photograph by Walter Lehrman. Courtesy of the Collection of Philip Whalen.
Page 237 Courtesy of Am Here Books.
Page 238 © Larry Keenan, 1967.
Page 240 Drawing by William S. Burroughs. Courtesy of the Allen Ginsberg Papers, Rare Book and Manuscript Library, Columbia University.
Page 242 Photograph by Allen Ginsberg. Copyright © 1994 NYC. All rights reserved.
Page 245 Courtesy of the Ohio State University Libraries, Rarebooks and Manuscripts.
Page 246 Photograph by Allen Ginsberg. Copyright © 1994 NYC. All rights reserved.
Page 247 Photograph by Allen Ginsberg. Copyright © 1994 NYC. All rights reserved.
Page 249 (left) Photograph by Jerry Stoll.

ABOUT THE AUTHOR

Dr. Steven Watson is an independent scholar and curator interested in the group dynamics of the twentieth-century avant-garde. He is the author of *The Harlem Renaissance: Hub of African-American Culture, 1920–1930*, and *Strange Bedfellows: The First American Avant-Garde*.